I Am Tecumseh!

WORKS by RUBEN SALAZ-M.

Tabloid

Tierra Amarilla Shootout

History

Cosmic: The La Raza Sketchbook

Educational Materials

Cosmic Posters (bilingual)
Indian Saga Posters

Children's Books

The Cosmic Reader of the Southwest-For Young People

In Spanish

La lectura cosmica del Suroeste - para los jovenes

Short Stories

Heartland: Stories of the Southwest

Novels (trilogy)

I Am Tecumseh! (Books I and II)

Dramas

Embassy Hostage: The Drama of Americans in Iran
Tonight or Never!
Padre Martinez of Taos

Essays (for USA TODAY)

I work in the World's Noblest Profession
They Do the Work We Refuse
Student Attacked

I Am Tecumseh!

Book II
of
a trilogy
by
Ruben Salaz - Marquez

Cosmic House
Albuquerque

For Leonard Peltier

Gwarth-e-lass
Leads-The-People

FOREWORD
from
Book I

...Tecumseh and his prisoner finally encountered the cabin the young warrior had been looking for. He dismounted, got Molly off her horse, and both walked toward the wegiwa.

"Keewaukoomeelaa!" shouted Tecumseh.

Molly saw another savage come to the door and peer out.

"Keewaukoomeelaa, brother Tecumseh."

"I have brought something for you," said Tecumseh.

"My gift to you."

Spybuck just looked at the girl.

Chapter 1

Spybuck ignored the Shemanese captive for several days after Tecumseh deposited her on his doorstep. The woman was cold and sullen, frightened but capable of desperate violence, he felt. The elderly housekeeper who cooked his meals ignored her totally as she went about her chores around the cabin.

Molly was indeed terrified but if she was to die at the hands of her barbaric, savage captors she would kill whomever she could to avenge herself and the murder of her father. She had heard tales of how captives were tortured and at times she shuddered inwardly but she would not give her captors the satisfaction of seeing her beg for mercy. *Lord rescue me!* she wailed inside herself when her courage faltered but outwardly she expressed no emotion. At every opportunity her cold eyes studied the cabin of her oppressor, its strange, gruesome contents which hung from walls and ceiling poles. There were herbs, bones, vessels of powders, gourds, rattles and other paraphernalia which were lost on her because she was totally out of her culture. She looked closely at the old crone who cooked, discovered where the knives were kept, decided the old bag would not harm her so the savage would be the only obstacle to freedom. But where would she escape to?! Where was she? Why had she been brought here instead of a regular village? Who was this strange fiend who lived in such isolation from the other savages? She had seen him looking at her, his brutish eyes devoid of feeling. It was as if he was looking at--nothing. This caused Molly acute anguish, a foreboding of something horrible.

1

At first Molly refused to eat but no one cared whether she did or not so when she became famished she devoured everything put before her. She noticed the savage drinking some kind of tea but none was ever offered her. She kept on the lookout for knives. For a week or so nothing was required of her. The desire for revenge softened a bit. She walked outside the cabin in leisurely fashion. It was then she noticed there was another cabin out back. The Indian would come and go from one to the other. She got the impression he was a witchdoctor or black magician. What a horrible creature! Other savages hailed him but they never entered where she was and their visits were usually brief.

Spybuck was fatigued from all the patients that had arrived in recent days, seeking his medical talents. Most of the previous night had been spent keeping solicitous vigil on a warrior who had suffered a painful gunshot wound in the stomach. White dawn walking the rim of the sky found him still alive, thanks to Spybuck's constant changing of the sassafras poultice. The juggler was an acknowledged master in the treatment of gunshot wounds but he had also sung and recited over the moaning warrior, thus soothing him during the delirium. The flower drug had enabled the poor man to get some sleep. Now Spybuck needed rest so during the day he took little catnaps until he decided it would be permissible to walk outside without endangering the life of his patient, so he walked outside.

Spybuck stretched some life back into his muscles then he saw his housekeeper come up to Molly, giving her a gourd with which to fetch *nepee,* water from the stream. The captive flung it to the ground, defiance on her face.

"You see," laughed the old woman as she chided Spybuck in Shawnee, "you have spoiled her in this short time. The Shemanese are a race apart." She picked up the gourd and unceremoniously slapped Molly cross the face with her other hand. The unexpected blow was more surprise than wallop.

Spybuck was too tired to be trifled with. "Now go fetch some water," ordered the juggler in his most commanding voice as he pointed with his knife to the stream. Molly followed the old crone, wishing to bash her skull open, but afraid of the tyrant's knife. She was a captive and could be killed at any moment on the slightest pretext. So she went to the stream and fetched water with the old hag. But she would not forget the slap.

Spybuck did not find the female very attractive but he had been without a woman because his medical duties precluded his going into the village. The Shemanese would have to do for the time being. But she had

2

such a stench about her. She would have to be bathed. The old house-keeper did not have the strength to force her into the stream so he would have to do it himself.

That afternoon Spybuck entered his cabin where the two women worked and said to the Shemanese: "You, come with me!" as he pointed to her, himself, the door. Molly understood the sign language, left the corn she had been grinding, obeying sullenly. The two walked out of the wegiwa toward the stream. Spybuck led the way, Molly wishing she had brought a weapon with which to slay her oppressor. He was too careless, she was certain she could kill him. The only problem would be to escape afterward. Where would she go? Maybe the men would make a dash into Indian country to rescue her and her sister! If they did she would kill this cocky savage herself and relish the act. But for now she would have to play possum, do what she was told, though the unintelligible gibberish of the hell-hounds rasped on her emotions.

"Take off your clothes and wash yourself," ordered Spybuck in Shawnee as he pointed. Molly looked at him innocently. "Get in the stream and bathe," said Spybuck. He took off his blanket, exposed his shoulders and torso, washed his face and underarms. "You go over there beyond the bend and wash," ordered the man.

It took all of Molly's willpower to hide her indignation. An ignorant, filthy savage wanted her to go in the stream and bathe?! The idea! And right there in front of him! Maybe she could brain him with a rock from the stream. Nothing would please her more than to see the monster's brains, if he had any, in a bloody mess on the ground. She pretended to do as she was told until she lost sight of her brutish oppressor behind a bush close to the stream. She spied a rock that was just the right size, pic-ked it up with both hands, walked around the bush toward the beast, hid-ing easily behind the great trees, approaching stealthily without detection. Molly was indeed a citizen of the frontier. She raised the rock over her head as Spybuck washed himself. He said, *"Nepwa?"* then moved sud-denly aside as the rock came down with crushing force where his head had been a moment before. "Lenawawe!" exclaimed the man, "Alive, very much alive!" He smiled and laughed as if he had been observing the antics of a child at play. " Since you will not bathe away the stink from your body I shall have to do it for you," he continued playfully in Shaw-nee. Molly felt now she would be killed for sure.

Spybuck grabbed the girl and immobilized her to him with one power-ful arm. With the other hand he raised her linsey-woolsey, getting it nearly off before Molly was aware. She struggled mightily but it was futility for the ogre was immensely strong. Too late she grabbed her

3

dress and when she did the material tore, Molly sprawling into the stream from her effort. Her underclothes were pulled away as she tried to get up, coughing and wiping the wet hair from her face. Spybuck now took handfuls of fine sand and rubbed her body, the woman fighting as she could. To the man's surprise, the woman's skin began to turn pink. Her scent was something like that of a wet turkey. Molly slapped the savage then tried to cover her nudity whereupon Spybuck grabbed her by the hair and put her under water for a moment, thus putting an end to her fighting.

Spybuck had never seen a Shemanese in the nude. He decided pink skin was not particularly attractive, rubbing all the while. When he got to her bod the woman fought back and had to be submersed once again. "Then you wash it," he said.

Molly had never felt such humiliation! An animal washing her with sand! How unhealthy! What crudity! Touching her privates! What degradation! And there was nothing she could do about it, not a damn thing! She wanted to cry but her spirit refused to let the brute gain the satisfaction of seeing her in tears. He could kill her, torture her, but she would not have her spirit broken. He had better kill her, soon, because she would get her revenge! She would kill this savage even if it cost her own life, *she swore it!*

Spybuck finished with the sand, rinsed her off, then stood back as if to admire his work, hands on hips, head tilting to one side then the other. Suddenly Molly was no longer afraid. The Indian's entire personality seemed to have undergone a radical change. Up to now Molly had been frightened to death by the ogre's isolated cabin and sinister mein. The other Indians who came to see him also appeared to fear her oppressor. He was so evil! She deduced he must be some kind of sorcerer, a wizard schooled in black magic of the forest depths. But now he looked-- playful. He wasn't going to hurt her, just mock her! The bastard! Ripping off her clothes and rubbing her raw! She would repay him in kind. Boldy she walked up to the animal and subitaneously pulled on his breech- cloth, which was all the man wore. The covering slipped away without resistance and Molly felt a quick elation at her successful revenge. But the victory was short lived for Molly suddenly realized the two were standing totally nude, the man's organ beginning to rise. Abruptly she became frightened again, walked backward too quickly, slipped and fell into the stream.

Spybuck laughed easily then pulled the woman out of the water, car- ried her in both arms out of the stream to a natural enclosure where a blanket was on the soft ground. He put her down, rubbing his hands over

4

her in order to dry her down a bit, stood up and did the same with his own body, his eyes on the woman as he chuckled boyishly.

Molly looked at the savage. His wide shoulders, heavy torso, strong waist, rock-hard thighs were hidden under a swarthy skin, which was all she could see. She did not know how to fight anymore so she closed her eyes and just laid there.

Spybuck noted the woman's cold, stony countenance. The demon was high, ready to probe the woman's passion. He took the woman's ankles and opened her legs wide. There was no resistance but neither was there enthusiasm, not even a bit of healthy lust...

Molly lay there, trembling slightly. Let him do his worst! Her jaw was set rigidly, her lips pursed. She didn't move. And nothing happened. She cracked open an eye, then looked up and found she was all by herself. The Indian wasn't around! In utter confusion she wrapped herself in the blanket and tried to decide what to do next.

Episode 2: Family Reunion

The journey was the most joyful imaginable. Puckeshinwa's family would be reunited in Missouri! It was led by Cheeseekau, universally respected as the "Shawnee Warrior," the Hector of the Shawnee nation. He had refused to become a chief because his sole ambition was to fight the Shemanese. His friend Blue Jacket had been elected chief and started his own town but the Shawnee Warrior lived only for the warpath. It was said around the campfires that Cheeseekau had killed more than 200 Shemanese to avenge the death of his beloved Tarmanee, that he vowed to kill four-hundred more. His feats of courage and daring were unequaled by any other warrior knight in the entire nation.

Tecumapease had wanted her husband Wasegoboah to make the trip with the family but when events prevented this she left her children with him and journeyed to Missouri. Tecumapease was well known in the Shawnee tribe for her levelness of mind and noble character. As leader of the Peace Women she was responsible for many good works which benefited the poor and helpless. Tecumapease was welcome wherever she went and Wasegoboah, whom Tecumseh admired greatly, was very proud of his wife and her achievements. During the trek to Missouri her good humor and abilities were constantly displayed as she joked, worked around the campfire, and loved her brothers and sisters with a passionate hug now and then. She was indeed the daughter of Methoataske. Her word was law, even for Cheeseekau, three years her senior. "My Shawnee Warrior," she would say to him, "be kind enough to gather some firewood that is dry tonight."

"How would the Noble Lady of the Shawnee have me stack it?" retorted Cheeseekau.

"Laulewasika, would you please educate my little *apetotha?*" Tecumapease asked of the youngest in the family.

"The tenderfoot is beyond help, alas!" replied twelve-year-old Laulewasika.

Sauwaseekau, the third born of Puckeshinwa's offspring, would laugh the most for in the family it was he who had the best sense of humor. He was not lacking in any wilderness skills. He could hunt and fight with the best of them for he had been tutored by Puckeshinwa and Cheeseekau. It was just that he enjoyed a good story, could tell one almost as well as the Grandfathers, and could be counted on for entertainment. There were those who believed it was difficult for Sauwaseekau to be part of such a distinguished Shawnee family. How could the third born of Chief Puckeshinwa and Methoataske surpass the Shawnee Warrior or his sister Tecumapease? But Sauwaseekau did not resent, he loved. He was the best story teller in the family, enjoying that special niche.

Okiskee, born after Sauwaseekau and before Tecumseh, was in Missouri with Methoataske, as was Kumskaukau, the second youngest male in the family.

Tecumseh was now twenty years old in 1788. In his own way he was the core of the family for he was a composite of everyone. He was heir to the heroic mold of Puckeshinwa, Blackfish, Joseph Brant, Cornstalk, Pontiac. His character was noble as Tecumapease had wished, his mind as sharp as the best Grandfathers could whet it, his warrior body as conditioned as Cheeseeekau and Sauwaseekau could make it. He was Tecumapease's favorite and he spent much time with her, even now that she was married with children of her own.

Tecumapease was the mother of the family in the absence of Methoataske. Nehaaeemo, a beautiful spirited woman, born after Tecumseh and before Kumskaukau, was a great help to her, much as Sauwaseekau had been to Cheeseekau. A Shawnee woman had a very high status in her society but there was still very much work to do for a family in the wilderness. Nehaaeemo was of marriageable age and never lacked for suitors.

The only family member Tecumapease worried about was the youngest, Laulewasika. Everyone had spoiled him inadvertently because he had never known his father and his mother had gone to Missouri when the Shawnee tribe split forever. Tecumapease was concerned with Laulewasika's temper tantrums and certain devious ways. Coupled with his great intelligence he could make much trouble for himself. Laulewasika had been the most difficult to manage. The sister had often wondered if things would have been the same had Laulewasika gone with his mother to Missouri. But she loved the poor little orphan, tantrums and all. Such was the character of Tecumapease.

The six made their way from the Ohio Country toward Missouri in leisurely fashion, enjoying Earth Mother and Sky Father as only citizens of nature could. They travelled overland from Wapakoneta to a tributary of the Wabash River then floated downstream. It would have been simpler to go down the Great Miami but that would have led to the Ohio much sooner and the treacherous Shemanese lurked throughout the river, posing great dangers to all Indians. The sons of Chief Puckeshinwa would not place their sisters in such peril so the family made its way down the Wabash.

At the confluence of the Tippecanoe and Wabash rivers the Shawnee travellers fell in with some French Canadian traders who were on their way to New Orleans to sell their furs. The master, a Frenchman named Vitelle, recognized the Shawnee Warrior and treated him with great deference for he knew how to talk to Indians: "It is with an open heart that we recieve your hands. Friendship stretches ours to yours and unites them together. Let us be as brothers. Join us and enrich us with your company."

At first Cheeseekau fastened his eyes on Vitelle and his men as a hawk on its prey but that passed quickly on seeing the traders were French. "The chain of friendship between us," replied Cheeseekau, "has ever been bright. We live as brothers in this wilderness kingdom. I pledge my warrior's arm to you and your men. We will share your company."

Tecumseh, the best student in the family, knew only a smattering of French but he was delighted by the songs the Frenchmen sang. Boatmen's songs were always light and cheerful, created to pass the time while rowing or paddling, generally embodying some little satire or witticism calculated to produce a spirited chorus. The master usually started the song while the men would chorus what he sang:

Par derriere chéz ma tante,
Par derriere chéz ma tante

(Chorus)

Il-y-a un coq qui chante,
Des pommes, des poires, des raves, des choux,
Des figues nouvelles, des raisins doux.
(Chorus)

7

The song continued for miles until the advice was given:

Ne prenez pas une noire,
Car elles aiment trop à boire,
Ne prenez pas une rousse,
Car elles sont trop jalouses.

The different qualifications were rehearsed, objected to, lengthened by interminable repetition of the chorus, and stopped only by the shout of the master—"Whoop la! à terre, à terre: pour la pipe!" which signified a rest stop. Like all voyageurs, these men had to halt their prodigious labor of rowing so every five or six miles they stopped to relax and smoke their pipes. Distances were thus measured by "pipes" instead of miles.

Most Indians knew at least a smattering of French because Frenchmen had begun the fur trade and many were still actively engaged in it, contacting the Indians often. Tecumseh quickly understood why there was no more exhilirating mode of travel than voyaging over these waters amid the splendiforous magnificence of nature with the measured strokes of the oar keeping time to the strains of "Le Rosier Blanc," "En roulant ma Boule," "Leve ton pied, ma jolie Bergere," and so many other he heard throughout the journey down the Wabash. He found himself comparing the French, English, and Shemanese. The French were beyond a doubt the most stalwart friends of the Indians. But why was it so? All were from across the Great Salt Water. Each had come as strangers to this great island of the Indians. It was that the French had endeared themselves while the English had not. And now the Shemanese had taken control of the seacoast and would kill their bloody way toward the setting sun, it appeared, if they were not stopped. He doubted an honorable peace could be maintained yet he hoped he was wrong. Maybe they should all stay with Methoataske in Missouri. No, their lives were in the Ohio country. But perchance if their mother really needed them for a while they could extend their visit.

"Pour le pipe!" bellowed Vitelle again as the boatmen paddled toward shore, the Shawnee following their example. Tecumseh liked the Frenchmen. Many times he had seen or heard of their courage, athletic powers, perserverance, and patience with privations. In their canoes, pirogues, or barges they penetrated the remotest of territories, the longest rivers, made the most difficult portages, and kept up trade and communication much as the Indians always had. Indeed, they were much like native people, accustomed to every species of exposure and deprivation, despising ease and luxury because they robbed people of character. They dressed in buckskin Indian style, armed themselves as hunters, and could exchange an oar for a rifle with perfect equanimity. Their complexions were like those of Indians for the sun hit them directly from the sky as well as indirectly form the water.

Tecumseh had seen the *coeur de bois* as they floated their picturesque boats past this village or that. They were poetic in appearance for the scenes were like the fairy tales which he had loved so much as a child: a beautiful spring morning, the verdant forest on either side, the mild, almost delicious temperature of the air, a delightful azure sky, crystal clear water over scurrying fish, rich bottom lands here, rolling bluffs there, the boats and occupants floating gently forward. But these idyllic scenes camouflaged the toils, dangers, and adventures which were part and parcel of a career on the waterways of the Great Spirit. Within a few minutes from such poetic wonders there could be attacks from thieving cutthroats, insidious rapids, or deadly falls with foaming waters.

While everyone rested on shore one of the Frenchmen, the one named Guardapie, took out his violin and played a rousing ditty. Some of the others began to dance, cracking jokes all the while, laughing uproariously. In time the master blew some familiar notes on his bugle, the charming sound reverberating down the Wabash, as a signal for the men to return to their boats and man the oars. Had Tecumseh been an impressionable youth instead of a maturing young man he might well have been tempted by such a lifestyle.

Down river a couple of days later the party came to a bank that jutted out into the water, making it very shallow. A great number of trees and protruding branches had lodged on the bank so that water rushing through them sounded like falls or rapids. Night camp was made on shore and just before all were going to sleep there was a tremendous noise accompanied by so violent an agitation of the river the boats swayed to the point of capsizing.

"Mon Dieu!" yelled the master Vitelle. "Que'est ce qu'il y a?" Cheeseekau, Sauwaseeka, and Tecumseh were already on their feet but the ground under them was swaying. They looked at the river, saw it agitated as if by a tremendous monster. The noise was inconceivably loud and terrific but the crash of falling trees could be distinguished.

"C'est un tremblement de terre!" yelled a Frenchman.

"Allons a terre!"

The tremors diminished but were followed by a succession of lightning flashes which approached with great rapidity. A cloud so dense as to resemble a solid body in the night, came up, lightning pouring through it at intervals.

"We must shelter ourselves quickly," yelled Tecumseh as he stumbled toward Tecumapease.

"Ward the rain off with a skin!" said Sauwaseekau as he threw some at his sisters first. Nehaaeemo screamed as lightning hit a tree close by, setting it on fire.

"It's a real gale!" said Cheeseekau. "We must stay together or we will be blown away." He was able to grab a long strip of rawhide and encircle the sisters with it. "Hang on" he said to his brothers as the rain came down in angry torrents. No one could see the Frenchmen as they peered from under the skins. The Shawnee hoped they had not been swept into the river.

"The boats!" yelled Laulewasika. "They must be secured!" He made as if to go toward them but Cheeseekau grabbed the youngster and would not loosen him. The *ulukaashee* had been moored by the shore but no one was going to check them now.

The storm raged for the better part of an hour then began to abate until all was calm. The family was uninjured so concern turned to the Frenchmen who, after their initial shock, had secured all boats to their mooring then covered themselves with skins. Everyone had weathered the storm admirably and congratulations were hearty. Survival was always an achievement.

The next morning the sun rose unobscured and everything was put out to dry. There were no discernible chasms caused by the quake though many trees had been uprooted.

"I never want to see the like again!" said Nehaaeemo.

"It wasn't so bad," commented Laulewasika. "I would have seen to the boats except for Cheeseekau."

"You are brave, little brother," said Tecumapease. She hoped wisdom would come with experience.

The shining sun and gentle breezes dried everything in a couple of days and the party was off again. When it came time to part with the Frenchmen the Shawnee family bid them a fond "Adieu" at the confluence of the Ohio and Mississippi. After buying some horses they set out overland for the last leg of their journey to Cape Girardeau and Sugar Creek. Cheeseekau was eternally vigilant for signs of danger, Sauwaseekau kept everyone entertained with jokes and stories, Tecumapease and Tecumseh saw to everyone's needs, and Laulewasika threw an occassional tantrum. When they crossed the mighty Father of Waters they knew their mother was a short distance away, expectation and happiness filling everyone's heart. Their approach to the village at Sugar Creek was unannounced but children gathered to look at the strangers.

"My boy," called out Cheeseekau to one of the older children, "can you inform me where lives Methoataske, wife of Puckeshinwa?"

"Sure," replied the lad, "down that way. Come on, I'll take you," he said as he trotted away, the other children at his heels.

"Methoataske, Methoataske!" chanted the children in unison. They came to a wegiwa where Okiskee and Kumskaukau came out to see about the commotion.

"Okiskee! Kumskaukau!" yelled Tecumapese in her happiness as she bolted from her mount and ran to them.

"Tecumapease!" returned her sister and brother. The others dismounted and rushed to them, the scene becoming a melee of hugs, warm embraces, closeness, tears from the females. The family entered the wegiwa to find Methoataske stirring some food in a large pot. At first she looked at everyone as if they were strangers, the family quieted momentarily by the apparent lack of reaction.

"I knew you were coming," said Methoataske calmly. "See, I have your food prepared. I am glad your journey was safe, that you are well. I look upon you, my heart is white again, and I smile."

Cheeseekau walked up to his mother and embraced her. "My first born," said Methoataske quietly. "Even from this great distance we have heard of our Shawnee Warrior." She rubbed Cheeseekau's face and hair as if he was a child.

At any other time the rest of the family would have remained astonished at Methoataske's lack of emotion but the years had been long so they crowded around the mother, embracing her, touching her as best they could all at once, telling her how they had missed her terribly all this time. Tears came to Methoataske and soon everyone wept, even the men. "Your father would have been very proud of you, my children. For all of you to come this long way together at one time. I have missed you so greatly! Would that you could live with me again. Perhaps I shall return with you."

"You will return with us, my mother!" said a jubilant Cheeseekau. His reactions were like the spring of the panther.

"I miss the Ohio country but do you know what is even deeper in my heart?" asked Methoataske wistfully.

"What, mother?" encouraged Tecumseh.

"I would like to return to the lands of the Creeks where my fathers were born."

"I shall take you wherever you wish," said Cheeseekau.

"I long for the ancient freedoms of our people," continued Methoataske. "But you, my beloved children, bring rest to my heart. I feel like

11

a leaf after a storm, when the wind is still. It is a pleasant sky above our heads this day. There is nothing to darken it. I hear nothing but pleasant words. The raven is not waiting for his prey. I hear no eagle scream."

"Come," interrupted Okiskee, accustomed to her mother's flights of fancy, "let us eat. You must be famished." She got bowls for everyone as the females immediately began to help. "It is absolutely amazing. Mother kept telling us she would soon be reunited with her family. We thought she was just wishing but somehow she knew, she knew."

While everyone ate Tecumapease took Okiskee aside and asked, "How has she been, honestly?"

"I think she is doing very well," answered Okiskee. "She broods much too much and she still loves our father, but moving here has been good for her mind. She often talks of returning to the Creeks so I guess she means it. I am certain she will return with you. I have a husband and two children now, I will be unable to return."

"Okiskee, how wonderful!" exclaimed Tecumapease as she hugged the younger sister. "I am dying to meet my nephews! Would that you could see my family also. The fragmentation of our tribe has been painful to everyone in so many ways."

"Hey you two," called Tecumseh, "come and eat! We need our sisters to cheer us."

Everyone chatted for the rest of the day and a good portion of the night. The following day Methoataske took her family out among the villagers and the basic question was: How are our people faring in the Ohio country?

Episode 3: Louisa St. Clair

The tribes had been told to assemble at Duncan's Falls for the treaty which would be effected this year, 1788. But Thayendanegea of the Mohawk Iroquois, known in English as Joseph Brant, led the movement which postponed the council and pressed to move it to another locale where the men would not be under the guns of General Harmar and his soldiers. Fort Harmar, across the river from Marietta, was selected as a better site and when Micheal Brant, son of the famous chief, came down the Tuscarawas and Muskingum trails with two hundred warriors he was selected to inform Governor St. Clair of the change.

Young Brant accepted the responsibility and rode with his warriors to Duncan's Falls. He had been educated well by his multi-talented father, even being sent to Shemanese schools in Philadelphia, so it would be no simple matter to trick him. Once at the Falls, Brant immediately posted sentries, made his encampment, sent two warriors with large white flags to Zanesville nine miles below to inform Governor St. Clair the tribes desired treaty preliminaries to be fixed at this time.

Louisa St. Clair, as bold as she was beautiful, was riding her spirited mount a distance from Zanesville when she noticed two redmen approaching. She saw the white flags so she rode toward the warriors.

The men stopped when they saw a lone rider approaching at a gallop. They lifted their flags high, waved them from side to side. A trick? Both smiled when the horseman reined up in front of them and turned out being a woman. "Message," said one of the Indians, "message for Governor St. Clair," waving the letter in front of Louisa.

"Come with me," said the comely young woman, "my father is in the fort." She rode lightly on her saddle as the Indians followed.

The gates of the fort opened to admit the trio as people gawked at the redskins, soldiers immediately surrounding the riders. The Indian with the letter held it in full view of everyone though he did not appear nervous.

"Louisa!" gasped her father as he came out of his quarters. The girl dismounted smartly and walked toward St. Clair.

"These Indians have a message for you, father. I'll bet its about the treaty."

A soldier took the envelope, handed it to the Governor. "Thank you," he said, then bowed slightly toward the Indians. "I shall read it and return with my answer. Please wait." The redskins remained on their horses as the St. Clairs entered their temporary quarters. The letter was short, containing nothing more than an invitation for St. Clair to come to Duncan's Falls and finalize details for the impending council, which was desired at Fort Harmar. It could be a trap, thought St. Clair to himself so as not to alarm Louisa. If they abducted me... he re-read the letter, decided it was legitimately innocuous with nary a glint of treachery. He set down the missive but Louisa snatched it up immediately and read it excitedly. Duncan's Falls. That's where the Indians were. It was signed "M. Brant." Could that be the Micheal Brant she had met in school?

St. Clair went outside and addressed the Indians. "I will send an answer with a ranger. You may expect him within a day or two. Tell Captain Brant I send my fondest regards. We meet soon." He raised his hand in farewell, the Indians did the same, turned their horses and rode calmly out of the stockade. "Get Hamilton Kerr," ordered St. Clair. "Ham is the ranger for this job." An orderly went to find the ranger while St. Clair went indoors to compose his reply.

Hamilton Kerr came to see Governor St. Clair that evening and received

St. Clair went outside and addressed the Indians. "I will send an answer with a ranger. You may expect him within a day or two. Tell Captain Brant I send my fondest regards. We meet soon." He raised his hand in farewell, the Indians did the same, turned their horses and rode calmly out of the stockade. "Get Hamilton Kerr," ordered St. Clair. "Ham is the ranger for this job." An orderly went to find the ranger while St. Clair went indoors to compose his reply.

Hamilton Kerr came to see Governor St. Clair tht evening and received his instructions. He was to contact the Indians and deliver a reply but he was also to reconnoiter the area for a possible ambush or trap. "I don't think trouble is brewing at this point," commented St. Clair, "but you never know with this race. I do not expect danger though you are the most competent ranger to handle it if it crops up. I can send additional men if you so desire."

"That will not be necessary, sir," remarked Hamilton as Louisa entered the room then exited immediately when she saw her father was in conference. "The tribes are peacefully disposed at this juncture."

"Yes. They were bold enough to send only two messengers. We shall demonstrate we need but one. Get a good night's rest and set out tomorrow. Return immediately after delivering the letter or I shall take it as a sign of trouble and send out a rescue mission."

"You may trust in me, sir," concluded Hamilton as he stood to leave. The two shook hands and said, "Good night."

"Father," said beauteous Louisa as she glided into the room when she saw her parent was alone, "why could I not have been born a man?"

The question more than its abruptness took St. Clair totally by surprise. "Bold one, what are you talking about?"

"Men have all the fun," said Louisa as she made a face. "Why could I not go instead of Ham? Simply because I am a woman! How unfair!"

"My child, we are not having fun, as you say. This is business of state. Surely you don't want to go out among the savages—"

"And why not? You taught me to ride and shoot and love the woods. You said this was our country. Now that I am of age all people expect of me is to marry and raise children. Why shouldn't I go out and scout? My soul needs adventure too."

The Governor looked at his daughter proudly but shaking his head slightly. "Come here, child," he said. A thousand men with Louisa's boldness and the Northwest Territory would belong to the United States in short order. Even Arthur, his oldest son, didn't have such zest for living. He loved Jane and Margaret, his two other daughters, but Louisa was in a class by herself. At a very tender age she had asked her father,

"But when am I going to be able to be a soldier?" Now she was saying the same thing once again. "I suppose you want me to let you go with Ham?"

"Instead of," said Louisa.

"Your mother would have me lashed to the stockade, now wouldn't she?"

"All right, with him then."

"You're still my big girl," said the father. "If anything happened to you I could never forgive myself. The savages—"

"We are not at war with the savages," interrupted Louisa, "there is no real danger or you would not send Ham out by himself and they would not have come here in the first place."

"Spying on me are you young lady?" said the Governor in the most imperious tone he could muster.

"You would find me a good spy, father," pleaded Louisa, "oh please let me go instead of Ham!"

"Get the 'instead of' out of your head." He kissed her affectionately on the forehead. "Now it's getting late and I have things to do."

"Oh all right," said Louisa as she kissed her father on the lips. "I'm still your best spy. Now don't stay up too late. You're no young buck, you know."

St. Clair made as if to strike her fanny whereupon Louisa bolted away, giggling. She went to her room then her father's words echoed in her mind: Get the instead of out of your head. She went to her trunk and pulled out her Indian clothes, laid them over the bedstead. She had trouble falling asleep that night, such was her excitement.

Episode 4: Micheal Brant and Louisa St. Clair

Hamilton Kerr didn't feel starting at the crack of dawn was necessary since Duncan's Falls was a bit more than a day's ride away. He didn't want to arrive at the Indian camp at sunup so he left at half past nine, his keen eye watchful for anything the trail might tell him. A short distance above Waterford the man reined in his horse sharply: tracks, very fresh, from an Indian pony. Immediately he veered off the trail, slid off his horse in the same motion that he readied his rifle for defense. He crouched then went to his knees and elbows, crept to the top of a bluff, keeping the river in sight all the while. Then he heard a woman laughing, got to his feet slowly, saw Louisa St. Clair, dressed Indian style, on her pony.

"I could have picked you off six times," laughed Louisa as the stupefied ranger walked back toward the trail and his horse.

"What on earth are you doing here?" asked Ham.

15

"I could have picked you off six times," laughed Louisa as the stupefied ranger walked back toward the trail and his horse.

"What on earth are you doing here?" asked Ham.

"I left before you did," said the young woman as she smiled radiantly. "Some of us are serious about our work."

"Get back to the stockade or your father will be coming out a-looking for you," ordered the scout.

"I'm going to Duncan's Falls to parley with the Indians," said Louisa with no little determination.

"There will be no parley, just delivery of a letter," said Hamilton as he pointed to a pouch on his saddle. " Does you father know you're here?"

"He does not mind if I accompany you. He refused to let me go alone. Now let's get moving before some white man sees you and mistakes you for an Indian."

"Louisa, now see here—"

The girl laughed the louder. "Goodness Ham! Okay, the red handkerchief for a turban, the hunting shirt, but a breechclout instead of pants. You must think your legs are a sight to see!"

What was Hamilton Kerr to do? She was afterall the Governor's daughter. If he had given permission it was not for the ranger to object. Ham took her pony by the bridle, led it up the trail, mounted his own horse and resumed his mission.

The two riders made good time, without incidents of note. The beauty of the wilderness was an omnipresent charm to Louisa and Ham admitted to himself he enjoyed her company. That night the two built a small campfire, supped from the dried venison the ranger carried. The horses were hobbled for the night and Louisa covered herself to sleep, rifle in hand under her blanket.

Ham looked at the girl as she dozed by the small fire. What were women coming to these days! But then Louisa was a breed apart, finding amusement and frolic in everything around her. She could ride a horse as well as most men. He had seen her mounting the wildest or most spirited animals, managing them with skill. She was a constant figure in the wilderness, dashing through the woodlands and open spaces at a full gallop, leaping over logs or other obstacles that presented themselves. During the winter when ice covered the Muskingum she could skate with the best of them, her speed equaled only by her grace. Everyone knew she could load and shoot her rifle like a woodsman, killing a squirrel from the highest tree or lopping off the head of a partridge. Always in the woods, she didn't seem to fear the savages lurking in them. Louisa St.

Clair was a rare spirit indeed, besides being the Governor's daughter. Hamilton Kerr did not forget that very important fact as he stared at the girl, protected by her snug blanket. He listened to the night, decided all was naturally calm, reached for his own blanket and was soon in a light sleep.

The next morning the two continued their journey and within a few hours after sunrise came into sight of the Indian camp. Hamilton stopped his mount, peered cautiously into the encampment, noting the prevailing atmosphere, definitely relaxed, of the savages as they walked around. He detected no evidence of sentries. Perhaps there were none—Louisa reached toward Ham's saddle, untied the dispatch pouch with a jerk, yanked it toward her then took off excitedly, her pony at a full gallop.

"Louisa no, don't!" yelled Hamilton as the girl headed directly into the Indian camp. He dared not follow at a gallop for the savages might think they were being attacked so he mustered all his will power and kept his horse at a walk.

Louisa had enough presence of mind to wave a white kerchief as she approached and entered the encampment. A number of rifles were readied but the white flag prevented instinctive defensive measures. Mounted warriors came up alongside her, slowed her pony to a walk, took the reins. She was now their prisoner and for a fleeting moment she was frightened. "I have a message for Captain Brant from Governor St. Clair," she said cooly. "I would speak with Brant."

The warriors remained impassive but secretly they were impressed with this courageous Shemanese woman dressed as an Indian maiden. But why send a female? Could it be a trick? Probably not, but maybe an insult.

"I have a message for Captain Brant," repeated Louisa, in full control of herself now and enjoying her temerity.

"My father is not among us," remarked a young warrior in full war panoply, "I am here in his stead."

Louisa looked at Micheal Brant, remembering how differently he had looked wearing civilized clothing. She concluded immediately that Brant was much more handsome in the clothes of his people. "Here is the letter for you then," remarked Louisa as she opened the pouch, handed over the envelope. "I remember you from Philadelphia," she added. The girl had never forgotten how perfectly at ease Micheal Brant had been that day at school, drinking tea from a dainty, fragile china cup then going outside to demonstrate how a tomahawk could be hurled with deadly accuracy. Impressionable Louisa learned from her older school chums Micheal Brant was more familiar with buckled shoes and cologne than the scent of cows which permeated so many American boys. She was also told the Brants were very wealthy, lived in a luxurious home, wore clothes tailor made of the finest material, had meals served on crisp Irish linen, and owned a host of slaves. These were savages?! Her one desire during the cotillion that night was to dance with Micheal Brant...

"What?" exclaimed Brant, visibly affected by her radiant gaze.

"Philadelphia," explained Louisa, "when you were visiting from college and I was a student in school. We were at the cotillion and introduced to each other."

"Then you are--"

"Louisa St. Clair."

"The Governor's daughter!" said Micheal Brant as flatly as he could.

"A lone rider is approaching," warned one of the men as all turned to look. Louisa had not understood the language but she turned to see Hamilton Kerr at the periphery of the camp. She waved her kerchief and Ham immediately waved his white flag in response. Brant issued an order and a number of warriors went out to meet the other messenger as Louisa explained who he was.

"I remember the cotillion," continued Micheal as he made a super-human effort to place the girl. There had been so many introductions that night! How could he have forgotten the daughter of St. Clair! "But there were so many people," he admitted honestly.

"It's all right," soothed Louisa as she flashed her beautiful smile, "I remember you and I haven't forgotten."

Micheal bowed gallantly, appreciating her magninimity. He motioned for his men to bring in the other rider then quickly read the letter. Its contents were simple and direct: Governor St. Clair could not come to Duncan's Falls but if the leaders of the various tribes wanted to meet at Fort Harmar, as he had been informed, he would join them there within ten suns. Micheal Brant was pleased for it was what the leaders sought. He smiled at Louisa, oblivious to the ranger.

"I risked my life to come see you," said Louisa, "and now I am going to ask for your aid in returning to Marietta where my father awaits us."

You have but to ask," chivalrously replied Brant.

"We feel we need some protection for the return trip," said Louisa. Hamilton kerr looked at her in puzzlement. "Might we impose upon you for a guard?"

"My people are a race who value personal courage," said Micheal,

18

"and I would be less than a gentleman to risk anything happening to so wondrous a maiden as the daughter of Governor St. Clair. I shall escort you to Marietta myself, along with some of my most trusted warriors."

"Then let us begin immediately," commented Hamilton Kerr.

Brant sent the governor's message on to the Indian leaders then selected the escort, instructing the others to await his return. Soon everyone was riding, Brant next to Louisa.

"Why did you risk your life as a messenger?" asked Micheal.

"I don't know," replied Louisa honestly, " I guess I wanted some adventure and ..."

"And?"

"And to see the Micheal Brant I met before," concluded Louisa. "But you didn't even remember me."

"But I will never forget you now," commented the man sincerely. Micheal's face was impassive but his eyes shined.

"What do you mean?"

"Like I said, our people value courage. Very few maidens would come to parley as you did. Especially dressed as you are. Where did you get that outfit?"

"Come now," chided Louisa playfully. "Your people wear our clothing on occassion, why should we not wear yours?"

"True," replied Micheal. "We both are only people after all."

"Tell me about your father," suggested Louisa. "My father says he is the greatest living man of your race."

"His basic concern is to obtain justice for our people. This treaty coming up will be most important in keeping the peace between our races."

"That is what my father is working for also."

The two discussed many issues during their ride and the evenings at the campfire. They found mutual acquaintances from the Philadelphia years and by the time they arrived at Marietta they were more than just attracted to each other, they were fast friends.

"Now it is you who must give us an escort," said Micheal as he saw a squad of soldiers coming out of the fort to investigate the approaching Indian party.

"Hamilton and I will ride up to them, you just keep this pace," said Louisa. "Come on Ham."

The two galloped to the squad, stopped their progress, waited until the Indians rode up. The warriors were surrounded and escorted into the stockade while numerous citizens gazed at them in wary silence. Louisa took Micheal to her father and explained how kind young Brant had

19

been. The Governor felt some kind of vibration emanating from his daughter but he had no time to specify it.

"Chief Brant, I appreciate you caring for my daughter's safety," began St. Clair, "especially during these times." He said nothing of her going without permission, *that* he would settle with the bold one. " It is our fondest wish both our people might live in peace and security. I am looking forward to meeting with your distinguished father and I shall certainly express my appreciation to him personally. Now there is food for your men and I would like you to grace us with your presence at my family's dinner table."

"I would be most honored," replied Micheal as he bowed slightly. " My only regret is that I did not bring the proper attire for such a function. Perhaps it would be better if we dined another time, at the treaty making perhaps—"

"No," interrupted Louisa. "I mean, you must be hungry. And I am dressed as you are. Let us dine as my father suggests." There was obvious enthusiasm in Louisa's voice.

"All right then," accepted Micheal, "we shall dine if it is your wish."

"Good," finished St. Clair, though he was puzzled with his daughter. "Louisa, be so kind as to inform your mother." The girl exited immediately and the two men talked pleasantly until Micheal excused himself to see to his men. St. Clair went to order their nourishment and when all the details were taken care of the Governor's family and Micheal Brant sat down to eat. The conversation was polite, Louisa could not keep her eyes off Micheal, and young Brant was pleasant and correct. St. Clair was impressed with the man but his thoughts were more on his father, whom he reckoned to be his principal antagonist at the upcoming treaty. When the occassion was finished Micheal expressed his thanks and gratitude to Mrs. St. Clair, bid everyone farewell, then mounted up and rode out of the stockade, escorted by soldiers and Louisa.

"My friend," said Micheal when it was time for the escort to turn back, "in this short time you have become more than my friend. I wish to see you again very soon."

Louisa offered her hand in farewell. "It is also my dearest wish. Come visit—" She caught herself. "We shall see each other again."

"Soon, dear friend," said Micheal as he took her hand in both of his. "You shall be in my thoughts until we meet again. Your touch is as light as a feather falling from an eagle's breast, your voice like the music of paddles stroking the blue waters of the lake. You have given me a joy which will light up the lodge circle as a new fire kindled in the eyes of my friends and kinfolk."

The Indians rode away, the soldiers returned to Marietta, Louisa remained alone, deeply touched by the poetry she had just heard. For some ineffable reason she wanted to cry. Micheal looked back several times, noting the girl had not moved. When he saw her the last time he waved a final farewell then disappeared at the head of his warriors. In his heart he felt the voice of Spring coming over the mountains, waking the earth with primrose stars and violets' breath. Then his feelings bounded like the deer pasturing free near the waving sprays of forest bough. Micheal Brant knew he was in love with Louisa St. Clair.

Episode 5: Treaty making.

Arthus St. Clair, Governor of the Northwest Territory, was confident he could accomplish what he had been instructed to do: hammer out a treaty which would insure white development of the rich lands north of the Ohio River. He looked at the assembled Indians as they passed around the calument, each puffing from it ceremoniously. Secretly he was impatient to begin but he understood that redmen had to fan their vanity with their own style of protocol before getting down to business. He stood up from where he had been sitting, allowing the Indians to scrutinize him. Of Scottish stock, he was tall, graceful, dignified in his resplendent military uniform. His hair was of a chestnut color, his blue-grey eyes had often been described as handsome, his complexion that of a typical blond. His nose was large but not overly prominent, his gaze constant, his jaw and mouth set with determination. He knew the savages were studying him yet he remained as impassive as they. He gave the redmen all the time they needed then began:

"I welcome you, O my chiefs, and I pray to the God of our fathers that what we accomplish here at Fort Harmar may lead to everlasting peace and friendship." St. Clair paused for the several translators to convey his message. "There is nothing greater to be hoped for than life and security for our women and children..." The Governor made his opening address then invited the Indians to speak their hearts before signing the new treaty which Congress empowered him to offer them.

Captain Hendrick of the Mohawk was the first to speak: "I have been delegated the task of informing Governor St. Clair and his commissioners that our brothers the Miamis, Kickapoos, Shawnee, as well as other members of the Confederacy have refused to attend these proceedings. It is clear they will countenance no cession of land north of our Ohio River. I wish to apologize to the Governor for their absence but I want him to understand that we have done all in our power to invite our countrymen to come here, listen to what is said

21

with an open heart, and partake of the festivities which the Governor has planned for us."

Captain Pipe of the Delaware spoke next: "We, the Delaware, along with our younger brothers, the Shawnee and the Mingo, have tried living along the waters of the Sandusky and the Maumee, which in ages past were only places for our winter hunts. Now we miss the waters of the Muskingum, the Scioto, the Great Miami. There the country is better for there is more game and the lands are excellent for corn. We want our brothers here present to know that we are uneasy where we are. We desire to return to our Ohio lands as rightful owners, which we are now and have always been, since time out of mind. No conquest has wrested these lands from us, and during the Revolution of the Longknives against the British we defended them successfully. The land cessions at Fort McIntosh and Fort Finney were invalid for they were not authorized by our Confederacy. These treaties were signed by individuals, not representatives assigned by the tribes. Furthermore, there were soldiers at their backs. Not one inch of our forest domain has been negotiated away nor honorably won on the field of battle. The Ohio River is the boundary between us and you and so this treaty must say."

Governor St. Clair now rose to answer: "General Wahington wants our people to live in peace, an honorable peace for us all. That is our purpose for gathering here. I have no authority to rescind or renegotiate any previous treaty. It is common knowledge that you made treaties with the British but you understand the American government is not bound by them. We threw the British on their backs, as you all know, during the war. It is unfortunate so many of you chose to side with the British. Be that as it may, the United States will allow you to occupy your lands. What more can we do to extend the chain of friendship?"

St. Clair glanced at General Harmar as he finished speaking. He knew Harmar felt this effort was wasted on Indians. They would come for the whiskey and the food but only a good thrashing on the field of battle would accomplish American aims.

Buckongahelas of the Delaware now spoke: "Our Confederacy must be respected as we respect yours. It would not do to sign treaties with separate states, ignoring your central government. So it will not do with us. You kindled your council fires where you thought proper, without consulting the Confederacy, when individuals signed the treaties of Fort Stanwix, Fort McIntosh, and Fort Finney. We told you about having a general conference with the entire Confederacy but instead you neglected our plan, effecting your aims covertly. I will tell you my heart clearly: all treaties must be with the whole of our confederacy and negotiations

22

must be carried on in the most open manner, without restraint or coercion from either side. This is the way business of state is carried on in this great island. If a cession of land is to be valid it must be made in the most public way and by the united voice of the Confederacy. We are one people with the same needs of the land. Any other treaty is void and of no effect because it will not be honored. We will fight to protect our lands."

General Harmar rose to speak: "My brothers, as you know, I am a soldier. You too are warriors, men who value courage and know what war is. You were led astray during the Revolution and you sided with the British. They lost the war, therefore it is only logical that you lost it also." There was a restless murmur as the translators delivered Harmar's message. "But in its generosity the United States has seen fit to allow you to retain your lands west of the Great Miami and Maumee Rivers. We could have dispossessed you, for such is the nature of war, but the People of the Eagle believe in justice, even for the vanquished. You still possess your best lands, you still have your tribes and customs. As victors we Americans claim some of the land. Why continue to fight, is there not sufficient land for everyone? These new lands have been surveyed and are now open to settlement. They are rightfully ours for we were the victors in war, which all understand. We have been magnanimous victors and now we want to consider you our friends and allies. You made a serious mistake with the British. Do not make one with the United States. Take up our hand in friendship so we may live in security."

Half King of the Wyandot spoke on behalf of his nation: "I am now between two fires for I must listen to you and to the back nations. Our Shawnee brothers have accused us of permitting our lands to be negotiated away from us at Fort Finney, that we permitted the surveys of their hunting grounds, that we did not resist. It is a simple matter for the back nations. They will not be the first to have their territory invaded, their villages burned, their women and children destitute and sobbing in pain."

St. Clair replied: "My brothers, war and destruction is the furthest thing from our mind. We are gathered to conclude a treaty of amity for so long as the sun shines and waters flow. We are strong. We have more hunting shirt men than there are leaves in the forest but our only desire is peace and honor. We must all live with our promises and the treaties made heretofore are not the purpose of this gathering. Peace and friendship are our concern." The Governor wanted Joseph Brant to address the gathering. He was certain the Indians were hopelessly divided.

Perhaps a blow could be struck that would end the Confederacy for all time. He looked at Brant, timing the silence carefully, then bowed at the Mohawk chieftain.

Joseph Brant knew he had been slightly outmaneuvered. But it was of no great importance. He got to his feet slowly and spoke: "We of the Confederacy have the same aims as Governor St. Clair. He speaks for the People of the Eagle, all of them. So must we talk for all our inhabitants of this great wilderness. We realize some of us are in immediate danger in case of attack." He nodded slightly toward Half King but his glance caught on Cornplanter, the Seneca who was his great rival among the Iroquois nations. "There are also others of our people who would never agree to the slightest compromise on the Ohio River boundary between our inhabitants and the people of the United States. Like every rational human being I too value peace and friendship. You all know I proposed a compromise boundary in order to preserve the peace, knowing I was risking alienation of both extremes in our Confederacy. But most of us are here and this gladdens my heart for we may speak with one voice to Governor St. Clair and his commissioners." Brant was satisfied. He had been forced to speak, had done so, and had said nothing that helped St. Clair with the proceedings. The burden was back on the Governor.

"My brothers, the great chief Thayendanegea of the Mohawk has spoken well," answered St. Clair, "and I am of the same happy heart to see us all here together in an effort to forge the chain of friendship. May the Great Spirit give us time to accomplish this goal. Now let us adjourn until tomorrow that we may begin the feast which we have prepared for you. I invite you all to partake of the gifts of the Great Spirit." The Governor walked out of the council hall toward the area where all kinds of meats were roasting in preparation for the Indians. The whiskey barrels were opened and all were encouraged to drink their fill. A couple of fiddlers supplied the music and the scene became complicated as the revelers, Indians or Shemanese, pursued their individual desires.

Micheal Brant was in the crowd that evening during the festivities, looking in vain for Louisa St. Clair. Finally he walked up to the Governor, asked if he could speak to him privately, succeeded in taking him aside.

"Sir," began Micheal, "I wish to marry your daughter."

St. Clair's main concern was the discovery that Brant and Cornplanter disliked each other intensely. If handled properly this could be very--

"What?" asked the Governor.

"I wish to marry Louisa," repeated Micheal.

At first St. Clair thought the Indian before him was drunk but then he noted the seriousness in young Brant's face. "My daughter has a mind of her own," said the father quickly, " as you might know. Or do you? I was unaware the two of you knew each other well."

"I can say I know her well enough to want her to be my wife," said Micheal.

St. Clair concealed his astonishment well. Louisa had never expressed an interest in the son of Chief Brant. Why, the Governor hardly even knew his name. He marvelled at the young man's confidence.

"I have not been able to forget her since she rode into our camp," confessed Micheal. "I can protect her and care for her well."

"I have no doubt about that, my boy," conceded St. Clair. "But it is quite beyond me to marry off my daughter without preparations."

"The union would be good for our two peoples," said Brant. "With your permission I will ask Louisa for her hand."

"You must forgive me, this comes like a lightning bolt out of the clear blue sky. My thoughts are on the treaty. While I am very concerned over Louisa it is she who has the final say. I would not want to be accused of marrying off my daughter for the sake of political convenience. You are free to speak your heart to Louisa and I am certain you will understand that at this juncture my prime concern is the treaty.

"Of course," said Micheal, "thank you. I have not been able to find her this evening. Will she be in attendance?"

"I would think she would be here but I was not informed as to her plans. She likes to be in the thick of things so it would be a good guess she will show up."

"I shall find her then. Thank you sir," said Micheal as he walked away in search of the woman he wanted to marry.

Episode 6: The Treaty

The following day the grand council was reconvened and addressed first by Governor St. Clair: "My brothers, I come to you this day with a determination that you understand we do not have authority to change boundaries between our people and yours. The country northwest of the Ohio has already been surveyed and is ready to be sold to settlers from the United States. Your people signed treaties which gave us the right to do so and my government has borne the expense of surveying. I am here to cultivate a good understanding with you and if anyone is sowing seeds of discord between us it is not I. And as to our right, ask the British who deluded you with professions of friendship. They were owners of the northwest country according to their own declarations and we threw the redcoats on their backs. Now the people of the Eagle want to enjoy what is theirs by right of conquest. We do not demand you get out of the territory, though we are not preventing you from migrating to good lands on the other side of the Mississippi as some of your good people have done. We ask that you allow us to live peaceable in our settlements."

St. Clair's opening comment and his haughty demeanor angered the assembled Indians. Joseph Brant replied: "Why were we not told when we sent word to your Congress that there was no possibility of making any alterations respecting the boundary line? I understand all too well now why you rejected even my proposed compromise line. If I had seen it sooner it would have saved us a great deal of trouble and fatigue. Governor, as you well know, we native people are the possessors of the soil north of the Ohio. By the law of nations we cannot be dispossessed. You may take by conquest what the British owned but remember in 1763 they set aside Indian lands in perpetuity. We have already gone over this and I shall not go over it again. If we find there is no other means left but that you must and will have our entire country we now tell you we have our feelings and our Great Spirit. We must leave future events to His will. He knows and understands the hearts of all men. We are peaceably inclined and nothing is further from our hearts than entering into a war. Treaties are insufficient to cover the hand of aggression. If the road becomes bloody it will be the doing of your country and your people." Brant then walked out of the council house followed by the other Mohawks in the group. They gathered their belongings, climbed on their horses and rode out of Fort Harmar. Micheal and some of his Chippewa followers remained behind because they were unaware their chief had washed his hands of the treaty making.

St. Clair and the commissioners were able to prevent the other Indians from bolting away, appealing to Brant's enemies to hold the gathering together. The strategy worked.

Shendeta the Wyandot sought to describe the Indian view of how native people had been cheated of their lands: "I dreamed of the past some time ago and I wish to share with you the feeling of that dream. I saw that the Wyandot nation were the first men the Great Spirit placed on this island. The Delaware were the second. The Wyandots sent the Delawares to the seashore to maintain vigil and see what creatures came out of the water. The first creatures he saw were the French. Then, some time later he spied the British. They asked to remain only one night on shore. With the Delawares as emissaries the Wyandot gave their permission. The British then became very persuasive when they begged for just a little bit of ground on which to make a fire, 'as much as one of our cowhides would cover,' they said. The British were pitiful and Wyandot moved with compassion, so the piteous request was granted. The British then gave the Delawares some liquor and made them foolish enough to lose their senses for a while. Now they cut the cowhide into thin strips which they used to enclose a considerable amount of land. When the Delawares came to their senses and saw what happened they knew they had been cheated. All they could say was 'Is this the way you are going to treat me always while you remain in our country?' The selfrighteous British denied they had cheated the Delawares, that they were merely taking what was rightfully theirs by agreement." Shendeta looked at St. Clair, General Harmar, the other commissioners. Either they were unaware of what he was saying or they did not understand the allegory. "The next generation of British decided they would buy more land," continued the speaker, "just a small strip they assured everyone, as much as a man could walk in one day. Again they brought much whiskey to celebrate the event, even if the Delawares had not agreed to anything. They gave much firewater to all. Now the British had hired their swiftest runners and these covered a great deal of land that day. Title was deman-ded of the Indians in order to comply with the promises made, they asserted, during the festivities, pointing out what great expense they had gone to for the celebration. Since then the British and the People of the Eagle have continued to take the land. I cannot explain how you have advanced so far into this country for I have not dreamt of it."

General Harmar was visibly irritated with all this talk of dreams. "Truly," he began, "if this is what we have been meeting for our time has been spent to very little purpose. If you were cheated by the British it is not the fault of the Americans for we were not allowed to make decisions on Indian affairs. Take your complaints to the British. You fought for them, they lost, and by all rights you should be grateful for our treatment of you when we continue to offer our friendship. I am a soldier, accus-tomed to speaking plainly. You joined the British king against, us, call-ing him father. We have overcome him. He has cast you off and given us your country. Our Congress, in its bounty and mercy, offers you peace and a country. We have told you our terms and these will not alter because they are just and liberal. We now tell you, if you are unwise and refuse these terms you may depart in peace. You shall have provisions with which to return to your towns and no man shall touch you. Then we shall consider ourselves free from all ties of protection. You may depend on the United States to protect its citizens and distress your obstinate nations. It rests now with you. Peace is in your power. Make your choices like men! We tell you plainly this country belongs to the Americans. Our blood will defend and protect it. You should be thankful for our forgiveness and offers of kindness instead of black wampum belts!"

Cornplanter was quick to reply: "Do not misunderstand us, my father. I want peace as fervently as you and I have seen that you treat your children with justice for you promised to allow my nation to retain its hunting grounds on the upper Allegheny as well as promoting trade and teaching us your style of agriculture. Father, you have now grown so big and strong that none of us can injure you. I hope you look up towards Heaven and return thanks to the Spirit for your greatness. Father, you say this land is yours. I hope you will take pity on the native inhabitants of this country as they took pity on your ancestors when they first arrived on this island."

Duentete next launched into a denunciation of Brant: "What Chief Brant has done is of no effect. There is not one grain of truth in anything he says. It was his fault we could not meet sooner to get this good work moving as we are at present about. We think it is the Mohawk who is doing the contrary work. It was Brant and the western nations who held council, the Mohawk telling these people nothing could be done with the United States that would be equitable, that now their only choice was peace or war. If they chose war he would help them but if they were for peace he would acquiesce. They declared for war against the Americans, Brant and his people striking Fort Pitt, the others striking here. Brant also did all within his power to prevent the pro-American Indians from attending this council."

St. Clair asked Chief Duentete: "What will your Wyandot do if Brant should be foolish enough to strike at the Americans?"

"It was the Six Nations," returned Duentete, "who caused this unsettling situation. They are the cause of the mischief done at the council fire." He looked directly at Cornplanter. "You, brothers of the Six Nations, you drew your sword and stuck it into the ground for the Quiatenon nation, desiring them to strike the United States. Further, it was you who originally sold lands to the British, the Kentucky lands south of the Ohio, lands which were not yours to sell because you did not occupy nor hunt on. Therefore I will let the brothers of the Six Nations answer the question of Governor St. Clair."

With Brant gone, Cornplanter was the leading chief present for the Iroquois delegation. He was visibly angry as he spoke: "Our younger brothers the Wyandot have given much more support to Brant than has the Seneca nation. When the Americans called us to the treaty making at Fort Stanwix in 1784 it was Brant and the Wyandot who spread the word that members of the Confederacy should attend. My people and I had no choice but to make peace with the Americans but you different nations blamed me and accused me of selling your lands. That never disturbed me in the least because it was not true. If I had become angry it would have been harmful to all of you, my younger brothers. I took pity on you and I rose from my council fire and went to the great council of the Thirteen Fires. The British had ceded our lands to the Americans. This I could not help. Brant is the friend of the British, why did he not counsel them to the contrary?!'' Cornplanter drew himself up and with great dignity announced, "I now tell you that I take Brant and set him down in his chair at home and he shall not stir out of his house! We will keep him there fast, he shall no more run about amongst the nations, disturbing them and causing trouble." He drew out a long string of wampum. "I recommend peace with the Americans. We will hold this end and I put it on you shoulders." He walked over to Wauatam of the Ojibwa nation, placed it on the man's shoulder. Wauatam turned as if away, causing the wampum to fall to the floor. Cornplanter was impassive but he added: "We have been a long time talking. I have advised you for yor own good. I will now leave you to decide matters for yourselves," leaving the council house immediately.

St. Clair dispatched Harmar after the disgruntled Cornplanter. Now the Governor was certain Indian disunity would enable him to dictate the terms of any treaty he wished to make. Indeed, he could probably set them to killing each other, though internecine warfare was not desireable at this juncture. Within the next two days he negotiated two separate treaties, one with the Iroquois, the other with the more westerly tribes. The jealousy existing between the Indians made a mockery of Brant's premise that they were one people. He felt he had achieved the objective of securing the Northwest Territory for sale, the revenue from which would remove the United States from the threat of bankruptcy. The divisions between the various tribes, all jealous of each other, played right into St. Clair's hands. When the treaties were hammered out the Indians' dilemma was summed up by Shendeta when he pleaded for a reconsideration of terms:

"Governor St. Clair, you have charge of all this land and I hope you will satisfy the minds of all who are uneasy. We want the Ohio River as a permanent boundary just like we want your friendship and protection. We are a poor, helpless people. We do not know how to read or write and we do not know for certain what we sign in this treaty. The strings of wampum are the books we read by. It is the request of all nations here present to you, to have pity and compassion on them. Think how hard it would be on the women and children to lose the remaining part of their country. Let the Ohio be the boundary as it was concluded before with the British. The individuals who signed the other treaties were not representatives. Take pity on a poor, helpless people. I am a foolish old man but with a dream of happy living."

St. Clair now sought to close the concil. "This is our treaty of peace and friendship. Touch the quill and we shall all live in happiness. We cannot revoke previous treaties. If you are for peace all you must do is touch the quill." The Indians acquiesed and the council fire was covered.

The Treaty of Fort Harmar was basically an endorsement of the treaties of Fort Stanwix and Fort McIntosh which were the legal basis for United States takeover of the Northwest Territory. St. Clair closed the council with the following words:

"I fervently pray to the Great God that the peace we have established may be perpetual, that He will be pleased to bless the good works we have been about and to extend to your nations the glorious light of the Gospel, of peace, and the blessings of civilization, that they may increase and prosper. That He will grant us to live in unity like brothers, and that our children may grow up and flourish like the young tree and there be none to make them afraid."

Episode 7: Micheal and Louisa

Micheal Brant had to go find Louisa St. Clair at Marietta, a short distance across the Muskingum from Fort Harmar. It was two days before Christmas. There were many other Indians in town because the grand council had just ended. A big snowfall had covered everything like a white buffalo robe and people hustled this way and that. Young Brant accidently ran into Louisa in front of the General Store late that afternoon.

"Hello!" called Micheal as he attracted the young woman's attention. "I would speak with you a moment."

"You go in," Louisa said to her sisters, "I'll be right along. Hello yourself, Chief Brant, and merry Christmas!"

"Yes, merry Christmas," returned Micheal. "Come, let us walk this way. You did not attend the festivities at Fort Harmar. I kept looking for you."

"No, I couldn't go but I did a lot of baking for you," said Louisa. "Believe me, we were kept busy." She looked at Micheal, searching the seriousness that ruled his face. Then it softened a bit as he noted her glance.

"You are beautiful in European clothing too," he said. "I couldn't leave without giving you a Christmas present. And I wanted to talk to you..."

"I was hoping you wouldn't leave without saying goodbye. I'm sure you know all about Christmas. It's our grandest time of year." Louisa saw a number of Indians leaving for home. "Why not stay with us and celebrate Christmas?" she blurted impulsively.

"I wish I could, bold one," said Micheal. "I should have gone sooner. There is much discontent with the treaty. I must return with my men. But I had to see you first. There are so many people about."

"Are those your warriors over there?" Louisa referred to a group of about ten men on their horses, waiting. Micheal nodded. "They must be cold. Why not have them dismount and—"

"No, we have been ordered to leave Marietta this afternoon and we must obey."

"Well then, I will escort you down the road a ways," said fair Louisa. "How would you take to a sleigh ride?"

"Fine, but I don't have one."

"Well I do," said the girl, "or at least my father does. He uses it because of the gout, you know. I'll borrow it and we'll go for a ride, just the two of us. I'll be right back." She walked quickly to her house while Micheal went to fetch the present which was tied to his saddle blanket straps.

"We must leave soon, Micheal," said Yellow Jacket. "There is something in the air, I don't like it." Old Yellow Jacket and the other warriors were responsible for young Brant's safety. It would not do to have Chief Brant's son held as a hostage.

"Always worrying," admonished Micheal good naturedly. "I must see this woman a while longer. Lead my horse, I will ride in the sleigh."

Everyone thus waited for Louisa to arrive and nothing else was said. Yellow Jacket stared at the Longknives as they went about their business. There was something about their manner... as if to say they had the Indians running as squirrels over a smooth log... he didn't like it. Louisa finally appeared, driving a team of horses from the sleigh, reining them to a halt in front of Micheal.

"Come on, jump in," said the girl.

Micheal did her bidding. "This is for you, here," he said as he placed a large package wrapped in plain brown paper on her lap.

"Shall I open it now or do I wait for Christmas?"

"Open it."

"Then you drive," she said as she handed him the reins. Micheal took them, got the horses moving with a "Whup!" and guided them out of the stockade.

"I almost forgot to mention," said Louisa as she opened the package carefully, "father insisted I take some men along. They'll be following us directly."

"Don't worry about it, my men will protect us."

"Oh what a beautiful blanket!" exclaimed radiant Louisa as she discovered what her present was.

"It will keep you warm and perhaps you will remember me on these cold winter nights."

"I would anyway but thank you so much. I'm glad you remembered me. Here, I have something for you." She reached into a pocket and handed him a locket. "Open it."

Micheal did so and found inside a beautiful drawing of Louisa. "It is exquisite, just like you. I will carry it with me always."

"I hoped you'd like it."

"I asked your father for permission," began Micheal but due to a sharp turn in the road he noticed his men a distance behind the sleigh but ominously there was a group of riders behind them. "We're being followed," said Micheal, "twice."

Louisa turned. "Father wouldn't let me come out alone. They're of no importance. You were saying?"

Micheal saw his warriors stopping, evidently desiring the Shemanese should catch up with them. Yellow Jacket never did like the idea of being followed.

"You were saying?" repeated Louisa.

"Excuse me, I was just hoping our people will keep their heads." He looked at the girl, wrapped in his blanket. "I would take you for my wife," he said directly, "if you will have me.'

Louisa was not al all astonished. She kissed him lightly on the lips but said nothing for a moment. Then, very seriously, "Here we are parting, going our separate ways during Christmas, and you want us to marry? How ironicly incongruent. When will I see you again? How far away are you going? Will there be war between our people or will everyone live in peace?"

"Louisa, I cannot answer for the future except that I speak from the heart, here and now." He put an arm around her as the sun began to set, casting a red glow over the snow-clad earth. "Be my wife and we shall never part. Come live with me and the rainbow will lead to our doorstep."

"I wish I could give you an answer, dear Micheal. I feel so strongly for you. I felt it years ago in school and it has never left me. But I just can't give you an answer at this moment. There would be so many things to work out, adjust. I do want to see you, I must, and I belong to no other but at this instant I don't know what to say."

"I require nothing of you except what is in your heart," said Micheal. He kissed her softly on the lips, embracing her strongly with one arm. The ecstasy of the moment was broken by the crack of a rifle. The two in the sleigh turned around to see warriors and soldiers looking at each other then peering into the surrounding woods. Micheal drove quickly to his men. "What happened?" he asked of Yellow Jacket.

"Someone shot at us from the timber," replied the warrior. Everyone was now ready to defend himself as the Shemanese rode up.

"Louisa, you all right?" asked Hamilton Kerr.

"Of course," she replied.

"We must all be getting back," said Ham.

"Go ahead, I'll be right behind you," said Louisa. Micheal instructed Yellow Jacket to leave his horse and wait up ahead for him.

"You have not given me a proper answer," said Micheal when both groups were out of earshot. He looked at Louisa but he cast furtive glances at the woods. Whoever the sniper was he hadn't been shooting at the Shemanese.

"Please give me some time, dear Micheal," pleaded Louisa. "I would have to prepare my family."

"And I mine," said a jubilant Micheal, "and prepare them I will." He kissed her passionately then stepped out of the sleigh and mounted up. "I will return as quickly as possible. No matter what happens you and your family can always count on my friendship." He leaned over and kissed Louisa once more.

"Micheal, I wish you weren't leaving me. What if I went with you right now?" she said boldly, fire in her eye, passion in her body.

"Your men would follow us forever," laughed Micheal. "Believe in me. I will be in touch with you as quickly as I can. Till then, know that I have given you my heart." He rode quickly away to his waiting warriors and all dashed off into their wilderness kingdom.

Episode 8: Spybuck and Molly

Molly was now large with child. She hated herself the bigger she got. She hated the stinking savage for treating her as his wife, hated his presence, despised his officious physical attentions which gave her no rest, hated the cold cabin, hated the food, hated everything and everybody! It had been a cold, snowy winter, white and dreary. When the voice of Spring could be heard she had given up hope of being rescued. The only thing on her mind was that she would give birth to a halfbreed little bastard conceived in rape by the brutish murderers of her family! She had tried to kill her abductors, tried to hurt them, irritate them, and finally all she could accomplish was to ignore them. She grew increasingly withdrawn after she tried to burn down the cabin. All was futility. What a prison was this forest! It mattered not if it was snow white or emerald green. The myriads of trees were the most effective bars imaginable. Kentucky might as well have been on the moon, so far removed it was. How could the men have forgotten about her?! Why had they not followed and killed all these cruel, murdering hell-hounds? And now, what could she hope for if by some miracle she was rescued? Who would want her? No one. No one! If only she could see her sister! But she didn't even know where she was. Probably living in this same kind of hell, if she wasn't already dead...

Molly decided there was only one choice. This day she took a lengthy rawhide thong, tested it for strength, calmly walked out of the cabin where she would not be observed by anyone. In the forest she found an appropriate tree, climbed a little ways up as best she could, secured the leather to a branch, the other end around her neck, and let herself fall. Her feet brushed the ground but her attention was jerked to her neck where she felt excruciating pain until she lost consciousness and was no more.

Spybuck found Molly a few hours later. At first he was hesitant to go near her but then he realized the taboo of death by hanging was merely a superstition of his people so he went up to her and cut her down. He fetched a blanket, covered the crazy woman in it, then carried her to a quiet place and dug a grave. The Shemanese had been so difficult, so deranged. He would have gotten rid of her himself but there had been no opportunity. Well, now she was gone forever. He felt no remorse at her demise. She was relatively worthless to him while living, despite his efforts to make her acquiesce to her new life. He vowed never to take another Shemanese female. They were absolutely devoid of sexual passions.

Episode 9: Return Journey

Methoataske journeyed with her family when they left Sugar Creek. Okiskee remained behind with her husband, as did Kumskaukau who wanted to travel west. Everyone else returned, jubilant that Methoataske was with them for a while before Cheeseekau took her to the land of the Creeks.

The party travelled through the Cahokia area and there Tecumseh made everyone rest for a few days while he inspected the famous mounds. He walked about explaining things as the Grandfather had done with him years ago...

"Grandfather, where did these huge mounds of earth come from?" asked Tecumseh as the two clambered up the Serpent Mound. The old man proved more agile than the youngster had thought for up to now conversation between the two had been in the Grandfather's wegiwa or the environs of the village. This was their first visit to the mounds and Tecumseh was impressed that such an elderly scholar could also be a model woodsman.

"They were built by the pioneers of our people," replied the Grandfather, just a little out of breath. "Today we call them the Mound Builders because these structures are their most obvious legacy to us."

"Why did they build these mounds?"

"We don't really understand why," confessed the Grandfather. "It is one of the many mysteries of our race. Some say they are burial grounds. Others say they were part of religious belief and ceremony. There are those who say great chiefs had them built for the totems of their clans. I do not know. The important thing, Tecumseh, is that they are here and they prove the greatness of our people."

"I do not understand, Grandfather."

"The Mound Builders and all their greatness were your ancestors in the misty long ago," explained the elder. "They were citizens of these great valleys, citizens with feathers in their hair, moccasins on their feet, courage in their hearts, talent in their brains and hands. Once, many many moons ago when I was only a young man I had occasion to study proof of the Builders' greatness. A rampaging stream washed away part of a mound that contained remains of a Mound Builder. I was frightened by the discovery for you know we respect the dead departed but my curiosity got the best of me for I too was a serious student. Within myself I asked permission of the Great Spirit to allow me to study the uncovered artifacts. That night I had a vision in which the water brought all things in the mound right up to my very doorstep. Water, life giving element of the Great Spirit, gave me the permission which I sought so the next day I gave thanks and began to work in earnest. I discovered a breechcloth woven in a wondrous way with such a beautifully designed fabric, the like of which I have never seen again.

There were ornaments of copper, of bear teeth, pearls, all intricately carved with designs unknown to me."

"Where are these artifacts, Grandfather?" asked a spellbound Tecumseh.

"I will show them to you when you are ready," replied the scholar. "The mound Builders were probably the first receivers of corn, squash, beans, and pumpkins, gifts from the Great Spirit. They were also given tobacco and taught to praise the Great Mysterious by smoking. Many individuals have found pipes believed to belong to the Builders. They are distinctive caluments carved to resemble intertwined necks of wild geese or perching owls and parrots, or squirrels sitting on their haunches munching nuts. Each one is a work of art and that is why any chief worthy of the name wants to have one."

"And the women?" asked Tecumseh. "My sisters says a nation can be judged by the accomplishments of its women."

"Tecumapease is correct," replied the elder as he began to walk, the lad following him excitedly. "The women of the Mound Builders must have been highly accomplished to keep up with the men. They possessed a variety of cooking utensils so they must have been experts in that art. I have no way of knowing what role they played in the government of nations but it must have been important for our traditions stress the value of women in national life."

"Where are the Mound Builders now, Grandfather?"

"That is also one of the great mysteries of our people. Legend has it that different clans went their separate ways over all this great island, becoming the progenitors of Indians everywhere. If that is true what does it teach us?"

Tecumseh reacted without hesitation: "That we are all brothers and sisters."

"That is correct," congratulated the Grandfather. "We are all related no matter how far away we find our people. The Creator willed that we populate our Earth Mother and we did so, changing as we went, according to necessities and exigencies of time and place. This happened in a time out of mind, so long ago many of our people have forgotten we are one race of people."

"How large is our island, Grandfather?"

"I cannot speak with exactness. I know some of our people live in eternal snow while others know nothing but Sun Father. I feel the Mound Builders must have been the first Indians, the first citizens of this great land willed to us by the Ruler of Destinies."

"I do not understand how they could have moved so much earth," *exclaimed Tecumseh as they walked on the high mound.*

"When you are older perhaps you will be privileged to see a number of mounds," said the Grandfather. "Some are thirty feet high, a hundred feet wide, and more than two hundred feet long, in shapes of serpents, turtles, birds. Evidently the people had time to carry the necessary earth.

"So many baskets!" exclaimed an awed Tecumseh.

"Many, many baskets, my son," agreed the Grandfather, "and much security in which to work. Perhaps the Mound people were all peaceful, without enemies. Only in such an enviornment could the mounds have been built."

"Grandfather, I am proud to be an Indian," said Tecumseh as he glowed through his beautiful skin and shining eyes. "If only we could revive the wisdom of the Mound Builders and share it with all our nations." The boy reflected quickly: "Of course, I do not know how it would be if there were no warriors."

"We must all live in our time, my son," soothed the teacher. "We can recapture the glory of the Mound Builders only through our minds. Ours is a society which values the warrior and his courage. We cannot change that anymore than we can alter the past. But perhaps we can study, learn the wisdom of our ancients, and better channel our courage, thus elevating our character as a people. I believe such would be pleasing to the Great Spirit. We cannot move mountains but our people were able to build gigantic mounds, preserving their memory for all time. It will be up to you and your generation to elevate the character of our people so we may continue to enjoy the gifts of the Great Spirit..."

After Cahokia the family stopped for a leisurely rest at Shawneetown in the Illinois country. The village was inhabited by Shawnee as well as innumerable refugees from many tribes. It was amazing how many people recognized the Shawnee Warrior for Cheeseekau was truly a champion of his people. A cabin was provided for the family and the men were invited to join a short buffalo hunt to provide meat for the villagers. They accepted, relishing the action.

On the day of the outing Cheeseekau, Sauwaseekau, and Tecumseh mounted their borrowed horses and joined the others at the appointed hour, when dawn was walking a glowing orange path in the horizon. Jonatah, the hunt leader, said a prayer for success then all rode out of town. Along about mid-morning Tecumseh pointed to three dark spots on the horizon. They were diminitive, not larger than mice in the great distance. "Is that what we hunt?" asked Tecumseh, showing deference to the leader. The morning atmosphere had a smokey tint and the sun was just getting bright enough to warm the drooping flowers into their winsome beauty. Even for the practiced Indian eye surrounding objects in the distance were difficult to ascertain.

"Let us approach," said Jonatah, his piercing eyes taking on a somewhat jovial air, or so Tecumseh thought. All galloped their horses and in due time the hunters saw the buffalo flying through the air! "There are your buffalo, brother Tecumseh," said Jonatah, "galloping toward the sun!"

Everyone laughed uproariously, including Tecumseh. The black objects had been myriads of crows on the ground, the murky atmosphere providing a proper setting for the illusion.

"You can have the hump ribs!" teased Cheeseekau.

"I'll take the tongue!" added Sauwaseekau.

"Me for the marrow bones!"

Finally Tecumseh said, "When the people back in the village hear about the flying buffalo we'll all eat crow."

"No, we won't mention anything about it," said Jonatah and all quickly agreed the incident would not be funny back home, especially if they returned empty handed. "Look," he said. There were more dark spots on the prairie and the sun was now bright enough to recognize them for real buffalo.

The hunters rode for an hour toward their prey then began moves for concealment as they advanced, bending low over the necks of their steeds, winding about among hollows and broken places until the buffalo were between them and the wind. No one spoke, all orders being given by hand. The buffalo were perfectly tranquil, some munching grass while others laid on it. The hunters strung their bows then charged into the herd, letting loose their most blood-curdling warcries, Tecumseh's being the strongest of all. The buffalo displayed great consternation for the surprise had been complete. Their large eyes gazed at the intruders for a few moments then the animals tossed their horns and sped away at great speed.

Tecumseh got alongside a buffalo, shooting an arrow into the heart. The animal did not come down so he shot again and then a third time before the king of the plains went head over heels to the prairie sod. The young hunter looked to the other side, spied a fleeing animal, gave enthusiastic chase. When he got close enough he let fly his deadly missles and the buffalo went down. He unleashed a victorious warcry then gave chase to a third animal. Just as he was getting into proper range he felt his horse slip out from under him and before Tecumseh knew what was happening he hit the ground, the horse falling on his leg, then the most searing pain he had ever felt in his life. Tecumseh's world became dark, his only awareness being his leg and side as he lost consciousness.

The Shawnee hunter would have been in mortal danger laying prostrate on the prairie had the buffalo herd been coming up but luckily there were no animals to stampede over him. He came to and was greeted by excruciating pain in his thigh. He knew it was broken as he rubbed it lightly. Due to the pain he did not think of yelling for help.

Sauwaseekau noticed a riderless horse as he gave chase to a buffalo and brought it down. He looked around, averted the charge of an enraged bull, then peered at the horse closely. *Was that not Tecumseh's mount?* he asked himself. The bull came at him again and Sauwaseekau lit out to get away when he spied his brother on the prairie. "Tecumseh!"

His brother raised an arm. It proved an exertion. Sauwaseekau directed his pony and was by his brother's side within moments. He saw the leg. "Broken?"

"Yes," replied Tecumseh, pain etched in his face.

"We must get it set." Sauwaseekau yelled the Help! cry to bring in the other hunters. It was then he noticed the approach of the enraged bull which had tried to gore him. The animal stopped a short distance from the two beings on foot, began goring the ground with his short, curved horns. Perhaps it was the presence of the hunting horse that made the bull hesitate but there was no time to lose for Tecumseh could not defend himself in his condition. "This is going to hurt but you must get on that horse and ride!" commanded Sauwaseekau. "Come, get on the good leg and hang on to the saddle."

The buffalo bull threw dirt and grass high into the air with his horns then charged men and horse. Tecumseh grabbed the mane, doing his utmost to mount but even with his brother's help he could not accomplish the task. He hung on as the horse side-stepped the bull. Sauwaseekau burst forth with the Shawnee warcry to get the bull's attention. He clapped his hands, stomped his feet and in short order the bull charged him. The man feinted to one side then ducked to the other. Displaying amazing agility the bull turned quickly, gored the ground and came in with another charge at Sauwaseekau. He sidestepped once more but the beast came much closer this time. "Ride away!" he told Tecumseh. Sauwaseekau was in a real predicament: he knew he could not run for the buffalo would overtake him and rip him open with those murderous curved horns.

Tecumseh was unable to mount the horse and finally he sprawled painfully back to the ground. A curious thing now took place: with Tecumseh off the horse's back, the steed went to the aid of Sauwaseekau, drawing the buffalo bull's attention. The king of the plains became confused as to which antagonist he should attack, going at one while the other threatened him. When the bull stopped to consider what to do Sauwaseekau bounded onto the horse's back and voiced a warcry. The animal saw an object laying on the prairie but just then a horse and rider darted in front of him as others approached. Enough was enough. The bull scampered away to rejoin his own kind. Sauwaseekau came back to his brother, dismounted as he saw the others arriving on the scene. "I will return when I have downed that bull," said Sauwaseekau.

"No, said Tecumseh, "he was brave. Let him live. That is some horse there..."

Cheeseekau was the first to dismount and look at Tecumseh. The Shawnee Warrior knew it was bad the moment he saw how his brother lay on the prairie. "The leg?"

"Yes, that is some pony," agreed Sauwaseekau.

Cheeseekau did not understand. "We'll have to get it set."

"Jonatah has had experience," said one of the other hunters.

When the leader arrived he informed Tecumseh he could not claim expertise.

"Go ahead," said Tecumseh.

Splints were prepared quickly, leather straps to hold them in place. "This is going to hurt," said Jonatah as he began to set the bone. Tecumseh closed his eyes, sweat poured from his face, but he uttered not a sound. Jonatah had spoken true when he stated he was no expert. At last the bone was set, splints secured, the thigh wrapped carefully to insure immobilization.

Tecumseh's brothers cut short their hunt and returned him immediately to Sawneetown where he was nursed by his mother and sisters. Villagers came to see him by the score, including elderly scholars and women who brought much good food with them. The handsome Shawnee quickly won them over with his good manners, sincerity, intelligence.

Tecumseh's convalesence posed a dilemma for his family. It would be a while before he could travel. The family did not wish to leave Shawneetown without him but finally Tecumseh told them: "Go ahead with your journey. It should not be long before I am with you again. There are many Grandfathers here and I have asked permission to study with them. As soon as I am healed I will follow your trail."

The family acceded to his entreaties. Cheeseekau would take Methoataske to the land of the Creeks, Sauwaseekau would lead everyone else to the Ohio country. On the day of departure Tecumseh hugged and was hugged by everyone before they mounted their horses and rode out of Shawneetown.

At first Tecumseh was in great pain as he hobbled around the village but he enjoyed meeting the people. There was much buffalo meat and corn was plentiful. Everyone lived in peace and tranquility. There was no threat of imminent danger as usually hung in the very air of Ohio. He understood why the people had fled their native land. There were several beautiful maidens who smiled at him as he hobbled around on crutches. Tecumseh's primary concern was the throbbing in his thigh for the slightest miscalculation of foot sent arrows of pain into the side of his body, a fact which led him to believe the bone had not been set properly.

Tecumseh learned which were the most illustrious tribal scholars and one day approached them for permission to study with them: "O Great Ancestors, from the people I come, eating the food of all men. I am the thoughts of my nation. I have few talents so I search for intelligence. To cross a river we make use of canoes, so in life we must listen to wise men. Grandfathers, ancestors of the nation, your intelligence is as high above me as the clouds. Let me benefit by coming to your side and communicate to me how my life may be preserved."

The three elders, a Delaware, Wyandot, and Shawnee, were impressed with the young man after they asked him various questions intended to ascertain his acumen. "What would you like to discuss this day?" asked the Delaware.

"Tell me about the Shemanese and their claims to Indian land," suggested Tecumseh.

"I have had many dealings with the Shemanese and I believe I understand them," began the Delaware. "I have known them in peace and war. Most of the Longknives cannot be trusted during either circumstance."

"I concur," said the Shawnee and the Wyandot also nodded his assent.

"On the surface it is difficult to understand why the Longknives behave the way they do," continued the Delaware, "but the matter is not all that complicated when investigated thoroughly. The Shemanese want the land and will have it by fair means or foul. Granted, among all people there are good and bad but there are few Shemanese like Brother Onas,* for example. At least I have not met them and I am looking from this high hill of old age."

"Tecumseh," said the Shawnee Elder, "it will depend on your gen-

* William Penn

41

eration to face the Shemanese for a permanent solution between the two races. Their deadliest weapon, in my opinion, is their propensity for lying. They are also convinced their way of living is vastly superior to ours."

"The French were not haughty with us," said the Wyandot, "but the British were and the People of the Eagle are the worst of all. They accuse us of not being able to till the soil and that according to the Great Book we do not have rights."

"I cannot understand a Great Book that would permit all the killing and thievery perpetrated by the Shemanese," commented Tecumseh as he shifted his painful leg.

"It is simple," remarked the Delaware, "they have the Great Book but do not live by it. Hypocrisy is easy to detect. The culture of the Longknives is based on greed, lies, and agressive militancy if they think they have the advantage."

"I would also add a hoodwinked ignorance," said the Wyandot. "The Longknives will gaze at our huge crops of corn, squash, beans, melons, then turn right around and accuse us of not tilling the earth. They did not have these crops before they came to these shores yet they will tell us we must learn to till the earth if we are to survive! Remember Tecumseh, nothing is stronger than a lie. There is no deadlier foe."

"The Shemanese are sinister," said the Delaware as he prepared a pipe, lit it, then passed it around for all to puff on, "because they attack you physically as well as mentally, emotionally, culturally. I can only guess at what makes them so active in their machinations and it is that they are not Lenni Lenape, original people, not a race that has existed unchanged since then dawn of time. They are tipified by mongrelism. Look at us, any of our tribes, and you will find the same characteristics. Look at the Shemanese, their features so varied, the hair on their heads, the colors of their eyes, different shading of skin... all denote a mongrel mixture of ancestry."

"Before the Shemanese came," said the Shawnee, "we were the only existing race on this great island. We were content with the beasts of the forests and fields, the fish of the river and sea, the birds of the air, all gifts from the Great Spirit. We were supreme among our fellow creatures and Manito was content with us."

"When the Shemanese landed on our shores," continued the Delaware, "we had to teach them the arts of hunting, trapping, and fishing, all but unknown to them. These activities require a versatility and craftsmanship superior to that of the farmer, shopkeeper, or mechanic which are the basis for the Shemanese lifestyle. Their plants, tools, and domestic animals are tame and easily controlled compared to our wild game. We educate our young by taking them out into the wilderness, which is the actual process of living. We do not place them in artificial situations in order to educate them. Our system produces hunters, trappers, warriors, and from the most successful emanate our chiefs, orators, and wisemen. We do not need written laws for that also is false because they can be easily manipulated. Instead we rely on long established habits and customs. Even the greatest tribute to our people that they render willing obedience. In our lifestyle age confers rank, wisdom gives power, and moral goodness secures title to universal respect."

"Grandfather," said Tecumseh, "why is it the Great Spirit gave the Good Book to the Longknives?"

"They are the ones who need it the most," replied the Delaware. "For genuine integrity, bravery, hospitality, and I would add mercy among our own, the people have very high standing. The Great Spirit knew of the wicked disposition of the Longknives so he gave them the Good Book and taught them how to read it in hopes then would not destroy the world. He felt we Indians had sufficient discernment supplied in our character to enable us to distinguish good from evil."

"All we need," said the Shawnee Elder, "are the great forces of nature in order to feel a sense of peace and justice. We attained contentment and that gave us hospitality, good will, and general disposition for sharing in common with one another. The Master of Life made the Earth and all it contains for the good of mankind. Everything was given in common to the sons and daughters of men and women. Whatever lives on land, grows on it, all in the rivers and lakes, everything was given to everyone and everyone is entitled to his share."

"I once firmly believed," said the Wyandot, "that we could maintain our civilization alongside that of the Longknives. We were able to do so with the French because they respected us and our property. But the English and now the Americans want the land. They care not for our customs and traditions. I and my people were naive to believe we could live in harmony. Their aggressions and bad faith have bewildered me and forced me to indignation. The People of the Eagle are dangerous, powerful enemies because they use every manner of weapon against our people: vice, lies, whiskey, ignorance, smallpox, pretended friendships, venereal diseases, humiliation, and glib, specious treaties which cloak their aggressions. They love to kill more than they like to fight. Their weapons are designed to allow great distance between them and their enemies. They do not enjoy fighting up close. That is why the ambush is so successful against them."

"Our border lands," said the Delaware, "are now pathetic frontiers of drunkenness, debauchery, and disease. The old beliefs have vitiated by contact with the Shemanese religion. We have been divided in order to facilitate the military conquest which is always shrouded in protestations of friendship. Tribe is set against tribe, clan against clan, brother against brother. Our natural way of living has become a source of humiliation and our people do not seem able to withstand the onslaught. And always there are scuffles, fights, and murders whenever riffraff of the Shemanese triumph with their chicanery and false values."

The wings of night shuddered, spreading their diaphanous veil of darkness. Shadows lengthened out of sight as stardust fell, illuminating lost trails of yesterday where warriors walked along star-filled paths.

"I must learn about the treaties Shemanese have used to take the land," said Tecumseh.

"That is quite complicated," said the Delaware, "but we will untangle them for you. Open your ears and listen with your brain, not your heart. The French made no large purchases of land from us. They bought tiny parcels on which to build defensive forts and some trading houses. The British then became jealous and sought to control the fur trade, which caused open war between the two foreigners. Most of the tribes sided with the French but the British succeeded in throwing the Frenchmen on their backs. But we were unaffected because we had not been conquered, just our allies. So when the peace of 1763 was signed the only transfer of land possible was the forts and trading houses, which was nothing at all. The tribes began trading with the British, though they still had much love for the French."

"Then in 1768," continued the Wyandot Elder, "the Five Nations made the treaty of Fort Stanwix in which they granted lands south of the Ohio River to the British, with whom they had ever been close."

"Brother," said the Delaware, "we must not forget that in 1763 the British proclaimed a law which said all lands west of the Allegheny Mountains were undisputed Indian territory. The Alleghenies were to be the barrier between the two peoples for all time."

"When the Five Nations sold the land south of the Spay-lay-wi-theepi," said the Shawnee, "they did us a great injustice for those territories belonged to us, the Wyandot, western Delaware, the Miami, and Kickapoo, as well as other nations who used them to hunt. The Iroquois had no authority to sell the lands of other tribes but the British accepted the deal as legal and binding. It was a good thing they did not ask brothers for the whole of this great island or they might have laid claim to all lands created by the Master of Life. Impoverished Long knives descended into the country south of the Ohio, destroying the game wantonly and killing us with similar lack of compunction. Finally Cornstalk led us against Lord Dunmore in 1774. We stopped one army but the second was more numerous than the first so we lost our Kentucky homeland forever."

Tecumseh had knowledge of this last account so he appreciated the Grandfather's bitterness as he recounted the loss.

"Now we find ourselves in an ever worsening situation,"said the Delaware. "We are told because we sided with the British during the Revolution we have lost title to our lands. If the Longknives lived by law, even if it was their law, we native inhabitants would be fairly secure, but they do not. It is logical the Thirteen Fires are entitled to possess what was owned by the British, who in turn could take what was under French jurisdiction, which was merely a pittance. We were not conquered, Tecumseh. When we met the Longknives at Blue Licks, for example, we destroyed their forces and remained in possession of our lands above the Ohio. The People of the Eagle are the most covetous of all for they accept all that was won from the British and demand everything owned by us on the pretext that we allied ourselves with the British king. Do not believe that we have no land because we fought to protect our country from their encroachments. We destroyed their forces in battle and they have no rights to our country. What they do have is the right to treat with us. That they did win from the British, but only that."

"Mark my words," said the Wyandot, "with such people treaties are of no worth. They are just an excuse, a justification with which to rouse their soldiers to come into our land and kill us. The Longknives will cross the Ohio and lay claim to its rich territories. They will bribe some of our people into signing a treaty to cede land then invade it amid great bloodshed, calling us 'savages' all the while. Soon there will be another war in the Ohio country, then another and another until one side is exhausted."

"Grandfathers," asked Tecumseh, "could we not blend our cultures and live in peace?" He was thinking of Steve Ruddell and many like him who lived happily in the wilderness.

"I tried," said the Delaware, "and could not. The Longknives do not understand the influence of nature, by and large. They call it 'savage mind.' They do not understand we live according to nature, enduring its attendant inconveniences but glorying in the poetry of nature. The Longknives seek to control nature. They bring their axes and chop down an entire forest, calling it progress. Myriads of them have become Indians but I do not know of many Indians who have been able to change into their way of living." The Grandfather scrutinized Tecumseh. "Remember always that we live as Nature's inhabitants, not its guests. The house of the so-called 'civilized man' is in reality his prison while Nature is our freedom. Without it we die."

"What then do they mean by 'civilization'?" asked Tecumseh.

"To the People of the Eagle civilization is an axe, a wagon, a musket," replied the Delaware. "He believes these things are of utmost importance because they give him power. He cares not for his soul, compared with what he calls civilization. He cares not for Nature unless he can control it. He is avaricious to the extreme about the land but not for its beauty or the life he can live on it. He greeds for it because he can rent it, sell it, exploit it. Sometimes I felt across the Salt Water there must have been no land, such is their covetousness for it. They are willing to die for it and thousands have at our hands when we protect what is ours. We of this great island are far from perfect, Tecumseh, and you must always strive to improve our character if we are to survive but never tolerate the Longknives' ideas that we are brutes, foul and unclean in life and thought. Above all you must never be a 'pet Indian,' for such is the life of the blackfaces whom the Longknives enslave."

The flickering fire compelled Tecumseh to say, "I do not wish to keep you up until dawn walks the rim of the sky. If I may come again tomorrow I shall let my Grandfathers sleep tonight." He got to his feet after a minor struggle.

"We will be here whenever you wish, my son," said the Wyandot.

"Until tomorrow then," said Tecumseh as he bowed slightly and hobbled out of the wegiwa toward his own quarters.

"Keewaukoomeelaa," said a pretty maiden. "I have been waiting to speak with you."

Tecumseh peered through the darkness, recognized Anungaee, whom he had met through his sister. "Good evening. I did not know you were here." Tecumseh's foot hit something in the dark, sending a sharp pain through his leg, making him wince perceptibly.

"Here, let me help you," said Anungaee as she put an arm around his waist opposite the crutch.

"Thank you," replied Tecumseh, "it is not far to my cabin."

"I know, but will you have no super?"

"I have not had the greatest appetite of late."

"A warrior must eat. You need a wife to care for you."

"You sound like the women in my family," said Tecumseh.

"Is that bad?"

"No, of course not. A wife is a good thing."

46

"Thing?"

"I mean everyone needs a good wife," said Tecumseh as he smiled at the maiden.

"Then why are you not married?" asked Anungaee.

"I am not exactly a Grandfather yet. There is time. Besides," he said playfully, "right now I am in no condition to provide for a woman."

"Will you be spending all your evenings with the Grandfathers?"

"No, not all, I guess. But while I am laid up I might as well study."

"This leg breaking was a good omen then?"

"I don't know that I would say that," answered Tecumseh.

"There is your cabin," said Anungaee. "The food I brought you is stone cold by now. I will warm it after I build a cooking fire."

"No, you don't have to trouble yourself so much."

"It is no trouble," said Anungaee as she helped him through the door. "Perhaps someday I will need your help."

"I will be most happy to repay you," said Tecumseh as the two entered the cabin.

"You will leave us when your leg is healthy again?"

"Yes, I guess I must return to the Ohio country. But I would not mind living here."

"Perhaps I can make you forget about Ohio. That country is so full of trouble. Here there is peace... and love." Anungaee hugged him with both arms now that the two were in the privacy of the cabin.

Episode 10: President Washington

"Mr. President, Secretary Knox and Colonel Willett," said the secretary to President Washington as he showed the men in.

"Thank you," said Washington. "Good morning, gentlemen," he said as he shook hands with both. "Come, let us sit over here by the window. I trust you will have some tea?" he said as he poured three cups, handing one to each of his visitors.

"Thank you, Mr. President," said Secretary of War Knox as Colonel Willett bowed slightly.

"Gentlemen, I need your advice on the Indian problem," said Washington, getting down to business immediately. The President could not afford the luxury of wasting time. The new United States were teetering on the brink of revolution, bankruptcy, disaster. "I want to know exactly what are the rights of the Indians in the Northwest Territory and how each of you feel we should handle the situation."

"I have been in contact with Joseph Brant of the Mohawk nation," said Knox as he sipped his tea. "He is the most influential Indian in the country, of course, and he understands that under international law the Indians are prior occupants of soil. The land cannot be taken from them unless by their free consent or if they are conquered militarily in a justified war. To dispossess them on any other principle would be a gross violation of fundamental laws of nations and that distributive justice which is the glory of the United States."

"Justice to the Indians must be and will be the cornerstone of our dealings with them so long as I am part of this administration," said Washington definitively.

"Chief Brant maintains Britain did not have valid title to lands north of the Ohio River," said Knox as Colonel Willett listened attentively. "Therefore we could receive no title from them, he asserts, because all the British had was an exclusive right to treat with the Indians. Because of our victory we now have that right and no one could deny us in a court of international law."

"Though we conquered the English I would be the first to concede their savage allies have not been conquered," said Washington, shuddering inwardly as he thought of Braddock's defeat many years ago. "The Northwest Territory is not safe for settlement according to reports coming in. People continue to lose their lives and property at the hands of marauding Indians. This in itself is justification for declaring war on the hostile tribes, is it not?"

Colonel Willett spoke for the first time: "Perhaps I should be an advocate for them, just for purposes of debate, Mr. President." Washington nodded approval. "Our people cannot go into their territories, take their lands, then declare war on them when they rise in defense of what they consider to be their native soil."

"True," declared Washington.

"Then, gentlemen," said Knox, "we are indeed on the horns of a dilemma for if our nation is to grow we must have the land or forever stay on the eastern side of the Alleghenies. Before we become total philanthropists let us remember that our country is the only bastion of freedom in the world. What will we tell the untold numbers of people who come here looking for liberty if there is no land for them? Soon our little country will be as crowded as Europe itself."

"Then we must purchase those territories," said Washington. But no one knew better than he the government was bankrupt for all practical purposes. Indeed, it was sale of the Northwest land to settlers that would prevent financial collapse.

"I sincerely believe we have endured enough provocation if we wish to declare war," said Knox.

"I would hate to do that," replied Washington.

"I share those sentiments," added Colonel Willett.

"What other choice is there?" asked Knox. "It is a question of survival, them or us. That's what it all boils down to, gentlemen. We can study the issue, investigate, form committees, listen to recommendations, everything. But it all comes down to them or us."

The President knew Willett understood Indians and how they fought so he asked him: "Would you accept the commission of Brigadier General if we had to fight?"

"It has always been my opinion," replied the Colonel, "that our United States ought to avoid an Indian war. I believe this to be the wisest policy. The reasons alleged in support of war have never convinced me in justice. From my knowledge and experience with these people I am certain it is not difficult to preserve peace with them. I am fully cognizant of the fact there are bad men among them and these will at times commit acts which deserve punishment. But to go to war with the whole nation is not the way to punish them."

"What do you suggest, then, Colonel?" asked Knox.

"Most of the Indians I have any knowledge of are conceited and vain," continued Willett. "By feeding their vanity you gain their good opinion and this in time procures their esteem and affection. They will then deliver up the recalcitrants among their own race. By conciliating their good will you can render them susceptible to almost any impression. They are suspicious yet they are credulous. They are vengeful because their family ties are so strong. They think a great deal and have in general firm notions of right and wrong. They frequently exhibit proofs of grateful minds. Like all humankind, they are not free from chicanery and intrigue, yet if their vanity is properly humored and if they are treated with justice it is no difficult matter to come to reasonable terms with them. The intercourse I have had with these people, the treatment I have myself received from them, and which I have known others to receive, make me an advocate for them. To fight with them would be the last thing I desire."

"Colonel, you are not saying they are unbeatable?" asked Washington.

"Not at all. Speaking quite frankly, based on my own experience, I do not conceive it difficult to beat them when brought to action. In small parties they scatter themselves along a frontier and that is when they are the most troublesome, downright dangerous. That kind of warfare is their forte and they are truly tremendous, probably without equal anywhere in the world. But when they attempt anything in large bodies, not-withstanding their great dexterity in the wilderness and the advantage they usually derive from the admirable position they take, they are easily vanquished."

"Well then how would you fight them?" asked Knox.

"In marching through woods, where troops are exposed to attacks from Indians, particular attention should be paid not only to the mode and line of march, but also to extend small parties and single men far on the flanks, in front and rear. But whenever a serious attack is made, which is usually furious, an instantaneous charge, with huzzaing suf-ficiently loud to drown out the yells the Indians themselves make, will never fail to repel them. And this stroke repeated and pursued, will inevitably terminate in victory. But remember," cautioned the man whose sincerity was unquestioned by either listener, "victories over Indians are always costly and defeats are the most horrible imaginable. No, the dubious honors of fighting and beating Indians are not what I aspire after. If in any way I could be instrumental in effecting and main-taining peace with them, it would be a source of great gratification to me."

"It might well be we will call on you for service," said President Washington. The trio continued to chat throughout the morning for sur-vival was the most serious of issues. Genocide for the Indians was not a pleasant alternative in Washington's mind. Even amalgamation was preferable but that would take time and the government needed money to survive now. Besides, people would go into Indian territory even at the cost of their lives. Washington had done this himself after 1763 in a land speculating business venture. Landless people always wanted land, it was their only hope and salvation. Treaties were the only way to avoid war but would the Indians honor them? He doubted the validity of the treaty executed by St. Clair for the most warlike tribes had not participated.

By the time Knox and Willett left the President his thoughts were clear: the United States would purchase Indian lands whenever poss-ible. They would make treaties to preserve the peace. But if the tribes continued their depredations as they had in the Ohio country they would be considered enemies and treated as such. Washington went to his desk and wrote a letter to St. Clair, authorizing the Governor to strike at hos-tile tribes if there was no alternative at keeping the peace.

Episode 11: Micheal visits Louisa

Yellow Jacket felt uncomfortable in his Shemanese clothes as he rode alongside Micheal. The older man had promised young Brant's father he would protect the boy but riding into Marietta in broad daylight was really asking for trouble. All this just to see a woman! And not just any woman, but the daughter of the Governor himself! "I hope you know what your're doing," said Yellow Jacket to Micheal in his native Mohawk.

"Talk English," snapped Micheal in a whisper. "You know there's nobody here but us Longknives." The young man smiled as Yellow Jacket shook his head. He noted other riders going in and out of the Marietta stockade so he felt there was no great danger. Perhaps war was imminent, perhaps it wasn't. Micheal had vowed to see Louisa and see her he would! The wings of night were ready to veil the earth as the two rode calmly into the village. Their entrance caused no commotion and Yellow Jacket breathed easier, his face impassive. No one scrutinized them, the frontiersman clothing working in their favor as Micheal had planned.

"Howdy," said Micheal as he greeted some villagers walking by. The two riders dismounted, walked to where someone was addressing a large crowd about some religious revival which would be held for the first time in Marietta. Micheal paid little attention to the speaker as he looked intently at the crowd to see if by chance Louisa St. Clair was present. Yellow Jacket also scrutinized the assembly but for a different reason: at the first sign of danger he had to get Micheal on his horse and make a run for it. Even if they were not discovered they still had to get out of town before the stockade gate was locked for the night, unless they spent the night in Marietta. Young Brant either was not thinking or didn't care. Of couse not, he was in love! Love would get him down the North Star trail right into the Shadowland if Yellow Jacket wasn't careful enough for both of them.

Micheal didn't find Louisa in the crowd so he walked toward the Governor's house in hopes of seeing her. Yellow Jacket walked behind with the horses, the old warrior making certain he covered his face with the animals whenever anyone came close. Abruptly he got the uncomfortable feeling someone was following him. He could not call out to Micheal... so he opted to lead the animals away from Micheal to see if the horse and rider behind him followed him or young Brant. He veered off toward a stable, the individual behind him still. Yellow Jacket loosened his knife then sneaked a look at his pursuer: a woman in an

Indian outfit sat atop a lathered horse... Louisa St. Clair. Yellow Jacket stopped and whistled for Micheal.

Louisa hadn't been aware of the man and two horses in front of her. Even the whistle hardly registered for her mind was far away. She rode up to the stable, dismounted, then led her mount into the building where she unsaddled and began brushing the animal. Then she heard:

"Does my Indian princess need help?"

"Micheal!" said Louisa as she turned with a start, putting her hand to her heart. "What are you doing here? There is talk of war. You are in mortal danger if discovered!"

"I told you I would return for you," he said candidly, "to make you my wife. Here I am, if you will have me."

Louisa rushed into his arms, embracing him passionately then kissing him softly. "You have been in my thoughts—"

"Riders coming this way," said Yellow Jacket as he hurried into the barn.

"Hide," said Louisa to him, "over there. Micheal, come, into the loft, quickly!"

The two scampered up, bounced over the hay then burroughed into it next to the wall by a little window.

"No one followed us," said Micheal in a whisper as he peered out a portion of the window. "Must be some passerby." The two pressed close to each other as a deep orange glare colored the horizon and weakened as Night Warrior took control of the earth.

"Will your people go to war?" asked Louisa in a delicious whisper. Her tone of voice was a stark contrast to the content of her question. "I hope you're not spying on us."

"No, I'm not spying, silly," replied Micheal. "You're as bad as Yellow Jacket! Maybe you two would make a better pair—"

"I'm sorry," blurted Louisa. She hugged him and Micheal became very aware of her warmth. "It's just so many rumors flying around. One doesn't know what to believe."

"There is no war in my heart," said Micheal. "I want you to come live with me and be my wife. I will care for you and cherish you always. I will provide for you well."

Louisa began to cry softly. Micheal was completely taken aback. "My only wish is to make you happy."

"You have, dear Micheal, and I do love you."

"Then why the tears?"

"I don't know, I just don't know what to do," admitted Lousia, her beauty not marred by the tears. "What of my father?"

"He will always be your father, that will never change."

"What if there is war? Will your people accept me?"

"Of course," said Micheal as he tenderly wiped away her tears with a caressing finger.

"Or would we live with my people?"

"That is possible too. Would they accept me?"

"Why yes, of course. But if there is war... I don't know what would happen." Micheal kissed her lips and pressed her to him. She did not hold back. The future was extremely uncertain.

"LOUISA!" somebody yelled from below. The Governor's daughter knew the voice: Hamilton Kerr! If the ranger discovered Micheal or Yellow Jacket there was sure to be trouble. She hoped the warrior down below would not try anything foolish as both individuals in the loft held their breath. "There's her pony but she's not around," said another voice. "Maybe she's in the crowd with the revivalist. Come on, don't worry, she's probably out there."

"She didn't finish tending her pony," said Hamilton. "You go on and I'll do some brushing. It's been ridden pretty hard."

Darn that Ham! thought Louisa, though he was a true friend. Micheal worked his right hand down to his hip, struggling to unsheathe his knife, just in case. Louisa didn't know what to think for a moment. She grabbed his hand then realized Micheal was readying his knife. She could not speak for Ham's ears were as sharp as any Indian's. She shook her head and pushed on Micheal's hand. She opened her eyes wide then closed them in obvious supplication as she shook her head. Micheal stopped. They could not talk. Neither could they move for the hay would crackle so they just lay there in silence listening to the brush on the horse. Louisa and Micheal kissed tenderly then more and more passionately. Other sounds came in from the grounds as horses walked by, people called to each other, everything normal. Hamilton Kerr finally finished with the horse, put it in a stall, then walked out of the stable.

"He's gone!" breathed Louisa. She moved her body slightly but to Micheal the whole world was quaking.

"Will you be my wife?" whispered Micheal.

"You know that is what I wish but I cannot go away with you."

"Then what do you want me to do with myself?"

"Be my love as I am yours," answered Louisa. "I cannot know the future."

"It was my desire to make you my wife tonight." The stable was getting quite dark.

"Micheal, we must away," Yellow Jacket was heard to say from below. "Come on, before they lock the gates!"

"Always someone in the way!" said Louisa desperately.

"Yellow Jacket is right, as usual," said Micheal as he began to move out from her warmth. "If there is war... will you wait for me?"

"Do not talk of war. I hate war! All I care about is holding you close to me." She hung on to him as long as she could then released him so reluctantly.

"Would that I could live here at Marietta," said Micheal as he helped her up. His heart was heavy but inexplicably he did not feel resentful toward the fate which had brought them together. "I will come to see you again. If there is war it might be a long time. Perhaps you will already be married."

"Oh hush up!" admonished Louisa, close to tears. "I wish I could sneak through the lines to see you. I would if I could." She kissed him again. "Will war break out?"

"Will your people vacate all lands north of the Ohio?" asked Micheal. "Will you leave Marietta and burn it to the ground?" Louisa made no answer. "But know this: you have filled my heart. When you look to the sky and see Mother Moon growing to fulness think of my heart which yearns for your love. Even winter's chilly breeze will ever spread a blanket of hope for our rapture. The moon's rays will carry a mingling of love and laughter to every swaying forest bough and there, like the flowers waiting for spring, when we are free our spirits will become as one."

"Micheal, hurry," said Yellow Jacket.

"I will see you whenever possible," said Micheal. "Make sure you don't shoot any Indians before you find out who they are. It could be me tapping on your window, or one of my messengers." He kissed her for the last time then both descended the ladder.

"I'll ride with you to the gates," said Louisa.

"No," said Yellow Jacket, "in the dark they could mistake you for an Indian, dressed as you are."

An ironic smile formed on Micheal's lips. "We will mount up and ride out calmly," he said, "alone. I will not put you in more danger than I already have. Perhaps it would be better if you didn't even come out of the stable."

"I will walk behind you," said Louisa bold and beauteous. "Don't worry about anything."

The two men went outside, mounted their horses, walked them toward the stockade gates. There was still a large crowd listening to the evangelist. Few noticed the two riders being followed by St. Clair's daughter dressed as an Indian maiden. The gates were being closed as the riders

54

went through them.

"Hey fellers, we're lockin' up; gimme the signal when you come back. Careful, out there's Indians skulking around."

Micheal waved at the two men closing the gates but said nothing. He turned around to look at Louisa, standing alone, her hand going up quickly in a furtive wave. He could not see the tears which flooded her eyes.

"What do you think would have happened," said Micheal in Mohawk when they were a ways from the stockade, "if we had been discovered?"

"If they didn't shoot us on the spot," replied Yellow Jacket, "they would have thrown us in their jail."

"Then what?"

"Then the girl would have helped us escape."

Episode 12: Spybuck's Adventure

Spybuck scanned the large assembly around the council fire. The night was extremely pleasant, neither too cool nor too warm. Various orators would get up to speak then Little Turtle would ask the tribes to take up the hatchet against the encroaching Shemanese. Good! The Shawnee could not defend the land alone forever. Besides, the excitement attracted the more adventurous women... The large crowd sat in circular rows around the fire but as yet the juggler had spoken to no one. His eyes searched the various groups of women who stood here and there. There had to be someone adventurous enough to reach the heights of passion. If he could find her the journey would turn out worthwhile. But there were so many people...the search might be difficult. Crowds were always a problem. He decided to move about, listening to what people said, stopped by a group of women but made no effort to include himself in their number.

An orator arose and began to speak as Spybuck walked further, finally leaning against a tree. His magnificent blanket glowed in the soft moonlight as he listened.

"You are Spybuck," said a feminine voice.

The juggler turned and saw the female. Even in the moonlight Spybuck noted how well she was dressed, the toga-blanket giving her an exquisite touch.

"Yes, and the moon spirit has sent you to me," replied the man.

"Have you come to gather courage to fight the Shemanese?" she asked.

"We all do what we must, or can," he replied.

"I know what you must, but I don't know what you can," said the woman. Spybuck was genuinely surprised. She sounded like him! Or was she mocking him? No, she was merely spirited. Suddenly he decided on a strategy and said:

"You are too much for me, dear maiden. You must speak more plainly if this poor man is to appreciate you fully." Good, he had surprised her a bit. "If we must fight the Shemanese, well and good, but tonight there is no battle but the moon bathing your passion in love hues."

The woman became silent and expressionless. Spybuck felt confident that he was stalking the proper path. "I do not know your name but the moon spirit surely knows you well for she compliments your glowing beauty."

"The moon shines on all."

"But glows only on some," added Spybuck. "I can see your warmth comes from deep within."

The woman looked at him, unafraid, self-possessed, but teasing no longer. "How could you possibly know what is deep within, wizard? My only wish is for a drink of water, nothing more."

"There is a beautiful spring a short distance through the forest," said Spybuck. "I would show it to you but I came to hear Little Turtle's oration."

"That is what we all came for," said the woman.

"But of course, we also came to enjoy our brothers and sisters. Perhaps we could go get you that drink and return before his oration. Nature is strong with needs that must be quenched.

The woman looked boldly at him.

"How did you know my name?" asked Spybuck.

"I too am an herbalist."

"Ah, then we are colleagues," said Spybuck. "Come, let us go to the spring that we may return quickly." He put an arm around her shoulders, tenderly, confidently. She could have easily broken away but after a moment of indecision she bumped softly into his hip and walked with him into the forest.

"How far did you say it was?" she asked. "I would not have you miss the Turtle's oration." Her tone contrasted her former teasing.

"Just a pleasant ways yonder," said Spybuck as he held the woman with his arm. "The water is cool and pure, delightful." As they walked away from the council gathering Spybuck became aware of her hip touching his. His entire body began to warm for the woman, though she was unaware of him, ostensibly. But then women could pretend so much better than men. She was nearly as tall as he, her body firm and becoming warmer, he hoped. He pretended to trip on a small root, pulling the woman closer to him. "Excuse my clumsiness, dear sister," he said as he pulled gently on the woman's shoulders, bringing her around in front of him in order to embrace her. She did not flinch. Quite the contrary, she brought her hips into his. Or was it Spybuck's wishful thinking? He rubbed his pubic bone on hers and the woman gulped as if startled anticipation had been disrobed. Spybuck's breechclout began to fill as the woman pressed herself ecstatically toward the provocation. The juggler now glimpsed a novel idea: was this woman seducing him? He smiled inwardly and said, "Come, let us walk further and off this path."

The woman did not resist but neither did she relinquish with apparent reluctance. Maybe he should let her boff him. Then he decided it would be folly to trust the woman to take the initiative merely to fan his ego. There was no sense losing a passionate encounter over mere vanity. As the two walked through the forest there were slivers of moonlight dancing on the couple and Spybuck thought the woman was sneaking glances at his breechclout. It heightened the expectation.

"You still have not told me your name," whispered Spybuck. The two were now a good distance from the beaten path to the spring, surrounded by trees as they walked.

"I shall let you give me a name."

"Good. Let me see," he said as he stopped walking, putting his hands under the blanket and raising them up her sides as far as they could go," shall I name you for your beauty or some worthy deed?" Her doeskin dress was up to the lower thighs.

Drums were heard from the distance of the council fire. The night was scented with nature and moonbeams swayed through the trees until they plunged into immovable surfaces.

"I shall leave that to you," said the woman as she put her hands on his shoulders under the toga-blanket Spybuck wore. She rubbed his deltoids softly then grabbed them tenderly, leaned back and allowed her passion to touch Spybuck's breechclout, titillating his bod to grope further.

Spybuck wanted to lean her down to the earth but instead he pulled her to him, kissing her neck, shoulder, down to her breast which he could not fully reach because of the doeskin.

"Let us walk further," said the woman, "the night is so beautiful."

"It is passionate," observed Spybuck, "and passion is the deepest form of beauty." The two continued to walk but now they embraced tightly. Except for the distant drums there was nary a sound behind their footsteps.

"I love drums and little bells," said the woman.

"Drums I have supplied you," responded Spybuck, "for bells I must wait another time."

"I have some with me," she said as they walked through a large moonbeam.

"I would hear them. Where are they?" asked Spybuck as he stopped walking. He had bided enough time.

The woman looked at him calmly then took the edge of his breechclout, removed it with a skillful twist and pull. Spybuck put his hands on his hips and stood there, moonbeams splashing on him. The woman took a couple more steps then turned to face him. Her hands moved expertly down the front of her dress and lay open the entire length of her body. The two had not lost eye contact during the proceedings and neither gazed at the other's bod. Spybuck now understood the woman had been out to seduce him from the start. He kept his hands on his hips, holding the woman's inspired eyes. He did not move forward but neither did the woman. Slowly he moved his right hand toward his bod, the woman following its progress with her eyes. Still she did not come forward. Suddenly his arm and hand extened toward the woman and she came slowly, exquisitely, as little bells, which must have been hanging from a fold in the open dress, tinkled their happiness. The woman came up close, caressed Spybuck's bod with her hand, then the rest of him. Suddenly she held on strongly, almost too tight, then put it to herself and pressed in the entire length. "OOOOhh!" she exclaimed ecstatically.

Now it was Spybuck who gulped unexpectedly, overcome by the warmth of her bod and body. The woman stood erect and still the penetration was totally complete and comfortable! The exhiliration was fascinating for such a position had never been so natural before.

"Ooooh!" said the woman as Spybuck withdrew most of his length then thrust once more, holding it deep within a few moments. He tried to take a breast in his mouth but could not quite reach so he rubbed softly with his hands until the woman's papillas jutted hard into his chest when he stopped and pressed her to him.

Spybuck grasped her strongly around her lower back, put his tongue to neck and shoulder, stopped moving his hips as his bod titillated with tensing strokes. "Don't stop!" whispered the woman as moonbeams churned through trees and branches to illuminate eyes that closed and opened wide, lips that pursed and filled out, skin that glistened with silvery perspiration, hair that swayed gently to and fro then side to side, hands that grasped to the threshold of passion pain, thighs that ached to move in strength instead of endurance, hips that pressed and struggled to

58

become pure ecstasy until the woman trembled across the heavens of fulfillment.

"Now I know your name," whispered Spybuck as he held her close and deep.

The woman rested for a moment, regained her composure, said, "I'll wager you don't."

"What do you want to bet?"

"Whatever you wish," she said as she regained her strength quickly.

"Once more."

"Just once?" The woman giggled as the bells again began to tinkle in unison.

"I will call you Standing Woman," said Spybuck.

"All that matters is that you like it," she said smiling as hips began to wave, undulate, gyrate. Spybuck kept up with her but with contrary motions which insured tinkling of the bells. Drums came again from the distance, converting into passionate thrusts in the night. Spybuck found himself wanting to look at her bod as it claimed his so he maneuvered her into a patch of moonlight. All he could see was the demon disappearing into the labyrinth of passion. Now there began the climb to the stars and his thighs trembled with the exertion. The woman was enticed along the starry trail where good fairies danced, veiled in the mystery of smoke rings until her strength united with that of Spybuck and burst forth in ravishing ecstasy!

Episode 13: Legend

"White Hawk lived in a remote part of the forest where birds and animals were abundant. The hunter was tall and manly with the fire of youth beaming from his eyes. He walked unafraid through the gloomiest woods and could follow the faintest tracks made by any of the numerous beasts. Every day he would return to his lodge with game for he was one of the most skillfull and celebrated hunters in the tribe.

"One day, going further from home than ever he had before, he found himself in an open section of the forest where he could see a great distance. It was the edge of a wide prairie covered with grass and flowers. Walking on in the pathless prairie he suddenly noticed a ring worn through the sod as if by footsteps following in a circle. Yet there was no path leading to it, no trace of footprints, not even a crushed leaf or broken twig.

"White Hawk was curious to know the meaning of this circle so he hid nearby in the tall grass and waited. In time he heard the faint sounds of music in the air. He looked up abruptly to see a small object coming down from the sky. At first it was a mere speck in the blue so far away it was but as it descended it grew in size and became a huge basket. When it landed he counted twelve beautiful maidens in it, maidens of the most enchanting beauty. They looked so much alike White Hawk surmised they were sisters. The music he heard had grown plainer and sweeter. Upon landing the maidens leaped out and began to dance in the prairie ring. Round and round they went and as they danced they reached out with sticks to a shining ball in the center of the ring, striking it as if it was a drum.

White Hawk was spellbound in his hiding place, gazing at the dancers' graceful motions. He admired them all but especially the smallest one who was probably the youngest. Finally he could control himself no longer: he rushed out and attemped to seize the youngest maiden. But the sisters had the quickness of birds, leaping back into their basket and lifting up into the azure sky.

White Hawk looked at them disappearing. "They are gone," he thought, "I shall see them no more!" Rather dejected he returned to his temporary lodge but could not rest so bright and early the next day he left his hunting camp and returned to the ring, praying fervently that he be allowed to talk to the maidens. His guardian spirit heard him and changed him into an opossum. He arrived at the ring and had not been waiting long when he saw the basket descending, the sweet music filling the air. The basket touched down and once again the maidens began to dance, looking even more beautiful than before.

Slowly the oppossum crept toward the ring, but the moment the sisters saw it they became startled and sprang into their basket. A short distance off the ground one of the elder sisters said: "Perhaps he has come to show us how the game is played on Earth."

"Oh no!" replied the youngest. "Let us be off quick!" The others picked up the chant and the basket rose out of sight.

White Hawk changed back into his own form again and walked sorrowfully back to his lodge. The night dragged on eternally but the next day the hunter returned to the ring. A short distance from it he found an old stump filled with mice. Thinking the sisters would not be frightened by such tiny creatures he brought the stump closer to the ring and prayed to have his form changed into a mouse. White Hawk's prayer was answered and he became one of the inhabitants of the stump. Soon music was heard and the sisters came down and began to dance.

"Look," said the youngest sister suspiciously, "that stump was not there before." Frightened, she ran toward the basket. But the others laughed and gathered around the stump, hitting it playfully with their sticks. As they did so the mice, including White Hawk, came running out. The sisters struck at the fleeing mice and killed all—except one, which was being chased by the youngest. As the maiden raised her stick to strike White Hawk regained his human form and clasped the young woman in his arms. The other sisters sprang to their basket and were quickly drawn up into their sky domain.

The little maiden cried but White Hawk used all his skills to please his bride and win her sincere affection. He wiped the tears from her eyes, told her of his many adventures as a hunter, and dwelt on the charms of a life on Earth as they walked to his hunting camp. He was tireless in his attentions and life in the lodge was glowing with joy. White Hawk was the happiest of men.

Winter and summer passed all too rapidly away in the lodge and happiness was increased by the addition of a beautiful boy. But the hunter's wife was a daughter of the stars and White Hawk could tell his woman longed to return to her father. He did not know how to handle the situation.

The beautiful woman had not forgotten the charm that would return her to the star kingdom. While her husband was out hunting she constructed a wicker basket, concealing it when he was home. She also collected such rarities from Earth as she thought would please her father, along with the most dainty kinds of foods. When the basket was ready she walked out to the prairie ring, taking her little son with her. They stepped into the basket and she began to sing. Carried by the wind, the music caught White Hawk's ear. How well he knew that voice! With all his fleetness of foot and quickness of spirit he sped to the prairie ring. But he did not make it in time, the basket rising out of reach.

"Come back, do not leave me!" he cried out but it was no use. The basket kept rising until it became a small speck and vanished into the blue. White Hawk bent his head down to the ground and wept.

He was miserable throughout the long winter and summer which followed. He mourned the loss of the wife whom he dearly loved but now he had also lost his son. In the meantime his wife lived in her home in the stars. She never forgot she had left a husband on Earth, though her activities were blissful amidst the twinkling orbs. Her son was a continual reminder of her husband and as the boy grew up he became anxious to visit his father and the country of his birth. He said as much to his Grandfather.

So it was one day that Star Father said to his daughter, "Go, my child, take your son down to his father. Ask him to come up and live with us. Tell him to bring along one of each kind of bird and animal he kills in his hunting."

Taking the boy with her the woman descended to the earth. White Hawk, who had moved his lodge to be close to the ring, heard her voice as she came down through the sky. His heart beat with love and forgiveness as his wife and son appeared in the basket. He clasped both of them in his arms and they told him they had come to take him with them to the stars.

When his wife told him of Star Father's request he set out with great eagerness to collect the gift. He spent whole days and nights searching out every unusual or beautiful animal and bird. When he was satisfied everything was carried to the basket and all ascended the heavens.

"There was great joy among the stars when the family arrived. Star Father invited all his people to a feast and when all were together he stated each could take whichever of the earthly gifts they liked best. Some chose a foot, some a wing, a tail, a claw. Now they could change into the form of that animal or bird whenever they wished, visiting the earth at will. White Hawk chose a white feather from his namesake, as did his wife and son. White Hawk then spread his wings and, followed by his wife and son, descended to Earth with the other birds and animals where they are found to this day."

Like everyone else around the council fire Tecumseh had listened to the story, enraptured by the Grandfather's tale. How wonderful it would be to visit the stars! Such had been his desires as a mere lad. They had not changed now that he was a young man. Tecumseh saw a stranger approach the Grandfather, tell him something, and other people began talking excitedly behind them. The Grandfather listened to the message then nodded his assent.

"Brothers and sisters," began the Elder, "forgive me for interrupting the story telling but I must communicate a most important message from Little Turtle, chief of the Miami in our Ohio country." The crowd murmured in expectation. "Warriors: the Shemanese have made settlements on our side of the Ohio. They are preparing an army to march into our country and take it by force. Here is the tomahawk." He lifted the hatchet for all to see: it was red. WAR! "If you would defend Indian land north of the Ohio Little Turtle asks you to remove there prepared to LIFT THE HATCHET AGAINST THE MURDERERS WHO ARE STALKING OUR COUNTRY!"

Tecumseh and all the warriors raised their tomahawks and warcries. WAR! It had to come sooner or later.

"Tecumseh!" cried Anungaee, struggling to be heard by the young man at her side.

He put his arm around the girl and walked away from the crowd toward his cabin.

"Your leg?" she asked.

"You know it is well, beautiful maiden," said Tecumseh as tenderly as he could, no small task considering the announcement of a few moments ago. " I should have gone home several moons ago but I chose to remain and study with the Grandfathers."

"Stay with me!" said Anungaee as she hugged him while they walked.

"How could I abandon my people?"

"I am your people, we are all your people," said the girl.

"Yes, and I will return," said Tecumseh, "but first I must fight the encroachers and do the will of the Master of Life."

"I knew you would go, I always knew," said Anungaee, tears filling her eyes. "Tomorrow?"

"Yes. But do not be hurt for doing what I must," soothed Tecumseh. "Dear one, do not honor me with tears. My father and my chiefs compel honor. Please understand. I must leave tomorrow."

"Then we have tonight," said Anungaee.

Chapter 2

Arthur St. Clair and General Josiah Harmar spent two months planning the campaign and now, September 26, 1790, Harmar was at the head of an army as it began the slow ascent up the Great Miami River. He had 1,133 militia, much touted Kentucky and Pennsylvania frontiersmen who could "shoot the eye out of a squirrel at fifty paces." General Harmar felt secure the men were bona fide riflemen for they had to be to inhabit the frontiers. There were also 320 Regulars, whom the frontiersmen held in universal contempt due to their notions of military discipline.

Harmar had been as efficient as possible in seeing to the repair of the frontiersmen's firearms, though the demand for such service appeared inordinate for men who prided themselves on the use of rifles. Many had personally told the General that recruiters had informed them all repairs would be made at Fort Washington, from where the army would jump off into Indian country. "It's about time the government did something to put the savages in line," one man had said to Harmar, "and I want to be in on the fun."

I'm glad you're here," Harmar had replied, "but where are your camp kettle and your axe?"

"Ain't got none," was the reply. "Can't kill an Indian with a kettle, now can ye?"

Everyone had laughed, including Harmar, but lack of a suitable federal comissary was a great hindrance in carrying war into savage country. So equipment was gathered wherever possible and weapons were repaired even while the army was moving.

Harmar was anxious to strike at the savages. He paced around in his boat, though there was not much room for walking. He peered at both shores, knowing his scouts were far up river in efforts to locate the enemy. He much preferred battlefields to council houses. The savages would have to be taught a lesson before they signed meaningful treaties. With close to 1500 men he hoped, nay, felt secure this was a lesson the Indians would never forget. He would whip them in battle, burn their towns, and destroy their food supplies. The savages would learn to appreciate the magnanimity of the United States. It was too late now. He thought ruefully: *I would hate to have all these frontiersmen chasing after me. Sure, they're an undisciplined lot and rowdy, but always spoiling for a fight with Indians. The savages won't be able to muster 1500 warriors. The men give the look of being on some sort of pleasure excursion but once we hit Indian country they will come through.*

General Harmar admired Governor St. Clair, who understood a war was inevitable. The Governor had come up with the strategem that General Hamtramck would come out of Fort Knox with his federal troops, 300 Kentucky militia, a few French from Vincennes, and ascend the Wabash River against the Ouiatenon and then later, if possible, effect a junction with Harmar in the Miami country. Harmar didn't feel invincible, he was too good a soldier for that, but he felt confident of victory. He had some time to think, for the advance was slow, about eight miles a day, because many of the men were without horses. But even if there had been a horse for everyone more speed would have been impossible for the meat supply was on the hoof and could not be overly hurried.

"Pull close to the shore," he ordered, "and let me walk with the men for a while," His personal staff of four did not relish the idea of walking as much as the general but they all got off the boat with him and followed his example. It was a good gesture for the frontiersmen as well as relief from monotony. Harmar walked crisply as he thought about St. Clair. He still found it hard to believe the Governor's favorite daughter, who could have her pick of anyone, was interested in the son of the head savage, Joseph Brant. Now Louisa was bold and independent but to come up with something like that! Harmar envisioned his men going into an Indian village and coming out with Louisa St. Clair as a prisoner of war. Perish the thought! It was better to send her back to Philadelphia, at least until the war was over.

By October 15 scouts returned to Harmar with intelligence that the army was just three days away from the Miami villages. The general detached Colonel Hardin with 650 men, sending them ahead to engage the savages afterwhich the main army would arrive and smash any further resistance. As Hardin carried out his duties Harmar gave orders to push the army hard so the attacking force would not be without reserves for very long.

Colonel Hardin arrived at the first Miami town to find it had been evacuated.

"Completely deserted," said the scout to Hardin. "Not even snipers or something to exchange shots with."

"All right, have the men occupy the village. We'll wait for the general. You two go on ahead," he said to his scouts, "to the next village and see if they're all massing there."

The scouts instantly reined their horses and rode.

Harmar brought in the main army the next day. The men were jubilant that their very presence had been enough to win the day. They walked through the village, taking what they needed or fancied. In time the scouts returned with information that there were five villages, all deserted. Harmar issued orders to destroy all five but privately he felt deprived of victory because the warriors could not be found.

There were about three hundred cabins in the villages. All were burned to the ground, nothing but smoking ashes remaining. All fruit trees were sought out and girdled. It was estimated twenty thousand bushels of corn were put to the torch. The Miami villages were thus wiped from the face of the earth.

Still the men were not satisfied. They wanted to kill Indians. Harmar sent out small groups for reconnaisance in attempts to locate bodies of defenders but none were successful. An Indian trail was discovered and Col. Hardin got permission to take 150 militiamen and 30 Regulars on a search and destroy mission.

Hardin rode at the head of his men who marched three abreast. But then most were frontiersmen so their walk did not resemble the marching gait of the Regulars.

"Can you imagine burning all the that corn?" said one militiaman to another as they walked.

"Hey, knock off the chatter back there," snapped the sergeant of the Regulars.

"Piss on 'em," said one of the men who had been talking, though he lowered his voice.

"Sure, we coulda loaded the horses then put it on the boats-"

Suddenly an explosion of muskets went off as if by prearranged signal and dozens of men tumbled through the air and fell to the ground.

"This way!" yelled Hardin as he led the men off the trail away from

66

the heaviest barrage. The Regulars obeyed instantly but the militamen hesitated for an instant then fled ignominiously back down the trail, panic stricken. It was as if the frontiersmen had been of one mind and body.

"ITS A TRAP!" screamed someone as the militia retreated post haste. The Regulars returned the fire but the second barrage destroyed half their already depleted numbers.

"Save yourself if you can!" ordered Col. Hardin when he saw how the cowardly Kentuckians and Pennsylvanians fled at the first onslaught. "Make your way back to the main camp! Every man for himself!" A private next to him was moaning so Hardin got the man, lifted him to his horse, jumped on behind the saddle and rode through the forest in retreat. Everyone took off running from the scene of the ambush but when Tecumseh came upon the site of the resistance he counted twenty-seven bodies. The young warrior had been surprised at the cowardice of the Shemanese but he remembered how Blackfish had advised him about the mind breaking down suddenly when an ambush is executed properly. And if the men were not properly trained a surprised enemy was as good as dead or captured. Some of the wounded Shemanese were captured and all the dead were scalped, although Tecumseh did not bother to take any hair. He sought Blue Jacket in order to be in on the next encounter. This had been only a skirmish for Tecumseh and the other warriors.

As Tecumseh walked to and fro he did not see a Shemanese, Ensign Armstrong, who had fallen behind and under a log in such a way as to prevent being seen. Armstrong saw what must have been hundreds of Indians and he thought for sure he was a goner, his only weapon being the knife he wore in his belt. But there were so many Indians around he dared not move and risk any kind of noise. Insects crawled on his cheek but with great will power he didn't move until it was pitch dark and he could make a successful escape from the site of battle. Other men also made hairbreadth escapes, which they related to the others when they eventually reached camp.

General Harmar now had to make a decision. Despite Hardin's skirmish, the army had accomplished its mission: destroy the Indian towns and all savages that could be construed as hostile. Would this action discourage the savages from attacking further traffic on the Ohio? Harmar could not be sure. Many of the men wanted to return home with victory tucked safely away. He mulled over it, called his officers together and asked for their opinions.

Col. Hardin spoke first: "Give me some men to engage the Indians in a real battle. I cannot consider this a victory until the savages are chastised in blood."

"I will go with him," said Major Willis. "The Indians will be returning to their villages to see what they can salvage. When they are there we can charge in and catch them by surprise."

The other officers were lukewarm about returning to Fort Washington without a definitive battle but they did maintain the men wanted to return home, considering their job done.

"All right," concluded General Harmar, "give the order to march for home. After we've been on the road two days, Hardin and Willis will return stealthily with four hundred men and engage the savages."

"Sir," said Hardin, "we don't have four hundred Regulars."

"No, you are to take militiamen," returned Harmar.

"Sir, I desire to take Regulars."

"All right then, take sixty Regulars and as many horses as you need. Good hunting." The council was ended.

The news broke quickly that the army was returning home, though the men were not as jubilant as when they marched in. There was also some difficulty in recruiting enough militiamen to return with Hardin and Willis to thrash the Indians in their own burned towns, but the necessary number was obtained and the four hundred stole back to the Miami villages.

The detachment was structured with the Regulars in the middle of the four hundred for Hardin had seen how ineffective the militia had been during the ambush. The men got to the first village, saw some Indians walking around and rushed in for the kill.

"Don't scatter!" ordered Hardin as the frontiersmen pursued this way and that after stray Indians. But the only ones to stay in a fighting unit were the Regulars, such was the glee of the militia in their pursuit. Major Willis went after his men as they pursued a body of Indians who retreated in a very disorderly fashion up the St. Joseph River. The frontiersmen let out the Kentucky yell, certain that victory was in their grasp when Little Turtle led his men out of the forest and pounced on the unsupported Regulars. The men fought bravely and in good military fashion but the odds were just too great. As a soldier thrust at an Indian with his bayonet another warrior would come up and tomahawk him from behind.

Tecumseh charged in from one side of the slaughter, tomahawk in one hand, warclub in the other, yelling fiercely all the while. He tripped over something, fell head over heels but was immediately back on his feet and swinging his weapons as it became necessary to cut his way through a mob of Shemanese, who did not stand long because there were too many warriors. Many of the warriors were painted red and black, causing horrendous fright among the militia and even the Regulars. Half the Indians fought from horseback and little bells hung down the left side of each animal's head, along with two narrow strips of red and white cloth which served as decorative pendants. Warcries, painted bodies, ominous bells, and flying pendants terrorized even the horses of the militia, making it most difficult to control them.

The militiamen who had pursued up the river were now pursued in turn, many being killed, some fleeing into the woods in hopes of escape to the main army. When the battle was over Little Turtle informed the assembled Indians that 183 Shemanese had been killed in defense of the homeland, and more than a score of wounded had been captured.

General Harmar and the main army made it back to Fort Washington in safety. He made a full report to Governor St. Clair and then wrote the official report to Secretary of War Knox: "The substance of the work is this; our loss was heavy, but the headquarters of iniquity were broken up..." He reported the expedition was successful, though it cost the lives of many men and courageous officers like Major Willis.

Some individuals at Philadelphia were not satisfied with Harmar's report. The Indian raids not only continued but became worse for they now believed they could handle the Longknives militarily. Pennsylvania Senator William Maclay remarked in Congress: "The ill-fortune of the Harmar affair breaks through all the coloring that it has been given. The report of the expedition looks finely on paper, but were we to view the green bones and scattered fragments of our defeat on the actual field, it would leave very different ideas in our minds. This is a vile business and my surmise is that it is much viler."

In time Harmar was smartly rebuked by Secretary Knox and ordered to demand a court of inquiry, which the General did. The investigation was held and Harmar eventually vindicated but he felt like resigning his commisssion. The official report to President Washington said the fault lay not in Harmar's leadership but in the fact that untrained militia formed the backbone of his army. No one publicized the fact that American frontiersmen, at least the ones with Josiah Harmar, were as lacking in courage as they were in discipline when it got down to actually fighting Indians. Congress decided to finance another expedition, tripling the amount allocated for Harmar's. Washington chose Arthur St. Clair as commander of the army and authorized him to call up three thousand men. Futhermore, precautions were taken to assure a large nucleus of Regulars, thus needing fewer militia-frontiersmen.

Episode 2: Lewis Wetzel

Tecumseh was just one of the many warriors who stopped at Little Turtle's village, Kekionga, before returning home with Sinnamantha and the others of Blue Jacket's contingent. All the tribesmen were heartened by the victory over the invader for it proved that Indians, some even without thunder weapons, could repel the Shemanese encroachers if the warriors united. The basic problem now was to get relief for the Miamis for their food supplies had been destroyed. Runners were sent to all neighboring tribes asking that any surplus of corn be sent to Little Turtle's people and all who could complied. The villages would be rebuilt before the onset of winter and the Shemanese sent out individuals to try to work things out with the Indians at the council fires instead of the battle field. But the tribesmen would not treat for anything if it was not understood beforehand that the Ohio River must forever be the boundary between the two races. The Americans were not ready to concede this so negotiations proved ineffective. And during this period there was constant fighting, guerrilla style.

One autumn day Lewis Wetzel shouldered his rifle and plunged into the woods, vowing not to return home until he had increased his store of scalps. He looked at the Muskingum River as he walked though he had gazed at it many times, this region being his favorite area for hunting and scalp taking. He walked all day, saw many signs, but encountered no Indians until toward evening he saw smoke in the distance, just a small curling stream only an experienced woodsman would notice. Wetzel made his way slowly, peering this way and that to ascertain if fiendish guards had been posted. He saw none and by nightfall he found the place where four Indians rested their swarthy forms by the small fire. The odds were not good but the savages were sleeping, or so it appeared, even if it was not late yet, so Wetzel decided to take them on.

After pulling back the flintlock to be able to fire it immediately, he laid down his rifle quietly, got his knife in one hand, tomahawk in the other, and made his way secretly into the encampment. He knew there were no sentries so he raised the axe and brought it down on a savage skull as he let out a terrific yell. The skull broke open like a melon. Wetzel swung at another Indian as he tried to rise, with the same result. A third savage, still half asleep and confused by the yelling, was sent to hell by Wetzel's large hunting knife with a deadly stab to the stomach. The fourth devil got to his feet and fled into the darkness without attempting resistance.

Wetzel was breathing heavily from his exertion but his concern was whether or not the last savage would return. The stabbed Indian was more dead than alive but still writhing in agony. Wetzel scalped him then stabbed him several times more. He took his axe and smashed the hellhounds skull then scalped the other two savages and wrought additional mutilation on their dead bodies, making sure to break the collar bones and axe the genitalia. The camp was a bloody mess when Wetzel went to collect his rifle but he had three more scalps to show the folks back home at Mingo Bottom.

When asked a couple of days later as to his success he replied, "Fair. I treed four red dogs but one of them got away with his tail between his legs."

"Better not let General Harmar get a hold of you," said one of the men as Wetzel and Veach Dicherson leaned against a building.

"What's up?" asked Lewis Wetzel. "He still trying to make a peace treaty after they whipped him?"

"Yeah, he sure is. Even has some chiefs going down to the fort. Wants to sign a peace with the noble red men."

"Is that a fact?" said Veach. "Well just maybe Lewis and I should go too so as we can make sure them Indians tell the truth."

"Sounds good to me," added Lewis in his laconic fashion. But his eyes sparkled in a frightening way as they first did when his entire family was slaughtered before his eyes many years ago.

The next day the two men secreted themselves between Fort Harmar and the spot where the Indians were encamped. Along about midmorning Wetzel's sharp ears heard hoofbeats in the distance. "That's them, I'll betcha," he said as he peered into the distance from behind his tree a ways from the road the Indians would use to arrive at the fort.

"I'll get the one in the lead," said Veach.

Wetzel saw the first Indian. He was the influential savage called "George Washington" by the whites. Lewis decided to make certain the dog never rode again so he drew a bead on him too. "Get ready for a quick re-load," said Lewis as the hammers were drawn back.

Both men knew George Washington was peaceably disposed but it mattered little as Wetzel counted "One, two, three" and both men pulled their triggers, the muskets spitting forth their deadly missles. But the rider continued on his horse toward the fort. Neither man could believe they had missed such a target! Then the rider bent over forward, nearly falling off his horse but not quite.

"Got him!" said the two men in relief.

"Shall we take another?" asked Veach as he re-loaded quickly.

"No, they're liable to see the smoke the second time around," cautioned Lewis though he reloaded also. "Let's get outta here. We'll be all right back at Mingo Bottom." The two men jumped on their horses and made their way back through the woods without further incidents.

General Harmar himself received the delegation of Indians as they rode into the fort. "Welcome, welcome my friends. It makes my heart happy to-"

George Washington fell from his saddle at the feet of the General. "What's the meaning of this?" asked Harmar. Then he saw the blood on the man's torso and abdomen. "Good Lord! Medic!" yelled the General. "Get a doctor over here on the double!"

The chief died that afternoon. The Indians had seen for themselves what perfidy was and no treaty could possibly hope to succeed. Harmar told the assembled Indians: "I give you my word as a warrior that when I find the perpetrators of this crime I shall bring them to justice. I have already sent out patrols to reconnoiter and investigate as to the identity of the murderers. They shall be executed for this breach of trust, this act of cowardice!"

The unfortunate affair was considered a good joke among the frontiersmen and settlers at Mingo Bottom so they took no pains to conceal the names of Lewis Wetzel and Veach Dickerson. The news reached Harmar within a few days and upon receipt of the intelligence he directed Captain Kingsbury to take a company of men and bring in the offenders.

Kingsbury took the soldiers to Mingo Bottom only to learn the men were all out to a shooting match.

"Is Lewis Wetzel with them?" asked the captain of his informant, an older man.

"Reckon so."

"Whereabouts is this match being held?"

"Down the road a piece on the other side of them two hills."

"Thank you. Men, let's grab a quick bite to eat here then we will continue. Dismount," ordered the captian as the old man walked away from the soldiers. When he was out of their sight he stopped a boy and told him to let Wetzel know the soldiers were after him. The boy went for his pony, put a bridle on him then jumped on his bare back and rode out of the village as nonchalantly as he could. He made it to the locale where the men were shooting and informed everyone about the soldiers.

The men became ebullient with the news. What the hell! That one of their number, a leader at that, who had saved more women and children from death than there were soldiers at Fort Harmar, should be arrested and hung for simply killing a red dog right out of the forest!

"Lewis, if they take you they're going to have to do it over my dead

72

body!" said one of the men.

"Same here!" chorused a number of others. Indeed, every man present was willing to save Lewis and Veach, devil take the consequences.

"I'll tell you what we'll do," said one tall fellow, "instead of waiting for that bastard Kingsbury and his boys let's go out and meet them!"

"We can ambush them easy while they're coming down the road."

"We can wipe out the entire company before they know what hit 'em!'

Major McMahon was present, dressed in his civilian clothes. He was part of the army but he knew the men and their frontier psychology. "Hold up a minute, now hold it up!"

"McMahon has something to say," cautioned a calmer individual in the crowd. "Let him speak his piece."

"Now fellows let's not go kill each other over some stinking Indian," began McMahon. "We're here to pacify the country, not make it run red with civil war. Now my idea is to go talk to Kingsbury, let him know the situation here and suggest he withdraw with his company before he loses all his men. All I ask is that you remain here while I go intercept Kingsbury. If I can't prevail on him then he'll be coming down the road for your pleasure. Will you give me your word?"

"Sounds okay to me."

"Fair enough."

All agreed so McMahon got on his horse and rode. Everyone waited with impatience for they were in dead earnest: if the military tried to take Wetzel or Dickerson there would be plenty of hot lead to greet them.

Kingsbury's company of soldiers never showed up. Lewis Wetzel considered this a personal victory and an endorsement for his Indian fighting. "I appreciate your support," he said to everyone as he shook hands with as many men as possible, "and if you're ever in a bind count on me. It's a shame we had to stop the shooting match cause I woulda whipped you all!" The afternoon ended on that gleeful note.

Episode 3: Tecumseh meets Frank

Tecumseh lead five warriors when he moved commando fashion against the supply train headed for the Shemanese army being built up at Fort Washington. The group crossed the Ohio below the mouth of the Hocking River and made camp. Big Fish was posted as sentry, two men were instructed to make the camp while the others, including Tecumseh, were to hunt for food. All were famished as the party was out of provisions. The leaves on the ground were so dry game was startled even

73

from a distance. Tecumseh struck off by himself in the direction of a Shemanese settlement which he knew was in the vicinity. He watched for game or anything edible but saw nothing until his ears told him that off to his right something walked through the woods. He put an arrow to his bow, not wanting to make thunder with his musket, and waited for a while. A man, no, a boy, appeared, walking aimlessly, but that didn't make sense. Ah, it was a blackface, about twelve years old. Tecumseh relaxed a bit but kept his bow ready in case others followed.

The boy seemed to be alone so when he came close Tecumseh stepped out form behind his cover and said in English "You lad, what are you doing out here alone?"

The boys eyes shone bright and large in his sudden fright. Right there in front of him was an Indian speaking English! "What?!" is all the lad could muster.

"Don't you know it is dangerous to be out alone by yourself?"

"Yessir. I mean, my master lets me."

"Where is this master?" asked Tecumseh.

"Back in Belleville, sir."

"And what might your name be?"

"They calls me Frank."

"Okay, Frank, what do you say you come with me and my men so you never have to have another master as long as you live?" He saw the hesitation in the boy's face. "We will not hurt you. We are all brothers."

"Wells, I gess'n it would be betta than being a slave," stammered Frank.

"Then come back to camp with me," said Tecumseh. "My men are out hunting. Perhaps they have found some game to roast for eating. Come on."

Frank realized he had no choice so he walked alongside the Indian. He couldn't help staring at him for he had never seen a wild Indian before. Tecumseh smiled at the lad as he continued searching the woods for game. He found none and when the two walked into camp they learned the other hunters had been able to bag only one poor tortoise, which was divided equally seven ways.

After the small morsel was eaten Tecumseh said, "Let us not camp here, there is no game and we will starve. If we move on we will encounter some food." Everyone agreed so the Indians climbed on their horses, Tecumseh pulling Frank on behind him. "As soon as we can we will get you your own horse so your can ride like the others," he said. "Would you like that?"

"Course," responded Frank.

The men rode for several hours until Tecumseh, riding point, noticed a trail of animals so clearly defined it could have been read at night. There were six or seven horses and quite of number of cows! This delighted Tecumseh for it was exactly what Chief Blue Jacket had sent him and his commandos out to do: kill Shemanese wherever possible and commandeer all supplies. Their famished condition would make their wits even sharper in the encounter that would follow. Darkness was casting its wings over the country as Tecumseh gave his men the sign not to make any kind of noise. He forgot about Frank sitting behind him as he followed the trail. When Tecumseh knew the Shemanese party was extremely close he reined in his mount, stopped the warriors, dismounted and went on alone, signing for the others to remain where they were.

The leader of the party was a man named Carpenter. His ten year old son and five men comprised the group that was bringing up beef cattle and milk cows to Paul Fearing, commissary to the United States troops in the West. Carpenter had come to a small creek within half a mile of the Ohio about six miles above Marietta on the Virginia side. He decided to make camp by the creek because the woods were rich with pea vines and the grass was lush. The cattle were allowed to roam while the horses were hobbled and turned out in the creek bottom. The men prepared a hearty supper, the atmosphere was jovial, and no guards were posted since whites were continually plying the waters of the Ohio, Marietta being so close. Carpenter believed it would be an audacious Indian indeed who tried to attack in this vicinity. When the men finished supper they talked a while then threw more wood on the fire, spread their blankets, and laid down to sleep.

Tecumseh watched every move the Shemanese made. He could have ordered an immediate attack but he decided against it because some of the stock might be lost. Besides, sleeping men were not enemies, only those who could kill. He watched the camp a while longer then returned to his men.

"We will attack at dawn," said Tecumseh in Shawnee. "We are equal in numbers. It should be no problem to surprise them. They have no sentries posted."

"Why not take them now and get something to eat?" asked Big Fish.

"Your stomach shall be filled soon enough, Steve," replied Tecumseh, using the man's Shemanese name.

"You could have brought us some food," said Tall Oak, continuing Big Fish's banter.

"Let us sleep," said Tecumseh, "we must be up before dawn to get into position. I will take the first watch." He walked a ways toward Carpenter's camp then made himself comfortable, his eyes and ears sensitive to the slightest warning in the night. When he was relieved by Tall Oak he walked even further then rolled up in his blanket and slept until something within told him it was time to awaken his men, which he did immediately.

Everyone, including Frank, walked to the attack, weapons ready. Tecumseh led his men to a fallen timber from which everyone could look down into Carpenter's camp. The Shemanese still slept soundly and the horizon to the east was dark but dawn was beginning to walk the rim of the sky. Tecumseh now motioned for Frank to follow him up the ridge. They walked in silence until Tecumseh turned and informed him quietly, "I am sorry to have to do this but I must tie you up while we attack. Do not make any sound, for your own safety." He tied the boy to a sapling and put a gag in his mouth. "Now I will come untie you immediately after we take the enemy, have no fear." He checked that the rawhide was not overly tight. "Stay here until I return, understand?" asked Tecumseh. Frank nodded and Tecumseh headed back down the ridge as the sun was stronger in the horizon.

Carpenter's men still weren't awake when Tecumseh returned so he and his warriors watched them as dawn began to break, casting back the dark wings of night. They readied their muskets, the four that had them, as the men began to stir. One Shemanese got up, put more wood on the dying fire and said, "Come on fellows, up and at 'em. Let's say our devotions then rustle up some breakfast." The others stretched, yawned, rubbed their limbs, then stood up to pray.

Four shots rang out as the sun poured into the camp. Carpenter, his son, and one other man fell to the ground as the morning air filled with terrifying warcries as the Indians charged down into the emcampment. A Shemanese was tomahawked into oblivion but the others fled precipitously, thus preserving their lives. Tecumseh now realized he should have encircled the little camp in order to get all the Shemanese.

"Big Fish, take three men and make certain no one returns from any direction," said Tecumseh. "Then let's gather the animals and be on our way." The men all looked at him. "All right, we'll eat quickly then make tracks. But keep your vigilance about you. Anyone could have heard the shots." He looked around in all directions for a counter-attack was possible at any time. Tall Oak rummaged around items left by the Shemanese and found their food: jerked venison, biscuits, coffee. A quick meal was prepared.

"Now we have a horse for Frank," said Tecumseh. "I'll go get the lad while you brew the coffee," he said to Tall Oak and struck out toward the ridge. He arrived there momentarily but Frank was not in sight. Evidently he had witnessed the affray below and decided he wanted no part of the Indians. Tecumseh shook his head in disbelief. How could the black-face prefer his life of slavery to Indian freedom? Would he inform on their whereabouts? It didn't matter. The party would be long gone with the rich booty of animals before the Shemanese could come out looking for them. Tecumseh returned to camp and ate quickly with his men. The first one to finish went to retrieve the Shawnee horses from where they had been secreted.

One of the dead Shemanese was scalped by Tall Oak but the bodies of Carpenter and his son were taken aside. Their hair was left in tact and new moccasins were put on their feet. Their bodies were then wrapped properly in new blankets. This was done at Tecumseh's direction because the year before at Marietta Carpenter had repaired an Indian's gun and refused payment for the service. News of kindness to an Indian was never forgotten by the tribesmen of the frontier. The body of the boy was snuggled next to that of his father, Tecumseh's final tribute of respect.

Episode 4: Laulewasika

"Laulewasika, would you go get us some water, apetotha?" asked Tecumapease of her youngest brother. "It is no good to wait until every jar is empty."

Laulewasika had been sitting on the floor of the cabin as if in deep meditation. "Yes, of course." He got to his feet, grabbed the earthenware jug and walked out of the wegiwa.

Tecumapease knew he had been drinking already, though she thought her younger brother believed he was fooling her. Perhaps she should follow to discover where he had the jug hidden? No, she did not wish to be sneaky. She could even have sent one of the children after him but it would be better to talk to him, not betray him into a confrontation. Something was wrong in Laulewasika's emotional life. She wished Tecumseh could work with him more often.

Laulewasika walked through the village at a leisurely pace, going to the spring that flowed from the side of a little hill. He suddenly detoured into the woods and walked to the place where he had the firewater hidden. How he enjoyed the fiery liquid! His mouth salivated in expectation as he looked around to ascertain intruding eyes were not watching where his private treasure was hidden. He set down the jar, unearthed the leaves and dirt which exposed covering of rawhide then pulled out the jug. He looked around one more time, undid the cork, put the jug to his lips and took a deep swig. "Aaagh," he said as the fiery draught made its way down. He sat against a tree and smiled complacently. He was sure no other man his age, fifteen summers, could drink as he! Some men hunted, others warred, he could drink. This was his second visit to his cache today and it was barely noon. Life was good. He missed his brothers and sisters but there was always Tecumapease and his nieces and nephews to take up the slack. He took another drink then corked the jug. *Enough for today. A while. Better put it back and go for.. the water. Water is good...too. Dizzy. Clear up when I walk.*

Laulewasika reburied the jug carefully, picked up the water jar and walked slowly toward the spring. When he saw other people he ignored them as if in deep thought. His head cleared and the dizzying effect dissipated by the time he put the jug into the clear waterhole. He looked at his reflection, blinked, then smiled pleasantly. With his hands he brought some water to his lips and drank. Now he was ready to take his sister the water. He picked up the jug and made it to the wegiwa without talking to anyone.

"Laulewasika, it is time you and I sat down to talk," began Tecumapease when the boy entered the cabin and put the jug down in a corner.

"Talk?" said Laulewasika. "What about?"

"You. You must know how people talk about you. They say you neither hunt nor fight, just drink whenever you have the opportunity."

"It is a crime to gossip," observed Laulewasika. "What are you going to cook?"

"Sofka," replied Tecumapease, knowing her brother considered it one of his favorite foods, "or maybe I will make it into *osah-saw-bo*. Which would you rather have.?"

Laulewasika was indecisive but finaly he said, "How about a little of both?"

"We shall see," said Tecumapease as she put the flinty corn into the deep mortar and began braying it with the pestle. "Put a couple more sticks on the fire to boil that water, would you please?" Laulewasika complied, being in the mood to cooperate with his sister. "Why do you drink?" asked Tecumapease candidly.

Laulewasika merely shook his shoulders. "Why does anyone drink?"

Tecumapease continued pounding with the pestle, intermittently stopping to inspect if the skin covering of the grain was sufficiently broken in order to separate it from the kernels. "Little brother, I know you were left adrift early in life. I realize you never knew our wonderful father and that mother has never been the same since his death."

"I shall always treasure you," said Laulewasika sincerely, "because you have been mother and father to me."

Tecumapease was slightly surprised her younger brother would say that. "You know I love you because I have cared for you."

"Though I know your love for Tecumseh is of a stronger nature."

Tecumapease was really taken aback now, though she showed nothing in her countenance, continuing with the corn pounding. "You are different human beings, little brother. I do not love you less."

"I want you to love my brothers," answered Laulewasika, enabling her to continue with what was on her mind. "I miss them too." He sat and looked at his sister. "If we are to blame anyone, let it be the Long-knives for destroying us with their merciless encroachments into our lands."

"The old ones say people drink because they are insecure."

"Do you think I am?"

"I must ask you," replied Tecumapease. "No one is more intelligent than you in this family."

"Not even Tecumseh?"

"Not even Tecumseh," said the woman sincerely.

"Sometimes I feel...lonely," said Laulewasika frankly. "I feel... rejected somehow. Not by you, dear sister," he added quickly. "I do not feel I was intended for the warpath. I do not enjoy hunting."

"How will you survive if you do not hunt?" asked Tecumapease.

"I do not know. The Great Spirit must show me what my destiny will be."

"Drinking and drunkenness will not bring you closer to the Great Mysterious," observed Tecumapease. "That will only break your health."

Laulewasika was known for his mercurial moods but his emotions did not jump this day. "What do you suggest? And don't tell me to quit drinking."

"Then what can anyone say?" Tecumapease inspected the corn and decided it was ready for the next step. "Bring me the law-as-quah-thi-ka."

Laulewasika looked around for the wafter, the broad, shallow, woven basket. He saw it and fetched it for his sister, who put the corn into it. "I'll take it outside," he said.

"Okay."

The two went out of the wegiwa and Tecumapease watched while Laulewasika threw the corn into the air so the skins could be blown away in the breeze, then caught it again in the wafter.

"I do not know what to tell you, then," continued Tecumapease as she watched. "I guess all I can do is communicate my concern."

"Do not worry. I will take care of myself." He stopped his work momentarily. "Do you know what? I am going to be the greatest member of this illustrious family."

Tecumapease wrinkled her brow and forehead in disbelief of her ears. "We all wish you to be illustrious but explain how you will accomplish such a feat."

"That I do not know," said Laulewasika in all earnestness, "but I feel it in my bones." He began to throw the corn again. "Yes, I know, father was the chief at Piqua, mother gave birth to us all, Cheeseekau is the famous Shawnee Warrior without equal, you will someday be the Beloved Woman, and Tecumseh excels at all he does but believe me, I shall be the most famous of all."

Tecumapease was greatly encouraged by Laulewasika's earnestness but she did not draw attention to it. Instead she got the wafter, inspected the corn, decided it was ready and said, "Okay, let's go put it into the boiling water," and the two re-entered the wegiwa. She poured the corn into the kettle. "I wish you had an idea of what you wanted to do but this day I will make a pact with you: it is my fervent wish that you become the greatest of Puckeshinwa's family, famous throughout the many lands of our people. I challenge you to bring your vision to fruition." She stirred the corn as the water began to turn white.

"I shall also be known among the Shemanese," continued Laulewasika.

This surprised Tecumapease and tended to dispel the hope that her brother was sincerely resolved to improve himself. "Why the Longknives? They are our enemies, murderers of your father and thousands of our people!"

"Now you're sounding like mother," chided Laulewasika.

For a moment Tecumapease lost control of herself after having her hopes dashed. She regained her composure instantly. "I mean, if you become a noteworthy individual among our people that will be enough."

"Our destiny is interwoven with theirs."

Tecumapease knew her brother had not received the education given Tecumseh and yet Laulewasika could make the most profound observations for one whom the Grandfathers had not tutored directly. "I do not understand how," she replied.

"I cannot explain it but I feel it," said Laulewasika.

Tecumapease put her arms around the boy. "Please stop your drinking, Laulewasika. Please put an end to it so you can live up to your vision."

"I do not know if I can," he said simply as he returned the embrace. "Its's just that when I feel... low... at least I don't get falling down drunk.. all the time."

Tecumapease smiled in understanding at her brother then went back to the boiling kettle. The corn would take a while yet. 'I think I shall make osah-saw-bo instead. I will get the nuts if you pound them for me."

"Sure."

Tecumapease fetched some walnuts and pecans, put them into the mortar since they had already been shelled, and Laulewasika smashed them with the pestle. He stopped suddenly and asked, "Do you think I am crazy?"

"Of course not. Remember, from this day on we have a pact and I am duty bound to help you. We are flesh and blood, your greatness is my greatness. But remember: your shame also must come to rest on my shoulders. I would feel better if you were apprenticed."

Laulewasika pounded the nut meats until Tecumapease thought they were ready, taking them and putting them in the kettle. "In a little time I shall have some delicious food for you, apetotha. I thank you for your help."

"I will return later," said Laulewasika as he headed for the flap which served as the door of the wegiwa.

"Don't forget our pact, little brother," said Tecumapease as the boy disappeared.

Episode 5: Red

By August of 1791 there were thousands of men at Fort Washington as well as a quarter of that number of women. Arthur St. Clair could do little about so many women, many of whom sold their favors to the soldiers and intended to follow the army right into the Indian country. The Governor, also serving as Major-General, was concerned that his supplies with which to wage the war were not coming in on schedule. Further tardiness would seriously impede entry into Indian territory, especially if an early winter eventuated. The march from Fort Washington would be a long one into the north country and snow on the ground would be disaster. St. Clair oversaw the proper storage of all supplies and equipment, the billeting of the men who would win the Northwest Territory for the United States and make it safe for civilization.

Of the hundreds of women who gravitated to the fort there were many comely or distinctive in appearance. One in particular attracted much attention from the soldiers for in reality the men had nothing to do but wait for St. Clair to give the order to march. She was a striking redhead who, unlike the other women, wore pants every so often instead of dresses. As she strolled through the fort on this errand or that, heads turned to watch her pass. No one really knew where she had came from, some saying she was from Philadelphia, others New York, even faraway Boston. Her pants were very snug around her voluptuous thighs and hips, as was the blouse which was pleasingly structured by her bust and shoulders. She became known as "Red" for she would not give her name to anyone. Even the women with whom she became acquainted called her Red and soon everyone heard rumors about the woman who became the most popular female at Fort Washington. At first she bestowed her favors on anyone with a dollar but when she was in great demand she required the man take a bath and pay her with one Spanish doubloon. This cut down her business considerably for the frontiersmen resented taking baths almost as much as doubloons were scarce. But Red didn't care about cutting down on her professional activities because she liked selection almost as much as real money, of which the United States money was not, being only paper. Spanish pieces of eight were the key to Red's night long passions and the lucky few who experienced them served to encourage the others to get their hands on "real money" in order to sleep with her.

"That's the one you want," whispered one man to another as the two stopped to look at Red as she walked on the other side of the flagpole. "One night with her will make a man outta anybody."

Rutherford stared at the woman. "The Spanish gold lady, eh?" he said to his buddy. "But where am I gonna get a doubloon? You only find those in deep waters."

"There are some floating around," responded Albert. "If you're lucky at cards I saw some the other night."

"I'll bet every damned rascal in this army is drooling over them. I guess I'll just settle for some other gal. Look over there at that covey of quail. Once you get 'em in the dark they're all the same anyhow."

The two scrutinized the women, sizing up who they'd pick if they had their druthers. Rutherford decided on the dark haired one, Albert's gaze wandered back to Red. "Those pants.. looks like she was poured into 'em. And they didn't know when to stop pouring."

"Look at the teats on the dark one," said Rutherford. "Come on, let's set up some action for tonight before we die of boredom in this lousy fort.

They're going into the tavern. Come on, forget about that Red wench! You can't afford it so quit dreaming. Let's get us one of the others." He grabbed Albert by the sleeve and yanked him in the direction of the tavern.

"Okay, but I'm gonna get into that if it's the last thing I do," vowed Albert, still looking at the woman as he walked away from her. For a moment he thought she was looking at him but then other people got in the way and he lost sight of her.

The two men walked into the dimly lighted tavern and though it was scarcely past midday the place was jampacked and doing uproarious business. There were not nearly as many women as men but everyone was busy and boisterous.

"Hey mister bartender, let's have some refills over here!"

"Now honey, let's not get too serious before I see your money. I could demand a doubloon, you know."

"Yeah, and you'd have to take in laundry or starve to death!" said the man gleefully.

"When do you think St. Clair is going to unleash us?" asked a soldier of his comrades.

"Who cares? Them Indians will keep," was the reply.

Albert and Rutherford walked around looking for a place to sit but found none so they went to the makeshift bar and got some drinks and just stood there. Bawdy jokes and stories were punctuated with hilarious laughter, smoke filled the large room as stray slits of daylight penetrated here and there through the log walls.

"Hey," said Rutherford, "there comes your woman."

"What?" asked Albert.

"Over at the door, the Red wench."

Albert looked and sure enough the voluptuous woman in pants was coming in with another female. Everyone who saw her, including the women, stopped the chatter and just looked as the two made their way to the bar, stopping by Albert and his buddy.

"Hi soldier," said the lady with Red, "would you buy a gal a drink?"

Albert was looking at Red and probably never heard the woman. "We sure will," hastened Rutherford. "What's your pleasure?"

"Whiskey, I guess," said the woman. "How about you, Red?"

She nodded lackadaisical approval, making a bit of a face as she did so. Albert could not take his eyes off her. Even in the dim light he saw how voluptuous her body appeared with its curving thighs, tiny waist, full busoms. Her shoulder structure intrigued him for the muscles were full as they relaxed under her blouse.

"Who's paying?" said the bartender for the second time.

"I am," said Red as she dug a coin out of her pocket, struggling with the tight fitting pants.

"Right here," said Rutherford as he made the man take the money quickly. "Now let's find a place to sit?"

"Sounds good," said the other woman.

"And your name is?" lingered Rutherford.

"Jo. This here's Red."

Rutherford introduced himself and Albert, who was a little more alert now though he still couldn't take his eyes off Red. She ignored him, at least on the surface, as she looked around the raunchy little tavern. The foursome walked in search of chairs but none were available.

"We could go outside," suggested Rutherford half-heartedly.

"Let's," said Jo. "Red?"

"Okay."

The four exited and immediately Rutherford and Jo broke off from the other two as they talked quietly to each other. Red and Albert walked in silence and found themselves alone.

"Do you want to go someplace?" asked Albert, slightly hesitant.

Red looked at him for the first time. What had he said his name was? He was young, probably not more than twenty-one. No money. Just a nice kid. "What do you have in mind?" she asked quietly.

"Maybe you'd like to walk outside the fort, in the woods."

"I guess, for a little while, to relax. I love the forest."

Albert now became enthusiastic. "Same here. That's why I came, to see the country."

"You an Indian fighter?" There was much activity in the fort in order to prepare for the push into the Indian country.

"Not yet, but I hope to get my chance." They walked away from where the militia were billeted in tents outside the fort. Albert was extremely aware of Red's physical presence and if he could have he would have looked at her from all angles as they walked but he made a herculean effort and controlled himself. Red walked briskly, as if she was going somewhere definite. "And you?" asked Albert.

"Me?" laughed Red. "No, I'm not a fighter." She giggled like a schoolgirl.

"Oh, then what are you?" Albert saw the woman's face become serious immediately, which also wiped the smile from his own face. "I'm sorry," he blurted, "I didn't mean to pry."

Red looked at him, comprehending no coarseness was meant. "It's okay. Look at that forest! I could live there forever!"

Albert was slightly confused. He knew Red was a prostitute, beautiful but still a prostitute. But here she was walking through the woods as if she was an ordinary person! His upbringing would not countenance the idea that a whore was also a human being, though he would not have been able to articulate subtleties at the moment.

"Are you experienced with women?" asked Red, knowing instinctively he was not.

"Of course," replied Albert. "Well...not really," he admitted. "Is that bad?"

"No. Just part of living, I guess. What beautiful country! I don't blame the Indians for fighting for it."

Albert was unbalanced by Red's candor and impetuosity, her rapid change of thought. He decided it would be better to remain silent and listen to her talk. Would she try to charge him a doubloon? He didn't have one. "It's our country now," he said, "and St. Clair has a treaty to prove it, but the savages won't honor it. So we're going in to take what's ours." He looked at Red's hair, her face, milk-white skin, shoulders that beckoned massage... and then his eyes fixed on her breasts, hidden under the blouse but still so apparent against the bulging cloth. How large they were! He had not noticed until now that he was up close.

"There are treaties," said Red, "and there are treaties."

"You have to take what's yours," said Albert. He decided the woman was built so perfectly, her various parts so well proportioned, that none stood out in bold relief as happened with some women. He wanted to reach over and touch a breast but instead put his arm around Red's shoulders.

"The trick is to decide what's yours," continued Red, oblivious to the man's arm.

"What a beautiful woman you are," said Albert, gaining confidence with every step.

"You are a nice young man," said Red as she stopped walking, "much too nice for some old Indian war." She kissed him full on the lips, her arms around him tightly.

Albert was taken aback by the sudden kiss and surprised by the strength of her arms. Why, it was like a wrestler's grasp! But the pressure from her breasts dug into him erotically and his manhood swelled under his clothing.

"I just want your friendship," whispered Red, "nothing else."

Albert hardly even heard, so aroused was he. He put his right hand to her left breast and carressed it tenderly.

"Please don't," said Red, "let's just be friends for a while."

Albert could not stop. He unbuttoned her shirt without serious opposition on Red's part, looked at the beautiful breasts, then took both in his hands, caressing them gently.

"You'd better quit that while you still can," said Red.

"I can't," said Albert, controlling the ecstasy as well as he could.

Red looked to see if anybody else was around, saw no one, so she pulled the man's head down to her breast. He took it in his mouth, titillated the nipple with his tongue. Her hand sought his bod, found it under his clothing, then quickly she undid his pants, grasping the fullness in such a way and with such dextrous motions that Albert climaxed within a minute, Red being careful the stream did not touch her clothing.

Albert was totally confused as he let go of her breasts and tried to re-button himself quickly. "I'm sorry," he stammered, "I didn't know I was that close."

"Don't think twice about it," said Red as she buttoned her shirt, no expression of any kind on her face. "I really wanted to walk. Come on, let's go back."

Albert regretted those beautiful breasts were being covered up again but he said nothing for a moment as they began to return to the fort.

"Someday I'm going to live in the forest," said Red as if nothing had happened.

"I'll win you one," said Albert.

Red smiled, exposing a magnificent set of white, even teeth. Albert was overawed with her beauty! What must the rest of her be like! He would get some doubloons if it killed him!

"And how many Indians will you have to kill for a forest, you silly boy?" asked Red playfully.

"As many as necessary."

Episode 6: St. Clair's Army invades.

On September 17 St. Clair gave the order for the army to march to Ludlow's Station, five miles above Fort Washington. There he waited for the infernal supplies which still had not arrived in sufficient amounts. There was some good news, however: General Richard Butler, second in command, arrived with his reenforcements, making the grand army a force of 3300 men.

"General Butler, glad to see you," said the Governor as he shook the man's hand. "Your delay has been most deleterious."

"Sir," responded Butler, "I have followed Secretary Knox's orders to the letter. I had to disband the militia in Pittsburgh before I could recruit my force-"

"I do not mean to criticize, sir," replied St. Clair, "our principal foe is the weather."

"I have no control over that, Governor," continued Butler, stung with his commander's greeting, unaware of the difficulties St. Clair had been through. "When I finally had my troops the government had no boats ready to move men or supplies expeditiously down the river. We can't swim down the Ohio."

"Of couse not, General. Come, let us walk through the camp, and I'll show you what we're up against." The two meandered throughout the large encampment.

"At least we have enough men," said Butler, mollified somewhat. "No Indian force will be able to withstand us."

"I agree," said St. Clair. "We have them outstripped numerically and our weapons are superior. Look at that cannon. But I'd like to hang our quartermaster. Of all the horses he brought in for us not a dozen are available for the campaign!"

"How so?" asked Butler.

"The horses were entrusted to men who had not the slightest knowledge about caring for them. They weren't hobbled at night, not even belled, so they strayed off. I hope to heaven we don't see them in the savages' camp! Those that didn't run off were fed in such a way as to have to compete for the food so they kicked and fought each other. We had to shoot some, they were injured so badly."

Butler shook his head in dismay.

"We requisitioned twenty-five hundred axes," continued St. Clair as he walked up to a tent and picked up the axe leaning against it. "We got fifty. Fifty! Look at this sheeting," he said as he ran his hand down the material. "Rain soaks right through it. Store the powder inside it and it becomes inefficient at best, maybe totally unserviceable. Perhaps we should have put the men to work at making bows and arrows," he said ruefully. Butler didn't crack a smile.

"We ordered saddles for the pack animals. They sent us cavalry saddles. Quite a mess, wouldn't you say?"

"I quite agree," said Butler.

"But we shall prevail, thanks to the men," continued St. Clair. "They are frontiersmen bred to arms. Some even brought their wives with them."

Butler had noticed the large number of women in camp. "Do you think it is wise, sir, to allow women into the Indian country? It could be a very dangerous-"

"These men are rugged individualists, General," interupted St. Clair, "not typical army personnel. If their woman can handle themselves on the frontier they figure they can do the same with an army around them. Why, my own daughter wanted to come along. Had to force her to go to Philadelphia for a while. I was afraid she'd ride into the enemy camp herself!"

"Yes sir," remarked Butler. "I will send out scouts to try to locate the whereabouts of the savages."

"Not yet, General, we have a long march before thinking of reconnaisance. I'll give the order to move out at dawn. We'll build some fortifications along the way-"

"Sir," interrupted Butler, "it is getting late in the season. Perhaps we should engage the enemy first then build the forts."

"Yes, it will be something to discuss as we progress on the march. That might be quite valid, considering our late start."

Butler resented the inference, if that is what St. Clair endeavored to communicate, that his contingent had held up the army, but he said nothing further.

The two parted without establishing any degree of amity after their walk through the encampment. Orders were given to break camp at dawn the following morning and the huge army obeyed, lumbering northward into Indian country. The militiamen thoroughly enjoyed the march into these unknown lands. Many sharpshooters went out to hunt but most returned empty handed for the game was frightened off by so much commotion. Speed was not of the essence, though it was getting late in the season, for it was necessary for the army to exert much energy in acquiring forage for horses and cattle. Frost had killed much of the grass.

Every morning the animals would have to be gathered and the march would have to be halted early in the afternoon in order to let them wander about to find food, causing quotidian delays. And everything was being watched.

Tecumseh was the leader of a group of five scouts, one of the many parties that kept a constant vigil on the invading force. He was impressed with the size of the army but he was astonished as to its behavior. It seemed more like a migration than an invasion, so many people wandering around helter-skelter. When the Shemanese stopped to build a war village in the vicinity of the Great Miami River Tecumseh sent one of his men to report to Blue Jacket, one of the Chiefs masterminding the strategy, along with Little Turtle of the Miami and Buckongoaelas of the Delaware. Nothing escaped Tecumseh's attention or scrutiny.

Fort Hamilton was built amid the grumbling of the militiamen. "We came out here to fight Indians, not build forts for the government," said one discontented frontiersmen on a logging detail. "If I had known we was going to be the niggers I woulda stayed home and fought the savages by myself." He lifted his end of a heavy log unto the wagon.

"We're getting paid," said the sergeant in charge, "to serve."

"Well," said another man as he strained under the load, "we're really serving."

"Don't let it get you down," said someone else, "you can always look forward to a night with the gals. Maybe you'll get lucky and wind up with Red!"

"You don't need luck, just a doubloon!"

"Fat chance of me getting a doubloon. Next thing you'll be saying is that Butler and St. Clair are best of buddies."

"Worst, not best. Come on, let's take these logs back."

Fort Hamilton was built and garrisoned. The army continued northward onOctober 12, cutting its way through the dense forest until St. Clair came to a likely spot for another fort and ordered the men to build the structure, calling it Fort Jefferson. Many men refused to work and there was talk of deserting.

St. Clair got his staff together and addressed his officers in council: "You are to inform the men that deserters shall be considered traitors in the face of battle. My orders from the President are to erect these forts and insubordination will not be tolerated at any level." A heavy silence hung in the air as St. Clair paused momentarily. He knew his general staff was racked with dissension. "Any individual or individuals deserting will be brought back and whipped. You are to keep your men in line until their enlistments are up. That is all."

Two days later, with the fort no where close to completion, three hundred militiamen deserted in a body. When St. Clair learned about it he called Major Hamtramck in and told him: "I want you to take the First Regiment and bring them back! We shall make an example of them. I have also been informed the deserters intend to comandeer the supplies which are being sent for the army. You are to make haste and see to it this does not happen! Get your men and leave immediately."

"Yes sir," replied Hamtramck. He saluted and exited the tent.

St. Clair now entertained grave doubts about the militia. He had no tally of how many had deserted before this but he knew it was a large number. He was puzzled for he had believed the militia were frontiersmen, the backbone of America. As he thought about the situation he knew his health was deteriorating, no matter how determined he was to lead the army to victory. The gout was worsening but he would not give the army to Butler, no matter how ill he became, short of being bed-ridden. He walked out of his tent and supervised the building of the fort.

Tecumseh led miniscule hit and run attacks along the flanks of the huge army but these snipings weren't even worthy of being referred to as skirmishes. He reported to Blue Jacket that, in his opinion, the invaders were over-confident and ripe for a well executed ambush.

St. Clair pushed himself and his men hard. Within a week Fort Jefferson was built up enough to secure men and supplies so he gave the army the order to march northward after leaving a garrison and construction details to continue building. Despite previous difficulties, St. Clair was confident all would be well. On November 2, 1791, the army came to a small branch of the Wabash River, and there completed camp. The following day the creek was the heart of the commanding piece of ground and the troops were situated in two lines behind the creek. The first line, commanded by General Butler and his batallion commanders Clarke, Patterson, & Butler were about seventy yards ahead of the second line battalions of Bedinger and Gaither, plus the Second Regiment of Col. Darke. The right flank was secured by the creek, a steep embankment, and Faulkner's corps. Most of the calvary and their pickets covered the left flank. The militia and most of the women were allowed to cross the creek and make camp, in the same fashion, about a quarter of a mile from the Regulars.

A light snow began to fall and in the Indian headquarters. Little Turtle knew it was what he had been waiting for. Now there would be no shadows for the Shemanese to hide in. The invaders were in a steel trap which would soon turn the snow red in their own blood. He gave the order to get the warriors into position and to take no prisoners.

That evening St. Clair got together with Major Ferguson and decided where the breastworks should be thrown up. "As soon as the First Regiment comes back we will seek and destroy the enemy," finished St. Clair. "You may begin the works first thing tomorrow."

"Yes sir," replied Major Ferguson. "I hope you will be feeling better, sir."

"Thank you, Major, I will be fine. Good night." St. Clair was reallly ill now. He went to his blankets, wrapped himself up in them, and tried to sleep.

Ferguson walked in the direction of a large bonfire, ready to snap at whoever had started such a conflagration in the heart of Indian country. But then he saw General Butler in the crowd around the fire and passed by without saying anything.

"If he doesn't send out some scouts tomorrow I will have to talk to him," said Butler. "We've got to discover where the Indians are hiding."

"I wonder if they haven't already found us," said one of his men.

"We'll be the first to know when they do, gentlemen, I assure you," said General Butler. "Let's get some sleep."

The men disbanded and went to their tents. Sentries were posted throughout the camp, including that of the militia, though they were more relaxed as they shuffled from one little campfire to the next. As the night wore on the only noise was an occasional laugh or giggle piercing the night air.

Albert and Rutherford walked through the militia camp in search of Red but she was not to be found. "Better go look in the officers' tents," said one woman when she heard the men calling the woman. "There're the ones with hot money on a cold November night."

"I've got to disagree," answered Rutherford.

"Well honey, let's see whatcha got," said the woman.

"Come on, let's go," said Albert.

"You go on ahead," said Rutherford, "I'll see you later."

Albert decided to walk around in hopes of seeing Red so he left his buddy and walked from fire to fire but he did not see the woman. He crossed the creek and looked through the entire camp of the Regulars with the same results. Damn her! She was probably holed up for the night already. He waited a while longer then finally decided to give it up, guessing it was around midnight. Then he noticed some men at General Butler's tent, calling for him to wake up. He walked in their direction.

"What is it?" asked Butler from within.

"It's me, Captain Slough," said the excited officer.

"Hang on just a minute, Jacob," said the General. He had sent Slough out to protect the horses from Indians who might try to steal some then forgot about him. "Yes, Captain, what's up?" said Butler as he came out of the tent putting on his jacket. "Oh, hello, William," he said to Colonel Oldham of the militia who stood next to Slough.

"Indians sir, lots of 'em," blurted Slough.

"Where abouts?" asked Butler.

"We never made it to the horses. I saw a large group about a mile from here so we hid in the woods to let them pass. When I thought it was safe to make more headway I started to move when we saw another band of more than a hundred savages going east of the other group. I thought we'd be attacked so I waited a goodly while. Sure enough, another large warparty passed us by. We lit out for camp when the coast was clear. Iffen we'd been discovered our scalps would be hanging from a savage's belt right now. Those woods are crawling with Indians!"

"Looks like we'll be attacked in the morning," said Colonel Oldham.

"Could you see what tribes they were?" asked Butler.

"Beats hell outta me," replied Slough. "All I know is there's a powerful lot of them."

"I'm glad you managed to elude them, Captain."

"Me too," said Slough, "now I'll go over and inform St. Clair. We've got to get ready."

General Butler stood silent a few moments, looking at the ground all the while. Then he said, "I commend you for your courage and vigilance. You must be quite tired so go on ahead and get some rest. Leave everything to me."

"Thank you, sir, I could use it," finished Slough as he walked away toward the militia billets and was quickly swallowed up in the night.

Albert had heard everything. An attack was probable in the morning! He had to find Red and warn her! But where was she?! He ran back to the militia encampment but the woman was still not in her tent. He wandered around in great desperation, quite a contrast from the rest of the encampment. "We're going to be attacked tomorrow!" he said to a couple of men who were boiling some coffee over a small fire.

"That a fact?" asked a bearded militiaman.

"We just got word of it," said Albert. "Have you seen Red?"

The two laughed out loud. "She doing the attacking?"

"She can come get it any time," said the other.

"It's true!" said Albert desperately, realizing he had destroyed the force of his assertion.

"Well then go tell St. Clair," said one of the men.

"I'm sure he's already been told," replied Albert.

"Then he'll sound the call," finished the man as he sipped on his hot coffee. "Better find your Red and make her stop."

"Not that nympho," said the other.

Albert walked away in disgust. He walked through the whole encampment one more time then gave up his search. He went to his tent and prepared his gear as best he could by the light of the small fire outside. When he was ready, he lay down, wrapped himself in his blankets but could not sleep. He had never fought Indians before. The army was large enough to take care of itself. He was ready. But he couldn't sleep. Maybe it wasn't so. Maybe the savages wouldn't attack tomorrow. There had been no awakening of the camp, no drums sounding the alarm. The night was calm and peaceful. Too quiet? His mind was working overtime so he unwrapped himself and went outside. As he threw a couple more pieces of wood on the fire he looked up and saw Red walking toward her tent.

Was it really her?! He got up and ran after the phantom but it really was the woman. "Red!" said Albert in a loud whisper.

The woman turned to see a man running toward her. Quickly she bent over and pulled a knife from her boot.

"It's me, Albert!"

Red waited for the man. "What do you want?" she said in an unfriendly tone.

"Nothing," said Albert quickly, "except to tell you we're going to be attacked tomorrow."

"We've heard rumors since we left Fort Washington," she said as she continued to walk. "Why are you so sure?"

Albert related what had transpired earlier. "I want to protect you," he finished. "Your tent is at the edge of the woods."

Red was a good judge of men, or at least she thought she was. Albert really believed what he said, it wasn't just a ruse. "Well, what do you want me to do, move in with you?"

"Well... yes."

Red stopped walking and looked at the man. "All right, just until morning. First let's go get a couple of things." They walked to her tent, she brought out a few items, notably a saddle bag where she kept her money. "I feel silly, sort of."

"No reason to," said Albert as they walked. He was calm now not the least bit nervous or excited.

"So you're going to protect me from the Indians, but who's going to protect me from you?" Albert offered no remark as he peered into the dark woods. Suddenly Red was a bit frightened. "Do you really think they're out there? It's so quiet."

"Don't worry. It's still a few hours to sunup. We'll be all right." They walked to Albert's tent, Rutherford was not there. Something was amiss, Albert could feel it, but the alarm had not been sounded so he kept his forebodings to himself.

"Why did you come to warn me?" asked Red as she sat down on the blanket. "Did you want something?"

"Because... I care about you," replied Albert. Even as he was filled with agitation and notwithstanding the dim light that entered through the tent opening he was struck by the woman's beauty. What a waste of a life! She would have been such a beautiful wife for... someone.

"And if I died tomorrow?" asked Red playfully.

"Don't talk like that," snapped Albert. "You're not in Boston or New York or wherever the hell you're from. Everybody's out on a lark, including you."

"I don't understand why you're angry with me," said Red like a little girl. "I just want to be happy."

"Then why are you... a whore?" There, he had said it.

Red became disturbingly serious but she did not leave the tent. "We must be what we are, you, me, everybody. What are you doing here, trying to steal Indian land? Are you a thief?"

"I don't think so."

"Well I do. This whole army is a whore and you and I are no better," said Red, visibly angry. "I don't matter any more than anyone else."

"I didn't mean to hurt your feelings. I care about you, is all. I don't know why but I knew it the first time I laid eyes on you. I didn't have any of your precious Spanish money then and I still don't. Just as well."

Red became calm now and slightly amused. "What do you mean?"

"Never mind. Go on, get some sleep." He lay down on Rutherford's side of the tent.

"No, I'm serious. What do you mean? Answer me."

Albert lay quiet for a time, then "I wouldn't want to buy it. I would have you for a wife." He was amazed he could speak so frankly. He had signed on with the expedition as a young man looking for adventure but instead he had experienced love.

Now it was Red's turn to remain silent. Men had always loved her but she would not allow herself to love in return. So passion had become a business and love had always cooled. What should she tell this fine young man? "How well do you know yourself?"

"Go to sleep."

"I can sleep tomorrow. Come here."

"Sleep. I have no gold," said Albert, regreting the remark the moment it left his lips. There was silence in the tent until Red's bag of coins landed on Albert.

"There's all the gold you want," said Red, "help yourself." Still Albert did not react so the woman got on her hands and knees and laid beside him, her arms grasping him gently.

"I want you, not gold, not land, just you," Albert finally said as he put his arms around her after covering both with a blanket. He kissed her gently on the cheek, the bridge of the nose, the forehead, then full on the lips. "Now let's rest," he said. Physical passion had become meaningless as they tried to sleep but all they could accomplish was listening for ominous sounds in the night.

Episode 7: The Battle

The following morning the Regulars were dismissed from parade half an hour before sunrise. As the sun began to streak the heavens and the men thought of getting some breakfast a terrific yell came out of the forest as the militia camp began to stir. Musket shots rang out in volleys as the frontiersmen came out of their tents. Most who showed themselves were immediately shot down and their death agonies struck terror in most who heard them. The Indians charged into the camp and began a bloody hand-to-hand battle that destroyed what little resistance there was. The militiamen fled pell-mell toward the Regulars' camp, the Indians right on their heels. Tecumseh was one of the first three Indians to rush into the Shemanese camp, striking with tomahawk in one hand, warclub in the other. He saw myriads of women running helter-skelter so he avoided them, controlling his fury in order to focus on the men, on whom he showed no mercy. A Shemanese lunged at him feebly but the assailant was despatched by another Indian from the side.

Within a few moments the entire militia was in panic-stricken flight toward the main encampment. The Regulars had formed their lines immediately on hearing volleys of musket fire but they had to let their confused, terror-ridden comrades in, thus opening for the Indians also. Tecumseh was now in the lead of the warriors. Three soldiers struck at him with whatever they had in hand, everyone going down in the melee, but other Indians were quickly on top of the invaders, crushing their skulls that sounded like melons striking the ground. Tecumseh felt no wounds so he got to his feet and continued his charge into the Shemanese encampment.

"Fire that artillery!" ordered General Butler.

Tecumseh heard the man and searched quickly to find the big guns. They could easily turn the tide of battle. A big roar came over from one side as the cannon belched death into the woods so Tecumseh yelled, "Stop the big guns!" in a voice that carried above the din as he darted toward them amid the acrid smoke, screams, groans, shrieks of horses, warcries, musketfire. He came to one cannon just as a soldier was bending forward to light the fuse but Tecumseh buried his tomahawk into the man's arm. The scream was cut short by his warclub to the man's head. This was one cannon that would not fire again today! Instantaneously he got the idea to turn the big gun around and fire it into the ranks of Shemanese but he was knocked off his feet by an undistinguishable blow from he knew not what direction. Groggy, he blinked several times until his vision cleared then saw Spybuck bending over him.

"You all right?" asked the juggler-medicine man.

"I'm okay. You should not be on the front lines. Get back for the sake of the wounded."

"My power is strong this day," replied Spybuck as he tried to discern what was the nature of Tecumseh's wound. He could find nothing obvious.

"I am all right. WE MUST HOLD THE BIG GUNS!" he yelled. He threw himself at the soldiers who also rallied to the cannon, cutting, slicing, hacking his way clear of the hated encroachers.

"Stand and fight you cowards!" yelled General Butler at the fleeing militiamen who raced by him. Some of the Regulars held their positions in the terrifying confusion, their officers courageously holding them under control. St. Clair was in the thick of the battle, though extremely ill, giving orders to close the formations as soon as the frontiersmen raced in. He got on his horse, an easy target for any marksman.

Micheal Brant saw the Governor from the Indian lines. "Shoot his horse!" he yelled at his contingent of Mohawks. "Don't kill him!" The warriors of his tribe understood but others did not. The horse was quickly shot from under him and a rifle ball knocked off his hat.

A withering fire kept the artillery quiet. Artillerists displayed great courage in efforts to use the great guns but they were mowed down by the scores for their efforts. When there was no volley and the Shemanese renewed their efforts the warriors threw themselves upon the soldiers and died or hacked their enemies to pieces, completing the work of death on the cannons themselves. Never had the soldiers seen such fury and daring! They began to give ground slowly as the warriors threw themselves at the battalions in great numbers.

St. Clair gave up on the artillery when he saw the slaughter around the cannon. Everywhere there were screaming savages firing from the woods, springing from tree to tree with incrediable speed, refusing to give the riflemen a target. A second animal was shot out from under the Governor.

"Get me another horse!" yelled St. Clair.

"General, stay on the ground!"

"Get me a horse, THAT'S AN ORDER!" He knew the men were almost beyond control at this point, he had to let them see him. "Where's Butler?" he asked of his aide.

"I don't know sir!"

St. Clair mounted up and rode away from the artillery. The riflefire was doing no good whatsoever. "FIX BAYONETTS!" he ordered. "Use the big knife! Colonel Darke, charge them from your side!" Once more the Governor's horse fell dead under him as Darke led his men in an impetuous charge at the head of the left wing, driving the savages back about four hundred yards. But then he was in danger of being cut off from the rest of the force so he stopped and received a withering volley that decimated his men.

Col. Oldham was standing beside a great tree and St. Clair ordered him to follow Darke. Oldham must have been in a state of shock for his eyes were wide and hollow-looking as he shook his head in refusal. "That's suicide! Damn it, I won't do it!" he concluded as a bullet tore away the back portion of his skull.

"Come on, men," yelled St. Clair to Oldham's soldiers, "fix bayonets and follow me!" He hobbled to the attack as soldiers dropped like flies around him. Miraculously, the Governor received not a scratch.

"Retreat!" ordered Drake and the men obeyed instantly. It was in effect an attack to the rear for clouds of warriors hung around the entire Shemanese camp.

St. Clair ordered other bayonet charges, which were attended with temporary success but also with severe loss, especially of officers. Not once were the soldiers able to keep the ground that had been so costly to take. Finally it was apparent most of the officers had fallen and the troops, Regulars and militiamen, began to huddle in despair, some even weeping. They were shot down with no resistance.

"Open a road to the rear," the Governor ordered Col. Darke, "and sound the retreat," he said to the drummer. The road was opened after frenzied fighting. The moment the men heard the call to retreat they literally threw away their weapons and ran as fast as their panic spurred them, often stumbling over their own comrades or knocking slower ones aside.

Spybuck was riding a horse to a side of the disorderly retreat when suddenly another horse and rider appeared from out of the smoke and collided roughly with his own, both animals and riders sprawling to the ground after hitting a tree. Spybuck was slightly dazed as he swung a tomahawk at the other rider but he missed and the individual swung some kind of a bag at him, striking him in the chest. It was a female, a flaming red-headed female!

Red quickly drew her knife from her boot and swung at the savage desperatley but he side-stepped, caught her arm, wrenched the knife loose, picked her up and smashed her to the ground. But Red bounced right back up and threw herself at the Indian, biting, scratching, trying to kick his groin.

Another Indian came up behind the two. He grabbed Red from the hair and yanked her to the ground. He was going to swing his tomahawk but Spybuck caught his upward swing and yelled, "DON'T. This is my prisoner."

"Fine," said the other warrior, who went on quickly to combat the invaders who now retreated in such ignominious haste.

Another warrior rushed after a Shemanese officer with flowing white hair. The warrior caught up with the officer, grabbed him by the hair and set to tomahawk the skull when the hair, all of it, was yanked off. The dumbfounded warrior stopped in his tracks to examine the unexpected prize: a white wig. The fleeing officer thus escaped. The warrior scrutinized the magical hair bonnet, put it on his own head, and got back into the fight.

Spybuck and Red just looked at each other. She thought she was dead for sure but why didn't the savage end it all immediately? She looked at her bag full of money, real money, and now it was so meaningless. But was it?! An idea flashed through her mind. She took her bag slowly, deliberately. The savage said something in a menacing tone but she got the bag and put it close to him. Then she jingled it a couple of times.

"Take it," said Red, "take it. This is yours. A fortune, take it!" She leaned back against a tree as she sat. It was useless, he didn't understand she wanted to trade her life for the doubloons. But then why should he? He was in control of both. The army had been destroyed. What a host of cowards! The vaunted American frontiersmen had even run over the women in their panic! "All right, go ahead, kill me! Come on, get it over with!

Spybuck looked at the woman as he grabbed her by the hair. What an unusual color. He took out his knife. The female was unafraid. Was she worth more as a scalp or as a woman? He ran his other hand over her face. She was weeping but still she would not be conquered by death. She would be his prisoner. Perhaps she could be trained to be of worth. Not much chance of it, being a Shemanese, but perhaps. He stood her up, tied a strip of rawhide to her wrist and looked for a place to rest in order to avoid being killed by a chance shot.

Red did not know what was on the savage's mind but her first effort was to retrieve her bag. She yanked on the rawhide until the savage let her have her way. He caught the bridle of a horse and put the female between him and the animal. He did not want a warrior to catch sight of that red hair and shoot his prisoner in a moment of passion.

The warriors pursued the fleeing army for about four miles. The road was strewn with rifles, axes, powder horns, lead, and other accoutrements of war. The frontiersmen had had their fill of fighting Indians. The warriors ceased their chase when they were sure the invaders were not regrouping for another assault. Besides, the entire camp had been left with rich booty, including hundreds of horses, and each warrior wanted a share.

Tecumseh was among the last to give up the chase but when he returned to the battlefield he was affected by the carnage. There must have been more than five hundred bodies in what had been the Shemanese encampment! For a moment he thought he was going to vomit. Warriors walked throughout the camp and woods, tomahawking all the wounded to put them out of their misery. "You came to steal our land," said one Indian exultantly, "so this is the land you have won!" and he filled the dead Shemanese's mouth with dirt. Tecumseh saw Spybuck and the woman he had taken captive, a red-haired paleskin. Up to now he had seen no other captives.

"Tecumseh, come here a moment," called Spybuck. The young warrior walked over to the medicine man as a crowd was gathering around him and the woman. "I must tend to some of the wounded," said Spybuck. "Watch my prisoner for me," and he was gone quickly.

Tecumseh nodded his assent.

"Death to the Shemanese!" growled one warrior menacingly as he grabbed his tomahawk.

"This is not your captive nor mine," said Tecumseh calmly. He thought of putting her up on the horse which she held but decided against it because she could be picked off with a rifle shot.

"We vowed to fight to the death!"

"The fight is over," said Tecumseh. "I fought to the death also, but now we have won. This captive is charged to my safekeeping. We have had enough death and destruction. Besides, this woman belongs to the juggler, Spybuck."

With that the warriors dispersed immediately. Jugglers could talk to the devil! There was plenty of other booty around.

Red knew her life had been a straw in the wind for a moment, though she could not understand the savages. But she said, "Thank you," anyway.

"You are welcome," replied Tecumseh.

"You speak English?!" blurted Red. She looked at the savage, younger than her captor, about Albert's age. Poor Albert! He was among the few who tried to stand and fight when the militia fled with their tails tucked in terror. "Help me to my people and I will reward you," Red said earnestly.

"You do not belong to me," answered Tecumseh.

Red's only ray of hope vanished with the Indian's answer. She would have to wait and see what would be her fate. At least she was alive! And she held the bag of doubloons firmly in hand.

The next few days were spent dividing the booty. A big council was held on the third night with Little Turtle, Blue Jacket, and Buckongahelas as guests of honor. Warriors sang, recounted their exploits, rejoiced in the defense of their homeland. Finally Little Turtle rose to speak. Tecumseh would have preferred Blue Jacket but after all, Little Turtle had been the principal chief against the invaders both this year and last:

"My fellow warriors, we can now return to our homes, secure that our women and children are protected in their lives as bequeathed to them by the Great Spirit. Our people everywhere throughout this great island owe you a debt as great as the dawning sun, a cornfield in tassel, a purple sunset, the silvered moon. When you return to your brothers and sisters spread the news of our great victory over the rapacious Shemanese who would take our lands. Let our people know so long as we unite as patriots we shall not feel the heel of the oppressor on our throats. Hold fast to the chain of friendship among our people and brighten your hatchets with vigilance. Your brothers the Miamis could not have withstood the onslaught of the oppressor without you our brothers of the Delaware, Shawnee, Mohawk..." A cheer went up with the mention of each tribe who had heeded the call to arms. "We were a thousand strong and we defeated an army much larger than our own. Let us always remember and sing of this exploit of a free, indomitable people! We have endured enough. The boundary between us and the Shemanese must forever be the Ohio River! The snow clad warrior will soon ride forcefully out of his kingdom in the north country. Let us return to our loved ones but always continue our vigilance for such is the eternal price of liberty. Farewell, warriors of freedom!"

Episode 8: Red and Spybuck

Red expected to be assaulted or gang raped after the savages finished with their council fire but no such thing happened. She was forced to share the same tent with her captor but the man slept without the slightest awareness of her. Red was frightened but she refused to show such emotion to the savages. When she finally slept it was the only emotional freedom she experienced.

The following day she was put on a horse and lead away by a large group of savages evidently returning to their village. She could not find the young warrior who spoke English but she did not think her life was in immediate danger. *They probably want me for a slave,* she thought to herself. Maybe, if she survived, she would be repatriated when the army thrashed the Indians next time. Or killed during the attack. She didn't like that thought. She looked at her captor but all she could see was the blanket he wore for it was cold. At least he had given her a blanket with which to stay warm. Perhaps she should consider herself lucky. So many women were shot down. And the cowardly men stomped right over them trying to escape the Indians they had vowed to kill! And they were supposed to be fighters! What hypocrites!

Groups of Indians separated at various points during the homeward journey and in time Red found herself in sole company of her captor as he approached two cabins secreted in the woods. The man dismounted easily, stretched his arms and legs, then bent over and touched the ground several times with his palms. He walked over to Red, pulled her off her horse and said something in Shawnee.

"I don't talk Indian," said Red.

Spybuck knew a few words in English and French but for all practical purposes he spoke only Shawnee. So he pointed to the pack horse, walked over to it and motioned for the woman to unpack it. Red got the message, tried to undo the rawhide that held everything together but couldn't so she pulled on the bundle in an effort to bring everything down. She succeeded and things started to fall on the ground.

Spybuck shook his head in disgust. Red looked at him, really looked at him for the first time. His skin was swarthy but he really was an attractive sort. Even handsome, perhaps, in a wild sort of way, with that thick, long, black hair. He was powerfully muscled, perhaps a bit on the heavy side, but not to distraction. Spybuck ignored the woman as he undid the rawhide straps. As soon as he did everything sprawled to the ground, including the woman's bag of coins. Red sprang to pick them up quickly. Spybuck whistled toward the cabin and in a while a wrinkled elderly woman came out, greeted the man with "Keewaukoomeela" and began to pick up everything to take inside. Red wondered how long ago this other woman had been taken captive and earnestly hoped it hadn't been recently if that's what she would soon look like.

"Spybuck does not learn," giggled the old crone.

"I hope the kettle is high," was Spybuck's only comment as he walked into the wegiwa.

Red gathered everything she could and took all inside. She looked around at the cabin and was intrigued. What a strange place, almost sinister. She forgot who she was as she wandered around. She was not afraid, so engulfed was she by the cabin's contents. Spybuck walked up to her, gave her a bowl and made motions for her to help herself to the food in the kettle. She did, and both ate without particular attention to the other. After eating Spybuck lay down to rest on his robes. It was good to sleep on something besides the ground for a change. He was not suited for the warpath. Henceforth he would disregard the titters and

101

remarks of Standing Woman, whoever she was. That was another thing, there were no women on the warpath, excepting the skinny, pale variety, in whom he had no interest. Maybe he should have taken the scalp of this one and done with it... but she had good spirit... and he could not resist wiping the tears from her eyes... enough carnage...

Red knew when the man was asleep. Perhaps she could find an axe and smash his head open? No, there was no place to go. And somebody would scalp her on the way. So she put a bit more wood on the small fire as the afternoon ended. She had never been able to stand the cold. There were pouches that she opened undisturbed, the man remaining asleep and the old woman not in the cabin. There must have been dozens of different herbs in pouches and baskets. Red smelled all of them, tasted some. One in particular she liked so she placed it in a handy place and took a pinch every so often. She put more wood on the fire as evening set in, not feeling the least bit tired. She opened a basket and found a skull staring back at her. She controlled her initial fright as she covered it, peering in the direction of the sleeping man. The firelight danced on the walls and off objects which hung from rafters. It struck her that as yet she had found no liquor. Then she spied a tomahawk under a skin of something. She grasped it, walked over to the sleeping man, raised the weapon high, and considered everything equal now that she had spared his life as he had done with her. She returned the tomahawk to its place, took another pinch of the delicious powder. Suddenly she felt tired. How could it be when she had been so energetic moments before? No matter. She saw some blankets and glided over to them, fluttering down smoothly, becoming one with her covering. She slept, or thought she did, for it was as if she was looking at herself, watching yet beckoning. Moments later, or so it seemed, she awoke, picked herself up and raised her hands as if to reach the heavens! She felt restrained by her clothing so she took off every stitch she was wearing. Somewhere far in the distance she heard the strains of a flute as she started to bend her body this way and that, reaching with her arms, thrusting with her hips, lifting a knee to her face, jutting out with her foot. All was done smoothly, deliberately, passionately but with delicacy.

Spybuck awoke as the woman danced with sensual abandon. At first he thought it was a vision, a visitation from the spirit world. But as he became fully awake the red hair informed him it was reality. He was now totally refreshed by his sleep as he watched the woman dance, sitting up to do so. Perhaps she had lost her mind but then her body captured all his attention: her calves were rounded, as were her thighs which quivered ecstatically. Her pompis was extremely well formed, the flesh rounding voluptuously then contracting to thrust her hips forward. Her waist seemed quite small, accenting her upper body and especially her breasts, which were large yet firm on her chest with not the slightest hint of sag. Her shoulders where broad and could have been described as muscled, they were formed so well, which Spybuck assumed was necessary to carry those marvelous breasts the way she did. The woman's red hair looked wild at times and the intensity of the dance made her pale skin glisten in the small fire that remained. Spybuck quickly put another stick on to throw more light on the vision that greeted him this night.

The woman danced toward Spybuck with long, slow movements. She put a foot to his chest, pressing him gently to the floor. The female's eyes shined brightly but appeared devoid of earthliness. Yes, that was it, they reminded him of celestial radiance, a star making a hole in the night.

Red was aware only of an immense physical levitation, an unchained sensation that made her believe she could fly. She stepped on the man's chest with all of her weight then sprang off it suddenly, causing Spybuck an intense pain in his rib cage. But his attention had been on her pubic hair, not the pain. Never had he seen such a covering of hair, and so red! So thick it was it reminded him of the buffalo. Perhaps this woman was not like the other Shemanese, so cold and cruel with life. He felt his breechclout restraining his bod. Perhaps he would dance with the woman. Would that break the spell she was under? He'd risk it, but first he stood up, walked over to the washing jar and washed himself with a cloth. When he was done he shed all his clothing and approached the woman.

Red saw the man standing there, his manhood asking to be engulfed, but first she grabbed his black hair from the temples and in an amazing feat jumped high enough to encircle his neck with her legs. She let go her hands, letting arms hang at her sides. Spybuck was now interested in this unpredictable female. He turned his head and nipped at whatever flesh he could reach, then he started turning round and round, his eyes riveted on the woman's breasts then on her sensual face. He was becoming dizzy as he continued to turn but he did not want the female to fall so he slowed down and tried to hold her with his arms. He nearly fell from the dizzyness or was it the excitement of the woman's bod on his chest? He wanted to thrust into her but first he would have to undo her legs from around his neck and shoulders. He stopped turning completely, lowered her gently to the floor whereupon she quickly let go with her legs and got on her feet. Had she come out of the spell? Spybuck thought she might be teasing him but when he stood up she weaved up to him, threw her right leg around his pompis, grabbed his bod with her left hand and put it to her own. The penetration was slight, just enough to make Spybuck's cravings peak a little higher. This was maddening for there had been no women on the warpath. He became more aggressive in his strength, grasping her into him, feeling his bod engulfed by moist warmth. "Eeeeh!" gasped the woman, not in ecstasy but in pain. Notwithstanding the deliciousness Spybuck released her, realizing he had used muscle, not persuasion, to penetrate her. What was happening to him? He was acting like an adolescent out of control. So what, she was only a Shemanese... but first she was a woman, and he was a man. He would make her peak and force would not be necessary.

Spybuck bent over a little and took a bosom in his mouth, exciting the nipple in every fashion he could until it went soft. *Strange,* he thought. He took the other breast, which was firm almost to the point of hardness, the nipple hardest of all, and after a while it softened like the other, which he caressed with his hand to find it tense as a working muscle. So he calmed it down with his mouth, the only way, evidently, it could be done. Red took his bod with her hand, gently pulled it to herself, Spybuck therefore being unable to work on those magnificent breasts. The woman rubbed herself with him then used her index finger to swell the head until Spybuck was ready to force her up and put her down on the sleeping robes. He grasped her strongly with his arms, she uttered that painful sound again but as Spybuck began to penetrate warmth the demon shot forth its joy juice, making him tremble in ecstasy and disappointment. Indeed, he had been without a woman too long! Or was it that this woman handled him as if he was an adolescent? The momentary ecstasy past. He felt nothing but disgust. He looked at the woman full in the face. She was still under the spell. Anyway that's what he thought. She'd better be. For this to happen to him who thought he knew women so well. What a disgrace. Perhaps she would not remember anything. There he was, already under her control. And a Shemanese to boot! Rather sheepishly he picked her up, put her down on his sleeping robes, lay down beside her, covered them both, and tried to get some sleep. His passion was far from spent. He would teach her what passion really was! And a miserable captive had made him feel like this?! But secretly, very secretly, he was intrigued by this robust, pale, red-headed female.

Episode 9: McClellan attacks Tecumseh

The defeat of St. Clair resounded throughout the territories east of the

Father of Waters. The Shemanese were terrified that attacks would be made on their settlements and many fled the border areas for safer locales. The Indians were fired with a tremendous zeal to defend their culture against the invaders. The confederacy preached by Joseph Brant of the Mohawk was now a reality and petty disagreements were forgotten. All the tribes of the Northwest had participated in St. Clair's defeat, including the Delaware and Wyandot who long ago had turned their backs on the Confederacy.

Tecumseh's group of ten men and a boy camped on Loramie Creek was just one of the many commando groups operating in the Ohio country this December. The trees stood covered with snow just before dawn and the cold brought all the men to the small fire Tecumseh had begun. The men huddled over the warmth, smoking and talking about the great victory.

"There were rifles and powder horns all the way to their fort," said one warrior as he smoked, "thrown away. We should have followed them and destroyed them all. They ran like deer in their terror..."

Robert McClellan was camped a short distance away from the Indian party, leading thirty-five men on his own commando raid. McClellan had been a scout for St. Clair and the defeat at the hands of savages rankled deeply. He wanted to atone for his people's loss and there were few who were better at fighting Indians in their own way.

"They don't know we're here, boys," McClellan was saying to his men, "and there's not more than a dozen of 'em, so we shouldn't have much problem." McClellan was relishing the approaching engagement as he fired up his men. He was short of stature but long on personal courage that countenanced no fear. His rippling muscles made him the equal of most men and his agility had often been the talk of the frontier. "Let's go so we can be in position as the sun comes up. Careful how you walk in the snow. These savages can hear a leaf in the wind. Walk quick."

McClellan got his men into position without being discovered. The trees were in the way so a volley would not destroy the savages as he had hoped. He motioned for some of his men to go around one side, another group opposite, he and the remainder in the middle. Then they closed in for the kill.

Tecumseh was enjoying the life-giving warmth of the fire along with everyone else when a shot rang out. "Get your RIFLES, we are attacked," he said. Everyone quickly sprang for their weapons. "Groups of two," ordered Tecumseh, "get behind cover and alternate your shots."

Bullets were whizzing through the forest but no one seemed to be hit. "They come from the south!" yelled Tecumseh, his voice carrying easily. "Feather Down," he said to the boy, "run north in to the forest. Go!" The boy lit out immediately but much to Tecumseh's dismay Black Turkey was also fleeing to safety. "GET YOURSELF BACK OR I'LL COME GET YOU MYSELF!" yelled Tecumseh angrily. "HELP DEFEND YOUR BROTHERS!" The man stopped running. "NOW!" Black Turkey retraced his steps, zig-zagging to avoid being picked off. When he got into position he picked up his musket and started firing.

McClellan and his men moved in closer, or tried to, as the savages returned their fire. The surprise attack had not been successful but the sheer force of numbers must inevitably conquer. A man right next to McClellan was hit and fell backward into the snow. "Close in on 'em form all sides!" yelled the leader but the Indians kept them at bay with deadly stings that hit the mark or came disturbingly close. McClellan, experienced Indian fighter notwithstanding, was stunned that the savages who a few minutes before were huddled around a fire, calmly smoking, could not be taken by surprise and destroyed in one swoop! "Charge in!" he yelled, taking the lead himself in a display of reckless courage for which he was well known. His musket was shot out of his hands and as he scurried for cover he saw another of his men suffer a mortal wound. That was two dead. How many wounded? Was a mere skirmish worth so many lives?

"REGROUP!" yelled McClellan. A retreat ensued during which Black Turkey gave hot pursuit, wounding two more Shemanese as they fled.

Tecumseh hollered "CHASE!" and all the warriors pursued as the Shemanese fled across the snow. After following in a hard run Tecumseh stopped, put his musket up to aim at a slow Shemanese but the trigger broke, allowing the man to scurry to safety. "ENOUGH!" yelled Tecumseh, concerned that a trap might develop if the chase continued. "Let us return to camp. I will scout to make certain they do not double back to surprise us." He struck off by himself. The tracks in the snow showed the Shemanese kept going away form the hornets' nest they had stirred up. Tecumseh now walked at a perpendicular angle to the tracks in order to see if the Shemanese would try to circle back but there were no prints anywhere in the snow. He felt reasonably sure the fighting was over for this day so he returned to camp.

Tecumseh's men greeted him with handshakes when he returned. They dearly admired his cool courage in the face of the sudden attack, enough there even for his fellow warriors.

"No one killed," reported Big Fish, the Sinnamantha, "and only two wounded, neither seriously."

Black Turkey had received a flesh wound on the side.

"My brother," said Tecumseh to Black Turkey, "I must congratulate you for your ardor during the fight. Your musket sent out death when you fired it and you were the first to chase when the Shemanese fled like partridge across the snow."

"Thank you, my chief," replied Black Turkey. His initial flight was totally erased from everyone's memory by his subsequent bravery and aggressiveness. He knew it had been Tecumseh's courage and conduct that saved his reputation as a warrior, perhaps even his life and that of the others. If Tecumseh had run it could have been disaster. The leader's conduct had been responsible for the group's confidence.

"Let us eat and be on our way," said Tecumseh. As he munched on his ration of jerked meat his mind wandered back to his first battle. He had tasted panic as a lad. He was no stranger to Black Turkey's initial fright therefore censure never even entered his mind. The man had recovered and even distinguished himself in the face of superior numbers. All his men were now imbued with the spirit to win and defend their homeland against the encroachers.

Episode 10: Louisa visits President Washington

President George Washington re-read the sentence: "The astonishing success of a few Indians, not more than 1040, who have opposed and destroyed the whole American force, will probably cause a more numerous collection of Indians—" In despair he let the letter fall to his desk. The memory of Braddock's horrible defeat thrust itself into his mind. Now St. Clair! One thing was certain: the United States would have to handle the Indians or forever remain east of the Appalachian Mountains! The British were pressing for a neutral Indian barrier state north of the Ohio. Washington was constantly being encouraged to make the British stop supporting their savage allies but that was beyond the President's power, unless war was declared. And if the United States were being vanquished by Indians, what would happen if the British entered the struggle? He was sure of only one thing: the Indians would have to be defeated militarily or there would be no westward expansion for his tiny republic.

"What a horrible business!" said Washington aloud. He had not wanted an Indian war. His veterans of the Revolution had been so confident of victory! Harmar thrown back. St. Clair annihilated. The United States bankrupt. If the Northwestern lands could not be sold there was no salvation in sight. Treaties had not achieved ownership of the land.

Yet the land had been surveyed for sale. How ludicrous!

Perhaps the United States could do without the Northwest Territory? No, that was not possible. Too much money had been spent acquiring it. But a compromise would have to be worked out. If the Indians would allow the Americans to keep what had already been surveyed or sold... Washington decided there was no other course of action. The Indians could keep all their lands, the tracts not already sold to the Ohio Company or the Symmes Associates.

But what if the savages refused? The tribes were riding a crest of success. If they insisted on the Ohio River boundary, what then? Washington knew there was no other recourse but another war. While he had proven he was no military genius during the Revolution he was enough of a realist to know that brute force was the cornerstone of civilization. He had to ready another expedition, larger and better prepared than all the others. This would be it. Another defeat would render the United States absolutely impotent, easy prey for any country who wanted to attack it. The British might easily return and subjugate the States. And whom would he choose to led the troops? There was Henry Lee. Perhaps Rufus Putnam. Anthony Wayne. Wilkinson. Any number of candidates. But the selection had to be perfect this time. The life of the tiny republic lay in the balance.

"Mr. President," interrupted Washington's secretary, "there is a young lady who insists on seeing you for a moment."

"Oh?" said the President, coming out of his thoughts, "I didn't realize I had any appointments."

"You don't sir," he said, "but she demands to see you, claims you're old friends. Says her name is Louisa St. Clair."

Washington smiled. "Send her in."

Beauteous Louisa walked into the President's office, noting its quite humble decor. "General Washington, good day sir. I hope you will excuse this unexpected call. I hoped you wouldn't be too busy—"

"I'm never too busy," said Washington. "Your father and I are comrades in arms and in the near future I am afraid I will need the arms of your generation to help me along."

First in war, first in peace, first in the hearts of his countrymen! came into Louisa's mind. In all the world ther were kings, queens, and George Washington.

"What may I do for you, Louisa?" asked the President. The girl reminded him of Sally Fairfax, in a way.

"Sir, I am very concerned for my father," said Louisa. "He did not send me here, mind you, I came of my own accord. People are saying he should be court martialed, that he is incompetent, that he was responsible for the death of his army."

President Washington did not know if the girl was ready for tears or battle, such was her intensity. What spunk! With people like these he felt better about the fate of his tiny country and began to come out of the depression he had been feeling all day. "Come now, Governor St. Clair has my full confidence and nothing is going to change that."

"Is there going to be a court of inquiry?" asked Louisa.

"Of course not. Why, if there were courts for every military failure I should still be embroiled in them. You must not listen to idle chatter. Your father is a brave, intelligent man who has done great service for his country. One man seldom wins a battle, or loses it. Rest assured that he has my entire friendship and confidence at his disposal."

Louisa felt much better. She believed George Washington would not lie to her. "What of the Indians?"

Washington was puzzled by her question. "The Indians? From all I hear they are quite jubilant."

"Will they be punished? Their leaders?"

"If we must wage war it is unfortunate for everyone," replied Washington. "I hope the Indians don't take it into their heads to punish our leaders," he remarked ruefully.

"No, I don't mean it that way," said Louisa quickly. "The Indians are just defending their lands."

"The situation is quite complex," conceded Washington. "But rest assured your father is not the first general to lose a battle and be critized for it. When you see him express my sincerest regards."

"He doesn't know I'm here," confessed Louisa, "and please don't ever tell him. He would be embarassed."

"I shall let you in on a secret," said Washington. "I know how much property your family lost giving service to our country during the Revolution. I will try to have the Congress award him a penison when this all blows over. Please say nothing to him at this juncture since it is not definite. But I will do my best to effect such deserved reimbursement. Will you be returning to Marietta soon?"

"I hope so. It was my father's idea to send me here but if he doesn't call me soon I shall just up and return." Louisa stood up to leave. "Thank you for seeing me without an appointment, Mr. President. I needed to talk to you very badly."

"I'm glad you did," replied Washington as he rose and put an arm around the girl as both walked to the door, "and don't worry about anything. The Indian war is just a temporary reverse, God willing."

"Thank you, sir," said Louisa and impetuously she kissed him on the cheek. "Goodbye." She walked out of the office, paid no attention to the other people who were waiting around, went out into the street, her thoughts a cloud of torment. *Micheal, Micheal! How can I ever hope to see you after this?!* She walked slowly. What if her father had been among the dead? Was Micheal among the warriors? What if he was killed?! Or maybe some terrible wound? How could she possibly hope to marry someone who had helped destroy her father's army? It would kill her father. Her heart was breaking as she realized she could never see Micheal Brant again.

Episode 11: Nehaaeemo meets George Ironsides

Nehaaeemo, two years younger than her brother Tecumseh, walked into the trader's store in hope of buying some ribbon for her hair to use at the frolic dance this evening. Everyone was so elated with the warriors' victory a dance could have been called every night and the people would have attended. She looked up from the broadcloth which had caught her eye to see a new face staring at her, a man younger than the old trader who was talking to some people in a corner of the large room.

"May I help you?" asked the young man. His stare was ignored by the woman as she shook her head and continued searching the items with her bright eyes. "Excuse me, you don't know me," said the man, "my name is George Ironsides. I am Mr. Johnson's new partner."

"Keewaukoomeelaa," said Nehaaeemo pleasantly.

"I speak only a little Shawnee," confessed George Ironsides, though he was not apologizing. "Uh, do you speak any English?"

"Little," replied Nehaaeemo. "Aah," she said as she spied the ribbon she wanted, dark blue as a strip of night. She put down the beaver skin she had brought in, took the ribbon in hand and knew it was what she wanted. "How much trade?" she asked in English.

George kept staring at the young woman, her brilliant eyes, coal-black hair, dusky skin, emerald teeth, the nobility of her bearing, her soft doeskin dress.

"How much trade?" repeated Nehaaeemo.

"Oh, well, excuse me," said George, though he seemed quite confident in his behavior, "let's see... that ribbon is brand new, I just brought it in a week ago. For you, I will make a gift of it to you."

"Gift? Trade," said Nehaaeemo as she pointed to the beaver skin.

"No, for you it is a gift. Here, take it and remember your friend George Ironsides. The price is that you say my name."

Nehaaeemo smiled brightly. The man was crazy. "Jorg Ainsides," she said good naturedly.

"Fine, take the ribbon, it is yours," said George. Nehaaeemo took the ribbon and tried to give the man the beaverskin but he would not take it so she shrugged her shoulders and simply walked out of the store with her gift. George came to the door and watched her walk away.

"Hey, Ainsides," called Claude Johnson after a few minutes as he walked up to his new partner, "we are traders, not philanthropists."

"Claude, I will never cheat the Indians just because it can be done," said George.

"That's not as easy as you might think," replied Claude, "believe me. I've been trying for the last twenty years and have never been able to beat them. Here, let's move this over there. These people know what they want and they know what they'll pay for it."

"Who was that girl?" asked George.

"That little filly you'd better be careful with," cautioned the old trader, "unless you have marriage in mind. And even then you'd better watch it."

"How so?"

"You ever heard of the guy they call the Shawnee Warrior?" George nodded assent. "That there's his little sister. Her father was the chief at Old Piqua. Pretty gal, ain't she. But her family doesn't like white folks much."

"Where is the Shawnee Warrior?"

"Somewhere down South, fighting the whites. But she's got other brothers here. You don't want to fool with that little lassie. There's plenty of others around. Oh oh," he muttered almost inaudibly, "here comes trouble."

George looked up to see an Indian and a red-haired woman entering the store. The Indian was Shawnee but the woman was obviously white, though she didn't look like any miserable captive. The man stood while the woman came up to Johnson and said, "I'd like some coffee, please."

"Yes Mam," said Claude quickly, "I have all you'll ever want right here. How about a little sugar just to sweeten it a bit, or some fresh honey?"

George looked at her Indian clothes, noting how comfortable the woman looked in them: silver ear rings, a necklace of silver and different colored stones, her red hair in two braids which hung past her shoulders, her doeskin dress embroidered with various designs, all of them colorful, tasseled sleeves, embroideries even on her moccassins. She didn't look like any captive, no sir. He turned his attention to the man: tall, straight, a slightly bored expression on his face, a beautiful tri-cornered blanket

111

worn like some emperor's toga. His eyes took in everything at a glance and the Indian seemed to realize George was scrutinizing him the same as the old trader riveted his eyes on the woman.

"Do you have any underclothes or could you get some?" asked the woman of the trader.

Claude's face reddened noticeably and for a moment he was at a loss for words. "Uh, no, I don't get much call for.. that," he mumbled. "Perhaps I could...uh, special order...well, I don't know that I could."

"When you find out, let me know," said Red, not the least bit timid. "What do I owe you?"

George got busy with moving more items as he continued to look at the man and woman, both of whom ignored him completely. When they left the the store he walked over to Claude and asked, "Who in the world is that?"

"That's the medicine man, Spybuck. He's supposed to be a wizard, a juggler. Practices witchcraft, can evoke demons and all that. People are afraid of him, lots of stories about him. But I'll tell you one thing, he's got some woman with him, I shit you not. I'd like to know who she is and what she's doing with him. Paid me with Spanish money. If I wasn't so old that's the wench I'd go after. Old or not, maybe I'll do it anyway. Enough to make my blood boil!"

George had to laugh. He had thought the other woman just as attractive, in a different sort of way. "What was the name of the other one, the sister of the Shawnee Warrior?"

"Name's Nehaaeemo. But remember, there's plenty other women around. We're in business to make money. Now there's lots of advantages to having an Indian wife but a man has to be careful or the tribe will run you out. We're on their land and there word is law if a decision is made against you. Forget Nehaaeemo if its going to lead to business troubles."

"No, I don't want any trouble, rest assured," said George. *But I will see that girl,* he thought to himself. There was something about her, a strong attraction. The white woman was attractive also but her Indian was obviously an insuperable obstacle. Perhaps there was someone in Nehaaeemo's life? "Is she married?" he asked Claude.

"I don't think so. She comes here alone or with family. I've seen many a young buck with eyes for her, though. But women are women the world over. They have more rights here than in civilization."

George Ironsides would make it a point to attend the frolic dance this night.

Episode 12: Kenton attacks Tecumseh

Luther Calvin rode at the head of a column of thirty-seven men this spring day in 1792. If the horses taken by the Indians were not recaptured he was a ruined man, or close to it. He looked hard at the ground now that the retrieving force was north of the Ohio in Indian country. "Simon, there to the left, a blind man could follow that trail."

Simon Kenton had been picked by Calvin for joint command since the frontiersman was the most famous Indian fighter in the group. "Sure enough. Fresh tracks. Indians not far away, maybe a few miles at best."

"Let's send out a scouting party," said Pel, who rode behind Kenton and who had been the most sanguinary personality on the Kentucky side of the river, making sure everybody knew what he would do to the savages when he caught up to them.

"Hang loose," said Calvin. "We've got to close the gap first. You'll get your chance."

"Damn right I will, but not like St. Clair's army," continued Pel. "No more ambushes for this frontiersman. Horse flesh isn't more important than my hair.

The group rode on in somber silence for about five miles. St. Clair's defeat and slaughter had driven a wedge of fear throughout the frontier as far east as Pittsburgh. Few individuals on the border had been able to shrug it off emotionally and Calvin's expedition grew more apprehensive as the afternoon waned.

"I say we stop right here and send out scouts!" hissed Pel as he reined in his mount.

"All right, all right," conceded Calvin, "let's make camp here and reconnoiter. We're not going to lose this trail, though, even in the dark."

The men dismounted and made a temporary camp. "Let's get plenty of firewood," said Spencer Calvin, Luther's eighteen year old son, "so we won't be afraid of the dark."

Most of the men laughed but Pel looked at the young man and said, "What the hell do you mean by that?"

Spencer looked at Pel. "Whatever you think I meant by it, mister."

"You afraid of the dark?" asked Pel. "That what you referring to?"

"I ain't no coward," replied Spencer, "and I want to hear you say the same."

"Why you little pup!" exploded Pel as he walked up to Spencer and

113

pushed him roughly to the ground. Spencer picked himself up quickly and rammed Pel's midsection with his head, both men sprawling to the ground, punching, kicking, choking.

"Here now," said Kenton as he and several others did their utmost to separate the two antagonists. "Cut it out, we can do all the fighting we want with Indians, not each other!" The men were pried apart and forceably restrained.

"I'm calling you a coward, loud mouth!" said Spencer as they held him down. "Big talk so long as no Indian is around but the instant you cross the Ohio your backbone turns to jelly!"

"Let me at him!" yelled Pel. "Little fart doesn't know what a fight is and he thinks he's going to parade into Indian country! Let go, damn it!"

"All right, let him go!" ordered Luther Calvin. "Now listen to me, both of you and everybody else. I don't want anybody here who doesn't want to be here. This here's a voluntary expedition to help a neighbor out just like we've always done in the past. This is no army and nothing is required of nobody!" He made a line in the earth with the heel of his boot. "There. Now I'm going on, even if it's alone. Those of you who want to come with me step across that line. Those of you who want to return home, I wish you good luck and no hard feelings."

Captain Luther Calvin was a respected man. Twenty-one men crossed the line to continue the quest into Indian country. Fifteen decided to turn back toward home. They mounted their horses in stony silence and Pel lead them back toward the Ohio crossing.

"No hard feelings," repeated Calvin as he gave the fifteen a quick wave of the hand. "All right boys, let's finish making camp. We'll be getting an early start come dawn."

The night proved uneventful, though sentires were posted, and the next day pursuit was resumed. Along about mid-morning the riders heard a bell like that used on horses to find them after being turned out to graze. Instantly everyone darted off the trail in search of protective cover.

"Simon, look," whispered Calvin as he saw an Indian riding toward them in careless fashion. Kenton had already seen him and was preparing to shoot him down, even though he was much more than a hundred yards away.

"Let me do it," said young Spencer Calvin.

"All right, do it," replied Kenton, aware that the young man needed some bolstering.

The shot rang out and the Indian pitched out of his horse. The men waited to see if any other savages came out but none did. They rode and searched for the Indian, found him dead. "Good shot," said one of the men to young Calvin.

"Now let's get some scouts to find the Indian camp," said Kenton. Two men volunteered quickly and were off in stealthy fashion. The dead Indian was scalped in short order and the men took souvenirs as they desired.

The scouts returned an hour later: "Big Indian camp up ahead. They're all sitting around, talking and laughing. Looks like they're waiting for somebody."

"Could be reenforcements," said one of the men.

Everyone mounted up hurriedly and before anyone could say anything further the whole detail of twenty-two men lashed their horses in retreat and did not stop until they were several miles from the dead Indian.

Kenton finally put a halt to everyone's flight. The horses were winded anyway. "I don't think we'll be pursued," he said to Calvin. "They were too far away to hear Spencer's shot. Let's collect our wits and plan some strategy." It seemed to be the respite everyone needed.

"It's gonna get dark soon," began Calvin. "Let's have a go at them in the dark. Maybe we can pick most of them off around their fires. Simon, what do you say we split up and attack from two sides while some of us are getting the horse herd?"

"Sounds good," replied Kenton. "I'll take ten men or so, you take the others and send one to drive the horses."

The men mounted up and rode back the way they had come.

"No moon tonight," commented Spencer Calvin as the woods began to look dark and ominous.

"Hold up, everybody," said Kenton and the detail halted instantly. "We're gonna need a password in the dark. What do you say we use *Boone?* Fire at anything moving that doesn't respond with the countersign."

The riders peered into the darkness, led by the scouts who had discovered the Indian camp, but nothing showed itself. The inky blackness served them well for they could not be picked off with savage impunity as they rode. The scouts came to a point in the trail where they dismounted.

"The horses are over yonder," whispered one to Captain Calvin, "in the bottoms."

"Spencer, you go after the horses," said the elder Calvin. "Simon, you take your men that way, I'll go this way."

Spencer had wanted to attack the Indian camp but the horse herd was the most important target right now so he obeyed without comment. Both parties got as close as they dared, which was close enough to see maybe nine warriors lounging here and there. One savage was well silhouetted by the fire. The first shot hit him and he fell over the small blaze.

Tecumseh had been lying under some pine trees outside the camp. Though he was the informal sentinel the approach of the enemy had not been detected until one of his men had been shot. "Sinnamatha!" he yelled out in Shawnee, "charge them and cover me!" With that he ran toward the attackers' position, his only weapon the warclub which he was never without. The other warriors came out of their temporary bark tents as Big Fish sounded the warcry. The fight was confusing because the night was so dark.

"Boone," Tecumseh heard one of the Shemanese uttering in the darkness.

"Boone!" yelled Tecumseh loud enough for his men to hear him. "Boone," he said in a loud whisper as both groups of combatants used the countersign to the enormous consternation of the Shemanese. Tecumseh saw a form in front of him, "Boone!" he whispered again then sprang at the man, delivering a powerful blow with his warclub to the enemy's head, squashing it like a melon.

More warriors came to help in the fray. Simon Kenton heard his password coming at him from all directions. Instead of firing and possibly killing some of his own men he quickly decided to retreat. "Let's get out of here!" he said to those around him and everyone fled. Calvin's group heard men smashing through the bushes so they took to their heels.

Alexander McIntyre, one of Kenton's scouts, was able to get an Indian horse because the animal had been tied to a tree. When the retreat began McIntyre tried to mount up but the animal became spooked and would not allow it. So the man led the horse away on foot while the rest of his party hot-footed it desperately to where the horses were secreted, mounted and continued their flight at top speed.

Tecumseh would not allow pursuit in the darkness. "Let us see to the injured man," he said. But the warrior had received a mortal wound and was dead. He was wrapped in a new blanket for the trip back to Wapakoneta and burial.

The next morning it was learned Sinnamatha's horse had been taken.

"Let's go get it back," suggested Tecumseh with vengeful determination. Sinnamatha and two others volunteered to go with him and the quartet was off as dawn began to walk the horizon. The trail was not hard

To follow and Tecumseh pursued it relentlessly until close to midday McIntyre was spied cooking meat over a small fire. Tecumseh dismounted and walked boldly into sight. McIntyre froze for the barest instant than grabbed his rifle and ran! Tecumseh and two warriors gave chase immediately.

They ran over a hundred yards, the Indians gaining on the scout, when suddenly McIntyre stopped, turned around, and raised his gun to fire. He saw two Indians quickly darting behind trees but the one that had been in the lead zigzagged a couple of times and crushed into him where he stood. Tecumseh grappled with McIntyre on the ground, put a fierce hold on him and quickly had him immobilized, a prisoner. The other two warriors now came forward and McIntyre resisted no more. He was tied securely and all returned to the Shawnee encampment.

Tecumseh and his prisoner were welcomed back in camp. One Shemanese had been killed, by Tecumseh's warclub, one warrior had fallen, another was missing, but now the prisoner would make it a Shawnee victory. It was generally agreed the Shemanese attackers had been more numerous than the Indian party.

"Let us eat and take our horses home," said Tecumseh. "Did you get them together?" he asked Whistling Pine.

"Uh, no, they scattered," stammered the warrior.

"And you did not retrieve them, after all this time?" said Tecumseh, a bit peeved. "We routed the Shemanese once, we could do it again if need be, but not with timidity," he admonished. "Sinnamatha and I will go for the horses. You *men* get some food ready." He and the Big Fish left camp without another word, grabbing some jerky from the meat pouch.

The horses were gathered and returned to camp by late afternoon. Tecumseh was beginning to feel the fatigue of his efforts so he stretched after he dismounted and was about to lay on the grass when he saw the Shemanese prisoner covered with an old blanket. "What happened to my prisoner?" he asked immediately as he walked over to the prostrate form on the earth.

"He was executed," answered Rolling Thunder.

Tecumseh threw off the blanket and saw the man's limbs were still tied. "What manner of warriors are you?" challenged Tecumseh. "This is an act of COWARDS!"

The Shawnees were taken aback. Prisoners were often executed unless it was decided to save them for the gauntlet or other feats of courage.

"This was my prisoner!" continued Tecumseh. "How dare you dispose of him without my approval? How are we to defend our country if

117

that is the brand of courage we live by? Answer me!"

"The Shemanese are the enemy in our land," said Whistling Pine. "If they can kill us under any circumstance-"

"Yes, I know that is truth. But no warrior riding with me will ever commit such acts of cowardice. I killed with my warclub and my only regret is the enemy fled like mice when we answered their challenge for I would have destroyed more. But that is the heat of battle where there are only victors or vanquished. Killing a captive that is tied and helpless is murder, unworthy of anyone who calls himself a warrior. We are better than that, the Shemanese notwithstanding. We kill only to defend the homeland while the Shemanese kill to steal it from us. Now I want the solemn pledge of everyone here present that a prisoner will never be murdered in cold blood while you have strength to speak up. Give me your promise from the heart."

All the men uttered their consent and approval. They mounted up and drove the horse herd before them, secure in the belief their leader was destined to be a great chief.

Episode 13: Tecumseh goes South

"Then we both have something to tell him," said Tecumapease to Nehaaeemo as the two women prepared the supper which was to be Tecumseh's farewell. Tomorrow he and thirty warriors would ride to the Cherokee country in answer to Cheeseekau's request for help against the Longknives in the South.

"But I don't know how to tell him," said Nehaaeemo. "He is so against intermarriage."

"Just be straightforward. Tell him: George Ironsides, the trader, asked me to marry up with him. George is a good man an I am going to accept his offer."

"Then he will grab me by the hair," continued Nehaaeemo, "and throw me right through the wall of the wegiwa!"

"Silly, he would do no such thing," laughed Tecumpease. "But I don't know what he'll do with Laulewasika. I am at my wits end with that little brother. All he wants to do is drink! If only father had lived to train him properly. And he says he will one day be the greatest of father's children. It breaks my heart to see him in such condition."

"My sister, you have done your very best with him and all of us," said Nehaaeemo. "You must not feel bad. Perhaps Laulewasika will find himself soon."

"I hope so. The other day he got in an argument with Wasegoboah.

118

My poor husband just sat there and took the abuse until I ordered Laulewasika out of the cabin. It was then he suggested he accompany Tecumseh to the south to help Cheeseekau fight."

"I'm glad you didn't encourage him to go," said Nehaaeemo. "Who knows how long they'll be gone. That is one thing about a trader: he must be at home if he is to sell his wares. I do not want my husband going away for long periods of time."

"I hope your husband-to-be wants the same thing. What shall I tell Tecumseh about our youngest brother?"

"Perhaps Laulewasika should go south with him?" said Nehaaeemo. "Might do him good to get away. A chance to grow up."

"The warpath is no place to grow up," observed Tecumapease. "Do you know the only aptitude Laulewasika shows? He likes to help cure the sick. Perhaps if we apprentice him to a healer..."

"Tecumseh is good friends with that Spybuck man. Perhaps-"

"Don't even mention that man's name," said Tecumapease quickly. "Our younger brother is bad off enough with firewater. I don't want him burned as a sorcerer."

"What sorcery!" said Nehaaeemo derisively. "All this talk of witch-craft and demons any time someone mentions Spybuck. Everyone shuns him until they need him for a cure. He's got everyone afraid of him so he can do what he wants!"

"What are you talking about?" asked Tecumapease in amazement. "Have you ever been around that man?"

"I've seen him about in the village, but not much lately. He has a Shemanese woman living with him now. I've seen them a couple of times when I was visiting with George. They only talk to the traders."

"Good," said Tecumapease as she continued with the preparation of the *ne-pan-wi tak-u-wha*. The soft milky mush was almost ready for the baking kettle. "You stay away from both of them."

"Do you really believe in witches, elder sister?" asked Nehaaeemo.

"You have not seen the things I have. Go see if you think Tecumseh should take more *gol-tha-wa-li*. It's over there by the blanket."

Nehaaeemo went to the buckskin bag, opened it, withdrew the smaller bag inside it. "Seems to be a good supply, but better too much than not enough. Let's give him another ration." The corn meal, when stirred into a cup of water, made a good drink as well as a nourishing meal in an emergency, ideal for warriors on the hunt or warpath. Kept dry it would serve indefinitely. "Well I wish I could see something with my own eyes. All I ever hear is stories."

"You will change some ideas when you are married."

"I am glad Cheeseekau is not here," confessed Nehaaeemo. "Tecumseh is bad enough."

"Do not talk about your brothers that way. Yes, I know what you mean. They have ever protected us and that is their only desire. Why do you wish to marry a Britisher? I'm not criticizing, you know I accept you as you are. Just tell me why."

"I will marry my Sky Eyes because... I want to."

"All right, stubborn, but you have not answered my question," said Tecumapease.

Nehaaeemo became more serious. "He treats me well. He lives among our people. He does not like the Longknives. I can take care of him."

"Do you love him as I love Wasegoboah, as mother loved father?" asked the older sister.

"Certain relationships are rare," conceded Nehaaeemo. "I can grow to love Sky Eyes. I think he will be a good husband and with time he will be precious to me the way father was to mother."

"What if he leaves our country?"

"I don't know."

"What if he leaves you behind when he leaves?"

"What if, what if," said Nehaaeemo with some irritation, "I cannot see into the future. All I ask is that you stand by me. I owe you such a great debt already for being a mother to us all. Help me now, help me with Tecumseh especially, to make him understand that I am of age to live my life as I see fit."

"All I want is your happiness," concluded Tecumapease. "Be aware of what could happen is all I'm asking. Perhaps it is good. And I will continue to ask your help with Laulewasika."

"You shall have it, I promise," said Nehaaeemo.

"Have what," asked Tecumseh as he entered the wegiwa, "supper?"

"Of course, older brother" said Nehaaeemo happily. Had he heard any part of the conversation? She threw her arms around his broad shoulders.

"Oh oh, little sister wants something," teased Tecumseh, unaware the woman had some grave news for him. "Maybe I'd better get supper first, eh?"

"Are all your warriors ready for tomorrow's departure?" asked Tecumapease. "I wish Laulewasika was going with you."

"It will be a long journey," observed Tecumseh. "Ah, here is little brother now," he said as Laulewasika entered with Wasegoboah, the children coming in after them. The wegiwa filled with happiness.

"Come, let us eat," said Tecumapease as she scattered the children away from the cooking fire. Bowls were passed out to everyone then Nehaaeemo and Tecumapease served the meat, soup, and corn. Everyone sat on the floor and asked questions of Tecumseh as to his itinerary. Everyone could see the young warrior was anxious to set off.

"We shall take Cornstalk's route into the south country," said Tecumseh between mouthfuls.

"Why do they call it Cornstalk's route?" asked his eldest niece.

"Because Cornstalk travelled that road when he went to recruit warriors to fight against Dunmore," answered Tecumseh. "He took with him the great purple war belt of the Shawnee nation. It was six inches wide and nine feet long. During his speeches he would pour vermilion on it to represent blood, putting fire into the warriors."

"Will you see Grandmother?" asked another niece.

"Yes, I am anxious to see her again. Maybe I will make her come back with us. Through Cheeseekau I will meet the Cherokee brothers, through mother I will acquaint myself with the Creeks. Both are fighting the Longknives."

"What happens if we are invaded here again?" asked Wasegoboah.

"I guess you and Laulewasika can defend the homeland without me," said Tecumseh as he relished his last home-cooked meal for a while. He was on the abstemious side but he loved his sister's cooking.

Laulewasika smiled at his brother's comment. The lad was totally sober and had been that way since Tecumseh's return from the warpath. "See, Wasegoboah, it is all left up to you and me now," he said in jest.

"It is good," replied Wasegoboah in all seriousness.

"Some day you will encounter your destiny," said Tecumseh, "and do honor to your father's name and your people."

"Uncle," asked Tecumseh's oldest nephew, "Where did you learn about the purple war belt?"

"By studying with the Grandfathers, as you must do if you are to educate yourself," answered Tecumseh. "Only through such education can you have pride in yourself and your people. The Grandfathers will tell you about our history, about your Grandfather Puckeshinwa and your uncle the Shawnee Warrior. You must study and learn all your father has to teach you, as well as what your mother has to shape your character."

"How about you, why don't you educate us?"

"I will, when I return."

"Or when he's a little old man and no longer is called to the warpath," observed Nehaaeemo, looking for some opening with which to tell her brother she wanted to marry George Ironsides. She looked at Tecumapease but the older sister made no comment. Indeed, the children talked more with Tecumseh than anyone else. They wanted to know how many were in the war party, who was going, where they were going to meet Uncle Cheeseekau, why Grandmother Methoataske was so far from her family, and on until Tecumapease curtailed their inquisitiveness.

"Enough, enough or your uncle will be weary before he begins his journey. My brother, I would speak with you for a moment."

"I must see to the horses" said Tecumseh, "why not walk with me to the horse compound?"

Tecumapease nodded and both went out of the wegiwa. "It is Laulewasika," began the venerated sister, "I am concerned about his drinking and lack of inclination for making something of himself."

"I have talked to little brother," said Tecumseh, "but I don't know how much good I have done. He told me he wanted to be a healer so I asked Spybuck to take him under his wing."

"Oh, not Spybuck!" gasped Tecumapease.

"Do not worry, sister, it will be all right," was all Tecumseh could say. "I would not condone it if something could go wrong." Tecumseh could not reveal to his sister that Spybuck's sinister reputation rested more on Shawnee belief in witchcraft than actual fact and behavior. He had worked his way out of superstition yet he understood most of his tribe was still mired in it to some degree. "Send Laulewasika to the medicine man periodically and let us hope he will gain some knowledge about the healing arts."

"All right, if that is your wish."

"What do you wish me to tell mother?"

Tecumapease walked silently for a moment then put an arm around her brother. "Tell her we love her with filled hearts, just as we love you, apetotha." She stopped and hugged her little brother, now so big and strong. "You must return to us. I don't know why but Cheeseekau I do not feel will return to the Ohio country, nor will mother. But you must return to us for you are our destiny. You will meet many people, perhaps even take a wife, but you must never leave the Ohio forever. I long to see the day when people call you 'Chief of the Beautiful River.' Do you remember when you were little, everybody wanted you to be something different?" The two continued walking again, arm in arm, as Tecumseh nodded. "All I ever wanted was for you to be good to the people. That is still my heartfelt wish. We have beaten the Longknives in battle..." She thought of Nehaaeemo marrying a Britisher. "--but our people are in dire need of good leadership and someday that mantle of responsibility might fall to you. As you ride south think that someday you will have to be the Puckeshinwa, the Cornstalk, the Pontiac of our people. This crusade to help our brothers and sisters in the south will clarify your duties here in the Ohio country. I believe the Great Spirit has chosen you for special tasks. Always pray for guidance from the great Mysterious and give thanks for the many legacies bequeathed to you from His hands. My apetotha, you are destiny's warrior. We are all as simple and complex as Mother Earth so do not tempt unnecessary dangers, my Tecumseh, for if you do not return my heart will be empty to the end of my days."

Chapter 3

Cheeseekau looked at the fresh prints and knew the pair had to be close by. He had guessed from the beginning the two were superior woodsmen but they had been unable to elude his tenacious tracking. The Shawnee Warrior had noted every sign: the moss on a rock that had been trodden by a human foot, pebbles disturbed, twigs broken by some weight, or leaves that were flatter than others around them, all of which Cheeseekau could perceive without stopping to scrutinize. There, to the right, a slight rustle of sound then deadly silence. Cheeseekau wondered if an ambush had been planned by his prey. Could they know he was following them all this time? He stepped softly behind a tree and listened calmly. *Click.* Someone's musket was ready to fire, the hammer being pulled back. So they knew where he was. But they didn't know how many pursuers there were. Still, Cheeseekau was uncertain as to their exact positions. He was sure only of one thing: there were two murderers to his right somewhere. He had to flush them out. He could hear the sound of running water further on but nothing else in the green forest was alive this day. Cheeseekau vowed either one Shawnee or two Shemanese would be dead by sunset. He brought back the hammer on his musket, feeling the enemy already knew where he was. He took his tomahawk firmly in one hand then flipped it underhand into a tree some twenty feet away: thud! BANG! rang out two muskets almost in unison and Chee- seekau saw where the enemy was hidden. Instantly he charged the posi- tion, crashing through the brush and voicing the most horrendous warcry he could muster: EEEEEaaaaiiii! The two men were getting to their feet as Cheeseekau came into sight. One quickly went for his axe and as he leaned back to throw the Shawnee Warrior's rifle boomed its missle of death, the man tumbling backward forcefully. The other man saw the Indian, realized he could not reload in time, so he reached for his knife quickly and stood his ground.

Cheeseekau smiled through the acrid blue smoke as it rose skyward. He put down his musket and calmly reached for his own knife. "You and me, Shemanese," he taunted.

"No, Injun, just me," replied the white man.

Cheeseekau crouched slightly as he approached, wondering if the Shemanese had some other firearm to use. But none was in evidence as the two men feinted and parried preliminaries to their mortal combat. The Shawnee Warrior went down to one knee in an effort to cut at the man's legs but the bearded one sidestepped with great agility. Cheeseekau came up with a stick for his free hand and swung it mightily at the man's knife hand, wresting it from his grasp. He expected the unarmed man to flee but much to the warrior's surprise he did not, though he moved backward warily.

Cheeseekau looked at the man cooly, perhaps Tecumseh's age, then took his knife by the blade and flung it at a tree behind him where it stuck violently. The combat would be weaponless! The white man was large and muscular, a fitting opponent for the Shawnee Warrior, though there was disparity in their ages. Perhaps the Shemanese was older than he looked.

Cheeseekau charged into the man, received a blow on the shoulder, grabbed his antagonist as both rolled on the ground over and over, Cheeseekau coming up with a strangle hold. The man's eyes opened wide as his air diminished but then he put both his hands on one of Cheeseekau's wrist and managed to break the hold. Immediately he delivered a kick aimed at the groin but the Shawnee Warrior took it on his thigh as he jumped up to avoid the blow. The Shemanese now turned and ran but Cheeseekau saw his object: the tomahawk stuck to the tree! Instantly he ran after the man, catching him just as he put his hand on the tomahawk to yank it out. Cheeseekau butted him with his head, dazing the Shemanese long enough to grasp his throat and squeeze, *squeeze* with all his strength. The man went limp and when the Shawnee Warrior knew he was dead he let the corpse crumple to the ground. He took his tomahawk then rested against the tree, breathing heavily. Two more, two more. What was the count now, about three hundred? Years ago he had vowed vengenance...two hundred men for his sweetheart, one hundred for each of her parents. *You must stop taking desperate chances on the warpath,* his warrior's instinct cautioned him as it had so often in the past. He had won again, the odds notwithstanding. But *no matter how much blood he spilled his woman did not return,* except in visions. The path of vengeance was gratifying only in emptiness.

Cheeseekau hoped Tecumseh had received his message. Perhaps his younger brother could... save him? No. The Shemanese had forced his life to be spent on the warpath. But if he wanted it so, why was he tempting the fates? Was it confidence in his warrior prowess or was it a death wish? The Shawnee Warrior knew not. At the moment he cared not for his job was unfinished this day. He retrieved his knife and rifle along with the firearms of the dead Shemanese, putting them in a pile for the time being. He dragged the dead men to different trees, stood them up and tied them from around the throat with rawhide straps so they would remain upright. With their own knives he cut the hunting shirts from the chests then buried the knives into their solar plexus, the handles standing out grotesquely from their gruesome white skins. Next he fetched the Shemanese tomahawks and buried each in the frontal skull of its owner. He knew the Shemanese usually mutilated the genitals of murdered Indians but Cheeseekau decided the scene was hideous enough without adding Shemanese touches. Finally he shot each corpse full of arrows. He collected the rifles, powder, and bullet pouches before he headed for home, not looking back. He was watchful for other enemies while his mind was occupied with the hope that his younger brother would bring many warriors to help with the war.

Episode 2: The Black Drink

Tecumseh had been most anxious to renew his ties with the southern Indians for his mother had always recounted stories about her brethren, encouraging him to visit them when he was a warrior. The day had finally come and now he was an important part of the Shawnee contigent that sat around the war kettle, along with hundreds of other warriors, as the *Ghigau,* the Cherokee equivalent of the "Beloved Woman," began to prepare the sacred Black Drink with which the warriors would purify themselves before taking the warpath against the *Unaka,* Cherokee for Shemanese.

The woman was radiant in her white deerskin clothes, trimmed in white swans' down, her lustrous black hair reflecting firelight this early evening as she moved around the kettle and the blaze under it. Her motion were traditional to the Cherokee and each of her movements was marked with a sweep of a white swan's wing, now slow and graceful, now

126

fast and sharp. Cheeseekau, sitting proudly next to his younger brother, had seen the Black Drink Ceremony several times but it was a totally new experience for Tecumseh and he was enthralled.

The woman chanted ancient songs as she danced around the fire, the swan's wing in perpetual motion. From a deerskin bag she drew a handful of salt and scattered it on the fire. Then she closed the bag and tossed it at the feet of Chief Glass. From another bag she drew out specially prepared yaupon leaves that had come from holly shrubs which grew on the sacred hills of the Cherokees, threw them in the kettle to simmer until the water was just the right color. Then each warrior would drink in order to purge himself so as to prevent injury and loss of life.

"You don't have to drink," whispered Cheeseekau to Tecumseh. "It is not our custom and might make you ill."

"I don't want to be sick but I will respect my peoples' custom by drinking just a bit," said Tecumseh. "Have you drunk?"

Cheeseekau nodded. "It is bitter and makes you vomit. Drink only a little. Your system will react strongly. Watch."

While the kettle simmered a pole was brought out and placed in a hole in the ground. Three sclaps dangled from the top of the pole and a painted warrior began to sing: "E-ha-e-yo-r-yo-he-YE-YE!" Everyone stood up and began to keep time in place, raising the right foot higher than the left. A group of lCherokees made a circle around the scalp pole and kettle and commenced to move to their right. Another group of warriors joined in, moving to the left. Now there appeared a scout outside both circles, all alone, but moving in the direction of the inner circle, using the same step but with a sneaky motion. At the chorus of the "YE YE!" all the dancers stopped and raised a weapon in the air, Tecumseh grasping his warclub and smashing enthusiastically at every YE YE! as did the large assembly of warriors, the martial spirit of the crowd thus being fanned to great heights.

Another scout now entered the dancing, making his way to the first one whom he engages in mock battle as they parry at each other with tomahawks. The sneaky scout falls and the winner yells out his victory amid the chorus of YE YE!, pretends to scalp the vanquished enemy and quickly runs to the scalp pole, placing the trophy on top.

The dancing now becomes more frantic with each YE YE! and warriors come up to the scalps and tear ferociously at them with hands or teeth, thus ending the dance. Now all who wish to purify themselves step up to the war kettle and are given of the Black Drink.

Tecumseh stood in line and took a very small amount of the bitter liquid. He walked back to his brother and the Shawnee contingent, most of whom had preferred not to partake of the Black Drink.

Chief Glass stood up to speak after everyone had drunk: "My brothers, my friends, my fellow warriors, open your ears for my message this night. You patriots of this great island realize better than anyone what we must do." He raised his tomahawk up high. "We have tried the white path of peace and were murdered on it. We have colored our faces with the blue of patience and seen it run red with blood from unprovoked attack. Our tribes have scattered like little birds before the eagle. But running have done them little good for tragedy and dispair track the prints of their moccasins. The assassins kill us with their smallpox or render us ugly for life with scars on our faces and souls. Drunkenness is rampant and frolic dances become orgies where drinkers fall into the fire, burning themselves and even dying. There are brawls, murders, thefts. Adultery goes unpunished as women become prostitutes to obtain liquor and men sell their wives and daughters for it."

"But now we have been purified by the Black Drink. No longer are we little birds before the eagle. Our brothers have made us strong! The Creeks are fighting by our side! We of the southern tribes welcome our brothers from the north, led by the famous Shawnee Warrior!" A great roar of approval went up from the warriors. "Together we shall turn on the invaders who encroach upon us at every turn, who live only for our death and their greed for our land, who speak with forked tongues, extending a peaceful hand to our hearts while another stabs from the back." He walked to the scalp pole and brought down his tomahawk into it. "In two suns, DEATH TO THE UNAKA!"

Another roar went up from the warriors and the evening was ended. The Black Drink was doing its work and the men had to finish their purification alone.

Episode 3: The Attack

Ziegler's Station was two miles from Bledsoe's Lick, thirty miles east of Nashville. Chiefs Glass and Turtle-at-Home led their many warriors to the little fortification, confident of an easy victory. There was a stockade around the houses but no blockhouse worthy of the name. By mid-afternoon Ziegler's Station was surrounded, awaiting the signal for attack. Cheeseekau was honored by being allowed to begin the engagement by firing the first shot: he spied a man walking outside the stockade, aimed carefully, and fired, bringing him down. Immediately the woods reverberated with volleys of blazing musketry. Nothing outside the stockade remained alive, whether human or animal. The defenders inside

128

the station replied in kind but their numbers were small compared to the attackers.

"We can take them at any time," observed Tecumseh, "if we scale the stockade."

"Yes," commented Cheeseekau, "if they have no big guns."

Word was passed down the Indain lines that the stockade would be stormed after sunset, for everyone to be deathly quiet to unnerve the Unaka until the night attack. The woods became silent. There seemed to be no activity inside Ziegler's Station either. Evidently they had no cannon and precious few riflemen because they did not take any kind of initiative. The sun went down in silence then as the evening darkened word was passed to the contingent leaders to pick several warriors to carry two lighted torches, one in each hand, for the assault over the stockade. It was a sight to frighten the most valiant of defenders as the forest erupted with spine chilling warcries and torches charged at the terror-stricken Unakas. Some Indians fired while others scaled the walls and the moving torches converted everyone into two by the interplay of shadows. There was scant resistance and the station was taken. Four Unakas lay dead, eighteen men, women, and children captured.

Tecumseh knew the skirmish was a minor one decided by the weight of numbers. He looked at the frightened captives, almost feeling sorry for them, especially the women and children. All were given to the Creek contingent. This was one aspect of warfare he was unfamiliar with: he had never been captured or enslaved. What would that be like? Probably a fate slightly preferable only to death. The blackface, Frank, must have returned to the Shemanese who enslaved him rather than living with the Shawnee. That had been most difficult to understand, how someone could choose slavery above freedom.

Everything of value was commandeered by the victorious warriors by the following day and Ziegler's Station was put to the torch, flames reaching hungrily into the sky. The victorious army now made its way toward Buchanan's Station, four miles south of Nashville. An encampment was made a judicious distance from Buchanan's and that evening there was much oratory around the council fire. Even Cheeseekau, not an orator by any stretch of the imagination, rose to speak when invited:

"We brothers of the north know full well how bloody is the heel of the invader. Puckeshinwa, Chief of Old Piqua and my beloved father was murdered by Shemanese right after the peace had been made with the governor of Virginia. We have all lost our dearest loved ones. WITH THESE HANDS I HAVE KILLED THREE HUNDRED SHEMANESE," he thundered with outstretched arms and knotted fists, "AND I WILL KILL THREE HUNDRED MORE! I will gorge myself with their blood then sit down and be happy. I can say nothing more except that each of you is free to follow my example." Cheeseekau returned to his place of honor among the leaders and chiefs.

Tecumseh sat with the warriors, his brother's venomous words making him more determined to fight valorously in order to win the respect his brother enjoyed and so justly deserved. The Shawnee Warrior was famous in the north as well as the southern nations. The young warrior listened attentively to every speaker and when the rhetoric finished he sought out Cheeseekau and the brothers walked to their bark tent to sleep.

Tecumseh was the first Shawnee up the next day so he stoked the embers of the small fire and by adding a bit of wood got it going again for breakfast if anyone wanted to roast a bit of meat. Other warriors began to do the same with their fires but Cheeseekau was not among the Shawnees he would lead this day against Buchanan's Station. The sun was up before he walked up to Tecumseh and said, "Let us get the warriors together, I have something to tell them."

"Ah, you're turning orator now?" joked Tecumseh. He gave the whistle for immediate gathering, every Shawnee coming immediately.

"Brothers," began Cheeseekau, "last evening I saw the sun set for the last time." Tecumseh looked at his brother, his serious demeanor, heard the ominous tone of his voice. "I saw its light shine upon the treetops, and the land, and the stream of water. I am never to look upon them again." Every Shawnee in camp became agitated. "No other evening will come for last night I heard the drums on the North Star trail and felt a bullet pierce my heart."

"No!" shouted Messahawa and several other warriors who from the beginning had been with Cheeseekau in the south country. Tecumseh could say nothing. "No!" repeated Messahawa, "if you have heard the drums we shall not fight this day!"

"My brothers," said Cheeseekau calmly, "we will fight and take the fort. what would our brothers say if we refused to fight? They would call us a bunch of timid old women. Destiny calls me and it cannot be changed. It is a good day to die. Everything is disharmony within me. There are no songs in my heart. Beauty has left our shining eyes, leaving only the vacant luster of death. My thoughts are bad. It is a good day to die. You are all free men, decide what you will. I must battle. I must prepare. I have spoken." Cheeseekau went to meditate and paint himself.

Tecumseh was perplexed and agitated like everyone else. Cheeseekau could be overpowered and kept a prisoner... that would not do. Perhaps he could be protected... but once the battle started it was impossible.

Messahawa walked over to Tecumseh: "He is your brother and respects you greatly. Perhaps you can convince him we need him alive more than we have to take the fort."

"Would that I could," said Tecumseh.

"Do something," said Messahawa.

"We must respect him," said Tecumseh simply. "Perhaps it will not be so. I will stay by his side."

"As will I," added Messahawa, realizing there was little anyone could do.

In a short time the order was given to move out to strike the enemy. The principal chief was the Cherokee John Watts, assisted by lesser chieftains Otter Lifter and Middle Stricker. There were no people encountered in the surrounding country and Tecumseh deduced correctly all had sought safety inside Buchanan's stockade. All cabins were burned on the way to the station. All cattle and horses were herded by the warriors. The attacking party arrived at the station shortly after dark.

"I believe they have some cannon," said John Watts as he conferred with the other chiefs and his advisors, Cheeseekau included. "The gates are open but they will be slammed shut when the see us. We must scale the stockade and fire the blockhouse." He looked at his men. That might be suicide. Let us surround the station and charge in as we did at Ziegler's.

"We could drive the animals toward the gates," suggested Cheeseekau. "With us behind them we might be able to get in and keep them open."

"We might prevail in the darkness," suggested Middle Stricker.

"Let's try it," said Watts. "I will take some picked warriors and follow the animals. Everyone else get your men quickly into positon and open fire as soon as the battle begins."

"I shall take some men with yours," volunteered Cheeseekau.

"The Shawnee Warrior is welcome to accompany me," replied John Watts.

The animals were brought up when the warriors had had enough time to get into position. In the darkness they were just a herd of cattle as they made their way to the stockade gate. They were twenty or thirty feet from the gate when the alarm was sounded by someone on the blockhouse roof:

"Indians, Indians! Close the gates, quick!" The Unaka fired his musket at the enemy, thus alerting the defenders inside the station and causing the warriors to open fire, the flashes lighting up everything for brief moments. The bullets proved ineffectual against the timbers of the stockade and blockhouse. The defenders responded with a cannon shot at the charging Indians, forcing them to run for cover.

Except Cheeseekau. Instead of fleeing he sprinted toward the stockade wall and leaned against it momentarily in safety. Then he made his way toward the blockhouse, staying close to the timbers so he could not be seen from above. He heard bullets crashing into the stockade wall but he resolved to climb it and get to the roof of the blockhouse. He could be picked off by the hated Unaka or a stray bullet from his own men might get him but he searched for a log on which to discover some sort of grip. He found one that was rough and slightly separated from the one next to it so he slung his musket behind him and made his painful way upward.

"Where is Cheeseekau?" yelled Tecumseh at Messahawa.

"I don't know," returned the brave as he squinted into the darkness. "I lost him after the cannon shot." He looked at the young warrior. "He was not hit."

A musket shot illuminated the top of the blockhouse very briefly. Everyone saw a warrior making his way up the wall. "Cheeseekau!" said Tecumseh, partly relieved his brother was alive, partly aghast at the danger he would soon put himself into at the top of the blockhouse. "Cover me!" said Tecumseh as he charged toward the stockade, bullets sounding around him, cattle and horses stampeding out of the darkness, numerous carcasses laying strewn in his path. He jumped behind a dead cow for momentary protection then made it to another closer position. A number of other warriors followed his example.

Cheeseekau was almost at the top of the stockade, nearly lost his grip and footing, but held on and peeped through the railing to see two Shemanese huddling low as they reloaded. The Shawnee Warrior girded himself for a fierce leap over the railing that ran along the edge of the blockhouse. With all his might he pulled himself up and over this last obstacle. He grabbed his tomahawk as he landed and split one man's skull open with it but the other sprang at him with a knife, his rifle not being ready to fire. Cheeseekau managed to grab the man's arm but he could not hold on to his tomahawk so he grappled with the Unaka as he tried to unsheathe his own knife.

Partisans on both sides knew there was a mortal combat ensuing on top of the blockhouse as flashes of light gave brief illumination to the struggle. Riflemen did not shoot in that direction for fear of hitting the wrong man so they shot at anything else that moved. With his great strength Cheeseekau kicked at the man with all his might and fell on top of him, rolling around the roof in herculean effort to control the Unaka's blade. They both would have fallen off had it not been for the railing. Finally Cheeseekau smashed his elbow into the man's face, drove his fist into it again and again until there was no resistance. He took his own knife and plunged it into the base of the throat. He caught his breath. If he could set the blockhouse on fire the battle would belong to his people. The wood was dry enough. With his knife he tried to make splinters for kindling, succeeding but knowing riflefire would soon be directed his way. He put down his knife and made a spark, blowing it into the small pile of splinters. It wouldn't light at first but the repeated sparks finally made it catch. However they also made him a target, bullets coming at him from Unaka muskets. There was a flicker then the flame began to grow. He remembered the sappy pine he carried in his pouch exactly for this purpose, got on his side to find it, grasped the sappy stick and placed it on the small fire. Instantly the pine burned brightly and as Cheeseekau lost his cover a bullet hit him in the chest. He knew it had penetrated a long way for he could not breathe. Another bullet caught him in the thigh as the kindling became a little blaze. He stood up in agony, another bullet knocking him over the railing.

The Shawnee Warrior fell to the ground and laid there as bullets struck all around him. "Don't give up!" he yelled hoarsely. "Take this fort and killlllll....Shemanese. Happy am I to die in battle...kill the murderers of our people...let the birds pick my bones...open air...Tarmanee...Tarmanee..." Cheeseekau lay dead.

A cannon shot prevented the Shawnee warriors from retrieving their leader's body immediately but when the assault was over Tecumseh led a party that rescued it. The attack was called off during the night and the warriors retreated out of the immediate vicinity. Even the victory at Ziegler's Station had not been worth the loss at Buchanan's. All the dead were carried out on litters but the death of Cheeseekau was a tremendous loss. His reputation alone had been such as to attract followers for a war party, not to mention his abilities as fighter and leader.

The following day all chiefs and numerous warriors came to express their condolences to Tecumseh for the loss of his brother. He accepted the homage for Cheeseekau had been a herculean figure for Indians everywhere. The body was prepared for burial then taken to a site at the foot of a beautiful rolling hill and buried according to Shawnee custom. Tecumseh spoke to the crowd: "Chiefs and warriors, do not grieve. Misfortunes will happen to the wisest and best of men. Death will come, and always out of season. It is the command of the Great Spirit and people must obey. What is past and cannot be prevented should not be grieved over. We are not discouraged or displeased because this misfortune occured in this country. Misfortunes grow everywhere, not just on this warpath. How unhappy am I that I could not have died this day instead of the warrior that lies before us. The trifling loss my nation would have sustained at my death would have been doubly repaid by the honors of the burial. It would have wiped away all regret. Instead of being covered with a cloud of sorrow the warriors would have felt the sunshine of joy in their hearts. Chiefs and warriors, your tribute this day has not been bestowed in vain. Your attentions shall not be forgotten. My nation shall know of the respect you paid the Shawnee Warrior and I personally vow to echo the sounds of your guns in battle."

Tecumseh was the last to touch his brother's breast and when he did his mother's voice rang out amid the peaceful scene: *"Tecumseh, you shall avenge the death of your slaughtered brethren! Your enemies near or afar will hear your name and tremble..."* His thoughts returned to that dreadful night so many years ago when he and Methoataske had found his dying father. The terror of the moment had never left his emotions. "Beloved brother," began Tecumseh in a small voice, "I swear I shall not leave this country before I have done something worthy of your courage and death. Now you are with our father and Cornstalk, Blackfish, and... Tarmanee," he prayed as tears brightened his eyes and began to roll down his cheeks. "Give me the strength to continue our struggle for survival and freedom. Show me how to care for our mother so that I may reach her spirit. Great Father of the universe, take unto you the soul of Cheeseekau your child that he might enjoy the peace and tranquility he could not find on Mother Earth, in whose bosom his body will become one with the unseen forces that surround us. Father, take pity." Tecumseh removed his hand and covered his brother's body with utmost reverence. Then he walked away from the site and other men came, lowered it into the grave, covered it up, camouflaging it to avoid discovery.

When everything was finished the Shawnee gathered in council and elected Tecumseh, the youngest in the group, as pipeholder, acknowledged leader. He addressed the men: "My fellow warriors, I am honored to follow in the place of Cheeseekau, though I admit freely I could never color the warpath as he did for so many years. I will remain in this country to fulfill my vow to avenge my brother and our people. You are free to accompany me or to return home to the north country across the Ohio if you have duties which beckon. I too will return in time but first I must inform my mother of the death of her son. Then the Unaka will have cause to grieve."

The entire contingent of Shawnee, close to sixty men, rode back to Will's Town and Tecumseh went to his mother's wegiwa. He found Methoataske sitting with a young girl, talking pleasantly. The moment Tecumseh walked into her presence Methoataske sensed tragedy for the gift of prescience abounded in Puckeshinwa's family.

"What is it?" asked Methoataske.

"Mother..." Tecumseh was moved into speechlessness.

"Puckeshinwa's...eldest son?" asked the woman as her face, so vibrant and alive the moment before, became hard in agony.

"I have bad news," Tecumseh blurted.

"Cheeseekau, Cheeseekau," said Methoataske in a pained voice. She stood up, threw her arms around Tecumseh and wept sorrowfully. Her son could not keep his eyes from shedding tears. "Where is he?" asked Methoataske, "why did you not bring him to me so that I could touch his heart for the last time? We stand a small island in the bosom of great waters. We are encircled, we are emcompassed. The evil spirits ride upon the blast and waters are disturbed. The waves rise, they press upon us, they will settle over us and we shall disappear forever. There is no peace in our land. Our fields are ours no more. There is no laughter in our cabins. The children are homeless. Who will live to mourn us? None. What marks our extermination? Nothing."

Tecumseh had no words with which to assuage his mother's pain. She was all the tribes of his people and their sufferings for the loss of family by violent death was an integral factor in the psyche of the American Indian. He held her and wept with her until Methoataske's tears were spent. Only then did he notice the girl his mother had been talking to. In her effort to console the woman she had embraced Methoataske and then when her emotions overcame her she had put her arms around both.

"Come, mother, rest on your sleeping robes," said Tecumseh tenderly as he led her to lay down. "That's it, rest."

"Don't leave me," whispered Methoataske desperately. "Puckeshinwa, my husband, will return tomorrow. He will want to see you."

"I will be right here, mother," said Tecumseh. She looked like a crumpled rag doll with a tear-stained face. "See, I am going to sit right here and talk to your guest while you rest. Sleep, my precious, sleep."

The girl came over and sat by them. Silence reigned supreme and one would have thought the world was all peace and tranquility. When Methoataske drifted off to sleep Tecumseh looked at the girl.

"I appreciate you being here with mother," he said. Even through the girl's tear stained face Tecumseh realized she was one of the most beautiful young maidens he had ever seen.

"I admire her so much," replied the girl, "I could spend my whole life talking to her. She has been like a mother to me."

"I appreciate you," said Tecumseh simply. "She...ah, has been known to have relapses but I hope she'll come out of it. She has before."

"I will care for her, don't worry. She has been saying she wants to go into the Creek country. I hope she stays here instead." The girl stared at Tecumseh but the young warrior was so concerned for his mother he was totally unaware. "You are Tecumseh," continued the girl in a very pleasant voice. "Your mother has told me much about all her children. I would so love to meet Tecumapease."

"When you come to the north country I will introduce you. You will love her as I do."

"Are you hungry? May I get you something to eat?" asked the girl.

"Not right now, perhaps later," answered Tecumseh. "If mother is all right I shall take the warpath in two days. Are there provisions anywhere?"

"Yes, your mother always kept things ready for...Cheeseekau. Must you go so quickly to the warpath?"

"Yes, my scouts are right now searching for the enemy. We must fight. Fetch me a wet cloth to wash mother's face, would you please?"

The girl did Tecumseh's bidding then noted how tenderly he cared for the woman. This man looked every bit the warrior but no enemy would take him seriously if he could be seen at this moment, gently wiping his mother's face. "Sleep, newethar," whispered Tecumseh, "sleep."

The following day Methoataske was coherent though in a deep depression. Her only comments were that she would soon be leaving to the Creek country, away from Ohio troubles. A large party of Creeks were leaving Will's Town, including some women and children, so Tecumseh made arrangements for his mother to travel with them. She seemed to be in control of herself and Tecumseh promised he would follow her into the land of the Creeks when he had fulfilled his vow against the Unaka.

"We will be using this town as our base of operations," explained Tecumseh to the girl whose name he had never thought to ask, "so we will return periodically." He had already said farewell to his mother, who would be leaving in a few days. "See that mother is happy and acquire anything additional she might need. I will return and repay you." He mounted his horse and smiled for the first time, touching his forehead in disbelief. "You have not told me your name, beautiful little sister, and I have been too much of a dullard to ask it. Please forgive and tell me."

"They call me Star Maiden," said the girl as she smiled.

"A beautiful name for my Cherokee friend. I will return to see you," finished Tecumseh then he was off with his contingent of thirty warriors.

Yes, Tecumseh, thought the girl as she waved, *come back to see me for someday you will be my husband.*

Episode 4: Tecumseh Fights

Tecumseh's scouts gave him information that caused him to divide his men into three squads in order to strike at the Unaka. They agreed to reunite within one moon and Tecumseh took his men toward Drake Creek where some Unaka lived in a cabin by a clearing. When the guerrillas arrived in the vicinity the horses were left far enough away so as not to give notice to the enemy and the commandos stalked the rest of the way on foot. Tecumseh saw three men working at clearing some land of trees. He signalled for five of his men to work their way toward the cabin and secure it, the others to come with him against the Unaka. The only sound was the axes biting into trees as the warriors approached undetected until they were close enough to be seen.

"Indians!" yelled one of the men as he ran for his rifle, "get the yaller devils!" They were his last words for Tecumseh shot him as he got to his rifle and positioned himself for a shot. His men shot the other Unaka where they stood terror-stricken, axes in hand. All three Unaka were scalped though Tecumseh ignored the hair of the alien he had shot in order to look to the cabin. His men were coming out of the structure, a woman and two children as prisoners.

The war party reunited and took from the cabin whatever struck each individual's fancy. Then it was set to the torch.

The Unaka woman wept, as did her children. "What will you do with us?" she asked of the savage who seemed to be the leader, "torture us and kill us?"

"My fight is not with women and children," said Tecumseh, "though we are as vermin to your people. Let us be gone," he said to his men in Shawnee as the cabin flames leaped high in the air.

"The woman!" yelled Messahawa as the female darted away in a futile gesture at escape. Tecumseh dropped what he was carrying and sprinted after her, grabbed her around the waist as her children cried "Mommie!" and carried her back to the group.

"You are in our power," said Tecumseh, "and nothing is going to hurt you. My men fight oppression, not families. Stay with your children and don't try to escape."

"Where is my husband?" asked the woman.

"Your husband is dead, just like my father and brother and so many of my people. But you have no feeling for them, just your losses."

"We did not come to kill," said the woman, "but your people won't leave us be."

"You come to our country, kill our animals, steal our land, and you want us to leave you in peace." Tecumseh became silent for talk was usless. The woman and her children were taken to the closest Chickamauga town and given over to the authorities there.

Tecumseh and his men came to acquire reputations as stalwart fighters, reviled by the Unaka and praised by the native nations. Unaka's were slain by the scores and, while some Shawnee were wounded, none were killed. Talk spread throughout Unaka settlements that a party of Indians led by some new devil chief was scourging the countryside and rewards were posted for his death or capture, along with any of his men. But the Unaka were unable even to discover his name, much less capture his scalp.

The following moon Tecumseh was encamped with ten men along a canebreak by the Tennessee River. Their larder had been depleted so time was taken for a hunt which proved successful and during the early evening everyone was busy with the meat, cutting it properly in order to dry some for future use, roasting some for immediate consumption. As the evening wore on the Indian camp was discovered by thirty Unaka, who stealthily closed in for the kill. A volley of muskets blazed into the calm evening but before the smoke had time to clear Tecumseh raised the warcry and hollered, "Into the canebreak! They're over to the right!" The warriors immediately grabbed their weapons and rallied to the prearranged area of the cane growth, Tecumseh firing the first shot in retaliation. The Unakas did not hit one single warrior with their preliminary volley. This was all but incredible that Unaka marksmanship could be so poor, especially when they prided themselves, as a prisoner once informed Tecumseh, in being able to shoot squirrels through the eye.

"Attack through the cane," said Tecumseh as he motioned for some warriors to follow him, "the rest of you keep up a hot fire." He led his men into what proved to be the Unaka's flank. Two were killed while the others panicked and took to their heels, leaving the bodies of their fallen comrades to be scalped.

The area was reconnoitered quickly. "It was a large group," said Lone Eagle, the best tracker with Tecumseh's guerrillas. "We should all be scalps dangling on lances," he continued, "for we were greatly outnumbered. I don't see how they ran away."

"They thought we filled the canebreak," observed Tecumseh, "and when we attacked the flank they must have believed it was another war-party. The Shemanese do not prefer to fight unless numbers are greatly in their favor."

"Unaka, not Shemanese," joked Messahawa who, along with the other warriors, understood Tecumseh's prearranged battle plan, formulated for just such an eventuality, was what had saved their lives and won the skirmish.

"Unaka, Shemanese, they're all the same," commented Tecumseh. "Now let's break camp and paddle away from here before the intruders gather some courage to come back and count our numbers." Everything was put in canoes and the commandos paddled down the Tennessee River.

Tecumseh led his warriors successfully through Georgia, Florida, Alabama, and Mississippi, fighting the Longknives whenever possible, meeting myriads of people and being hospitably welcomed by his brothers and sisters in the countless villages and towns he visited. When he was not fighting he delighted in the customs of his southern cousins, joined in their dances, listened to their myths and legends around the council fires, ate their foods, even wore their ceremonial costumes on occassion. Wherever he went he continued to be fascinated by the temple mounds which were much more numerous in this country than in his native Ohio. He came to admire the people first-hand, their religious zeal, rituals and ceremonies centered around corn, a sacred perpetual fire symbolizing the sun, observing that while details differed between north and south the basic pattern was quite similar: a people living in accordance with Earth Mother. Tecumseh also became familiar with the Creek Confederacy and was proud of it as a shining example of native statecraft. The Grandfathers he spoke to informed him there were more than fifty Creek towns with inhabitants numbering in the many thousands. Some towns were red, which meant they waged war, others were white, peace towns. The Creeks owned many blackfaces, excelled in communication, and traded goods far and wide. The Seminoles of Florida were an offshoot of the Creek people, Tecumseh learned when he visited the peninsula, and there were many runaway blackfaces who sought freedom in the land of the Seminole.

Everywhere the young Shawnee leader went he met women who

invited him to quit the warpath and stay to live. Tecumseh enjoyed these feminine beauties but none could keep him for very long. He simply was not interested in marriage at this particular time in his life. Besides, he could be killed by some treacherous Unaka at any time, making his wife a widow. So he spent time in towns and met innumerable personalities from all stations in life but his principal attachment was the warpath.

Tecumseh made a stop to deliver some horses and cattle in the town of Koasati when he heard the news that Blue Jacket of the Shawnee had sent a recruiter to enlist warriors to fight the invasion of the Longknives into the Ohio country. He gathered his warriors that same day and said, "My fellow warriors and clansmen, it is time to go defend the northern homeland. Let us have volunteers to inform the other Shawnee of the news and prepare ourselves for the return journey." Riders were chosen to find the various commando warparties while all others acquired the supplies everyone would need during the northward trek.

Tecumseh remained in Koasati while most of his men went out looking for the other Shawnee freedom fighters. He took on the role of recruiter, enlisting a few hot bloods for the upcoming northern war. he wished he could have visited Methoataske one more time, but she was now far away in the Alabama country among the Creek relatives. His tour of voluntary duty in the south ended when all his men came in. The group broke up into smaller units of five to ten men and headed north by different routes chosen by the warriors themselves. Tecumseh returned by the western Virginia route along the Greenbrier River, a favorite scenic area since the days of Cornstalk. As he rode his horse during the journey he kept a watchful eye out for possible trouble and his thoughts were heavy on the loss of Cheeseekau. He would have enjoyed his southern warpaths so much more if his brother were returning at his side! How would he break the news to Tecumapease and the rest of the family?

The trip went by uneventfully and Tecumseh's party of six warriors crossed the Ohio near the mouth of the Scioto River. "Ah," said Lone Eagle as soon as he touched Ohio ground, "it is good to be in the land of the brave again!"

"What do yu say we make camp up ahead and do a little hunting?" asked Tecumseh, as excited as anyone to be north of the Ohio again.

"Yes!" exclaimed one and all as they pranced around happily on their horses. A suitable campsite was found in a thick wood. "Ideal for defense," said Messahawa, trying to imitate Tecumseh's voice.

"Most important," chortled another warrior.

"Especially since we haven't even smelled a paleface since we left the

Creek country," added Lone Eagle.

"Well let's just see who gets some meat in camp first," said Tecumseh as he dismounted and began to gather wood for a small fire.

"Good, you be the apprentice and we will be the hunters!" With that the men fled into the woods, leaving Tecumseh with the horses and camp duties.

"Hey wait, I..." He smiled good naturedly when he realized all were out of sight. Ah well, he might as well make camp. First he secured the horses by unsaddling and hobbling them so they couldn't stray very far as they munched. Next he gathered some stones with which to circle the cooking fire and filled the area with pine needles and wood, ready for a spark when needed. Then he went about building some leantos for sleeping that night. The men returned with some meat and the camp settled down that late afternoon to a comfortable meal.

Simon Kenton and James Ward, the leaders of the Kentucky party who were in pursuit of the savages who had attacked and taken captive some prisoners from Bath County, all but stumbled straight into Tecumseh's camp. If Kenton had not noticed a small column of smoke rising above the trees...he didn't pursue the thought.

"Only about a half dozen," said Kenton to Ward as they crouched behind cover. "We can take them easy."

"Who are they?" asked James Ward.

"Looks like Shawnee," replied Kenton. "But they're not wearing any paint."

"Let's go bring the men."

"It's getting real dark," observed Kenton. "What do you say we wipe 'em out at dawn? Better than risk shooting each other."

"Okay, let's get back and plan a little strategy. These redskins aren't getting away so let them enjoy their last meal."

The Kentuckians retreated noiselessly and made it back to their own encampment without being detected. The plan was to leave the horses where they were and Kenton, Ward, and Baker would each take ten men and attack the savages from three different sides, pressing them into the large creek behind the Indian's camp. If they could shove them into the water they were sitting ducks. "Fire when you have enough light to aim by," advised Kenton to the assembled Kentuckians. "Now let's get some shuteye. I'll take first watch."

Few of the Kentuckians slept and at least an hour before dawn everyone made his silent way toward the Shawnee camp in exciting expectation. Their approach was again undetected, no small feat for a party of thirty-three men. Kenton motioned for Ward to take his men to the right, Baker to the left. He gave them time to get into position then led his avengers directly toward the enemy camp. He could not see if the savages were stirring for it was still too dark so he halted his men and waited. Suddenly he thought he heard the barking of a dog, peered out from behind a log and to his dismay saw Baker's men advancing in front of his own! A shot rang out from Ward's area and Tecumseh's warcry reverberated from tree to tree, awakening everyone in camp. Instantly the Shawnee darted for cover and returned the fire.

Tecumseh noted the attack was coming from the south and east. The creek was to his back but there were no attackers emanating from there or the west. The thick woods were appropriate cover but this led him to believe the attackers were on foot. They had stashed their horses somewhere, perhaps close by. "Messahawa, you and Lone Eagle go west quickly and see if you can locate their horses. If you find them cross the creek with the herd and give us the signal that you are ready. We will return home with many horses. Go quickly! And listen for our warcry." He yelled a tremendous warcry and the other warriors followed his example.

Tecumseh moved from tree to tree, his brothers doing the same, yelling all the while. The Shemanese were deceived into believing the savages were a much larger force than their actual number. "Go unhobble the horses and cross the creek with them," Tecumseh said to Buffalo Horn, "but keep up the warcry." He was now down to three men standing off the attackers but the three shot and re-loaded with enough rapidity to prevent the Shemanese from charging forward. Tecumseh saw a form moving and shot quickly, the man pitching backward and screaming his agony. Tecumseh was beginning to run low on powder as he shot and reloaded when he heard the whistle from the other side of the creek. "Come on," he said to his men "mount up on the other side of the water. Run quickly! I'll cover you."

"No, you come too."

"All right, let's go," said Tecumseh as the woods became still. The Kentuckians stopped firing. The lull enabled the Shawnees to cross the creek, mount their horses, and drive the captured horse herd in front of them.

Simon Kenton felt the Indians had given up the fight but one couldn't be sure with people who were so talented at ambushing. He led his men forward only to find the Indians had vanished. Then he heard a sound like thunder in the distance. The horses! The savages had captured the horse herd and made good their escape!

"Well, what do we do now? asked Ward. "It's a long walk to Kentucky."

Kenton just shook his head and gritted his teeth. He would never forget that warcry, a powerful agressive yell he knew had accosted his eardrums before. He didn't know the savage's name but he had to be some charmed devil chief!

Tecumseh and his men were in the highest of spirits as they rode the last leg of their return journey. The captured horses were good Kentucky mounts such as the Shemanese liked to brag about when they thought the Indians could not understand.

Tecumseh was the happiest of all. He now had a firm reputation as a fighter and patriot among several tribes of Indians. He was respected and more important he was confident he could lead warriors in defense of the homeland. He had always wanted to be a real leader and now his training was evident as he came into maturity, controlling the forces within himself. The many skirmishes he had fought, while minor and obscure, had proved he could lead men against great odds and still win victories. At this point he was by no means the leader of his people in their great island but he did understand they were confronted with a ruthless, avaricious enemy whose only wishes were Indian land and extermination of his people. He, like all free people in his world, must remain strong and alert or face annihilation.

Episode 5: Red and Spybuck

Laulewasika gathered the herbs as Spybuck directed. "In time I will teach you the use of all," commented Spybuck. "Let us return to the wegiwa and set the herbs to dry. Remember, you are not to discuss this knowledge with anyone. That is the first condition of your apprenticeship."

"Yes, understood and agreed," said Laulewasika who was now a young man and looked it. "By the way, Tecumseh wants me to communicate his regards. He will come to see you one of these days."

"Tecumseh, ah it is good he has returned," said Spybuck. "Perhaps the woman and I will visit next time we are in the village. It will make my heart glad to see my young friend."

Laulewasika wanted to talk about the woman but he realized it was not his place to question. She bothered him, somehow, he did not know why. Perhaps it was she was Shemanese. But Nehaaeemo had married the trader Ironsides and the Scotchman did not...concern him.

When the two arrived at Spybuck's wegiwa the juggler fetched a skin on which the herbs were spread to dry. "Return tomorrow," said Spybuck, "I have an assignment for you."

"Yes, of course," replied Laulewasika. "Until tomorrow."

Spybuck entered the cabin to find Red hiding right next to the door. "Boo!" she said, then she threw her arms around the man's neck and kissed him passionately on the lips, an act Spybuck had readily taken to under her tutelage. "You did not say you would be gone all day," Red whispered in English. Spybuck understood the words *you* and *day*.

"I have missed you," the man said in Shawnee, for Red had made a serious effort to learn the laguage. "Let us have a light supper for we must go to the forest ring tonight."

Red understood *supper, forest,* and *tonight,* so she quickly put some meat on the fire and served Spybuck his tea. Her behavior was a puzzlement to herself periodically for she had never in her life cared about men. Now that her life had taken the most drastic change imaginable, a captive among savages, she had encountered a measure of happiness. She would return to civilization at the first opportunity, of course, but her sojourn in the woods had not been the certain misery and cruel death she had been taught to expect. Was it Spybuck, her savage gentleman? She smiled inwardly at the irony of the thought. Or was it basically that she loved the forest and had been fortunate not to be hurt? Up to now all men had been dull and boring. But this savage wizard was...interesting, fascinating at times. Perhaps it wasn't Spybuck himself. Maybe it was how everyone feared his powers, whatever they were.

The Indians were so superstitious. He earned a good living, you had to say that for him and Red guessed he knew his medicine quite well. As a little girl she had been enthralled by stories of ghosts and witches. Since then her interest had always been piqued by the supernatural, though she didn't really believe in it. But she had learned her white neighbors really did. The idea struck her perhaps they were just as superstitious as the Indians!

"More drink," said Spybuck. "Is the meat ready?"

Red understood *drink* and *meat.* She gave him more tea and turned the meat as the man relaxed on the sleeping robe, watching the woman pleasantly. Red had been with Spybuck for going on three years. Had it been that long?! Christ! She wondered what had happened in civilization during her absence. By most standards she was a wealthy woman for she still had the greater portion of her gold doubloons. When she returned she would buy...what, a farm? And milk cows the rest of her life? No thank you. Perhaps a house of her own, with women working for her. But she would have to build up a clientele again. The thought of having to take on all comers turned her stomach. But then maybe she could go into some other business. A dress shop perhaps. She had always had an eye for clothes. The meat was ready so she served it to Spybuck, then lay down beside him, her hand supporting her head.

"Will you not eat?" asked Spybuck in Shawnee. Red shook her head slightly. She would not allow herself to get fat and ugly.

"How's my dickey-dope?" Red asked Spybuck, knowing he understood nothing of what she said. It was one of her favorite pastimes, perhaps an innocuous way of combating her captivity at the expense of her captor. "Say it: dickey-dope," instructed Red.

"Dickey-dope," repeated Spybuck dutifully. "You," he added as he laughed.

Was he on to her little game? No, he couldn't possibly understand. Darn him anyway. He always did something to keep her guessing. "Dickey-dope *you*," she said as she put her hand on his breechclout. Almost immediately his bod began to swell under her touch.

"You like, hey?" asked Spybuck for he also had tried to learn some English.

Red didn't answer for she wanted the man to finish his meal. Men were so alike. But then this savage had a few wrinkles she had never noticed in anyone else. Was he really a wizard? The idea intrigued her but she had never seen him perform anything magical, white or black. As a child she had been fascinated by witch stories but then her mind seemed to go blank on them for she heard none after age 12 or 13. Upon entering puberty she was taken over with other interests.

Spybuck finished his light meal and began to gather certain items. Red deduced he was going to conduct some sort of ceremony as he had so often in the past. Perhaps he had someone in the healing cabin. "Let us go bathe in order to purify ourselves this evening," said Spybuck in Shawnee. Red understood *bathe* and *evening* so she gathered a robe with which to cover herself and followed the man to the stream. The water was cold, goose bumps rising on her skin, but the washing was over quickly and the man and woman huddled together, the robe around them.

Spybuck held her close, rubbing her back and being titillated by her breasts and thighs. At first her scent had not been gratifying. She had the scent of hair about her but now either he no longer noticed or had gotten accustomed to it. Red took a little nip from his pectoral muscle and soon his bod began to rise in quest of warmth. Spybuck had been dead wrong about the Shemanese not being passionate. This woman was passion incarnate. He was almost ashamed of the fact that he had been with no other woman since he had taken Red captive. He thought he must be slowing down but he did not feel dissatisfaction. "Tonight you will see the powers of Spybuck," he said to the woman as he held her, her breasts titillating him with hard nipples which would not relax until his tongue softened them to normalcy. "Let us return to the wegiwa and prepare." He took each breast in his mouth for a few moments. "Come, the evening is spreading its dark wings about us."

Red was reluctant to halt her mounting passion but she did not communicate the slight irritation to Spybuck. After all, she was no child. She walked back to the cabin, dried herself off briskly, danced sensuously in front of Spybuck just to tease him, casting away his proffered embraces as he took the bait. So he went to a rawhide bag and pulled out the new outfit he wanted her to wear this evening. It was a gorgeous, red doeskin dress that buttoned down the front, replete with quills, shells, and brilliant beadwork. "Oh!" exclaimed Red as she stopped her teasing dance, utterly taken with the garment's beauty.

"You will wear this for the ceremony," said the juggler nonchalantly. Red had been in the company of men most of her life, attending the most fashionable events in cities where she had lived, but no costume previous to this had ever been more beautiful or created with more craftmanship. Spybuck looked at her disinterestedly but he realized the garment had made its desired impression. When Red noticed him she feigned only slight approval but it was too late to hide her happiness.

"What are you going to wear?" she asked, putting *you* and *wear* into Shawnee.

Spybuck pulled out a beautiful red blanket which had been decorated along the lines of the dress. It was every bit as beautiful as the dress and Red wished they were going to some fantastic social affair somewhere. They would have been the object of everyone's attention!

The two dressed at a leisurely pace and when they were ready to leave Spybuck lit the torch prepared for the walk through the forest. The wings of night shuddered as stardust fell, illuminating lost trails of imagination along with the torchlight which was more than sufficient to make their way through the silent woods, Red carrying a sack of items as instructed by Spybuck. After half an hour the two came to a circular clearing in the forest. Red looked at the place, a perfect circle made by nature for there was no evidence trees had been cut where grass now grew. Spybuck walked around the circle three times, the torch illuminating where he walked but darkening the furthest side in an eerie way. Red felt an evanescent fright but quickly imprisoned her emotions. Spybuck produced some wood with which to build a small fire in the exact center of the circle, lit it with the torch, then put out the torch by smothering it on the ground. He put a circle of rawhide for Red to sit on the ground, one for himself on the opposite side of the fire, motioning for the woman to be seated. He pulled a ceremonial pipe out of the bag, sat down, lit the pipe and puffed at it, raised it toward the heavens then passed it across the small flames to Red, who puffed at it several times and returned it to Spybuck.

Within a few minutes Red was feeling a bit dizzy, very aware of the fire, pipe, and Spybuck. The man began to sing a soothing melody as Red smoked again. She peered into the fire and to her astonishment saw a face looking up at her. She blinked but it did not go away. Spybuck took the pipe from her, stood up, placed the calumet where he had been sitting, and did a simple little dance, his magnificent blanket giving him the appearance of some majestic bird whose kingdom was the eternal heavens.

"You must not be seen with that old hag again!" shrilled her mother's voice. Red turned with a startled gesture. How could it possibly be the voice of her mother?!

"Tell me about that Mr. William, Grams. It was Red's own voice as a little girl!

"Aye, that William Gruff was a bad'un, he was." Now it was the voice of the wrinkled old lady she called Grams. Spybuck approached the fire, waved his hands over it and the flames grew brighter. Red saw herself in the flames, along with Grams. *"He had a pact with the devil, he did. An unfriendly man, hardly anyone talked to him. His only interest was money and gettin' rich. He thought I was a witch, he did!"* The old woman cackled a laugh. *"One night William got the idea of raising the devil in order to ask his help in gettin' more gold. He mixed all kinds of brews in his iron cauldron and chanted magic words over it. But nothing happened until he found a letter on the floor of his kitchen. It said the missing ingredient was human blood! If he would follow directions and add the blood of a murderer he would be successful in his devil raising spell. Finally the letter told him to go to the forest ring at exactly midnight.*

"The next night the moon was full and no creature was about. Bill felt compelled to leave his cabin and walk through the forest, which he did until he arrived at a circular clearing: this must be the forest ring of the letter! *he thought to himself. He looked for the devil and his fiends but there was nothing but grass, moonlight, and dark trees. He walked around the circle and noticed a stump. By it was a gun and a letter. He picked up both, opened the letter and found the name JACK REEFER, written in large red letters that seemed to be bleeding. So it was Reefer to be the victim, eh? Good! William returned to his cabin*

147

and the next morning started searchin' for Jack. He found him in the next town, watched him for a couple of days, then shot him at midnight in his bed. He loaded the carcass on a horse, covering it up expertly, and brought it back to his cabin. For three nights he poured Reefer's blood into the cauldron and on the third night a tremendous storm blew up and in a horrible flash of lightning the Devil appeared right out of the cauldron!

"William Gruff was terrified as he saw the demon from hellfire but the Devil took him by the arm and said 'I will give you all the money you ever wanted for the next ten years. At the end of that time you will be mine in the ring of the forest.' William was no longer frightened. Ten years? He could travel to the ends of the earth by then 'Okay,' said he, 'but I must never run out of money no matter what.'

'Agreed,' said the Devil and with a claw-like finger he made his mark on William's forehead. Then the demon disappeared without a trace. William found himself standing by his cauldron but now it was loaded with gold, pure gold!

"William Gruff moved out of town and travelled all over the world, wearing the finest clothes, drinking and gambling to his heart's content, buying anything that took his fancy, sometimes doing his utmost to spend every last gold piece but he couldn't. At the end of the ten years he was thousands of miles away on the other side of the earth but as his time drew near the Devil's mark on his forehead grew brighter and even began to bleed slightly. On the final night he felt himself floating in the air, back to the forest ring, back to damnation. At exactly midnight he found himself in the center of the ring surrounded by a circle of demons. A storm raged and when lightning split the sky the great Devil himself stood at Bill's side, the mark on Bill's face bleeding out of control. The ring became nothing but fire, the very earth opening up into the pit of hellfire as William Gruff screamed hideously. The next day the sun rose on a calm day to find William Gruff, lying in the middle of the forest ring, stonecold dead!"

Red shuddered with fear and fascination. Yet another figure appeared in the fire.

"What did the witch tell you about?" asked a bearded man from behind the table. The room was dark and young Red was frightened. Her clothes were too tight, her precocious body straining at them. "How could a nice little girl like you spend time with a witch?"

"Grams is not a witch, she is just an old lady," Red heard herself saying in a girl's voice.

"Are you a witch?"

"No sir."

148

"Do you know what happens to witches?" asked the man. "Do you read your Bible? It says, 'Thous shalt not suffer a witch to live.' My but it is warm in this room." The man removed his coat and unbuttoned his shirt a bit, hair becoming apparent under the garment. "Come over here and sit by me so we can straighten out this mess. You are a nice little girl, not a witch, but that wrinkled old lady will hang for her crimes. Come here."

Red timidly walked around the table.

"That's it, now sit on my lap and tell me you are not a daughter of witches."

"No sir, I am not a witch sir."

"Good, I knew it." The man put her on his lap, one arm around her, the other hand caressing her thigh gently, caressing higher and higher until it got to her groin. "You could not be a witch. You don't want to be hung by the neck now do you?"

"No sir," replied Red, "I never—" The man fondled her entire body and the girl began to shiver in fright compounded by confusion.

"There, that's a good girl. I'll report that everything is fine, no devil's possession here." Then the hairy man undid his pants and pressed himself at the girl's groin. The pressure didn't last long for Red felt a stickiness all over the area right through her underclothes. The man covered himself up quickly, pulled out a handkerchief and wiped at the girl. "Now say nothing of this and I will make a good report about you. You need not worry again, so long as you are silent. Just tell everyone the man said everything was going to be all right, that you answered all the questions properly. Is that clear?"

"Yes sir," answered Red, not as frightened anymore. This hairy man was like the boys at school! "Good day, sir."

Red laughed out loud, her mirth rising to the heavens as she titlted her head up and fell unto her back from her sitting position. When the ludicrous remembrance faded she lay there and saw a gorgeous sight: an angel stood at her feet, wings outspread, a beautiful smile on his face. The heavenly creature lifted her easily into his arm-like wings and Red caught his scent: corn. What a wonderful scent for an angel to have! She felt herself floating in the night breeze, high into the heavens, the ring in the forest diminishing into a tiny, illuminated dot. She became frightened and hung on tightly to the angel so as not to fall out of his arms. The celestial creature must have felt her fear because the sky ride ended with a smooth dive back into the forest ring. Red was relaxed now but she did not wish the angel to leave so she held him by an ankle. She looked up and saw his wings moving rhythmically as if trying to stay afloat in the air. She must keep him from forsaking her! But how?! She grabbed a wing, the feathers feeling like a blanket of green corn plumes. In the distance Red heard Indian drums, a flute, a gourd rattle. She looked at her angel's face: it was the color of earth, the beautiful, rich fruitful earth. She wanted to kiss the face but could not pull it down to her no matter how she struggled. Red decided to stand up, did so, pressing herself against the angel as she rose. Her movement caused the being to shed his celestial trappings and take on a richly colored human skin, very erotic to the touch. She felt the angel undressing her slowly, her carnality peaking expectantly. She wanted to speak but was unable to produce the words because the angel ran his tongue along her shoulder to the base of her head, making her thighs tingle and vibrate. Her breasts became ever so firm, the buds craving tongues of angels to alleviate the ecstatic torment of desire. She rubbed the soles of her feet on a cloud as the angel's tongue made its way down her spine. When it was slightly below her waist she pulled the angel's head to her lower abdomen and struggled to raise it to her breasts. It came up slowly then Red felt a warmth pressing between her thighs. She looked and saw the angel's brown muscular leg. But where was the angel's bod? Didn't angels...oh yes, there it was, flashing as it captured a ray of light straying across the universe. Her angel was complete and now he must charge her with his celestial life force in order to create a new race of demigods! She lay down on a tepid, furry cloud and watched the angel follow her with passionate deliberation, her pulsating body aware of the slightest movement above her. The angel shed its regal robes, bent over and took both buds in his mouth, relaxing each until he covered her with his entire being, his lips kissing her ear while his passion slowly became one with hers.

"*Keesh-arthwau Sho-ataa Ke-tar-kee-kee-ree:* Flaming Eagle of Delight," said Spybuck in the woman's ear over and over for such was the name her captor was giving her this evening. "You are the Flame of the Universe, the essence of Life Force. Together we are all."

Flaming Eagle of Delight heard the angel talking to her as he feel *everything* within, from her ankles to her forehead, throb with ecstasy, building, building, building to a crescendo of oneness with eternity! She rested a few moments then opened her eyes to see a vaguely familiar face above her, she wasn't quite sure whose. But her passion wasn't fully spent and her abdomen undulated rythmically and forcefully, her arms gripping the shoulders connected to the face now above, then at her ear, her neck, shoulder, breast, back to her ear and the soft murmur of "Flaming Eagle of Delight," until once more she began to climb the vault of the sky in quest of the Gates of Paradise which would swing open at her touch. There, there was the path, over that mound, and see the beautiful roses! She had never seen such petals before! And they felt so good on her body as they covered her, caressed her, scented her very soul! The light, there was the light getting bigger and bigger, stronger, blinding her until she closed her eyes and became engulfed by the powers of goodness! Flaming Eagle of Delight was so overwhelmed she cried deliriously until she relaxed and slept.

The following morning the sun peeped into the ring in the forest and found two human beings wrapped in each others arms, covered in comfortable blankets, sleeping contentedly as if the universe held not a care.

Episode 6: Greathouse

Taumee watched the party of Longknives as their boat touched the shore on the northern side. The gobbling of turkeys continued emanating from the woods and three of the men, rifles in hand, stepped off the boat and headed toward the birds. Another man on board, perhaps the leader, said something to them but Taumee did not understand much English so he disregarded the comment, as the three Shemanese appeared to do. "As soon as you hear the rifles, charge the boat," he said to his men, his instructions spreading quickly to his warriors, more than a hundred in all.

In a short while a volley of musket fire rang out and an avalanche of warcries filled the woods and shore as the warriors dashed toward the boat. The suddenness of the attack, its stark contrast from placid seconds before, momentarily froze the Shemanese on the boat, but then everyone sprang to defend themselves. A blazing volley wasted a number of them and drove the others for cover. The fleetest warriors jumped through the shallow water and made it on board while others secured the mooring chain. A short hand-to-hand combat ensued but the Indians greatly outnumbered the Shemanese, who were quickly made captive and pushed onto dry land.

Taumee counted the prisoners: four men, three women, six children. The boat was loaded with their belongings, rich booty, he hoped.

"Greathouse, Greathouse!' yelled Keetutaa, the oldest member of Taumee's warparty.

GREATHOUSE! The vile war criminal?! The murderer of Chief Logan's entire family! The beast was there, standing before the throng of Shawnee warriors.

"Jacob," said a woman, apparently his wife, "why are they saying our name like that?"

"I don't know honey, just leave things to me," said Jacob Greathouse. "My Shawnee brothers," he said, "nethathar, neethathar."

The Indians were in no mood for hypocrisy. Taumee walked up to Greathouse and struck him with a ramrod across the face. The big man fell to the ground then was struck repeatedly by a dozen warriors. Other Shemanese in the group were now cuffed and kicked about.

"Jacob!" screamed Greathouse's wife between blows. But there was nothing anyone could do.

"Tie them to the trees!" said Keetutaa as he cut a switch. The warriors became a mob and swept the Shemanese to the trees where each was tied securely around the wrists then, with upraised arms, secured to individual trees. Their clothes were cut from their backs and warriors took turns whipping them with switches which were soon dripping with blood. The women and children screamed in frightful pain.

"Let the children be," said Taumee.

"NO!" answered Ketutaa. "This murderer had no compassion whatsoever for the Mingo children. And Logan's sister, big with child, had the unborn cut out of her after they stretched her between two trees! All must die or I shall die this day!" challenged the old warrior in a frenzy of blood-thirsty revenge. The warriors voiced their approval, sealing the fate of all the Shemanese. The murder of Logan's family had long been a festering sore on every Indian's psyche and nothing could save Greathouse and his cohorts this day.

"It is well deserved," conceded Taumee, "and I will see to Greathouse and his wife in my own way," he said in ominous tones.

All the captives were whipped until they bled to death, except for Greathouse and his wife who were cut down before they became unconscious. They watched their companions die in great pain, saw them all scalped, even the youngest of the children.

"Have mercy!" said the Greathouse woman but her pleas went unheeded.

"We showed Daniel Boone mercy but you found none in your heart for the children at Ghnadenhutten!" replied one warrior in vehement Shawnee.

"Your husband has condemned you!" said another.

The two were taken to individual saplings, pushed against them roughly then dozens of avenging hands ripped every last shred of clothing from their bodies. The Greathouses stood stark naked, the woman crying softly.

"Put them on the ground and hold them tightly," said Taumee. The two were knocked to the ground and forced to lay face up. Taumee slashed an incision in Jacob Greathouse's lower abdomen then did the same with the woman, who screamed in pain. Both were taken to individual saplings, as Ketutaa approached Greathouse with his knife in hand. Taumee's slash had not been deep enough so while the murderer was held in his standing position Ketutaa's knife went through skin, muscle, fat, and finally the membrane of the intestine. Ketutaa cut the intestine, Greathouse screaming for the first time, and pulled it out slowly until there was enough to put around the sapling and lash it with rawhide. Then he went to the woman and did the same amid her intermittent screams.

"Jacob, WHY?!" she wailed in agony.

"Vermin, devils, fiends!" said Greathouse.

The woman didn't understand Shawnee and if any of the warriors understood enough English to explain none bothered to. It was obvious she had never been apprised of her husband's cruelties to the Indians, their women and children. She was now forced to walk around the sapling, her husband watching all the while, her insides literally wrapping themselves around the tree. The agony made her stop but prodding knives forced her to move again until finally with the small intestine completely outside her body, she died.

Now all the warriors turned their attention to the heinous Jacob Greathouse! What stupidity he possessed ever to set foot near Indian country again! He was prodded with knives and the small intestine came out snake-like from his abdomen, wrapping itself around the sapling. He made no sound, as if hypnotized by his guts as they unravelled before him. Now his large intestine began to show and blood vessels began to pop off and bleed profusely. "May you rot in hell forever!" hissed Jacob Greathouse as he paled beyond description. The ascending colon came out, then the transverse.

"You die for your crimes!" said an exultant Ketutaa. "Murderers! You are all murderers without a trace of human dignity and *you* are the worst. You make beasts of us all!"

Greathouse fell, emptying himself in the bloody process, death giving him mercy, deserved or undeserved.

"Let's get some fires started!' yelled one warrior. "They will all burn!" Wood was quickly gathered and placed around all the dead Shemanese. A spark was set to each pile and when there were coals the cavities of the Greathouses were filled with them. The warriors watched the corpses burn and when the stench was high they departed. Unlike the People of the Eagle in similar circumstances, the victims' genitalia had not been targets for torture or ridicule.

Episode7: The third invasion.

Little Turtle walked alongside his adopted son in silence. The conqueror of Harmar and St. Clair showed no signs of curiosity but then William Wells had not expected any from his foster father. When the two came to a secluded spot on the banks of the Maumee River the younger man said, "My father, we have long been friends and it has been my most cherished wish that we continue always. But our last fight against the Longknives jolted me into awareness of who and what I am."

Little Turtle looked at his son. There was no fire in the chieftain's piercing black eyes. He was not tall but he was brawny and well proportioned, his face expressive of a shrewd mind. "My son has fought well. Our nation sings your praises."

"It is my misfortune I was born to another nation of people," said Wells quietly. "I lie awake at night wondering if I have spilt the blood of my kin from Kentucky. I can no longer fight the Longknives for fear of killing my blood brothers and cousins. I say this: we are friends until sundown. When the sun touches the horizon we are enimies. You may take me prisoner now if you wish. You may have me killed if that is your desire. But I can no longer fight for the Miami nation. I am prepared to strike out immediately. Know that if you do not kill me I will join General Wayne's army."

Little Turtle smiled softly. "You have been my son all these years. I could not kill you this day or ever. But neither do I want you to go over to the enemy and fight against us. Have you not lived well with me?"

"Yes," said Wells, "you have been a good father to me and I would do everything in my power to keep you from harm. Neither can I wish to continue killng my blood relatives. I and those like me have been victimized because we have allegiances on both sides of the Ohio. It was not my choice to be brought here and yet I have learned to love you as a father. This is our last day together. The war has made us enemies."

"Why must you go immediately? Let us return to the village and I will give you a horse that you may travel more securely."

"No. The people would say you were aiding the Longknives," said Wells. "This way they cannot blame you. I just wanted to tell you my heart so you would not worry and grieve."

"A father's path is one of constant concern," said Little Turtle. "I cannot say you have made me happy with your decision."

"I am anything but happy," observed Wells. He put down his rifle and embraced Little Turtle. "I do what I must."

"Then go in moccassins of the eagle. I pray we shall never meet in combat for I know how well I have taught my son."

"Michikinikwa, my father, has no fear of any man, least of all his son." William Wells picked up his rifle and was quickly out of sight.

The chief of the Miami nation was heartsick with his son's decision. But his mind could understand what the young man said, even if his heart did not choose to. Little Turtle's mother was a Mohican and even though his father was a chief there were many who asserted Michikinikwa was a Mohican, since ancestry was traced matrilineally, and not eligible for chieftainship among the Miami. But the bold, wily Little Turtle proved himself many times over and when the time came he was elected chief. As he walked back to the village, very dejected over his adopted son's departure, the chief meditated deeply over recent events. He had lain in his cabin at night, listening to the wind and it whispered grave tidings. The Longknives had been turned back twice but they were coming again under a new chief who was aptly named the Blacksnake because he took his time in all he did. His scouts reported every move of the new invading army but no where had Little Turtle been able to discover some flaw through which to attack. Now his own son had gone to join the invaders! It must be an ill omen! Perhaps he should counsel peace? The nations were still flushed with their previous victories. How would they countenance a suggestion for working out a peace treaty? Or could the invaders be stopped a third time? Little Turtle fully understood that one major Indian loss would destroy the confederacy among the Northwest tribes. Then it would be peace on terms dictated by the Longknives. They would take the land, *all of it.* They would kill or drive away all the game. They would rip up the earth with their ploughs. All this was apparent to Little Turtle but what would happen to the people? This would be worst of all!

Perhaps he should counsel peace. It would require much courage but the worst that could happen was that his motion would not carry and the invader would have to be engaged in battle. As always the tribes would be outnumbered but they were fighting on home ground, with patriotic fervor. Perhaps they could win again... but this was tempting the fates. No one was victorious forever. And would the Longknives send yet another army if this one was defeated? If the tribes had suffered the carnage of the St. Clair battle it would have been most difficult to raise another army. How could the Longknives do it, apparently so easily? Yes, perhaps it would be better to make peace overtures to the Blacksnake before he coiled irrevocably.

Little Turtle sent out runners to the Delaware, Shawnee, Potawatomi, Ottawa, Chippewa, Wyandot and other chiefs to attend a grand council within one moon in order to discuss the Blacksnake and his invading army. They all arrived at Kekionga within the alotted time for all were aware of the imminent danger. Little Turtle opened the conference with the usual leisurely formalities. He gave special recognition to Blue Jacket of the Shawnee, Buckongahelos of the Delaware. After passing around the calumet Little Turtle got up to make the most important oration of his life:

"My brothers and warrior patriots: you have chosen me to lead our forces into battle twice before and I took on the responsibility willingly. Now we face the invader once more. We are apprised of his every move and I must admit the Blacksnake is the most dangerous of the paleface chiefs sent into our country. He takes time to train his men. He has many guns, many cannon, many horses. He puts huge stores of supplies in his war village. We have beaten the enemy every time under separate commanders. We cannot expect the same good fortune always to attend us." The gathered chiefs began to murmur their disapproval and dismay. "The Longknives are now led by a chief who never sleeps," continued Little Turtle, aware of how his listeners were reacting to his comments. "The day and the night are alike to him during the times he has marched on our villages. In spite of the watchfulness of our braves never have we been able to surprise him. Think well of it! There is something whispers to me it would be prudent to listen to offers of peace." Little Turtle's orations were never long winded, always brief and to the point like this one. But the Miami chieftain was totally unprepared for the reaction he received.

"Our brother has grown faint-hearted!"

"How can you imply we should listen to peace when you know we must lose our lands?!"

"Do you tremble like the oak whose roots have been wasted by many rains?"

"My brothers," said Little Turtle as he held a hand in the air, his black eyes piercing but his voice calm, "my forefathers kindled the first fire at Detroit and the Great Spirit charged them not to sell or part with our lands, but to preserve them for our children. Who among you will charge me with breaking this sacred responsibility?"

"We have heard your son has gone over to the Longknives," said Blue Jacket. "Perhaps you no longer wish to fight because of him?"

"My Shawnee brother should realize," retorted Little Turtle, "the voice of caution is not the voice of a coward. One can win wars with his brain, not just his blood."

156

"I know the Longknives," said Blue Jacket, "if we come to them with smooth words now they will consider us defeated. There is no alternative with such people. We must fight."

Little Turtle gave the Shawnee a piercing glance. He had heard stories about Blue Jacket's origin but had never paid them much heed. "I could ask Blue Jacket how he came to know the Longknives so well but that would resolve nothing. My adopted son has ever fought at my side. He will not be there when next we meet the Blacksnake. Life is complicated and we cannot waste time in explanations. I expect the invaders to come out of their winter hibernation and attack us in the spring. My heart is not white and neither is my skin. Whatever the decision of this council I shall abide by it."

For some reason Blue Jacket became noticeably angry. "My words are neither of a coward nor a madman. I do not know how to defend our lands against a covetous people who would have them except by WAR! If we had been able to make a treaty with justice we already would have done so. The Shawnee are my brothers! You nations are my brothers! I have no allegiance anywhere else. I have the greatest respect for our brother Little Turtle of the Miami. If his son is fighting for the Longknives I swear I will kill him as I would any other Shemanese! Only a coward can change allegiance! We will lure the Blacksnake to the post of the British and together we will hack him to pieces. Then with their help we shall drive the Longknives out of our country forever. I have spoken."

The chiefs discussed the issue for several days then reached a decision: the land north of the Ohio will not be given up, the Blacksnake would be engaged in battle as soon as the Snow Warrior retreated into the north country. The supreme commander for the allied tribes: Blue Jacket! Second in command: Buckongahelos of the Delaware. Little Turtle showed not the slightest emotion. True to his word, when he saw what was happening he said, "I shall be with my brothers when the battle cry pierces the air. We are fools to die like rabbits when the hungry wolves hunt them in the cold moon. But I am no coward. I shall die with you."

When the council ended Blue Jacket made quick tracks to his town and sent out word he wanted to see Tecumseh immediately. The young warrior heard of the call, went to see the chief and learned the supreme allied commander wanted him to be Chief of Scouts. "Your are to keep me informed of everything the Blacksnake does," said Blue Jacket to Tecumseh. "Your job will be highly crucial and I can think of no one who can do it better. Collect the men you want to help you. Remember, you are my eyes and ears."

Tecumseh picked an elite corp of scouts and the best horses available. The spring of 1794 came early and the Chief of Scouts orgainzed his men to cover much of the Ohio country along the Belle Riviere, the Beautiful River, though he personally stayed in the area of the Blacksnake's forts. Tecumseh's scouts scrutinized the river and its traffic as it passed between high timbered banks. The trees were alive with turkeys, great birds of an ash-gray color with copper necks. There were also many deer standing watchfully in the woods, nervously eyeing Shemanese flotillas as they sailed by, some of the men taking potshots at them from their barges but never seeing the Indians who observed them.

Tecumseh instructed his scouts to take note of any unusual activities occurring in the Shemanese towns on the northern side of the Ohio as far away as Marietta. At Marietta there were lovely vistas of flower-covered hills, forest glades where bloomed magnolias, spreading honeysuckle that sweetened the air for miles. When the forests thinned there developed a prairie with meadows green in tall grass which afforded more than ample cover for watchful waiting. The river was full of fish, especially white perch. The scouts learned Marietta was a huge supply base. The invaders would not be short of provisions.

The area around Gallipolis was also scouted but the people there were mostly French and therefore not anti-Indian so little time was spent there. Nothing was happening at Limestone so the scouts decided to concentrate on the Fort Washington locale and the regions north of it.

The Indians got as close as they could to the fort but it didn't take long to observe it was a beehive of military activity. War material was everywhere! But it was not filled with soldiers, who must already be further north.

Tecumseh spent his time watching the three forts built in the Indian country: Forts Hamilton, St. Clair, and Jefferson. He reported Hamilton was garrisoned by at least two-hundred soldiers, had four big bastions and kept watch from the cannon platform while men cut hay upon the extensive plain that lay about the structure. He wondered why the forts had not been attacked while they were being built. Now, with the hated cannon ready to rain death on his people, it would be impossible to dislodge them.

Fort St. Clair proved to be chiefly a storage stockade. Fort Jefferson, the furthest north, had been built on flat ground but a nearby range of hills would enable British cannon to destroy it when the time came.

Tecumseh made special note of the fact that very wide roads had been made between these outposts of aggression. It would not be difficult for the Shemanese to move their large vehicles and cannon on those roads. Huge quantities of stores were constantly arriving at Fort Jefferson, the stronghold nearest the Miami and Delaware villages on the Maumee River. Large herds of cows grazed on the prairies north of the fort and garrisons changed periodically. There were sentries everywhere. The Blacksnake did not sleep and Tecumseh and his scouts could not but conclude preparations were being made to push northward. This despite the Shemanese who communicated with neutral Indians about preventing war and signing a permanent peace! What duplicity the Longknives were capable of.

Tecumseh's men reported one afternoon that a company of Shemanese scouts were operating in the country. He learned that William Wells, the erstwhile adopted son of Little Turtle, was part of that group, and Tecumseh's blood boiled for a confrontation with the traitor. He had no way of knowing the leader of the scouts for the Blacksnake was none other than his former foster brother, Shatunte, now Captain Richard Sparks of the 7th United States Infantry. But Tecumseh had to turn his attention to the invading army when laborers began cutting another road into the north. Immediately he sent word to Blue Jacket. Perhaps an attack should be made on the road workers in order to stop the road which facilitated access into Indian land. Word came back to Tecumseh that the Georgia Unaka had launched another unprovoked attack against the Creeks. The war zone might very well spread all the way south.

The Blacksnake moved his army out of the fort. There must have been more than four thousand soldiers! Harmar and St. Clair had groped their way through the forest. This army travelled on a road with artillery and supply trains, spies on either side of the road. Every camp had patrols out at night, log barricades for protection, every move made with safety in mind. A huge encampment was made at a pleasant site on a beautiful peninsula on the banks of a winding creek and surrounded by rich prairie country. The soldiers' huts were guarded by a strong stockade, a wide trench, and a banquette inside the trench. The encampment was called *Greenville* by the Shemanese. Tecumseh felt it could not be successfully attacked. The Blacksnake was not finished yet: he built two more fortifications: Recovery at the scene of St. Clair's defeat, and Defiance further north. Then he waited for the Indians to react.

Tecumseh was eager to battle the invaders. In June of 1794 his scouts reported seeing 300 pack horses loaded with food going to Fort Recovery. He sent word to Blue Jacket and warriors came quickly to attack. The plan was patently simple: ambush from both sides. The pack train was being escorted by ninety riflemen but the Indians had overwhelming numbers as they positioned themselves along the trail. It was crucial for the pack train to progress all the way along the warriors' positions so the patriots were instructed not to fire until Blue Jacket himself took the first shot.

The warriors waited patiently as the riflemen came into view first, then the packers and their horses interspersed with riflemen throughout the convoy. Blue Jacket watched calmly from his position at the end, waiting for the approach of the Shemanese. In time they came into view and when the first rider was almost at point blank range he fired and brought the alien out of the saddle. Muskets blazed from both sides as Shemanese tumbled from horses, many animals being hit as they reared or fled out of control. Tecumseh fired and reloaded as quickly as possible, making every bullet count. The Blacksnake had uncoiled too far this time!

The Shemanese bugler sounded the signal for a full gallop toward Fort Recovery. It was their only chance. Most of the animals wandered off with their packs as the riflemen dashed for safety.

The blazing musketry was heard at the fort and mounted soldiers came out to help, engaging Blue Jacket's contingent first but the overwhelming number of Indians drove them back. When the smoke cleared there were more than twenty Shemanese dead on the ground and at least twice that number must have been wounded at such close range. The attack continued all the way to the fort as the Shemanese cut their way through Indian lines but if the survivors made it to Fort Recovery they were safe. The Indians laid siege to the fort but it was equipped with musket-proof doors and shutters, each fitted with embrasures for small howitzers. It also had a strong, fifteen-foot stockade, sunk deep into the ground, firmly fastened top and bottom. In addition, the land was cleared of trees for a thousand feet around the fort, the timber being used as abatis. The next morning Blue Jacket called off the seige. The real battle for the Northwest would come soon, everyone felt.

News came to Tecumseh that Governor Simcoe of Canada had renovated and garrisoned the old British stronghold called Fort Miamis at the rapids on the Maumee River. Up to now the Indian agent Alexander McKee had used the structure as a place to meet with the Indians and distribute presents. The renovated fort now combined a heavy land battery with powerful earthworks. Attackers would first have to cross a wide abatis, then leap a ditch and climb an elevated parapet before coming to the thick walls of the fort itself. Inside troops would be shielded while they mowed down the Shemanese either by musket volleys or cannon placed on the bastion platforms. It warmed the hearts of the allied tribes to see the British taking martial action. Besides, the fort safeguarded Detroit against attack because, Governor Simcoe reasoned, General Wayne would not be so foolish as to advance to Detroit with Fort Miamis in his rear, threatening his lines of supply and communication.

The entire country was now flying with rumors:

"The British are getting ready to unleash their entire military might against the Fifteen Fires!"

"All the speeches sent by Simcoe are red as blood. All the wampum and feathers are red. The war hatchets are bright red. Even the tobacco has been dyed red."

"The Indian Confederacy is now mustering 2,000 warriors!"

"Greenville itself will be attacked soon!"

The rumors reached Philadelphia for in the last days of June General Anthony Wayne received welcome instructions from Secretary of War Knox which read in part:

"If, in the course of your operations against the Indian enemy, it should become necessary to dislodge the party at the rapids of the Maumee, you are hereby authorized in the name of the President of the United States to do it. But no attempt ought to be made unless it shall promise complete success; An unsuccessful attempt would be attended with pernicious consequences."

General Anthony Wayne, sometimes called "Mad" by his detractors, the "Blacksnake" by his Indian adversaries, gave the order for the Legion of the United States to search out and destroy the enemy. The troops advanced in double column, with dragoons in front, at the rear, and on either flank. Scouts ranged far into the woods in order to prevent ambushes. Within supporting distance in the rear 1500 Kentucky mounted volunteers guarded communication lines. Because of the attack on Fort Recovery surprise was out of the question.

Blue Jacket called on British agents McKee and Caldwell to come through with more aid in keeping his warrior army together. There were not enough provisions to feed the warrior knights of the forest to begin with, and the Mackinac and Lake Indians, headed by the contingents of Chippewa, Wyandot, and Potawatomi were going home because they had acquired scalps and some prisoners. Ammunition was also going to run short. "You are certain the British will fight?" asked Blue Jacket point blank.

"You see me here with you," replied Alexander McKee. "Everything I own is at your disposal, including my life. Let us take all stores of food and give them to the warriors. That should check their exodus for a while."

William Caldwell said little for he had personally recruited volunteers from Detroit and was leading the contingent himself. "I am at your side."

"I put my life in your hands," said Blue Jacket. "I can see your hearts are good. I hope your government is telling all of us the truth. My warriors can not help but wonder why the king has not sent men into the field when the Longknives abuse him daily. My warriors request the king be strong and not neglect us. He must rise upon his feet and help us. He gave us the hatchet during the Revolution and we now return it to him to sharpen for us. The king must rub off the rust from where it has been buried in the leaves of our country. There is no time for delay or we will be undone."

"We will do everything in our power," said Caldwell, hoping the politicians would come through this time.

All three went out to council with the warriors and were fairly successful, being able to keep about 1300 Indians in the place where a tornado had knocked down hundreds of trees, now called Fallen Timbers.

Tecumseh's scouts captured a Longknife on August 17 and took him to Blue Jacket who thereby learned General Wayne would attack the following day. The warriors went into their ritual fasting, as was the custom before battle, but the Longknives did not show on the 18th nor on the 19th. The 20th looked like rain and the famished warriors believed there would be no attack this day either so between four- and five-hundred Indians left Fallen Timbers to ask for food at Fort Miamis four miles down river.

That afternoon Tecumseh and his scouts were the first to glimpse the invaders coming at the warriors at Fallen Timbers. Word was sent immediately to Blue Jacket and Tecumseh took his place with his warrior brothers, including his blood brother Sauwaseekau who was at his side. The mounted invaders were already within range but the Indians allowed them to get closer, closer, until a shot rang out and immediately the tall grass came alive with blazing flashes, throwing the Shemanese back if they had not already been knocked out of the saddle. The riders lashed their horses to the safety of the Legion but the front ranks of soldiers, hearing the blazing muskets, shrieks, and groans of those hit, became confused, broke, and ran.

The warriors reloaded their guns and waited. Soon another group of dragoons approached, huge broadswords shining in the sun, their horses jumping over smaller timbers, ramming their way forward in an effort to clear resistance from the tall grasses. Indian sharpshooters loosed another deadly volley and stopped the charge.

So far the warriors were ahead, the Legion of the United States hardly firing enough shots to do damage at all. The fallen timbers prevented the horse soldiers from being effective. Tecumseh was among those who waited expectantly for the third charge but this time it seemed the entire Shemanese army was descending on the front line, bayonets fixed. Shots rang out but the mass of soldiers just kept coming, forcing the warriors to fall back into the woods, the Shemanese yelling their battle cries all the while.

The warriors kept retreating but Tecumseh and Sauwaseekau set an example of desperate courage, taking a positon in a thicket and putting up a bloody defense. Tecumseh was reluctant to yield an inch though all about him was disaster. In his frenzy he rammed a bullet into his rifle before putting in the powder, making the weapon worthless until he could get it out, impossible during the heat of battle. "OUISCOT-TI!"yelled Tecumseh over and over, trying to inspire his men to throw back the hated enemy. "If I had a gun I would show you how to fight!"

"Here, use this!" said a warrior as he gave him a fowling piece.

Tecumseh used it for the remainder of the battle. More dragoons came into the battle but it was the infantry and their bayonets, backed by accurate fire, that was carrying the day for the encroachers. The main body of warriors was in retreat toward Fort Miamis when Tecumseh and Sauwaseekau spied a small Shemanese group with a field piece. "Let's get the horses!" said Tecumseh, the men around him directing their fire at the gunners, wasting all of them. They charged the position but Sauwaseekau pitched forward, taking a mortal wound. Tecumseh cut the traces, mounted one of them and lead the other away until he heard:

"Sauwaseekau has been hit!"

Tecumseh jumped off the horse and looked until he saw his brother's prostrate body. He knew his older brother was dead before he turned him over, picked him up as best he could, and took him to safety. Was all his family going to be killed defending the homeland?! "YOU SHALL AVENGE THE DEATH OF YOUR SLAUGHTERED BRETHREN!" Tecumseh was not unnerved but his heart was breaking as he secured his brother's body on the captured horse and headed for the refuge of Fort Miamis. The British had cannon and would make the battle something to talk about! *Yes, mother, Puckeshinwa, Cheeseekau, Sauwaseekau, all would be avenged!*

Tecumseh was among the last to arrive at the British fort. Much to his dismay, the gates were locked shut. "Let us in!" he yelled in his powerful voice, the horse that carried Sauwaseekau becoming frightened and rearing slightly.

"They have let no one in!" yelled a warrior from the side. "The British have deserted us! They do not mean to fight the Longknives! You must make your escape on your own."

The news cut through the Indian forces much more effectively than the Shemanese bayonets ever could have. It had all been nothing but RHETORIC! The allied tribes were ready to engage the Shemanese again for the battle at Fallen Timbers had been little more than a skirmish with few, though in the case of Tecumseh, dear, casualties. But if the British locked the gates this proved beyond a doubt the native people of this great island would have to wage a European style war without the aid of European weaponry. Tomahawks would not conquer cannon. Where would the Indians acquire gunpowder? The King of England would not keep his promises! What manner of king was he to break his promises to his red children?!

Major William Campbell, commander at Fort Miamis, sympathized with the redmen but he had his orders: Do nothing to provoke hostilities with General Wayne. He was to open fire only if the Americans tried to take the fort by assault. Blue Jacket had stood at the locked gates and sworn. Little Turtle asked at least to let in the wounded. A young warrior, an aide said his name was Tecumseh, had actually hacked at the gates with his tomahawk. Campbell stood by, unable to succor his allies of just hours before. The treachery rankled even in him for he was a military man but his first duty was to follow orders. He had made certain his men, standing on the wall watching the approach of the Legion of the United States, understood the orders in all clarity.

General Anthony Wayne purposely drew up his triumphant Legion in plain sight of the fort. "Lieutenant Harrison, let us you and I sally out and do some reconnoitering."

"It would be a pleasure," said William Henry Harrison, the general's young aide-de-camp.

The two rode up within pistol shot of the fort, looked around smiling, waved at the defenders within, then Wayne dismounted and, turning his back contemptuously, stooped and got a drink from a spring that bubbled amid the abatis. His men let out a hurrah that filled the countryside! Then Wayne and Harrison just stood there, waving to the maddened garrison within.

Campbell saw one of his captains seize a portfire to set off a gun at the two nonchalant Americans but Campbell raced toward him saying, "Touch that spark and I shall cut you down with my own sword!" He looked at the man, a good soldier. "I know, I would like to blast the bloody bastards myself!" Everything was calm on the wall after that. "Leave it to me," he said as he left the wall to send out a messenger. Campbell wrote out a quick note. "Get the white flag out," he instructed his orderly. "Take this to General Wayne."

"Shall I wait for an answer, sir?" asked the mounted horsemen as the dispatch pouch and white banner were handed to him.

"No, return upon delivery," answered Major Campbell. "Unlock the gates!"

The horse and rider exited and rode toward the two Americans. The Legion let out a tremendous roar when the men saw the white flag. Wayne and Harrison might have captured the British all by themselves!

There now occurred a series of note exchanges:

Campbell wanted to know "in what light I am to view your making such approaches to this garrison?"

Wayne: "If you are entitled to an answer the most full and satisfactory one was announced to you from the muzzles of my small arms."

Campbell: "Should you continue to approach my post in the threatening manner you are at this moment you must be prepared to suffer the consequences."

Wayne: "Neither the fort nor its guns could much impede the progress of the victorious army under my command."

Campbell: "My indispensable duty to my King and country and the honor of my profession will oblige me to have recourse to those measures which thousands of either nation may herafter have cause to regret and which I solemnly appeal to God, I have used my utmost endeavors to avert."

Wayne: "Your fortification is on American soil. I demand that you vacate it immediately and compliance will cause me to allow your men to repair to your own country without harm."

Campbell: "I certainly will not abandon this post."

Despite the bellicose bluster, neither commander wished to begin a new war so a stalemate ensued. Wayne set fire to all the cornfields and prairies within sight of the fort, hoping Campbell would sally out and fight but the British major ignored everything. Wayne camped his men just out of rifle range, stayed for a week hoping Campbell would do something but when he was satisfied the British were going to remain tame he led his men back to Fort Defiance.

There were no warriors to fight so Wayne ordered scorched earth marches on all the villages within striking distance. Cornfields were burned, gardens were totally destroyed, fruit trees were cut, cabins were set to the torch, stores of food were ruined, grass was burned to prevent Indian animals from foraging, even wild game was slaughtered to prevent it from falling into Indian hands. Forest fires were started in efforts to demoralize the Indians into accepting peace. Indeed, it seemed like the end of the world for nothing was left standing, including cabins owned by British traders like Alexander McKee, after the Legion of the United States passed through.

Antoine Lacelle, a French trader and Blue Jacket's brother in law, was found in the vicinity of Fallen Timbers, arrested, and taken to General Wayne himself for interrogation.

"You have aided and abetted the enemy, Monsieur Lacelle," began Wayne," but since you were not a combatant perhaps we can be lenient with you. All I need from you is the truth."

"Oui, monsieur general," replied Lacelle, obviously confused as to why he had been arrested.

"My aide-de-camp Lieutenant Harrison will record your testimony," said Wayne as he nodded to the young lieutenant "Who was the Indian leader at Fallen Timbers?"

"Blue Jacket of the Shawnee, monsieur," replied Lacelle immediately.

"What happened to Little Turtle?"

Lacelle explained how the Turtle had been deposed in council.

"I see," remarked Wayne. "How many warriors did Blue Jacket command?"

"In all there were about 900 warriors but only about 400 or so were in the battle at Fallen Timbers."

"Sir, I asked you for the truth," said Wayne with obvious irritaiton.

"Mon Dieu, monsieur, I speak only the truth."

Wayne motioned for Harrison to stop writing.

"You're a liar! If you do not tell me the truth I shall have you executed as a spy! Now tell me how many casualties the savages had?"

Lacelle did not know what to answer, totally intimidated by Wayne's rage. "Between thirty and forty killed, monsieur general."

"I have had enough of this!" said Wayne. "Lieutenant, put this man in chains and throw him in the stockade until he decides to tell the truth."

Harrison motioned for the Frenchman to walk in front of him. Once outside he communicated General Wayne's orders and shortly Antoine Lacelle was manacled hand and foot with heavy chains. He could barely walk into the makeshift stockade built of logs. As he sat in solitude he wondered why the American general had behaved as he did. Lacelle was a trader and as such he quickly perceived the American had not wanted to hear the information he was relaying. After one night in the stockade he told his guard, "Tell your general I will answer truthfully. I will give him the true facts of the battle."

Wayne got the message but he kept Lacelle in chains for two more days before granting him an audience. When the trader entered Wayne's cabin, still in chains, the general instructed him to sit, poured two glasses of wine, offered one to Lacelle. "Now," said Wayne, "I am told you wanted to speak with me." He nodded to Lt. Harrison to write every word of the man's testimony.

Lacelle took a sip of wine, the chains clanking incongruously. "The Indians had 2,000 warriors at the battle where your men chased them from the field," began the Frenchman. "They left behind around 400 slain, wheech was most unusual for the savages, as you know, mon general, for they perform great feats of courage to withdraw their dead."

Wayne nodded. "Was Little Turtle supreme commander?"

"No monsieur, Blue Jacket had replaced him, though the Turtle was eeen the battle."

"Hmmm. And how many British were fighting with the savages?"

"There were large numbers of Canadian militia, mon general, but I do not know exactly how many. They were led by Caldwell and it was said Simon Girty was there but I did not see him personally."

"Are the savages regrouping for another battle?"

"I do not theenk so, mon general," answered Lacelle. "When the gates were locked against the warriors by the Breetish it caused great demoralization. They had promised to help. They did not and even refused to care for the wounded. Typical Breetish perfidy!"

Wayne began to see perhaps this Frenchman could be used to good advantage. "I believe the British are at bottom of all tragedy in this country. What if I were to send you to speak to the tribes as an emissary for the United States?"

"Well, mon general, I have a wife and cheeldren, I must work."

"Of course, of course. I have the authority to grant you a license for trading. The British will soon be forced to retire from this territory and their traders will perforce go with them. Someone is going to pick up this lucrative trade. Perhaps it could be you, mon ami."

"Mon general, if I can be of service against the Breetish I would be most happy."

"I need some good men who are respected by the tribes," continued

167

Wayne, "to tell them to come in and sign a permanent peace. We must counter British lies and exhortations to make war. The Indians cannot win. War is simply the path to utter destruction and eventual annihilation. Do you agree?"

"Oui, mon general."

"Wonderful!" said Wayne. "Lt. Harrison, go see to it immediately that the chains are struck off this gentleman. Peace is in the horizon for this grand country."

"Mon general," said Lacelle, "I shall daily deliver my prayers to the Great Spirit above to turn the chiefs minds to good works that we may all leeve een happiness once more. They recognize the distress they are een and are ashamed. I geeve my word that I weell carry your message to all tribes of my acquaintance."

Anthony Wayne remained in his cabin, pleased events were going so well. He would make his report to Secretary Knox, using Lacelle's testimony as a basis. St. Clair's defeat had been avenged! He would have all the tribes sign a permanent peace but not until the spring. He would let them fully realize over the winter what kind of a predicament they were in. By spring even the most hostile elements would come in and sign a treaty. He would send his messages through men like Antoine Lacelle and Isaac Williams. The tribes would see how they had been misled by the British through men like Alexander McKee, Mathew Elliott, and William Caldwell. He offered peace and magnanimous treatment, burying the hatchet forever.

A Wyandot delegation came in to see General Wayne in November. He told them: "I hope and trust your eyes are now opened, and you will no longer suffer yourselves to be imposed on by the bad advice of those interested men who have so often deceived you and betrayed you into error by false promises. They never meant to assist you in fighting against the Fifteen Fires of the United States. How could they help you when a few short years ago we threw *them* on their backs? The British had neither the power nor the inclination to protect you. You have dearly experienced the truth of what I say, have you not?"

The Wyandot delegation replied the tribes sought only justice. They knew they had been deserted by they also realized the Longknives always demanded land as the price of peace.

"What will become of us?" people asked each other. Their only choice was to go to Greenville in the spring and work for as favorable a treaty as possible.

There was great hunger in the Ohio country that winter. Stores had been destroyed by the Longknives and game animals had fled before such a large concentration of people. Even the Longknives ran short of food and when supplies became scarce they wished they had captured corn and other foodstuffs instead of destroying them.

Episode 8: Treaty of Greenville

Tribal representatives began assembling at Greenville in June of 1795. By the looks of things it would be the grandest meeting ever held in the Northwest and it was certainly the most important council the United States had ever held with the Indians. All important chiefs and warriors would be there, except one: Tecumseh. He maintained he would not approve of anything that gave the Longknives land north of the Ohio. So he refused to attend the council and went with some of his friends to live on Buck Creek.

Representatives from eleven tribes were in attendance, however, totaling 1130 Indians from the Wyandot, Shawnee, Delaware, Chippewa, Ottawa, Potwwatomi, Miami, Wea, Piankeshaw, Kickapoo, and Kaskaskia. Wayne's officers wore resplendant uniforms but they were no comparison to the costumes of the various Indian representatives. General Wayne lit the council fire, welcomed the Indians in a short address, then delivered to each tribe a string of white wampum, emblematic of peace, then the council fire was "raked up" and the preliminary session was adjourned. Indian councils were long, drawn out affairs for leisure was part of aboriginal protocol. The next day Te-ta-boksn-ke of the Delaware replied to Wayne's speech of welcome and the council was again adjourned until the following day.

There were numerous chiefs and each had the right to speak so preliminary negotiations continued into July. The Delaware delegation reviewed events which led to the Greenville council, the first orator speaking thusly:

"The Ohio River was established as the permanent boundary between the British and the Indian nations during the Treaty of Fort Stanwix in 1768 in a council attended by 3,000 of our people. We people of this great island realize the grass on this earth grows for all but our grandfathers realized the British and French were struggling over control for land, our land. A Delaware chief once told a British emissary 'Why do not you and the French fight your battles on the sea? You come here only to cheat the poor Indians and take their land from them. We have obvious reason to believe you intend to drive us away and settle the country for yourselves. Why else would you come to fight on the land the Great Spirit has given us?' The British answered, 'We do not intend to take the land from you.' We are still hearing the same chant. We have defended ourselves and have spared none in the defense of our home-land. For this we are reviled as savages."

General Wayne did not comment as he listened to the interpreter.

Another chief rose and spoke: "The treaty council at Fort Stanwix left the Delaware and Shawnee very dissatisfied. The Five Nations, our Iroquois brothers, sold the land south of the Ohio to the British, though they did not live there nor hunt on it as did the Delaware and Shawnee. Actual villages were sold, the people having to move out. The Nations had no right to sell away the lands, especially for money which they did not share with the nations involved. The British informed us no white people could settle west of the Allegheny Mountains but they came any-way,men with the sticks and chains, surveying and settling. We defen-ded our land and finally war broke out, Dunmore coming with many young men in 1774. We lost our hunting grounds in Kentucky but land north of the Ohio was still Indian territory."

"During the war between the British and the Americans the tribes were advised to stay neutral at first but soon emissaries were in evey village telling us how the other side winning would be our ruination. The war caused much suffering among the Indians, especially the Delaware and Shawnee. The Moravian Christians, non-combatants one and all, were slaughtered at Gnadenhutten by Col. Williamson. The Shawnee had to leave their Scioto villages because of attacks by Clark, Bowman, and others. We asked the British for aid but none came. Even after the war ended there were soldiers coming from Kentucky to burn our towns. We thought we could live in peace but rumors flew like clouds. We tribes united to repel more invading armies under Harmar and St. Clair. There was always lack of food, trade relations were disrupted, supplies were difficult to secure, and valuable possessions like copper kettles, needles, knives, guns, powder, hatchets, shirts, blankets, and ornaments were always taken from us. All we had was our hunting to keep us alive. Then General Wayne came and we saw ample proof that our British brothers would not help. They can be called brothers no longer."

General Wayne stood up to comment: "I trust my brothers of the beautiful Ohio country now clearly see which people offer them the bright chain of friendship. We, the People of the Eagle, are your only hope for support and understanding. We could have driven you into the sea, for all the British cared! And I now have before me a treaty just signed with the British king wherein he pledges to vacate all the forts he now holds in the Ohio country!" There was an expression of surprise from the assembled Indians. "Yes, here it is in a treaty right before your very eyes. But we will not rely merely on the king's word. We have the Legion of the United States in the country that is rightfully ours. The British bad birds first ceded Indian lands to the United States but then kept their forts on our soil in order to stop us from doing justice for the Indian inhabitants, promoting mischief instead of justice. Yes, all this country south of the great lakes has been given up to America but we People of the Eagle are not lacking a sense of justice. We will not drive you like sheep away from your homes. You will keep your ancestral territories and live side by side with us. Soon we shall get to the work at hand." He waved Jay's Treaty in the air, the Indians expressing signs of shock. Even Wayne thought the inscrutable Indain countenance showed forlorn desperation.

"Brothers," continued Wayne, "I take you all by the hand. Now let me take a few moments to inform you of some measures I have taken for your convenience. I now give you up my exterior redoubts, to accommodate the different nations with council houses. My people are called in from them and you will allot them amongst you, as you may think proper. I take this opportunity also to acquaint you with some customs which we observe: upon firing our evening gun, all our men repair to their quarters. I wish your people to do the same. I know you will understand this measure of security. If you find any of my foolish young men troubling your camps after the signal I would thank you to tie them and escort them to me personally. I wish only to perserve good order and harmony." Wayne was cognizant of what had happened under General Harmar.

"I also want to explain what happened yesterday in order to dispel apprehension. It is a standing rule, in all our armies, upon any alarm or accident whatever, for our soldiers to repair instantly to their posts. When some rifles went off my alert warriors immediatley went to prepare for whatever trouble might have developed. As it turned out, there was no cause for alarm. Remember it is by my personal invitation that you are here and I stand pledged for your safety and security.

"It is also our practice to parade our men, morning and evening, and call every man by name. It is merely routine. And soon, on a festival which we celebrate every 4th of July, there will be some explosions of fireworks. It is part of our celebration with which we celebrate our independence from the British. It will not long delay this good work we are about and you might even enjoy it.

"I have nothing further to mention at this time. We intend to treat you well. The kettle is high. Let us all now go have a little drink. I trust your lodgings are quite comfortable. I will dine with you as numbers permit, first with those nations who came first into camp. Your plates have been heaped high and I want you to be content."

The procedure Wayne followed in his councils with the tribes conformed to the formal, unhurried pattern familiar to the chiefs. Everyone was encouraged to speak his mind frankly and openly. The camp was under extremely tight security and unknown parties, whether Longknife or Indian, were escorted to professed destinations inside Greenville. Men who had been enemies in the border warfare of the past twenty years now walked in the same camp. It was not until mid July that the treaty making got down to serious business. The council fire of the United States was kindled by Wayne in the council house, which stood on ground unstained by human blood. The peace calumet of the Fifteen Fires was then smoked by all, signifying preliminaries were over. Wayne and the Chiefs exchanged strings and belts of wampum to serve as records of friendship and attest to the validity of the statements that were to be made.

General Wayne informed the assembly his demands were no more than what many had already accepted at the Treaty of Ft. Harmar. He told them of the line that had been drawn as a boundary and the various small tracts of land within the remaining Indian country which were to be ceded. For all this, wishing to be fair, the tribes would receive many gifts and annuities. "...as long as rivers flow and grasses grow." Indian prisoners were to be released immediately and white prisoners within ninety days. Ten chiefs would have to remain in Greenville until all white prisoners living in the tribes should be surrendered up, all within 90 days.

The articles of the treaty were carefully interpreted to the various nations assembled. Various speakers, especially from the Delaware, Chippewa, Potawatomi and Wyandot, endorsed the treaty but emphasized they had not received enough payment for the lands which would be given up.

Little Turtle's was the only voice of dissent when he turned upon the other spokesmen in chagrin and said: "I am much surprised to find my brothers differ so much from me on this subject. Your conduct would lead one to suppose the Great Spirit, and your forefathers, have not given you the same charge given to us Miami. On the contrary, you act as if you have been directed to give land to any Longknife who wears a hat as quickly as he asks it of you. I expected this council to speak with one mind and one voice. I am sorry to observe you are unsettled and hasty in your conduct."

This speech began to build resistance to acceptance of the treaty as

172

explained by General Wayne. "Brothers," began one chief, "we have been told the United States want our land in exchange for a large sum of money or goods as was never given since the Shemanese set foot on this Island. Who among you will trade your land for money? There is no comparison between the two. Money to us is of no value and to many unknown. No consideration whatever can induce us to sell the lands on which we acquire sustenance for our women and children. We hope we may be easily removed and peace thereby assured.

"Brothers, we know these settlers are poor, extremely so, or they would never have ventured to live in a country which has been in continual trouble ever since they crossed the Ohio. Divide, therefore, this large sum of money, which you have offered us, among these settlers. Give to each a portion of what you say you would give to us annually, over and above this large sum of money. We are persuaded they would most readily accept it as compensation for the improvements they say they have made on the land. We will then be left in peace and your settlers will have conquered the poverty from which they fled."

Wayne replied it was too late to expel white settlers from their lands. The Legion could not be expelled either, he pointed out, and much treasure had been spent in pacifying the country. He re-read the boundary lines demanded by the United States and advised all to consider the only alternative was further war. The Wyandots, Delawares, and some Shawnees, not including Blue Jacket, asked for more time to consider the boundaries. Mashipinashiwish, the Chippewa chief, was impatient to leave for home and stated the Three Fires were in accord with Wayne's proposals and wanted "No further private council" over the matter. Two Potawatomi chiefs, Sun and New Corn, stated they were ready to sign the treaty right now. Tarhe, the Crane, acknowledged the United States were now masters over the land.

Blue Jacket of the Shawnee was mostly silent throughout the treaty. He was not an orator to begin with and British treachery had been his undoing. Secretly he had resolved to cease fighting forever but the loss of so much land was a heavy price indeed. He gave no major oration during the lengthy council.

As the days wore on Little Turtle made one more last effort to consolidate Indian opposition. Toward the end of July he arose and said, "Listen you chiefs and warriors! I expected to hear such demands for lands ever since we arrived. I have observed some of you are acting hastily. This is business of the greatest consequence to us all. It is an affair to which no one among us can give a final answer. Therefore, I hope we will take time to consider this matter, that we will unite in one opinion, and express it unanimously."

Then Masas got up and addressed General Wayne: "Elder Brother, you have asked who are the true owners of the lands now ceded to the People of the Eagle. I now tell you if any single nation should call itself the owner it is a lie. Our claim to the land is all equal. But our elder brother has conquered it.

"Brothers, let us have done trifling. Let us conclude this great work. Let us sign our names to the treaty as proposed and finish our business so we may continue with our lives.

"Elder Brother, if I can escape the snares of Mckee and his British bad birds I shall ascend as high as the falls of Sault Saint Marie and proclaim the good tidings to all our distant brothers in that region."

General Wayne did not hurry the Indians in any way. He heaped praises on those representatives who were in favor of signing, gave them the best of foods, extra rations of liquor, invited them to eat grand suppers with him and his top officers, even gave them horses. Medals were prized as highly as anything and Wayne distributed them with diplomatic expertise.

Little Turtle saw the battle as lost. Blue Jacket, so ready to council for war, had not done anything to keep the Indians united! What a travesty. Then he began working for his own tribe, as all others seemed to be doing, and got Wayne to believe the Eel River group of Miamis were a distinct tribe of their own, thus getting a double share of payment for his Miami.

On August 3, 1795, the Treaty of Greenville was signed by the leaders of the tribes: Blue Jacket, the Crane, New Corn, Leatherlips, Buckongahelos, Red Pole, Black Hoof, and Little Turtle, among many others. Little Turtle came up to the table the very last, saying to Wayne, "I will be the last to sign and the last to break it."

Blue Jacket appeared content. As he viewed the closing ceremoniers he reflected that only one major warrior had not affixed his name to the document: Tecumseh. His Chief of Scouts had not attended the proceedings. Blue Jacket resolved to go personally and tell him what the treaty stipulated.

General Wayne now acquired another name among the Indians. As his behavior before Fallen Timbers had caused them to describe him as the "Blacksnake" for his premeditation on all matters so now they called him "General Wabang," which meant "Tomorrow," for such was his constant reply when asked by the Indians when the presents were going to be distributed.

The Ohio country had finally been made safe for Shemanese settlers. The tribes now had ninety days in which to release all prisoners, a sign of good faith for which several hostages were kept at Greenville.

Episode 9: Repatriation

The scene at Fort Defiance was described as bedlam by Lt. William Henry Harrison, a personal observer for General Wayne. Hundreds of prisoners and former captives came or were brought in. The event attracted people from all over the border areas, looking for long lost family members. The population of the fort was tremendous during the repatriation period and there were many scenes lived out that would never be forgotten.

Repatriates were first taken to the military barracks where they gave their names, age, information on next of kin, where they had lived at the time of their capture. The adults were cooperative. It was the younger repatriates who caused problems.

One towheaded boy of about twelve or thirteen was brought into the fort bound hands and feet to a strong sapling that was carried at each end by mature Indians. "I will not stay with the Shemanese," screamed the boy in Shawnee as he struggled against his bonds and the sapling. His Indian mother walked at his side, trying to console him, advising him not to hurt himself. But she was weeping all the while.

"I will escape!" yelled the boy. "I will not live with the encroachers, I hate them! They killed my brother! How can you deliver me up like this?!"

"It is the law, my son," said one of the men who labored under the weight of the pole. "We must comply."

"I will not comply!" raged the boy in Shawnee. "You will see me dead before I become a Shemanese!"

"No!" admonished the Indian mother. "Do not even talk like that or I will disown you! Later, when you are older, you can come visit with your Indian family." Tears were flowing from the good woman's eyes. "You can come to your Indian mother... that I may hold you once more... and..." She couldn't continue.

"I have no mother but you," said the boy, calming down because the woman's hurt was obviously to the heart.

The boy was set down. "I am going to cut you loose," said the father. "You must not run away anymore. We have complied with the law and you must not shame us." It was obvious the man was also deeply moved.

Numerous Shemanese gathered around the little group and scrutinized the boy. Perhaps he was the little son lost ten years ago.

Big Cat, a Delaware, walked in quietly with his son of four years, John Brikell. "My beloved son," began the Big Cat, "you are old enough to make a choice. My son, there are the men the same color as yourself. There may be some of your blood kin here," he said as he waved at the crowd, "or they may be a great way off. You have lived with me this long time. I call on you now to say if I have not used you as a father would treat a son."

"It is so, my father," replied the young man.

"You have lived with me. You have hunted with me. But now our treaty says you must be free. If you choose to go with the people of your own color I have no right to say a word. But if you choose to stay with me, these people have no right to speak."

There was a heavy silence. Confusion reigned in Brikell's face and in his emotions.

"You are a good hunter," continued Big Cat as he placed his hands on the young man' shoulders. "You have been better to me than my own sons... I learned to lean on you like a staff. Now they tell me it is broken. You have the right to leave me and I am not to say a word... but I am ruined."

"Father... I have no words..." Tears streamed from young Brikell's eyes. "I must return... my blood kin..."

"Then you are free, my strong son," said Big Cat as he fought the tears. "It is I who am the prisoner... of my heart."

The two men embraced and wept openly.

Harrison moved on to another table where a white Indian was making a statement after being asked why he refused to be repatriated. Through a translator he said: "I do not know in what country I was taken, being extremely young. If I returned I would not know where to go. My attachment for this land is strong. That cord will not be broken. Let me entreat you People of the Eagle to regard us with feelings of kindness and when the hand of oppression rises against us you will be strong in your sense of justice. We ask you for nothing else. My people are dear to me and I could not leave them to wander about your world in search of blood kin. My destiny has been cast with the Chippewa, who insisted I come in alone so that I could make my own decision. If they suffer, so will I, if they prosper, I will rejoice. Let me once again ask you to regard us with feelings of kindness."

When the interpreter finished the Chippewa shook hands with all around him and walked out of Fort Defiance into the wilderness.

Spybuck and Flaming Eagle of Delight sat on their horses at the edge of the forest, looking calmly at the fort. The many hundreds of people all

176

over made it quite a panorama to behold. Both riders appeared calm in preparation for what had to take place, Spybuck's face set in an inscrutable mask.

"Well, shall we go in?" asked Flame in the best Shawnee she could muster.

Spybuck turned his eyes to the woman but said nothing.

"Why do you look at me like that?" inquired Flame. She had her money with her, the horse was her own, as was the pack horse behind her, and there were bags of clothing and blankets carried by two other horses, such was the quantity of so many prized possessions to take with her.

"Can I no longer look at Flame?" asked Spybuck in an expressionless voice.

"You know I didn't mean that," said the woman. "Talk to me."

"What is there to say."

"Well, ah, tell me that you are happy to be rid of me."

"You must make your own decisions," said Spybuck. "I have complied with the law in bringing you."

"The law. Ha!" said Flame. "If you-" but she stopped.

"If I what?"

"Nothing," she said, "come on, let's go."

They rode up to the fort, went into the stockade and dismounted. The two walked toward the scene of greatest commotion, attracting much attention as they strode up to one of the tables. Everyone marvelled at the beauty of the woman, obviously Shemanese but dressed so glamourously in a soft white doeskin dress, the man dressed in buckskin but draped with a beautiful blanket toga. All eyes turned toward them but especially did the Shemanese soldiers rivet their glances on the woman.

An officer came up to Flame where she stood in line and asked her, "May I help you mam? Come right this way with me, if you please."

Flame followed him to a table that was just being set up. The officer sat down behind the table and began asking questions, intending to write down the answers.

"I can write everything down, if you wish," suggested Flame. "Might save you some time."

"No problem, mam," replied the soldier cheerfully. "Out in this wilderness I've had nothing but time." His eyes shined as he continued to talk, bathing in the woman's beauty. "Your name please, and place of birth?"

Flame hesitated. Very few men had ever asked her name and none in the last few years. "Dawn," she said after controlling the temptation to give him her Shawnee name just to see his reaction.

"Dawn," repeated the man, "and your last name?"

"Johnson," she lied, feeling no need to give her surname.

"And where were you taken prisoner?"

"During the St. Clair battle."

"Was your husband killed?'

"I didn't come with a husband."

"I see," commented the man. "Do you have a profession to follow when you get back to civilization?"

Flame wasn't quite certain what he meant and the English came back in a halting manner, something she had not expected.

"I'll probably open some kind of business," she said.

"Who is that Indian over there?" asked the man as he pointed at Spybuck.

"He's the one who took me prisoner," replied Flame.

"Well we'll get rid of him in a hurry," said the man as he glared at Spybuck.

"That won't be necessary," said Flame, "I'll handle him. I don't want to create any problems."

"No problem, mam. Where do you intend to go upon your release?"

"I don't know."

"Cincinnati is a growing little town," said the man. "I'll be going that way pretty soon. You can travel with me, if you've a mind to."

"I don't know," repeated Flame. "Maybe I'll go to Philadelphia or New York."

The officer made some other comment but Flame walked away and returned to where Spybuck was standing. "Well," she said in broken Shawnee, "I guess that's that."

Spybuck continued to look at the man Flame had been talking with then said, "So you are really leaving?"

Flame was surprised. Spybuck had never come out and said he wanted her to stay. "Don't you want me to? I mean, I'm not trying to put words in your mouth."

"It was your decision to come here to be reunited with the Shemanese. I cannot keep you against your will. It is the law. Will you trade our life for some fine house?" Spybuck spoke very unemotionally and this irritated Flame for she was having difficulty deciding what she wanted to do.

"Come on, let's walk," she said, "people are staring."

"Perhaps if you would put on Shemanese clothes they would not stare," observed Spybuck as they began to walk through the crowd.

"What will you do without me?" asked Flame.

Now it was Spybuck's turn to be surprised. But then his eyes twinkled and he said, "Remember you a lot."

Flame laughed out loud, the laughter serving to release her emotions somewhat. "Oh sure, I can just see -" then she stopped when the idea hit her that Spybuck would be with another woman. Her expression became serious, her mood irritable.

"And you," asked Spybuck, "already with that Shemanese you were talking to? I should return home immediately so you can begin your new life."

"I am certain your pretty blanket will be warm soon, knowing you."

"You should talk. All you ever got to know was one part of me."

"That's not true."

"Yes it is," replied Spybuck, irritation creeping into his voice. Perhaps he should take her out into the woods and stab her with his knife. That would settle the issue once and for all.

"Well, are you complaining? Wasn't it good enough? Do you think you'll find better? Tell me!" demanded Flame, anger rising in her voice.

"If you wish to make a scene you must do it by yourself" said Spybuck calmly. "You Shemanese are such savages." He saw Flame was really upset and perhaps the woods were the best way out. "I am leaving this place. Change your clothes and become one with your people." He walked majestically to his horse, mounted, and rode out of the fort, adjusting the knife on his side as he rode.

Red looked for some rock or missle to hurl at him but found nothing. It was not like her to get upset over men. She was accustomed to having them upset over her! That savage! Didn't even know how to play the game! Damn him! She looked at him as he rode out of the gates, not even turning back to look at her. She hurled the worst obscenities she could produce within herself though they never came out of her mouth. She ran to her horse, mounted up and raced after Spybuck, trying to avoid the many people as best she could. Outside the fort she scanned every direction and saw the rider she was looking for, nearly into the woods. She dug her heels into the horse's sides and quickly caught up with her quarry. Spybuck turned calmly toward her as she reined up in a fury and struck his face. The unexpected blow nearly unhorsed the man. He grabbed at the woman as the horses squealed as if in combat. People from the fort turned to see what the ruckus was and a handful of soldiers ran to break up the fight.

Spybuck grabbed Flame and both tumbled off their horses. "Is this what you want?" said Spybuck as he unsheathed his knife and held it ready to strike. "Do you want to end it right here so that I can turn it on myself?"

Both were on their feet and Flame struck and clawed at him. "Yes, go ahead, use it! I dare you!" yelled Flame. She picked up a stick and swung at him, Spybuck dodging it easily and waving the knife wickedly, a snake ready to strike at the first propitious moment.

"Hold it, Injun, or you're dead!" yelled a soldier in English as the two combatants were surrounded.

"Drop the knife!" ordered Flame in Shawnee. Spybuck looked at the men, rifles pointed at him, so he dropped the weapon and began nonchalantly to dust himself off as if nothing had happened.

Flame picked up the knife quickly. "It's all right. Thank you," she said to the soldiers.

"You hurt?" one of them asked. Flame shook her head. "Sure?"

"Yes, let's get back to the fort and let this person continue on his way. It was my fault, I came and started it. Let him go."

"Get on your horse," said a soldier to Spybuck, "and don't let me catch your blanket ass around here again or I'll have your guts for garters!"

Spybuck understood nary a word but the message was clear. He looked at Flame calmly, mounted his horse, and disappeared into the forest.

Flame walked with the soldiers back into the fort. She looked at her hand and became aware it was tightly grasping Spybuck's knife. She turned to see... no, the forest had swallowed him up. She struggled to hold back tears. Good riddance! Maybe she *would* go to Philadelphia after all!

Episode 10: Harrison

Lt. William Henry Harrison finished his duties at Fort Defiance, asked for two weeks leave, had it granted by General Wayne, and went to Cincinnati to attend to a "personal situation." Actually his destination was North Bend, a little settlement sixteen miles west of Cincinnati, the outskirts of the little town where Anna Tuthill Symmes, the dark eyed, sedate daughter of Col. John Cleves Symmes, waited for him. She had already accepted his proposal of marriage. All that was needed was the venerable Colonel's permission. Harrison had met Anna Symmes while on leave at Lexington, Kentucky. The remarkably beautiful girl quickly captured his heart but it was not until later when he visited Ft. Washington on military business and sought out her companionship that he learned his deep attachment was returned. Now he was ready to ask old man Symmes for permission. Judge Symmes was an influential man in the Northwest Territory and his group of business men had bought 1,000,000 acres of land in 1788, years before the area had been made safe from Indians.

Harrison went to see Judge Symmes immediately without talking to Anna. The bronzed Lieutenant, in full military uniform, knocked on the door of the Symmes mansion, waited for a servant to let him in, requested an audience with the Judge, and was kept waiting until the man was ready to see him.

"Good afternoon, sir," began Harrison confidently.

"Ah, yes, Lt. Harrison, what brings you out this way?" asked Judge Symmes. "How is General Wayne these days?"

"He sends his regards, sir, but I wish to have a discussion with you on a most personal matter."

"Fine."

"I have fallen in love with your daughter, sir, and I wish to ask your permission to marry her."

"Well," exclaimed Symmes, "that's coming to the point, I should say. Good. No sense mincing words and wasting time. Time is valuable, you know, like anything else."

"Yessir," agreed Harrison.

"No."

"No?" repeated Harrison.

"No. You do not have my permission to marry Anna. How could you ever take care of her on a lieutenant's pay? What would you live in, a bark hut? Now I know your father was a man of high repute. You come from good stock. But you are not ready to take on a wife until you are financially secure. Now that's the way I look at it.

"But sir, your daughter bears the same feelings-"

"I'm the father here and I must care for my children. Now I must get ready to leave for Cincinnati on business. My answer is no and furthermore I order you to stop seeing my daughter. Now get out."

There was little else Harrison could do so he exited unceremoniously. All right, now it was up to Anna. His own feelings had not changed by Symmes rebuff. He rode out of North Bend but directed his horse to a wooded area where he dismounted and watched road traffic. It was not long until he saw the Judge riding toward Cincinnati. Harrison remounted when the man was safely out of sight and made his way quickly back to the Symmes manison.

"I would like to speak with Miss Anna," said Harrison to the servant who answered the door.

"I am sorry, suh, the Judge has left orders that—"

"Who is it, Frederick?" asked Anna's voice from within. She appeared at the door, a vision of dark-eyed loveliness, her small stature reminding Harrison of a china doll in some exquisite shop window. "Ah, it is you, William dearest." She came up to him and took both his hands in hers.

"I would speak with you, beautiful lady," said Harrison.

"Miss Anna, your father left instructions—"

"Don't trouble yourself, Frederick," said Anna, "I will talk to Daddy. Come in here to the parlor, William."

Frederick shook his head and left them alone. They could face the Judge on their own, he had done his best.

Harrison informed Anna as to what had transpired with her father.

"You poor dear," she said softly, then she kissed him on the lips. "Daddy is so direct sometimes."

"So it now depends on you. I love you totally and completely. If you will share my life, I am ready at this moment."

Anna loved her father dearly but she was of age and had a mind of her own. "If we run off we could be cut off without a penny."

"That would not trouble me in the slightest. God has given me a brain and a body. If He gives me you I will consider it the greatest gift of all."

"Poor Daddy is going to have a fit!" commented Anna. "Do you know Stephen Wood?"

"The Secretary of the Territory? I've heard his name."

"He's one of our tenants. And he's also a justice of the peace. He could marry us today, right this instant if he's home."

"I don't want to rush you or force you into any action you might regret later. But I'll saddle your horse myself if you are ready."

"Let's do it!"

Anna looked as beautiful as any bride when she exchanged vows with William in Stephen Wood's parlor. The couple was extremely joyous as they left his log house as husband and wife on their way to Fort Washington.

Two weeks later Harrison met his father-in-law at a dinner given in honor of General Wayne who was going to Philadelphia. The judge glared at the lieutenant who had eloped with his daughter but the only comment he made was, "Harrison, how do you intend to support my daughter?"

William fingered his scabbard and replied, "My sword is my means of support, sir."

Judge Symmes continued to glare at him throughout the supper.

General Wayne allowed Harrison to stay at Fort Washington instead of requiring him to accompany him to Philadelphia. William was very gratefull, as was Anna. She worked on her father until relations were cordial again.

In time William Henry Harrison was given command of the fort and he purchased 160 acres of land at North Bend. He began to get bored with the inactivity of the peace time Army so he got involved in business and politics. When he was given the post of Territorial Secretary he resigned his commission and threw himself wholeheartedly into politics. When his first son was born he named him after his father-in-law and won total acceptance into the Judge's good graces.

Episode 11: Tecumseh marries.

Tecumseh had been pressured by friends and family to take a wife and start a family. Now that he was living on Buck Creek and peace had been declared the pressure began all over again. Many Indians, some Shawnee but also many from other tribes, joined him and soon a little village sprang up and continued to grow. Word got out that he looked with contempt on the Treaty of Greenville or any document that allowed the Shemanese to ursurp land north of the Ohio. People came to listen to Tecumseh speak on his views and one individual who happened by was a woman named Manete. She was at least ten years older than Tecumseh, very light skinned because her father had been a Frenchman. Manete was deeply attracted to Tecumseh. Perhaps it was the excitment of trying to make the magnificent "catch" for the young warrior was considered the most eligible of bachelors. Manete began by being around him, never pressuring him with any action which would frighten him, engaging him in brief conversation, sometimes asking for minor help with this or that. When he was secure and feeling unthreatened she sent him food. In time he showed his appreciation by seeking out her company. She was no particular beauty and she was not a genius but she was older and the younger man benefited from her experience. Her lack of strong color he overlooked as he became acquainted with the woman and one day Manete confessed, "I love you and wish to marry up with you if that is your desire."

Tecumseh made no reply for a few moments then he looked at the woman and said, "I have been so long on the warpath I know little of love beyond family."

"You and I will be family," said Manete simply.

183

"I guess it is time I took such a step," said Tecumseh. "Perhaps it is the best way to immortality."

Preparations were made and within a short time the simple ceremony was recited:

"My footprints have come to meet the white pathways that lie before you," said Tecumseh.

"Sorrow and lonely pathways lie before us too," cautioned Manete.

"At my back upon the eternal white road will be the sound of your footsteps. I have come to share your soul."

"Then your thoughts are not to wander away. I have come to you. Your soul is to be mine."

"No more loneliness," said Tecumseh.

"Think of me from you soul," finished Manete, "for I am the endless pillar of time, the support of the nation. I am the star that guides men. I am the mother of all dying children. Let us have life together that we may endure as the rivers and the forests."

"I would have you for my wife," concluded Tecumseh.

And that is how the young warrior Tecumseh married Manete. They were happy but in time Manete came to resent Tecumseh's many activities that kept him so busy and away from home so much of the time. She did her best to control her feelings as she tried to understand her young, and increasingly famous, husband.

The village at Buck Creek grew faster than any other village of Indians and Blue Jacket, head chief of the Shawnee nation, sent a messenger to Tecumseh that he would visit within one moon. The great warrior of the Shawnee had promised to keep the peace and occassionally he heard rumors that Tecumseh's band, a composite from various tribes, had vowed to continue the fight against the Shemanese. He wanted to explain personally the articles of the Greenville work and have Tecumseh give him his word he would abide by all stipulations.

When the time came to travel to Buck Creek the older chief climbed on his horse and, followed by a small retinue of warriors, headed for the meeting with the young man people were referring to as "Chief of the Ohio." There could be no doubt Blue Jacket liked Tecumseh. Cheeseekau, Tecumseh's brother, had been Blue Jacket's best friend and companion through his growing years. Puckeshinwa had been like a father to him and because of these close ties Blue Jacket had observed Tecumseh as he grew and matured. There was no jealousy of the new young chief. Quite the contrary, talent and courage as possessed by Tecumseh was highly valued by all Indians. There was no doubt in Blue Jacket's mind Cheeseekau's brother was the outstanding young leader in the Ohio country. Tecumseh's bravery, the way he outwitted Simon Kenton twice, the crusade to the South country and his battles to avenge the death of Cheeseekau, the stern contempt bordering on hatred for the race of encroachers, all these things and many more were well known throughout the Indian villages since they were often the basis for conversation around campfires, especially now that peace had been declared. But the peace had to be kept. The Shawnee people had given their word and it was a point of great pride that a breach of trust was unknown in the tribe.

"Keewaukoomeelaa!" greeted Tecumseh joyfully as Blue Jacket rode up to his cabin. "Welcome, father!"

"It is indeed good to see you in such good health," said the chief after he dismounted and shook hands. "You have an attractive little village here."

"Not very many people, my chief, but it is growing."

"So I have heard."

"Come," said Tecumseh, "let us go in and smoke together." The two entered the cabin, Tecumseh introduced his wife.

"You honor our humble wegiwa with your presence," said Manete.

The two men sat down, Tecumseh lit the pipe, passed it to the older man. "Ah," said Blue Jacket as he relaxed. "You bring back so many good memories for me."

"We are all most happy to have you among us. We are also curious as to the reason for your visit."

"Very simple, my friend," began Blue Jacket. "You were not at the signing of the treaty." Tecumseh's expression hardened just a trifle. "I came to inform you as to its stipulations. I hope you will approve of them."

"Father, I cannot approve the loss of our land."

"Do you approve of peace?"

"Are they one and the same?"

"Yes, unfortunately," admitted Blue Jacket. "You were in the battle, Tecumseh. We lost good men that day, including Sauwaseekau your brother."

"We have not been destroyed," said Tecumseh calmly. "The battle was little more than a skirmish.

"Agreed," said Blue Jacket, "but without the British we have no weapons with which to win a war. Tomahawks cannot challenge cannon. You saw how the British refused to help us. The king cannot be trusted. Are we to die like fish washed up on the shore? Such is our condition without allies."

"My chief, do you believe the Shemanese will ever honor an imaginary line drawn across the flatlands of Ohio?"

"It is the law."

"The Shemanese understand no law beyond their own cupidity. The treaty did not prevent them from crossing the Ohio. It will not stop them from swallowing up the great lakes of our people."

"What you say is true," said Blue Jacket, "up to now. There is nothing else to do but hope both parties will live true to their word."

"There is little doubt about us. I desire that our leaders not shut their eyes when the Shemanese break the treaty."

"Tecumseh, no one knows the Longknives better than I. You are still a young man and many call you 'Chief of the Ohio,' placing their hopes on your shoulders. Their hope could be a great burden. The merciless hawk darting on a sparrow colors significantly when your people are the sparrows. I lead our nation to Fallen Timbers, confident of British help. We were the hawks against Harmar and St. Clair but against Wayne we were not the panthers springing toward the prey. We could have been annihilated! We, all of us, could have been just memories right now. I am the chief of the Shawnee nation. If we had been destroyed as St. Clair was our people would never have been able to stand again! The victors could have done what they wished with our women and children. Think of it. Your people call you 'Chief,' and rely on your judgment. Do not seal their doom, I implore you. It would drive you insane if you lead them all to bloody graves. The tears of the women and children would drown you in a flood of remorse.

"The Longknives sent three armies against us, each larger than the previous one. If we had lost as many people as St. Clair we could never have faced the next army. Even without such losses we could not win without the British. Learning that has been the hardest lesson in my life."

"Then what do you suggest, that we all become pet Indians?" asked Tecumseh.

"You are a chief," admonished Blue Jacket, "you can't allow yourself to be flighty because people will react to your words, whether they are good or vile. Your responsibility must force you to consider what you say, even how you say it. Shemanese are overrunning the country, as is their right under the treaty. I came to tell you what it said. The line runs..." Blue Jacket went over the entire document from memory and Tecumseh, always an excellent student, remembered every detail.

"They will never stick to it," said Tecumseh when Blue Jacket was finished.

"I want your word that you and your people will keep the peace," said Blue Jacket. "If you don't, we will all suffer."

"I cannot wage war. I will not fight so long as I am not attacked. I can pledge the same for my followers."

"I do not know what else to tell you," said Blue Jacket.

"I will keep the armistice as long as the Shemanese do," said Tecumseh. "I still remember how my father was murdered after another treaty was signed. That will not happen to me or my people."

"I understand and sympathize. No one family among our nation has paid more than yours for freedom. Perhaps I am getting old."

"Blue Jacket is the first warrior of the nation," said Tecumseh.

"We must walk the white path of peace. If you walk any other, I or the nation will be unable to help you."

"I understand," was all Tecumseh said. He was on his own and knew it. So be it. "I will never start any difficulties. You have my pledge."

"I accept it. Now I must be on my way," said Blue Jacket as he rose to leave.

Tecumseh walked out with the chief and bid him farewell. He wished he could have said something more pleasant, something to smooth over the waves of differing viewpoints, ideologies. But there was no way. Now that he knew all the specifics of the Greenville treaty he liked it even less. How could the leaders of his people leave hostages with the Shemanese?! This could not be condoned. A new leadership had to be developed. Indians could not be cowed into a degrading peace. Were the chiefs too timid for action?

Episode 12: Chief of the Ohio

The settlement at Buck Creek continued to attract dissidents from many tribes. A Shemanese town, called Urbana, began to grow nearby and Tecumseh made certain his people kept the peace but all were certain he would not stand idly by if the Longknives commited some atrocity against his people. Tecumseh's nature had been molded by contradicting personalities and events as well as the fires of many combats. He accepted leadership as a duty to his people. Decisions came quickly to him without the slightest hesitation. His immediate followers knew him as a generous, warmhearted, compassionate man to his friends. But if his authority was challenged he answered with a touch on the stem of his tomahawk, showing that behind his words was a developed, lithe, powerful body which could employ the cunning of a panther and strike with the venom of a snake. He did not feel compelled to explain his view point or purposes to anyone for no one had to accept him or live in his village if they didn't wish it. It was ample explanation to say, "I am Tecumseh," and let the citizen make up his own mind.

One morning Manete awoke and informed Tecumseh she was with child. Tecumseh was happy with the news, though he had not given much thought to becoming a father.

"Now we shall be immortal," said Manete, who alternated between pleasing and irritating him with nagging when she had to compete for his attention from his many activities.

"Good!" said Tecumseh. "I shall celebrate by making the rounds of my traps. Perhaps I can bring home some good beaver."

"I wish you could celebrate at home a little more often."

"I must do the things I must."

"Am I not a *must?*" asked Manete. "Why did you marry me, to abandon me?"

"Of course not."

"Then stay at home. We have enough meat. I have never seen so much wampum in one house. Why so much activity?"

"A man is a man. I will return shortly." He tried to embrace her but she threw his arms rudely away. "I will return." He left without looking back. Manete was becoming rather shrewish, he felt.

Tecumseh made the round of his traps, the last of which was placed in a stream which ran into Buck Creek. He walked noiselessly and from a distance he could see another Indian was in the process of trying to disconnect the chain in order to steal the trap. There was no mistake, it was an Indian, not a Shemanese. Tecumseh approached silently in order to cause no alarm. Just as the man was taking the trap out of the water he saw Tecumseh surveying him, loaded rifle in hand. Stealing was a heinous offense and the law said Tecumseh could shoot the thief on the spot with perfect justification. The man straightened up, expecting to be executed. This touch of nobility was enough for Tecumseh, who said:

"Don't be alarmed, brother, at my approach. I am come only to present you with this trap, of which I see you stand in greater need than I. You are entirely welcome to it. Here, take this gun also, as I perceive you have none of your own." So saying he delivered his gun and accoutrements, turned his back and headed toward Buck Creek.

The would-be thief did not know what to do, such was his confusion. He knew by all rights he should be lying dead in the mud this very instant. "Father!" he called out to his benefactor. "I am unworthy... of this fine weapon. I would return it to you."

"The rifle is yours," said Tecumseh, "use it well."

"I would be of service to you," exclaimed the man. "What is your name?"

"I am Tecumseh."

"Ah, my Chief of the Beautiful River. Let me live in your village and I shall follow you to the end of my days."

"All brothers are welcome at Buck Creek," said Tecumseh. The two walked to the village where Puckeshinwa and Methoataske's son was so deservedly the chief.

Manete became more difficult during the course of her pregnancy. She sometimes even taunted Tecumseh, telling him he was a little orphan looking for his parents. "And the people call you Chief of the Ohio! If they only knew you!"

"I wish you would not talk that way," said Tecumseh, tolerating her as best he could.

"Then why can't you drop that cold facade, at least in front of me?" pleaded Manete. "Why can't you warm up to me like any normal husband?"

"I have. I do my best to be a good husband. There are many burdens in being a chief. That is why Cheeseekau refused it."

"Yes, I know, you and your famous family!"

When Tecumseh became irritable he would leave the wegiwa. Besides, arguments were not good for a woman in Manete's condition. Perhaps her temperament would improve after the child was born.

Manete was delivered of a boy. He was named Pugeshashenwa. For the naming festival which would take place a group of young hunters came to Tecumseh and challenged him to a hunting contest in order to acquire meat for the entire village.

"A contest?" said Tecumseh as he faced the half dozen young men. "Now you think you can take on your chief, eh? All right, give me the guidelines. Make it easy on yourselves."

"Everyone goes his own way," said Pashaae, "for three days and returns with the skins to prove the kill."

"And the winner?" asked Tecumseh with a glint in his hazel eyes.

"Shall be proclaimed the best hunter in the village."

"Agreed!" said the chief. "When do we start?"

"Dawn tomorrow."

The hunters went to their wegiwas, each intent on being named the best hunter but especially desiring to outdo his chief. Tecumseh went back into his cabin, looked at the newborn Pugeshashenwa and talked softly to Manete. "You are feeling well?"

"I am all right," replied Manete. The baby's birth three days ago had taken much out of her. "Will you be a good father?"

"Now what kind of a question is that?"

"You must be a better father than you are a husband."

"Do you wish to start another fight to welcome our first born?" asked Tecumseh. "I would think you would behave a little differently now that you have this infant who must depend on you so completely."

"He has no uncles here to defend him," said Manete. Descent was always through the mother and her brothers were in charge of educating her male children.

"I am Tecumseh. My son needs no uncles. Would that my brothers were alive to see to his education and training."

"You are always boasting of your family."

"Manete, I do not understand why you must be so difficult," said Tecumseh, trying to control his irritaiton.

"I have to be me," replied the woman. "I was not born to privilege. My father had to work hard."

Tecumseh did his best to ignore her. He looked at the child. He was of a lighter skin than his father. "I see your father's imprint on this infant," said Tecumseh in an attempt to mollify his wife.

"Perhaps he will grow up to be like his grandfather."

The young chief shook his head. Even at a time like this Manete made caustic remarks. "Sleep tight, nekwethar. Tomorrow I go to the hunt so the villagers can come pay you homage."

Manete continued to talk but Tecumseh did his best to ignore her as he prepared his hunting equipment. "I don't want you to go," Manete finally said. "Let the others do the hunting. You stay here with your newborn."

"I have given my word." It appeared to do little good for Manete continued to nag at him. Finally the two went to sleep and Tecumseh was gone the next day before Manete awakened.

On the third day of the hunt the young men began to return with evidence of their kills. Most had three or four deerskins. When Pashaae returned with twelve everyone waited with great expectation. The chief would have to honor the winner! The afternoon began to wane as Tecumseh finally strode into the village leading three horses, all of them loaded with deerskins.

"Well," he remarked to the group of hunters as other villagers gathered, "have you lost your tongues as well as your arms? Come help me unload. We must go get the meat before it spoils."

"Ah, how many?" asked one of the hunters.

"Count them, my brothers," replied the chief.

There were *thirty* hides. "There are no deer left in the forest!" said a villager. "Our chief has powerful medicine indeed. Hail Tecumseh, Chief of the Ohio!"

"Hail, Chief of the Beautiful River!"

Episode 13: Big Baby

Abner Barrett looked at the newcomer from Kentucky. "Well of course there's Indians living by here. This here's their country too, you know. They come right in here to trade, same as you and the other people in Urbana."

"We don't have them living next to us in Kentuck," said the man, a squat, muscular individual obviously powerful. "Any of you folks ever have to fight 'em?"

No one in the small trading house, which was built as an adjunct to Barrett's house, replied.

"Wayne settled 'em down," said one man. "You'll be safe in Ohio. Pretty soon we'll have enough people for statehood."

"I heard lots of talk," said the newcomer, "about Indian fights and massacres. The family wants to settle here but I don't want them in any danger, women folk and all."

"No danger," said Abner Barrett, "though I wouldn't go around looking for trouble."

"Do they do a lot of drinking? I heard tell they get hotheaded real easy once they start lifting the jug."

"Yeah, we get a few sots in here," admitted Barrett, "white and red, but I won't do business with 'em."

"That's probably the best way to-" The words froze in the man's mouth as he saw an Indian step through the door and stand there, rifle in hand, knife on his hip, a stern commanding expression on his face as he surveyed everyone in the building.

Tecumseh stood five-foot-ten but seemed much taller because of his erect carriage. He wore buckskin and no ornaments. The Kentuckian began to tremble, actually tremble, when Tecumseh fixed his eyes on the newcomer and approached him slowly. "A big baby!" said Tecumseh jokingly as he slapped the man on the shoulder and back, "a big baby!"

Barrett and the other men laughed merrily as they saw the quaking Kentuckian. Tecumseh laughed out loud, revealing his unusually beautiful teeth. "Big Baby!" repeated Tecumseh for the third time. This reaction to him was a mocking revelation about the Shemanese. How could one lone Indian cause fear in a gathering of white men?

191

"What can I do for you today, chief?" asked Barrett.

"Lead for bullets," replied Tecumseh in English.

"Whatcha got to trade?"

"Skins. Outside."

"Okay, let's go see whacha got." The two stepped outside.

"Who is that?" asked the chagrined Kentuckian.

"Chief of a village over on Buck Creek. Tecumseh. Hear lotta stories about him."

"Tecum... what's that in English?"

"I heard people say it means 'Shooting Star.' He was in all the fights around these here parts."

Another stranger now came into the trading room. He too looked the part of hunter. "Good morning, gentlemen," he said casually.

"How do," replied the oldster who helped Abner Barrett. "What ya need this morning?"

"How about some good land for a starter?"

"That's what everybody's lookin' fer," replied the old man. "This country's the best place to look."

"Yes, I was here years ago. Name's James Galloway. Used to be a hunter for George Rogers Clark. I got some land coming to me so I thought I'd take a look-see before I brought the family up."

"How'd you get past that Injun outside?" whispered another man as he looked at the embarrassed Kentuckian. Galloway didn't understand why everyone laughed uproariously.

Episode 14: Divorce

"Here," said Tecumseh to Manete, "make a little pouch to carry my paint," as he gave her the materials.

The woman had been particularly sullen this day. "I cannot do that!" she cried as she threw the skin at her husband.

"All right, don't," said Tecumseh in a rare show of anger.

"Oh, all right, I'll find someone who can," said Manete.

"Don't bother, I can find someone myself. One of us must leave, we can no longer live like this. Take what you wish and go or stay here and I will move away."

Manete looked at her young husband, his real anger frightening her though he had never come close to hitting her. Had he just been a challenge to her? Did she really care for him? She did not understand him, this much she readily admitted to herself. He was haughty, always under control of his emotions, never letting down except perhaps right

TECUMTHA

now when the anger crept out. He was still the homeless orphan trying to build a fortress of protective reserve and self-control. It had been a maddening experience for her, trying to break down that cold wall! And she had not succeeded, even by giving him a son. "No," said Manete finally, "I will leave. But Pugeshashenwa goes with me."

"That is best for him now that he is an infant. But when he is ready to be educated he will come with me."

"You are always gone," said Manete scornfully. "Do you want your son to be an orphan also?"

"He will live with Tecumapease when he is ready to begin his education," said Tecumseh with finality. "Take whatever horses you wish, all your things and the boy's. There is also enough wampum. It is unfortunate...but I can say nothing." He left the cabin while Manete packed. He was thinking perhaps he was temperamentally unsuited for marriage. He would go visit Tecumapease and Wasegoboah. Perhaps he would wander around the sites of Old Piqua and Old Chillicothe. There were so many boyhood memories. Sinnamantha, the Big Fish, Steve Ruddell... where was he now, back with the Shemanese? Was he happy or did he too miss the old haunts? Suddenly he wanted to leave, ride away immediately. He returned to the wegiwa, packed a few things in silence, collected his hunting equipment, and walked out to the horse corral where he saddled his favorite animal and briskly rode out of the village.

Tecumseh wished he could ride far into the north contry where he might hunt the moose, the shy, vigilant moose which was more difficult to take than a deer or buffalo. Well then, why not go? He was free now. The thought of his family breaking up came back, though he tried to occupy his mind with something, anything, else. He had heard the moose was fleeter than the elk, that their hearing was imcomparable, distinguishing a hunter stepping on a twig even during a storm. Tecumseh had heard stories about how moose managed to elude hunters by staying under water for a lengthy time... No, he would not abandon his village merely because he was depressed. He would not flee to the north country... this time, but someday he would indeed like to match wits with the elusive, intelligent moose...

Tecumseh rode hard that day and did not consider stopping until the sun had made its full journey and was hiding behind the western horizon. The chief saw evidence that some sort of encampment lay ahead so he got his musket ready just in case. As he approached he noticed it was an Indian camp so he relaxed just a bit, though his gun was still in front of him. "Brothers!" called out Tecumseh to the Indians, who had no sentries posted, "I would enter your camp and share your meal if the kettle is high."

"Who is it?" inquired a man who sat by the small fire where some meat was roasting.

"A friend, my brother, a friend."

"Then enter, my friend," said the man, "and partake of our supper and company."

Tecumseh dismounted and looked at the people as he walked into camp. Ojibbeways. "Moneto has favored me this night," he said. "Let me unsaddle my horse so he may feed."

"Of course. The meat is not quite ready."

Tecumseh looked around as he worked on his animal. Four men, two women. One of the men was a bit elderly. "Where are you folks headed?"

"On our way to Buck Creek," said the older man.

"Buck Creek? You are only a day's ride away, or perhaps a day and a half."

"Are you from there?" asked one of the women as she came closer to the fire and inspected the meat.

"Yes, I live there," replied Tecumseh.

"We hope the chief will take us in," said another of the men as Tecumseh finished with his horse and approached the fire.

"I am certain he will," remarked Tecumseh.

"We have heard many stories of your chief," said the old man as he looked at Tecumseh, "all of them good. The other chiefs were frightened by General Wayne at Greenville. Tecumseh refused to attend and today is the only voice rising against the bartering away of our lands. He talks like a real leader, a true patriot of our country." The old man now introduced what turned out to he his family.

"I am happy to meet all of you," said Tecumseh as he shook hands with the men. "I--" at that instant Tecumseh's horse let out a wild whinny and the Shawnee reacted instinctively toward grabbing his gun and looking toward defending himself and the encampment.

"Calm yourself, my warrior," said the old man, whose name was Netnokwa, "it is only your horse meeting up with our own animals. I can see you have spent much time on the warpath. The country is at peace now or we would have posted guards."

"Yes, we are at peace. I guess habits are difficult to break," admitted Tecumseh.

"The meat is ready," said one of the women, wife of one of the younger men. The two women served everyone where they sat around the fire and all commenced eating.

"You travel alone," remarked Netnokwa to Tecumseh.

"Yes, father."

"Perhaps you will find company in some village," said the old man, a smile on his face. "Looking at your handsome person, I am certain you will not be rebuffed."

"Everyone is rebuffed at one time or another," remarked one of the females.

"It depends on how it is handled," added the other. The men just laughed. Except Tecumseh. He was too emotionally upset over his dead marriage.

"Have you heard the story of Mamondaginine, our Beau-man?" asked the old man. Tecumseh shook his head. "I shall tell it to you. Perhaps there is a moral to it. Once, in a village of the Ojibbeways, there lived a noted beauty who captured the heart of every young warrior and hunter who gazed on her loveliness. She was particularly admired by this Beau-man who becuase he was also quite handsome and took special care in adorning himself, thought he could win the love of this belle. 'Come,' he said to a friend one day when he felt sportive, 'let us pay court to the beautiful one. Perhaps she may fancy one of us.' So they went to her cabin, called her out and tried to engage her in conversation. But she wouldn't even listen to them, much less talk. When the Beau-man saw this insult he said, 'Rudeness should never be a part of beauty,' to which the maiden put together her thumb and three fingers, gracefully raised her hand toward him and opened them contemptuously in his face.

"Now this was supreme scorn and rejection. Beau-man became confused and withdrew abashed. His pride was deeply wounded. Even worse, others had seen the gesture and soon the incident became the talk of every lodge circle. Beau-man was of a sensitive disposition and the rejection preyed upon his mind. He became melancholy, moody, scarcely speaking a word for days at a time, eating little or no food. At last he became ill and had to stay in bed. Not even his friends could rouse him.

"The time came for moving camp but no persuasion could induce the young man to rise and prepare for departure. His relatives put some dried food within his reach and finally left him there, lying upon his deerskin couch. The last to leave was his companion who had been with him when the belle maiden rejected him. He implored Beau-man to leave with him but even his voice went unheeded. As his retiring footsteps faded the wilderness stillness and solitude engulfed him.

"Now the young man felt death must be lurking near for his thoughts were troubled within him. He began to pray to his guardian spirit, who heard his appeal and put into his mind a plan by which he might punish and humble the haughty girl who had brought him so low. But evil spirit now took hold of him, working on his mind, which soon roused him into action. Soon he recognized the strategem by which to wreak his revenge.

"Rising feebly from his couch he walked over the deserted camp, gathering all the bits of cloth, feathers, and other fancy scraps he could find. Soon he had a heap of gaudy, soiled stuff which he cleaned as best he could, putting them into the shape of a man, then clothing all of them with coat and leggins, trimmed with beads, decorated after the fashion of his tribesmen. He gave up his spare set of moccasins, which he garnished in the same way, got ready his bow and arrows, and a frontlet and feathers for the head. The entire creation was still very loose and rough looking so he searched for old bones and scraps of meat with which to seal the spaces. A light snow began falling so he mixed some with dirt in order to finish the sealing. Now the evil spirit breathed life into Beauman's creation and there before him stood Moowis, the Rag Man, a tall, wellframed man attired in gala costume.

'Follow me,' said Beau-man to Moowis, 'and I will tell you what to do.'

Together they followed the trail of the tribe, coming up to the main camp by evening when there was scant light to prevent looking closely. As they entered camp all were pleased to see young Beau-man, exclaiming now he looked more like his old self. But quickly all eyes turned to his companion: tall, silent, dignified, clothes so multicolored, his handsome person ornamented with such profusion and variety. The chief himself invited the stranger to his lodge and had prepared for him a feast of moose hump and the finest venison.

No one who saw the attractive stranger was more impressed than Mamonda, the beautiful maiden belle. She fell in love with him at first sight and implored her mother to invite him to their lodge for the following evening, which she did. Now Beau-man went with him, for it was under his patronage that Moowis had been introduced. But of course he had his own motive for going, now a complex mixture of desire for revenge and genuine admiration for the young woman. Perhaps, if Mamonda gave him attention...

No such thing occurred. Moowis attracted everyone's interest, every eye, every heart. He sat in the most prominent seat in front of the fire so he could be easily observed by all. But the heat began to make him uncomfortable. Now he worried that his original components were going to be disclosed by the fire until he pulled a boy to him, thus shielding himself from the direct heat. He shifted his position frequently and by turning this way and that, by dexterous maneuvers and timely remarks or questions, evaded the pressing invitation of his host to sit still and enjoy himself. At last he placed himself near the door of the lodge, and by so doing increasing Mamonda's admiration who felt only a brave spirit of great endurance could resist the paralysing cold in that part of the lodge.

In time Mamonda's mother insisted that Moowis cross to the innermost part of the lodge and take the coveted *Abinos,* the bridegroom's seat. Beau-man now knew he had no chance whatever. Moowis had triumphed. He therefore withdrew, as did the other guests, one by one. Moowis thus remained as family, husband of Mamonda.

Beau-man waited outside for the longest time, his heart full of vengeful satisfaction! The dart with which Mamonda had wounded so many others was soon to strike her own heart. Mamonda had married not a true man but an image!

As the morning dawned Moowis awoke, took his weapons and said, "I must go for I have important business to settle before I can settle myself in a lodge. There are many hills to mount and streams to cross before I come to the end of my journey."

"I will go with you, husband," said Mamonda.

"It is too far and you would not be able to withstand the toils and perils along the way."

"Nothing is so far that a wife cannot follow," said Mamonda courageously, "and there are no toils nor dangers that I am not ready and willing to share with you."

"All right, if you must," said Moowis, "but first I must bid my friend farewell." He went and told Beau-man the girl wished to accompany him on his journey. For a moment the rejected suitor was filled with pity and compassion. Such a beautiful woman, to cast herself away on an image when she might have been the very heart of a good lodge and a true man! Then the evil spirit whispered, "It is her own folly, she must submit to her fate. She has turned a deaf ear to you. *She must submit to her fate!*" Beau-man covered his face with his hands.

Moowis set forth, his wife following a safe distance behind as was the custom. The way was rough and difficult. She could not keep up with her husband's rapid pace. But she struggled hard and perservered in following him. Then the sun came out in all its strength. Moowis had been out of Mamonda's sight for some time now. The piercing heat began to dissolve his snow-knit body. He began to melt and fall to pieces. As the woman followed she began to find piece after piece of the raiment which she recognized as his. The ornaments by which she had been dazzled now caused her much puzzlement as she found them in her path. "Husband, wait!" she screamed.

She saw his moccasins, then his leggins, his coat, and the feathers of his head-dress. As the heat unbound them they fell asunder and returned to their original base condition. A high wind arose and swirled at Mamonda from all directions. She became confused and lost her way. Here and there she found a rag, a bone, a feather, a bead. "Moowis!" she would call, "I am lost! Help me or I perish!"

Mamonda spent the entire day searching in vain. She had lost every track and night overtook her weary and conquered by despair. "Moowis!" she wailed, "you have led me astray! Why have you deceived me! Do not leave me all alone, all alone. Moowis! Moowis!"

"There was no one to hear Mamonda's moaning," said the old story teller, "and she died in the woods of cold and hunger. Such is woman, impressed by images, and such is human nature."

Tecumseh had listened spellbound. When it came to hearing legends he was still a child in awe of the Grandfathers. Perhaps his recent divorce from Manete made this particular story more poignant and tragic. He shook his head sorrowfully but he did not know if it was for Beau-man, Mamonda, Manete... or Tecumseh. What had happened to his marriage? Had he married because of tribal pressure? He knew that was nothing on which to base a marriage. Perhaps then it was his own fault it turned out the way it did. Had he ever really cared for her? That was a difficult question... she was so helpful before marriage, so agreeable. Puckeshinwa and Methoataske became such legendary figures of love in their village. What magic was it that they did not pass on to their son?...

"Our guest does not seem to have liked the story," observed one of the women.

"No, my sister, it is not that," commented Tecumseh. "It was very moving in its tragedy." He looked at everyone around the fire. "Buck Creek is fortunate to count you as citizens."

"We did not hear your name, brother," said Netnokwa.

"I am Tecumseh. With your permission I shall retire in preparation for my long ride tomorrow."

The gathering acquiesced to losing such gracious company as the young Chief of the Ohio. Little wonder he had reacted in such military fashion when the horses whinnied. In small voices the group around the fire recounted his exploits far into the night...

Tecumseh bid Netnokwa farewell at the crack of dawn the next morning. He travelled leisurely and finally arrived at Wakaponeta. The

199

village had been burned during the late war but it had been rebuilt, though charred reminders were evident here and there.

"Keewaukoomeelaa!" said Tecumseh to his brother-in-law Wasegoboah when he spied him outside his wegiwa.

"Welcome, my brother!" said Wasegoboah exultantly as he put out his hand. "It is high time you come visit us!"

"I have missed all of you," said Tecumseh. "I trust my visit finds you well."

"Never better, my brother. Come, let us enter. Two sisters will be delighted to see you."

"Two?"

"Yes," explained Wasegoboah, "Nehaaeemo is here visiting."

The two men entered and when Tecumapease and Nehaaeemo saw their brother they let out a joyous cry and pounced on him with embraces. Tecumseh returned their affection happily.

"My!" exclaimed Tecumapease, "How proud would mother and father would be to hear everyone call you Chief of the Ohio! How wonderful we feel for you!" She hugged her brother one more time.

"I am part of only a little village," said Tecumseh. "People exaggerate."

"Wayne's victory over our people have made you national," said Wesegoboah. "You are no longer just a Shawnee. Now you represent all of the people on this great island who believe this is their land, a gift from the Great Spirit for all time. The chiefs sold our lands for a pittance and many are scorning them for their actions. They look to you for leadership in their quest to live their lives as they see fit, in the ways of their ancestors."

"Tecumseh my brother," began Nehaaemo, "many moons ago, before you went south to help Cheeseekau, I wanted to tell you about my impending marriage... to George Ironsides."

The happy smile died on Tecumseh's face. He knew these were not glad tidings by the way Nehaaeemo spoke.

"We have been very happy, George and I," she continued nervously. "We have a little one, a boy... I want him to meet his uncle as soon as you can come visit..." Nehaaeemo's face felt warm and she wiped her forehead with her palm.

"How could you have married a white man?" asked Tecumseh, calmly but obviously displeased. Tecumapease busied herself with food preparation and Wasegoboah withdrew to a corner of the large cabin. "The Shemanese murdered our father and killed two of your blood brothers, not to mention what they have done to all our people."

"He is a Britisher, not a Shemanese," protested Nehaaeemo nervously.

"The British closed the gates on us and refused to fight Wayne's army as they promised," said Teucmseh. "When will your husband lock you out of your cabin?"

"He cannot," said Nehaaeemo as she began to control herself. "I have rights and no one can take them from me. I am not a slave. George and I care for each other. My child is proof of what I say."

"And when will he return across the great salt water? Will he leave you and his child here to fend for yourself?" He scrutinized his younger sister. She did not look unhappy.

"He will go no where without me. I am no longer a child. He is a good man. You have but to meet him to see for yourself. Don't you wish to meet your little nephew?"

"Of course. And I want you to meet yours. Can your husband hunt?"

Nehaaeemo shook her head in disbelief. Was that all men thought about? "If a deer followed him home or died at our doorstep I am certain George would know what to do," said Nehaaeemo sarcastically. Tecumapease and Wasegoboah stared at the young woman. That was not the way to approach Tecumseh.

"Don't get cute," demanded Tecumseh. "If you care nothing—"

"Of course I care," interrupted Nehaaeemo as she threw her arms around her brother, "and that's why I want you to come see for yorself how we live and everything. Promise me that and I will be satisfied, nethaathar, my chief."

"Well," hesitated Tecumseh, "all right, but my nephew must not grow up to forget his Shawnee heritage."

"I would never allow that, oakeemau," said Nehaaeemo. "George wouldn't either."

"I too have unpleasant tidings," confessed Tecumseh. Wasegoboah and Temcumapease came closer. "I have dissolved the marrige with Manete..." He explained how it had been coming on and how it ended. "There is no chance for a reconciliation," he finished. Then he explained how he would like Pugeshenshewa to become part of the household when he was of age to begin his training and education.

"Of course," said Tecumapease, "bring me my nephew as quick as you can." Wasegoboah nodded his approval.

"Well," said Tecumseh, "if there is any more bad news we might as well hear it right away. It seems the day for it." He looked at Tecumapease. "What of Laulewasika?"

Chapter 4

Red unlocked the door of her ladies apparel shop on Chestnut Street, turned the doornob and let herself in. The "Closed" sign in the window was turned over to "Open," and another day began. Millicent would soon arrive, hopefully before the customers. She was already acting like the boss, even though the sale of the dress shop was not final for three days yet. Red thought she would like her new business, so different from her previous profession, and she had for a while but then creeping dissatisfaction set in. When she began to resent the customers and their assinine manners Red knew it was time to sell the shop to Millie. Perhaps she needed more excitement. That's what Millie said. A good man. Marriage. Children. But for certain a good man. Poor Millie! How many good men were there? Very few and far between. Even Millie's husband had made a pass at her. His only attraction was all the money he had. Ah well, if Millie was happy, so what?

As Red prepared the shop for the day she thought of the men she might have married... none, she decided triumphantly. She opened a drawer in her desk and there was the knife, a vicious looking instrument on its own but especially so in a ladies apparel shop. She took it by the handle, grasping it tightly as she often did. It was a quotidian reminder of her years in the forest. That Spybuck! Would he really have killed her with it? She often wondered about that. If she thought of any man it was mostly Spybuck. But that was only because he represented her years of captivity. Or because he was far away. Or because she had lived in such a different way during those years, being sexually active with just one man. All other men had been merely lucrative. She thought of none of them. But Spybuck... once he said, "To be alone is to hear the wind crying when all you ask is the warmth of a human fire."

"Good morning, glory!" said Millicent as she ambled into the shop.

"Good morning, Millie," said Red, coming out of her reverie.

"How is my ex-boss this morning?"

"Fine, just fine. Thinking what I'm going to do now that I retire. I know, 'Find a good man'," she chorused with Millie.

"Then you'll have someone to wear that box of fancy lingerie for," said Millicent. "Heavens, what's this world coming to. Reverend Watekins would have a fit!"

"I promise I'll never show them to the good Reverend," said Red.

"Well what are you going to do now that you are a lady of leisure?" asked Millicent. "Take a long trip? Europe is nice."

"Maybe I should. But not to Europe. Maybe the West."

"Oh, you and your forests. Aren't you afraid of those wild Indians? By the way, I've been meaning to tell you," said Millicent in a decidedly serious voice, "I have seen this man watching our place for the past couple of weeks. I turn the corner and he's a block away or I look out the door and he's standing at a distance. Same man all the time. Fancy suit.

"I haven't noticed anyone," said Red. "Probably just some husband too shy to wait around for his wife while she's buying her undies."

"I don't know, maybe. Good Lord, put that terrible thing away!" said Millicent as she saw the knife Red held. "We're not being attacked. You never did explain how you came on to such a thing. Looks... Indian, sort of."

"A friend gave it to me for protection once," said Red as she put it back in the drawer.

"Have you ever seen an Indian? I mean up close."

"Close? How close?" teased Red.

"You know what I mean," said Millie, "not touching close, silly. You're not that sort." She looked out the front window. "Look, there he is!"

"Indian?"

"No, silly, that well dressed man that keeps turning up. Look at him!"

Red peeped out the window and saw... whoever it was. She was certain she had never seen him before, that she remembered anyway.

"Good morning," said a customer as she came into the shop. Millie greeted her then when two other ladies walked in Red forgot about the well dressed man and tended to business.

When the sale papers were signed a few days later Red was paid and the money deposited in a bank. She had earned a tidy profit, proving she possessed good business sense but emotionally she was bored with shop keeping in Phiadelphia. As she relaxed in her apartment the day after the sale she was at a total loss as to what to do. Perhaps she should invest her money and let it work for her. There were all kinds of opportunities to invest in western lands. The poor Indians. Being robbed so speculators could make money off them. She wondered how Spybuck was, where he was living, how peace had affected him... *who he was living with.* Aah, who cared, she could always meet men. But the Indian had been... different. Sometimes she could still catch his scent of corn. How he made everyone fear him! She still remembered a lot of Shawnee. She caught herself thinking that if she returned to Ohio— That stopped her in her mental tracks. Return... to Spybuck?! What nons--- Was that what she wanted to do, return to Ohio and find Spybuck? "Happiness is the golden light which smoothes out the edges of harshness so everything is balanced on Mother Earth." She felt the buds hardening on her breasts. Something strange was coming over her. Part of her didn't like it. She grabbed a wrap and went outside for a walk.

She walked slowly, deep in thought, not hearing the first, "Good evening, madam." When Red finally became aware she saw a gentleman walking beside her.

"Excuse me," said Red, "do I know you?"

"No, madam, but that has been my loss."

Red noticed how fashionably dressed he was, and expensively.

"I would like to confer with you," said the man. "Would you care to accompany me for supper? Philadelphia is noted for its food and there is a good restaurant down the street."

"No, I'm not hungry," said Red easily. *What an amateurish approach,* she thought to herself.

"They serve very good food, like your mother used to make," continued the man. "And I think you would be interested in what I have to say, being a business woman. No problems, I assure you. Please, honor me."

"You have a business venture in mind? But I don't even know your name."

"Philip Georges, at your service. Come, a quick bite."

"Well, all right," said Red, "for just a few minutes." Perhaps there was a good investment in the offing.

They walked to the restuarant, sat down, ordered, and Georges got right to the point at Red's insistence.

"I propose to open a business establishment with you as directress," said Georges.

"And the nature of the business?" asked Red.

"Why, the oldest profession," said the man candidly. "I'll get you a stable of attractive women and with you to handle them we'll both be wealthy in a short time."

Red became icy cold. She thought it was going to be a valid business. How had this lout found out about her?! She wished she had been carrying Spybuck's knife. How happy she would have been to slit this nincompoop's throat!

Georges immediately noticed the change in the woman. "Come now," he said soothingly, "business is business. No point in being offended. There are still plenty of doubloons in the world."

Red quickly got a hold of herself. So he knew about her, so what? "I am not going to be around for very long," she said, "so I must refuse your offer."

"Oh?" said Philip Georges, "are you leaving our fair city of brotherly love?"

"Yes, I am."

"May I ask where?"

"That is none of your business," said Red easily, not upset.

"I wish you would consider my proposition. Don't be hasty. Talking never hurt anyone."

"I'm not interested," said Red as she stood to leave. "If you will excuse me--"

"No, I won't," said Georges as he grabbed her wrist with tremendous strength, forcing her to sit back down. "We ordered some food and it would be very un-lady-like for you to leave it all for me. If we cannot be partners in business let us at least be civil to each other. Please. Don't embarass me."

Red was not intimidated, though the man's strength had impressed her. How she wished she had brought Spybuck's knife in her purse! "All right," she said as the food was brought out and served, "but I will not tolerate bad manners."

"I would be the first to agree," said Georges. "Ah, this smells good. Eat up."

The two ate in silence but Red could feel the man scrutinizing her with noncommital eyes. "Are you sure you didn't mistake me for someone else?" she asked.

"Please, madam, at least credit me with intelligence." There was the barest twinkle in his eyes. "Your fame has travelled far and wide. And just looking at you I would say, deservedly so."

"I had not bumped into it before now."

"I did not mean to be rude. Please forgive me, my lady."

This pimp has his charm, there's no denying it, thought Red. "Have I met you before?"

"No, but I was one of your devotees from the afar, one of the many who could not get their hands on a doubloon."

"The Army?"

"Yes, St. Clairs's," replied Georges. "One of these days I will recount my adventures in the forest. But now my fortunes have changed." He reached into his pocket and put three doubloons on the table.

"Do you have a fascination for them?" she asked.

"Nothing compared to you."

Red didn't know quite how to take his repartee.

"If we cannot be business partners then at least let us be ... friends," suggested Georges.

"I am returning to Ohio to get married," said Red. The comment came out so easily it surprised her.

"Lucky devil," said Philip Georges, completely in stride. "Anybody I know?"

"I doubt it," replied Red.

"What does he do, an army man?"

"No, you might say he's a doctor." Red smiled pleasantly. Spybuck was certainly a doctor, and then some.

"Not much future in that, but then who am I to judge. I really wish you had listened to my offer. Could be quite lucrative, especially in the West."

"Oh, you wanted to start it up there? I thought you had Philadelphia in mind."

"No," said Georges, "too many here already. Perhaps I'll take passage with you. When are you leaving?"

"Within the week, as soon as I *finish* with the details." Red was absolutely amazed with herself. She really meant it! She would pack her things, take her money, and sail down the Ohio in search of Spybuck! Would he take her back? What if he was already married?

"If you'll tell me which boat you'll be on I shall sail with you," said Georges, evidently as quick to make a decision as Red. "But there is still time and I have these doubloons."

"What?"

"Why not?" asked the man.

"Exercise is not good after eating," admonished Red, a smile on her face.

"Come now, I went off to do my patriotic duty and got nothing for it. The least you could do is favor me with one night. All in the line of patriotism, of course."

"I've done my share," laughed Red, though she regretted her remark the instant she said it. She had been an upstanding business woman for some time now. Furthermore she must maintain her virtue for her prospective husband! What irony engulfed her. "I must be leaving now."

"If you will permit me, I will walk you back to your lodgings."

"If you like."

The two left the restaurant and returned to Red's apartment without much conversation. "Thank you very much. This was the most memorable lunch I ever had in Philadelphia."

Georges did not understand but it didn't bother him. "Good afternoon, madam. I hope to see you on board. What ship will you be taking?"

"Good afternoon," said Red as she closed the door without answering. Now that she was alone she could think. Did she really want to go find Spybuck?! Yes. Yes! She missed the man, actually missed him! Spybuck and his visions, spirits, and sacred things! Everything fell into place. She had been happy in the forest! She didn't want to be a whore ever again. This couldn't be accomplished anywhere that men might recognize her, Philip Georges had taught her that just now. But more important she wanted Spybuck! Georges was attractive, in a dandy sort of way, but she was not the least interested in him. Well, maybe a trifle, but nothing compared to Spybuck. Quickly she got some money and walked out in the direction of the wharf in order to book passage down the Ohio.

Episode 2: The Vision

Laulewasika endeavored to steady his hands as he took aim at the target with his bow and arrow. Twaaang! went the string as it propelled the shaft, wide of its mark. Laulewasika looked around sheepishly, though he knew no one was skulking around Spybuck's cabin to watch his efforts at marksmanship. He had been drinking, which he did whenever he could obtain firewater, and as yet he had not hit the target, though he continued pertinaciously in his efforts. *Why can I not be like the rest of my family?!* He asked this of himself over and over. *Why, because you are idle, that's why,* he voiced within his mind. Well that would change. He would take his bow and become a marksman! *A marksman like your father? What father... dead before I was born...* Twaaang! *My mother*

207

abandons me at five... drifting around while the Shemanese are burn-
ing the world... without Tecumapease I'd be a corpse covered with dirt
somewhere... firewater is the only friend I've ever had...

Laulewasika was not hitting the target so he concentrated on his next
effort, pulling back the bowstring, pressing his face close to aim better.
He loosed the string but the arrow split in two, part of the wood penetrating his eye. "Aaaaaaaaa," he screamed over and over in pain.

Spybuck heard his apprentice wailing and rushed out to see what
had happened.

"Cannot see!" yelled Laulewasika, "I'm blind, I'm blind!"

"Here I am, don't fret," soothed Spybuck. "Let me see." Blood was
in the eye. He wiped it away with a cloth and saw the irreparable damage
to the eyeball. Laulewasika was right, he would never see out of that eye
again. "Come on, let's go to the cabin." He kept the cloth on the eye and
guided the young man back to the wegiwa.

"My eye is gone," said Laulewasika sorrowfully.

Spybuck took him inside and bade him lay down after he cleansed the
wound, the thick sappy-like substance in the eyeball dripping out.
Laulewasika made no sound but Spybuck gave him a drug root to chew
on anyway. "Chew it and swallow it all," said the medicine man. The
wound was painful but between the drug and the firewater Laulewasika
soon drifted into a fitful sleep. He experienced a vision.

Laulewasika found himself journeying along a roadway charac-
terized by a different blaze of color as he walked. No other human beings
were about yet he heard voices in the distance. The horizon was illuminated as by a sunset while he walked, looking this way and that in confusion. He came to a fork in the road. "Turn to the right and reach
understanding, happiness, fulfillment," said a solitary voice. "Bend to
the left and you shall feel eternal misery. This fork is the condition of
your life and that of all my red children. Sinners must take the left fork.
But the Great Spirit will ever hold out His hand to those who wish to quit
their evil ways by choosing the right path, ceasing their wickedness and
doing good works. You, Laulewasika, son of Puckeshinwa and Methoataske, must repent for the sake of your people. Do not persist in the left
path. You have been shown your error, it leads to ultimate destruction.
The journey of life is slow until the traveller reaches the fork..."

Laulewasika was unafraid, the same feeling produced by drinking
much firewater. He stood at the fork, colors swirling around him, bidding this, beckoning that. Somehow he slipped off his feet and fell
toward the left fork. "So be it" said Laulewasika as he got up and walked
down the left branch. In a short time he saw three houses. From where he

stood he could see the right pathway, noticing the first and second houses were connected to the good road with small bypaths. He did not understand why it should be so.

The first house on the left pathway was totally green. It became a huge house, as large as a forest and in it Laulewasika saw tribe after tribe making war on each other. Guns were fired, arrows were sent with deadly accuracy, scalping knives plunged and came up crimson. Nation against nation, clan against clan, brother against brother. "No!" screamed Laulewasika, "you must stop this bloodshed. We are all children of the Great Spirit!" Some of the combatants heard his wailing, put down their weapons, walked to the byway and strode over to the good road, their wounds healing as they walked arm in arm with their brothers. Others further away continued their internecine battles for they could not hear Laulewasika. He tried to approach them but he fell to his knees. Try as he would he could not regain his feet so he crawled but progress was slow. Meanwhile, the fighting continued and a rivulet of blood colored Laulewasika's palms as he crawled. His buckskin clothes were unaffected. Only his hands turned blood red! He struggled to his feet and tried to wipe his hands clean but did not succeed until he brushed them on his buckskin clothes. The rivulet of blood had now become a strong stream. It swept him away screaming.

Suddenly Laulewasika found himself back on the roadway in front of the second house, a large red structure. In front was an army of ravenous dogs who rushed at him, forcing him to climb a tree to save his life. The animals growled viciously and waited for him to come down, obviously intending to tear him to pieces. At least he could contemplate the goings-on at the second house. He saw magicians and wizards going through their incantations and machinations, chanting their unholy verses, now in unison, now individually. Other people were in the house but when a wizard pointed to a certain individual a bolt of lightning struck him dead on the spot. Soon the other people fled in great fear but the sorcerer's evil powers caught up with them and they keeled over dead. He watched the corpse of one such victim and quickly the body took on a white light after which two people emerged from it, two *Shemanese* who sought refuge in the forest deep. Laulewasika observed how their numbers grew enormously. None wished to walk the bypath over to the good road on the right. "Desist!" wailed Laulewasika. "You are filling the dark woods with enemies who must soon outnumber us. Hear the word of the Great Spirit and cross over to goodness and peace!" Many Indians stopped and walked to the bypath.

"Do not listen to him!" screamed a red haired witch. She hurled a lightning bolt at Laulewasika, bringing the whole tree to the ground, thus forcing the vicious dogs to abandon their quarry. He was unhurt.

"You have been shown your error," returned Laulewasika. "Do not persist in your evil or face eternal destruction!" The red-haired witch sent another lightning bolt at him but many were walking the bypath in full confidence. The fire hit Laulewasika and exploded him down the roadway to the third house.

Here Laulewasika became confused. He could not tell what color the house was because it seemed to change every little while. It also appeared to move, evanescent like a mirage. Why did it have no byway like the other houses? There was no way to get in it, and no way back from it. Suddenly great shrieks escaped from the house and Laulewasika found himself inside it. He had never imagined such abject misery and damnation! Here were two drunken warriors, fighting to the death with knives that gleamed scarlet. There was a man beating a woman savagely, her screams filling the night, reverberating throughout a treacherous forest. Laulewasika covered his ears then lost his balance in a room that was ankle deep in vomit. "No!" wailed the suffering youngest son of Puckeshinwa as other victims approached him, all of them vomiting at him, the stench making him vomit in turn. He was drowning! With herculean effort he managed to make it through the door out of the vile room. He wiped the perspiration from his face only to be confronted by a myriad of people who were drinking themselves into a stupor. Their faces were scarred as if by smallpox and they had a ghastly appearance, as if ill unto death. Still they continued their drinking and one of the victims came forward to Laulewasika saying, "Come drink! We all know you love whiskey."

Laulewasika looked at the cup. The liquid looked like molten lead.

"No!" screamed Laulewasika. "I will not drink!"

"Drink!" commanded a chorus of victims. "Drink and be one with us!"

The sufferer closest to him tilted the cup and drank down the fiery liquid. Fire came out of his mouth and the whole room was engulfed in flames. Laulewasika ran out of the room screaming repentance, the flames licking at his moccasins.

Laulewasika raced back to the fork in the road and turned the other way this time. It was like walking through the forest on a pleasant day. Brothers and sisters from all nations greeted him cordially. There was good food, clean water to drink from sparkling brooks, animals for the taking. Surely this was the domain of the Great Spirit! A beautiful house stood at the end of the path. The scent of flowers was in every room, hap-

210

piness and contentment reigned throughout. "You are to bring my children to this dwelling," said a voice, gentle as the breeze, soothing to the ear, as a tender stream flowing. "You shall be the door of peace and tranquility..."

Laulewasika stood calmly as a beam of sunlight engulfed him. He raised his arms in worship and was imbued with strength for his mission.

Episode 3: The Letter

Louisa St. Clair looked absolutely stunning in her bridal gown as she tried it on. The seamstress could not stop complimenting her and by the time the fitting was over Louisa was glad to get out into the street and walk toward her father's office. A young Indian lad, perhaps ten years of age, walked up in front of her and gave her a white envelope without saying a word. Louisa took it without thinking and the boy disappeared around a corner before she knew what had happened. She had been made uncomfortable by the seamstress and the planned honeymoon in New York still needed detailing so when the laddie handed her the envelope... Well, what did it matter. She stopped walking, opened the envelope and read the brief note inside:

> When stardust falls and illuminates lost trails of yesterday my moccassin prints will not rejoice beside yours in the white pathways I hope are before you. A beautiful dream dies of sadness in the heart. The spirit of Spring is now hesitation upon syllables of sorrow for our love is a mist of shadows. Teardrops tremble in my eyes and I know it is you moving within my heart. Oh that I might weep with the rain and whirl away with the clouds! No matter how hard I try to forget, you always return to my thoughts and I know any smoke you see from a wood fire clinging to a November dawn in the Mohawk Valley will ever remind you of me. Farewell, dearest Louisa. May you ever walk in balance in the garden of the house of God.
>
> Micheal

Louisa re-read the missive, not because she did not immediately understand the Indian phraseology and meaning but because it was so emotionally beautiful. Then, much as she fought them, tears filled her eyes and ran down her cheeks. She clutched at the note and pressed it to her heart as if to stop a wound from bleeding. Passersby began to notice her so she stuck the paper in her purse and quickly went back into the seamstress' shop.

"My dear, what is wrong?" remarked the surprised woman as she looked up from her sewing.

"I... don't know... if I can..." blurted Louisa through her tears.

"Oh, I know, my dear, I know, marriage is such a big step and it unnerves us poor women. I've seen many a bride react just like you. There, there, come sit here and pull yourself together." The woman put her arm around Louisa, doing her best to calm the bride to be. "Everyone will remember you as the most beautiful of brides! Your husband is such a fortunate man. I'm sure he realizes you could have had your pick!"

And Louisa wept as if her heart would break.

Episode 4: The Galloway Family

James Galloway picked his farm land out of the Virginia Military Survey sections. The land was situated close to Old Chillicothe where Blackfish had been chief, between Oldtown and Yellow Springs. He had four sons and a daughter so it did not take long to build a home. Neighbors dropped by occassionally to lend a hand and the Galloways became quite popular in the area.

Galloway was a woodsman and hunter, a rugged man who had never raised his gun against an Indian or taken a scalp. The most violent encounter during his years of western service was against Simon Girty with whom he had fought hand to hand. Girty had managed to pull out a gun after the two had rolled around the ground, shouting, "Now Galloway, damn you, I've got you!" The ball passed through his shoulder and embedded itself in the back of his neck. Girty left him for dead. Galloway went faint from loss of blood but even in his critical condition he made it back to camp. Several years later the ball was removed by a cobbler.

James Galloway was perfectly at ease hunting in the forest or talking to the Shawnee still living at Old Chillicothe. They admired him in much the same way they respected the abilities of Daniel Boone. Galloway invited the Shawnee to visit him as he invited his own countrymen to drop over and his farm became a meeting place for both races to mingle.

The farm not only had a number of convenient pioneer tools and equipment but also the best library in the area, about three hundred books on a variety of subjects. The volumes had been carefully packaged, carried over the mountains by oxcart and down the Ohio by flat-boat until they came to rest in the Galloway home. Of all the children, 17 year old Rebecca, named after her mother, was the most studious for she poured over her father's books at every opportunity. She seldom neglected her chores around the house and the life of a pioneer woman was not easy by any means but there was always time to read, which was her passion. On occassion she would go with her father into Old Chillicothe and engage some of the women in conversation in an effort to learn Shawnee. She gave the impression of being mature beyond her tender years.

One day when the cabin was finished and comfortable Galloway told his wife, "I will make a little hunting trip into the forest."

His wife Rebecca asked, "How long will you be gone, husband?"

"Just a few days, not long."

Rebecca Galloway understood her husband had to spend time in the wilds, doing what he liked best: hunting. It nourished his spirit. She did not like him going off alone so much but she loved the man as well as sympathized with him. "Be careful, then, and bring us venison." She kissed him softly as he gathered his gear.

"No need to worry, wife, I'll return in a couple days," said Galloway. He went outside, saddled his horse and was into the freedom of the forest in a short while, Rebecca waving at him until he was out of sight.

Galloway rode away from population centers but he saw nothing until mid-afternoon when he spied some deer on a little ridge. He dismounted and stalked his way toward the animals, his rifle at the ready. One deer came into view but Galloway decided to get closer so he walked forward noiselessly. The animal was still feeding quietly. Suddenly the antlered head went up in alarm and the hunter realized he must get off a quick shot or lose him. Bang! Another rifle sounded over from Galloway's right. The deer went down kicking.

Within a few minutes Galloway saw an Indian walking toward his kill.

"Brother, that was a good shot," greeted Galloway, "and a might quicker than mine." He walked calmly toward the Indian, who seemed to be ready for treachery if it came his way. "Peace, brother," said Galloway as he put up his right palm, holding his rifle with the other. "My name is James Galloway. I live by Old Chillicothe village."

"Peace," said the Indian in English.

Galloway estimated the Indian was close to six feet tall. His complexion was not very dark, his hands and arms finely formed and muscular. As he came closer he thought the face was quite handsome, more oval than angular, his nose straight, a strong jaw. The eyes were clear, of a

213

deep hazel color, not quite inscrutable for the man appeared to be expecting some form of perfidy.

"I was after this animal too. Ah, a fine one," said Galloway.

"You may have meat if you are hungry," said the man.

"Thank you, ah..."

"I am Tecumseh."

"Pleased to make your acquaintance." Galloway offered his hand and Tecumseh shook it. He had heard stories about this man. Now that he met him he felt his face expressed power. "Do you hunt these parts often?"

"I grew up here," said Tecumseh, a bit more relaxed. There was something genuine about this man. "My sister lives in Chillicothe during part of the year."

"And you, sir?"

"I'm at Buck Creek but we will be moving to the Whitewater River headwaters when I return."

"I know the place," nodded Galloway. "If you wish I will help you skin this animal."

"That will not be necessary," began Tecumseh.

"No bother at all," interrupted Galloway as he pulled the animal into position.

Tecumseh acquiesced to Galloway's officious efforts and the two quickly accomplished the task at hand. They exchanged small talk durnig the skinning then upon finishing Tecumseh said, "I will make a present of this animal to you and your family."

Now it was James Galloway's turn to protest to no avail. "Well then, you must come home with me this very day and sup with us." Tecumseh accepted and with some steady riding the two were back at Galloway's cabin by sundown.

"I did not expect you so quickly," said a happy wife. Then she noticed the Indian coming into the cabin.

"This is Chief Tecumthe," said Galloway to his family, apparently just finished with supper, pronouncing the man's name as it was done in his native Shawnee.

"Pleased to meet you, sir," said Mrs. Galloway. She introduced her sons and then her daughter Becky.

"How do you do, Mr. Tikomfa...chief," stammered the girl.

Everyone chuckled, including Tecumseh. "I am fine," he said simply.

"Come, let me serve you some supper," said Mrs. Glloway as she motioned for the two men to sit at the table just vacated by the rest of the family.

214

"Tecumseh has made a present of a fine deer to us all," said Galloway. "You boys can do the butchering if there is light enough." said the man to his sons. "How is the hunting over at the Whitewater?" asked Galloway while the two waited for their food. Tecumseh held up his end of the polite conversation as he looked around the cabin. The stove on which the woman cooked peaked his interest until, in one corner of the room, where the golden haired girl was sitting when they had walked in, he saw hundreds of books, the talking leaves. How he would like to be able to decipher those talking leaves!

Becky helped her mother by setting the table for her father and his guest, stealing glances at the chief when she thought no one was looking. Why had she been so nervous at greeting him?! Other Indians had been there before. How was this one different? She looked at him closely for an instant. He was not nervous. Dark eyes, expressive lips, beautiful teeth. He appeared to be so dignified and well-mannered. His buskskin clothes fitted him so well...

"Yes, there is talk of holding a council at Urbana," said Galloway.

"Oh?" responded Tecumseh, genuinely surprised. His group of Indians were the only ones living in the area. "I had not heard of it before now."

"Some of our people new to this country become rather... nervous, you might say, around Indians. I guess they need some assurance that all is peaceful."

Tecumseh was cognizant of the tremendous influx of Shemanese into the Ohio country. His people had also become anxious and restless under the Shemanese's peace terms. That is why they had opted in council to move to the Whitewater, which was outside the Greenville line. "I have been hunting and visiting with my sister," said Tecumseh. "Perhaps that is why I was ignorant of the proposed council. But it is strange Tecumapease and Wasegoboah had not heard of it to mention it."

"Tecumapease?" interrupted Becky. "Is she your sister?"

"Why, yes, she is," answered Tecumseh.

"I have talked to her several times at Chillicothe."

"I have been asked to serve as an interpreter," said Galloway, "for the council. So I'll be there."

"Well then, perhaps I will too," said Tecumseh.

Episode 5: The Orator

The council was held in a grove six miles north of the Urbana settlement. As Tecumseh looked at the very large crowd he was slightly nervous for it was the very first time he would address an inter-racial crowd. Oratory had always been the highest art among his people but evidently the Shemanese also appreciated it for there must have been a couple of hundred in attendance. There were a number of chiefs there, all of whom would speak before Tecumseh, as was only proper for they were venerable due to age. His thoughts were on his mother... how he wished she could have been here this day! Now he would see if the Grandfathers had taught him well...

"Why do you wish to be an orator?" asked the Grandfather calmly.

"Because my mother says there is as much power in words as in a great river," replied Tecumseh.

"And how old are you now?"

"Eleven summers."

"Oratory is one of the basic strengths of our people," began the Grandfather. "We speak as we live, from the heart, hand in hand with the world of the Great Spirit. We employ logic in order to present a well reasoned oration."

"I do not understand logic, Grandfather."

"Logic is much like skinning a deer: you proceed from one part to another in orderly fashion. It is like the geese that fly in formation high in the sky. This the orator must do with words. Do you understand?"

"Yes, Grandfather."

"Good. The orator must speak in terms the listener understands. With our people it is Nature which gives images that stir our soul. What is more powerful than a mighty cataract, more beautiful than our forests, more delicate than a flower? Nothing. Our world is epic in breadth, eternal as time. Terms taken from our world can move the lazy, inspire the weak, convert men into heroes because Nature speaks from the depths of our race."

"I wish to speak the way my mother used to."

"Every orator has his own particular style. Above all you must be yourself. The art is to reach people and not all are alike. Use language that hearers will understand, employ words and thoughts that fire their minds and echo in their hearts. If your ideas are strong enough they will shape people's lives."

"But what if I have no great ideas, Grandfather?"

"Ideas are usually absent when people do not strive. If all is contentment or if all is suffocating misery, the sparks of genius will not be kindled. But do not concern yourself with great ideas. They will come if there is a need. Your responsibility is to unleash the secret magic of the spoken word. Your words must fan the senses and hearts of men and women..."

The afternoon waned into twilight so a small fire was kindled just before Tecumseh rose to speak. He had listened attentively to all speakers, Indian and Shemanese. Now it was his turn:

"Brothers from both sides of the Ohio," he began in Shawnee, "I welcome this opportunity to bury all rumors that danger wearing Indian moccasins spreads through the dark night. From beyond the crested mountains to this very spot where the sweet aroma of the forest is wafted through the shadows that come from sleepy hills casting their heaviness over stricken sage and woods there is no plan for war or mischief. Such thoughts expose a basic lack of knowledge about we inhabitants of the forest. But let me tell it like it really is: we are not only citizens but lords of the forest! The Amerindian is wanting for nothing. His are the deer, the elk, the waterfowl, the rivers which float his canoe, the trees which overshadow the grassy hills upon which he reposes during the heats of noon, the thickets where he rouses the sleeping bear, the prairie which gives vigor to his body. His home is disclosed by the curling smoke upon distant hills and the eyes of our people are cast upward in gratitude to the Great Spirit of all life for all these wondrous blessings of nature."

Tecumseh stopped occassionally for the translator, a French Canadian named Dechouset. The man was doing his best to interpret the word pictures and native conceptions, though it was an extremely difficult task. The back up interpreter, James Galloway, did not envy Dechouset at all.

"Those who have compared us to the Longknives say we live in forlorn conditions: no comfortable homes for our families to repose in, no *real* knowledge of agriculture, unable to manufacture cloth, dependent on the uncertain chase in the wilderness. But we ask no help of anyone for we have survived as the Ruler of Destinies taught us from the time of the first dawn, when all was green and fruitful. The Master of Life gave us this land and the power to follow its wildlife into the dark recesses of the forests even during an icy, dreary winter's day in the freezing climate of the Ohio country where snow lies on the ground nearly all winter. Accompany the Snow Warrior of the north country and what do you behold? A lonely forest of tall trees with ice-clad tops, the icy breath of the Snow Warrior roaring from limb to limb. Suddenly there is another sound: the pitiless howling of the ravenous wolf or the savage scream of the panther, who are also creatures of the Great Spirit, speaking in their peculiar way for food, shivering with cold, famished for sustenance, standing ready to devour whatsoever may come within reach of their claws. But look! There is another sound in the midst of this creation of animals and natural elements. Right there, beneath a few

217

slender poles and skins raised up from the frozen bosom of Mother Earth there is the weak cry of a little babe, cold but cuddling to its mother for protection, food, warmth. Those who would devour mother and child in the most ferocious manner stand at the very threshold of this habitation and are held at bay only by the mighty Amerindian hunter and father who must return momentarily from his appointed tasks of hunting and trapping, which are his liberties and perils willed by the Great Spirit. The father is only a man, small and weak as are all men, but he will not allow the devourers to claw and mangle this courageous family for the Ruler of Destinies created it for much nobler purposes."

The entire assembly was now hanging on Tecumseh's every word and gesture.

"We Amerindians of this great island ask not for the comforts of other people. We ask not for the Great Book, though we respect it. All we desire is to be left alone to enjoy what the Great Spirit has willed us: our Mother Earth, the animals of the great forests, sparkling river waters, the freedom to enjoy all in our own way. But there are those who say we cannot. There are those who maintain we have lost our birthright, our legacy, that the earth is no longer our mother. They tell us the land belongs to the People of the Eagle and the Fifteen Fires because they threw the British on their backs, thus conquering *our* land. Brothers from both sides of the Ohio, let us quickly review the course of events which have brought us to this juncture. The French were our first visitors to arrive from across the great salt water. They came to trade their goods for ours, which was pleasing to all concerned, at first. The French made no large purchases of land, just enough on which to build trading houses and forts and plant a little corn. These purchases were as a droplet of water from a great river. Then the British came wanting to trade for our furs and disagreements resulted in the French and British lifting the hatchet against each other. The French were driven away, despite the efforts of our great leader, Pontiac. Now the British were supreme among the foreign powers. But our people still remained in their lands, secure in their possessions because the French could transfer only their forts and trading houses to the British, not the land. Still the British filled the territory along the seacoasts. After Pontiac rose in defense of our land the British made it a law that no Shemanese could settle west of the Allegheny Mountains. Our people acquiesced, believing all lands past the Alleghenies were ours as long as rivers flowed and grasses grew. A big council was held then in 1768 at Fort Stanwix. Our cousins, the Five nations of Iroquois, ceded the lands south of the Ohio River to the British. For this they received many presents, we are told. Now the Five Nations did not live in the ceded lands. They had no great use for them though they claimed it as conquered territory because they had defeated the tribes who used it as hunting ground. In fact, the Miami, Delaware, Shawnee, Wyandot, and some other nations were in possession of the land. Trouble erupted because our people did not sanction the sale of their land by the Iroquois nations.

"Our great Chief Cornstalk lead us to war against the armies of Lord Dunmore from Virginia in 1774. My own father and some here present fought in that war. No one could claim a victory and peace was declared without any transfer of territory. In time the people of the colonies refused to obey the British king and war broke out. Each side told us to remain neutral but it was not long before both antagonists invited us to lift the hatchet. Cornstalk was treacherously murdered at Fort Randolph, causing many of our people to side with the British. We fought the Longknives and defeated them in Kentucky. There were many invasions and our people suffered greatly. But we answered with guerrilla raids in defense of encroachment on our land. What race of people will not defend to the death their rights to their homeland? When did we Amerindians ever wage war except on our native soil? Have we ever gone away from this great island and waged cruel and destructive war in some foreign land? Never! We have fought in defense of the graves of our fathers. Could we have done less? Of course not. We have pride as do all others of the human race.

"There were more treaties: second at Fort Stanwix, one at McIntosh, another at Finney, at Fort Harmar with Governor St. Clair. None of these were signed by authorized representatives of the Indian nations. At Stanwix there were guns at the backs of our people, at Fort McIntosh and Finney any Indian in the vicinity was invited to come receive presents merely for making his mark. Our principal chiefs like Joseph Brant, Little Turtle, Buckongahelas, Blue Jacket and hosts of others never attended. The whiskey barrel was a paramount participant. There was no peace. How could there be? A man cannot expect to expropriate a bear's lair without mortal combat. Since the land could not be taken under the cover of false treaties, armies were sent against us. General Harmar was thrown back in defeat. Governor St. Clair had his army annihilated with unspeakable carnage. War is a most cruel thing, my brothers and sisters! Who would not prefer the beams of peace?

"Then came the most difficult test of all. General Wayne brought in a huge army. The British deserted us, demoralizing our warriors after a brief skirmish at Fallen Timbers. Our chiefs capitulated and signed the Greenville treaty. Peace has cost us a great portion of our country. What

219

people have paid more than ours to insure the peace?! It is even worse when you understand, as we do, that the graves of our fathers are no longer ours. In my mind the boundary between our two people is the Ohio River. But the wings of night have shrouded our weapons. The hatchet is buried in a bottomless hole. Let us all live in a kingdom of sunshine. The past is behind a spreading veil of silence. Let us live like human beings who care, tend, and help other humans. Let us be guided by the Great Spirit where the rivers run free, the forests grow tall, where the plains are wide and spacious. I speak for my people when I invite you all to dance and restore the inner harmony of every individual here present as an effort to insure your own personal relationship with the Ruler of Destinies. Then we can all wear a rainbow for a bracelet and live in peace."

Tecumseh finished his oration amid deep silence. Then the entire group expressed its jubilation in a sudden burst of applause and approval. The Shemanese had been immeasureably impressed by Tecumseh's voice and the vigor of his arguments. The *Amerindians,* a new word coined by the young Ohio orator, were impressed with his imagery and grasp of historic details. The old chiefs crowded around him to shake his hand. Henceforth Tecumseh would be the spokesman for their tribes!

James Galloway and his daughter were among the first Shemanese to step forward with congratulations. "Quite a job!" said Galloway.

"Thank you, brother," replied Tecumseh.

"Mr. Tikomfa Chief," said Becky as she smiled brightly. Tecumseh chuckled and shook her hand also. "When will you come visit us?" she asked.

"I hope soon," he answered as other people sought to congratulate him. He spied Tecumapease and her husband Wasegoboah standing in the waiting crowd and made his way toward them slowly. Tecumapease's eyes glistened for she had always believed her little brother was special. Now she was convinced her mother would have been fully satisfied with Tecumseh's oratorical ability. What a great mind, what a beautiful nature belonged to her little brother! What pride and confidence shone through his handsome face as he presented his well-reasoned arguments. How strong his body appeared as he gestured for emphasis. What deep emotion he conveyed with his stern dignity, his soaring language flowing now gently now tumultuously from his very soul! When Tecumseh got to her she threw her arms around him and held him close.

"My heart is filled, son of Puckeshinwa and Methoataske," she whispered through her soft tears.

"Nothing would have been possible without you, beloved netheemaathar and neekeear."

Wasegoboah shook Tecumseh's hand as others crowded around to do the same. Abner Barrett came up, grasped the young chief's hand, and said, "You know, I wish you would speak in English a bit. I know you can. The rest of us would like to hear you in our language too."

"Grandfather, I have been learning the language of the Shemanese through some of my friends. Would it not be advantageous to be an orator in their language also?" The young Tecumseh searched his teacher's face.

"My young pupil is most ambitious," replied the Grandfather. "It is good to speak the language of other nations. If you continue to study and learn you will no doubt pick up much language from the People of the Eagle. But I would suggest if you ever become a spokesman for our people you must have pride in who you are and where you come from. It would not be a good reflection on our people if our orators chose to use an alien language."

"How so, Grandfather?"

"If we ourselves give precedence to another language are we not dishonoring our own? Our language is an integral part of our soul. It is perfectly acceptable to converse with aliens in their own language if one can do it. This I would recommend to you. But the orator is a cultural hero to us. Should our hero abandon the culture which produced him?"

"No, Grandfather, that would not do," replied Tecumseh.

"Always take pride in who you are and what you represent. Without self-respect there can be no happiness..."

Tecumseh quickly returned from the world of his student days and said to the waiting Abner Barrett: "I am shy of making a spectacle of myself. I would probably make too many shortcuts."

"Don't let it bother you," replied Abner jovially, "that's the way people speak around these here parts! Well I'd better let these folks shake your hand. I'm sure you'd rather talk to this pretty little lady anyhow. You drop over and see us real soon, now hear?"

Tecumseh looked at the woman who had been standing close to Barrett. He did not recognize the Shemanese.

"Do you remember me?" asked the woman.

"Forgive me, sister," said Tecumseh. She was very attractive in her Indian outfit and blanket.

"I am looking for Spybuck," said Red.

"Flame! Of course," said Tecumseh, "in all the confusion... Does Spybuck know you are here? He was immensely depressed when you left."

Red was elated with the remark! Perhaps, *just maybe* her trip had not been made in vain. "Is he... married?"

"Not that I know of," said Tecumseh, "but then I have not seen him for some time. As a matter of fact I wanted to invite him to come live with us. We are moving from the Whitewater to the White River in the Wabash valley. Our grandfathers the Delawares have given us some good land there."

"I need some help to find Spybuck," said Red. "If you could assist me--"

"Of course," said Tecumseh immediately. "He should not be hard to find, unless of course if he is hiding," he said smiling.

"He does not know I have returned," said Red seriously.

"Yes, wait with my sister and brother-in-law," suggested Tecumseh. "They are over there talking to the Galloways. I will be there shortly," he said as other individuals pressed in on him.

"Thanks," said Red. She made her way toward the little group and stood there, watching as some older Indians, probably chiefs, asked questions of Tecumseh.

The older chiefs, sachems, and sagamores had found a spokesman but they wanted to make certain he knew every detail of the Greenville Treaty. Notwithstanding Tecumseh's absence from the proceedings he was very familiar with all its stipulations. He was quized about previous treaties, which he had mentioned only as generalities during his oration, but Tecumseh knew all the details for them also. "How did one so young as yourself acquire such knowledge?" asked one of the chiefs.

"I have spent much time with the Grandfathers, my chief," replied Tecumseh.

"It has been time well spent, my son."

So it was that Tecumseh emerged from the Urbana Council as an orator of great power and persuasion. The Amerindians viewed him as their champion and the Shemanese, who translated his name into the allegorical "Shooting Star," as a responsible young leader to be reckoned with.

Episode 6: Reunion

Tecumseh asked around and learned Spybuck was in the Wapakoneta area so he took Red there. He also learned Laulewasika was the medicine man's apprentice, that he had lost an eye, and that he had given up drinking completely, good news for the entire family. So when Tecumseh and Red found Spybuck's cabin the young chief was anxious to talk to his younger brother.

"Keewaukoomeelaa!" shouted Tecumseh from outside the door.

"Enter!" said a feminine voice from within. Red was disappointed. Perhaps Spybuck had taken a wife...

The two went into the cabin to find Laulewasika working with some herbs, Spybuck meditating in a corner, a young woman preparing some food over the fire. The two men came forward and shook Tecumseh's hand but Spybuck seemed rather ill at ease when he saw Flame.

"Have you no greeting for me?" asked Red quietly. "I have come this long way seeking you."

"Welcome," said Spybuck. There was an awkward silence as Red stared at the woman doing the cooking.

"Come, netheemaathar," said Tecumseh to Laulewasika, "I would speak with you outside."

"I have much to tell you, nethaathar," replied the younger brother. "Tukwaukee," he said to the young woman, "come with us for I wish you to become acquainted with my brother."

The woman complied without speaking and all three exited, leaving Red and Spybuck alone.

"Well, have you nothing to say to me?" asked Red, teasing yet somehow hopeful. "Or perhaps Spybuck has forgotten me many moons ago."

"I am glad to see you."

"Is that your woman outside?" Red felt like kicking the man.

"That is Laulewasika's woman... but what business is it of yours? You wanted to leave and you left."

"You never asked me to stay," commented the woman softly, relieved.

"It was your choice to leave. The law said I had to give you up and I took you to the fort to comply. As I remember your reaction was to beat me with a stick."

"And yours was to pull a knife on me," said Red.

"Nonsense."

"Oh yeah? Look," she said as she took it from her carrying bag, "here it is. Do you still want to use it?"

"I suppose you came back just to return my knife?"

"I came back because... because..." Words failed. Spybuck didn't help her or make it any easier. "If I am in the way I can leave. I am no longer captive."

"You never were," said Spybuck, "except at the very beginning."

"Then what was I?" asked Red, suddenly having to fight her tears.

223

"You were my Flaming Eagle of Delight," he said as he moved toward her, "and I hope you are still."

Red threw her arms around Spybuck as tears filled her eyes. "I have missed you, I didn't know how much..."

"You have brought the sun back into my world," whispered the man as he held her close. "It has been clouds and mist since you abandoned me. You were gone but I saw you everywhere. You were the deep, shy water that conceals itself from the winter ice. You were the slow built sparrow's nest of infinite eggs and seasons. You were the absent mother of spring. As I saw flowers burst up through the earth you were the wild, fragile dancer in the wind. Your memory was the promise of next year in the autumn wind at odds with dispersing leaves. After my eyes go blind with years you will still be a vision of loveliness and passion. If ever you desert me again the human fire will perish forever."

"I will never leave again."

"We shall walk the sands of eternity side by side."

The couple stood in their embrace, much too affected emotionally to respond physically.

Outside under a tree and sitting on a log were the two brothers and the young woman Tukwaukee. Tecumseh asked his brother if he had really given up drinking. Yes, definitely and forever. Then Laulewasika related his vision, how it had left him so confused, how Tukwaukee had helped through the crisis.

"I am happy for you," said Tecumseh as he scrutinized his younger brother. The hankerchief he wore over his eye gave him a raffish appearance. "I appreciate your efforts with my brother, Tukwaukee."

"He is the son of a chief," said Tukwaukee. "He has the seed of greatness in him. If it is nurtured properly it will blossom powerfully."

"Why don't you come live with me at the White River?" asked Tecumseh of Laulewasika. "I want to create a village where our people can live in the traditions of our ancestors. Perhaps we could go visit our sister in Missouri."

"I believe I have been touched by the Great Spirit," said Laulewasika. "A tremendous force has been unleashed within me. I do not understand it yet but the secret to all is through religion. I am going south to visit what some of our people have described as a new way to praise the Master of Life."

"What is it?" asked Tecumseh.

"I do not know what the people call themselves. They are Shemanese and they dance their worship, perhaps much as we do. After I visit them perhaps my confusion will be explained to me. Then maybe Tukwaukee and I will join you on the White River where we can work for the good of our people."

Tecumseh was impressed with his brother. He was sincere, intense, away from the path of wicked ways. They spent some time together then Laulewasika was off to Turtle Creek. Tecumseh felt better about his younger brother. Methoataske had always been quite mystical.

Episode7: The Shakers

Laulewasika, travelling alone, arrived in time to see the tremendous crowd gathered for the occassion of the camp meeting. There were literally thousands of people in attendance! Hundreds of heavy wagons and carriages served as shelters but there were many people housed in tents. Laulewasika walked around the encampment, or rather, encampments, for there were different groups within the whole. Most were Shemanese but there were blackfaces and Indians here and there. He had never seen so many women and children, the former of which appeared to outnumber the men. One group began to sing a hymn that was to prove popular throughout the revival:

> Thy mercy, my God, is the theme of my song,
> The joy of my heart, and the boast of my tongue:
> Thy free grace alone, from the first to the last,
> Has won my affection, and bound my soul fast...

Laulewasika understood only an occasional word but the countenances of the singers were as expressive as words: sympathy, hope, fear, joy. He walked toward another group where a man was addressing a large crowd:

"He died accursed of God when his soul was separated from his body and the black flaming vultures of hell began to grasp him from every side. HEAR THE WRATH OF THE LORD UPON IMPENITENT SINNERS! All the evil crimes of this FOOL! stared him in the face as a lake of fire and brimstone opened to overwhelm him. The memories of well meaning sermons and the holy sacraments flashed like streams of forked lightening through his tortured soul. Then the realization that he had slighted the mercy and blood of the SON OF GOD, that he had despised and rejected him, was like a poisoned arrow piercing his heart. The foul fiends of HELL dragged him into the eternal gulf and as they did so the fool yelled, screamed, roared like the devil he was becoming! As he sunk into the boiling waves of hell the accursed sinners of Tyre and Sidon, of Sodom and Gomorrah, sprang to the right and left of him, making way that he might fall even lower than they to the deepest cavern of the flaming recesses of *hellfire*. Not only his body but his eternal soul is doomed to grovel in a sea burning hellfire until the end of time! The pain nearly drives him insane and he screams for mercy but there is none to hear him. 'I'll be damned!' it says. 'God damn his soul!' it says. Now the fool understands perfectly the meaning of those words he was so in the habit of using while on earth. He never reflected on their significance and he scoffed at those who did. But now the fool could tell you these words frightened even the stoutest devils and filled the flaming vaults of hell with the most hideous shrieks! Now the fool understands for the pain has caused him to survey his life and reflect on the many offers of salvation he refused, the manner in which he mispent his precious time and refused the means of grace. He hopes his father and mother and sisters and brothers or any of those persons who sat under the same means of grace with him, and whom he derided as fools, fanatics, HYPOC-RITES!, he hopes they will win salvation as emphatically as he has lost it for he is DAMNED IN HELL FOR ALL TIME!"

Laulewasika looked around, taking in more reaction than language. Groans were voiced from the large gathering.

"But perhaps you feel secure," continued the preacher, "perhaps you consider yourself far from hellfire and suffering." The man now went into the crowd, rounding his shoulders, bending over, moving on all four limbs. "I am the devil! He is right here amongst us, unseen but doing his evil work!" He moved throughout the seated crowd, snapping at some, grabbing others, now barking like a vicious dog. Then he stood up dramatically and screamed, "THE DEVIL IS AMONG US!"

Pandemonium broke loose as people screamed, prayed, exhorted, sang, shouted all at once as everyone stood up. Suddenly it seemed as if a huge cannon ball had been fired point blank at the crowd for a human swathe lay prostrate on the ground, knocked down by some unknown force. Groans filled the air as in battle. Some on the periphery tried to run away but they too were laid low by mystical forces, Laulewasika was convinced.

"BEHOLD THE POWER WHICH STRIKES CONVICTION TO THE HEART OF THE SINNER!" screamed the preacher through his tears. "Thus, O sinner! shall you drop into eternal damnation unless you forsake your sins and turn to the Lord!" The man's strength completely depleted, he fell to the ground pleading, "Mercy, mercy!"

A man wept to his wife and children, "Alas! We have been blind all our days! We are all going to hell together! Oh, we must seek religion, we must get into Christ or the gates of hell shall pull us through!"

226

People began to embrace each other as if the end was near. Those who had fallen were deathly pale, trembling, full of anxiety. Was this the Day of Judgment?! Some attempted to fly the scene panic-stricken but were knocked down or returned, inexplicably unable to make their escape.

Two little girls who could not have been more than ten years old cried out for mercy until one of them embraced the other and yelled, "O you little sinner, come to Christ! Take hold of His hand and promises! Trust in Him for he is able to save even the uttermost! O! I have found peace to my soul! O! Precious Savior, come just as you are! He will take away the stony heart and give you a heart of eternal flesh! You just give your heart to Christ right this instant! You are not a greater sinner than me! You need not wait another moment!"

The other little girl suddenly was showered with light as if a ray from Heaven shined on her. She lifted her arms heavenward and cried out in the most affecting manner, "O! here is another star of light!"

"Lord have mercy!"

Another little girl, perhaps about seven years old, spoke to the multitude from where she sat on a man's shoulders until she weakened and exhausted, leaned on the head of her bearer.

"Poor child," said a kind hearted old man to the side, "she should be laid down."

At this the little girl sat up, turned to him and said, "Don't call me poor for Christ is my brother, God my father, and I have a kingdom to inherit. Don't call me poor for I am rich in the blood of the Lamb."

"Stand still and see the salvation of God!" exclaimed a young man.

Laulewasika had never imagined such a sight. The very clouds seemed to separate and give way to the praises of the people of God ascending to the heavens. "Hallelujah!" from thousands of tongues rolled into eternity while hundreds of people lay prostrate on the ground begging for mercy. Laulewasika was standing in amazement when the unknown force knocked him to the ground. He felt an ineffable sensation throughout his entire body like that of hitting the inside elbow on a hard object. He began to tremble and quake where he lay.

"Holy, holy, holy, Lord God Almighty," shrieked someone next to him.

"Mother of God what distress!" moaned another.

"Jesus thou son of the most high God have mercy on us!"

Laulewasika knew not why he had been overcome with this strange whirlwind of sensation. He tried to sit up, succeeded after mortifying difficulty, the prickly sensation as if his limbs had fallen asleep becoming sharp then subsiding. He felt the blood rushing through his body, especially in the great arteries of the legs and arms. His heart became full as if it would burst. Now his hands and feet went cold and a tremendous desolation gripped him. He began to weep, tears rolling down his face. He wanted to scream but could not.

"I deserve hell but I cannot bear it!" yelled a woman's voice. "God would be infinetly just in sending me directly to hell!"

"I am lost forever! O, I see hell and the breath of the Lord like a stream of brimstone kindling it!"

A group of three men stood and sneered at the goings-on. One of them called out to his daughters, "When I get you home I'll whip you good and proper! Come on now, get off that ground..." He went over to where they lay but before he bent over he was knocked off his feet as if shot. His face began to perspire profusely where he lay, confusion gripping his entire being.

A preacher walked over to a young woman, a very attractive one under ordinary circumstances, in an effort to assuage her vociferous distress. "Hear the voice of the Lord!" said the preacher as he took her by the shoulders. "Salvation is at hand!"

"Such danger is sin!" wailed the woman.

"Take your hands off her!" ordered a man to the preacher.

"And who might you be, brother?" asked the preacher.

"I am a man. Just like you." He drew a fist in a threatening manner. "And I'm not your brother! Now take your hands off my woman."

"What is it you want?"

"I want to take her out of here," said the man.

"I am a friend," said the preacher.

"Don't provoke me to speak my mind."

"I am not afraid for you to do so. I have the testimony of my heart and mind."

"You and all like you are nothing but scoundrels!"

"You do not hurt me by saying so."

"Then I will do something to hurt you," responded the man threateningly but as he moved toward the preacher he was thrown violently to the earth by the unseen force.

"Repent!" yelled the preacher. Then to the woman: "Sister, do you need assistance?"

"I have been a great sinner," replied the woman. "Oh, I shall never get over it in this world! I can never be saved!"

"Yes, the hand of the Lord is being held out to you. Take it and the guilt in your mind and heart shall vanish forever. Pray, my sister, pray for forgiveness..."

Over to one side of the crowd a young woman began to whirl around like a top, continuing the movement until she fell to the ground. She began to jerk and others immediately were attacked by the same phenomena. Some well dressed ladies and gentlemen, who had not participated in any activity up to this point, merely watching, were overcome head to toe by the jerks. Dressed in their fine silks, jewelry and all such fashionable items, the first jerk saw their fashionable bonnets, caps, and combs fly off. So sudden would be the jerking of the head their long loose hair would crack with a sound resembling a wagoner's whip.

A group of rowdies had been drinking during the services, laughing and ridiculing the participants. The leader of the group, a stout man, shouted, "Damn you all to hell you're making! Damn all religion and damn all you hypocrites who ruin good people with your superstition!" He was then knocked down by the force and when he tried to run he was jerked so powerfully he could not stay on his feet. His fellows became terror-stricken and fled but not before they saw their leader jerk so violently his neck broke, the sound of the crack reaching those around him.

As some people jerked on the ground others went to and fro barking like dogs. They would rush from their places, bark in fits as they roamed around and in a while return, some foaming at the mouth while others growled, snapped their teeth, and scampered on all fours.

The participants seeking to glorify the Savior were in time drained of all energy, physical as well as emotional. As the day ended they made their ways to shelter under the care of friends or family. Laulewasika had only his blanket but he was grateful to spread it under a tree and rest upon it. The huge encampment settled down as the sun began to set but as the world was becoming veiled with darkness people began to sing:

> "I long to see the happy time
> When sinners all come flocking home
> To taste the riches of His love
> And to enjoy the realms above.

Small bonfires were lit by the various groups. Individuals got up to share their salvation with their friends and neighbors. Preachers gave special sermons and candles in hand lit up faces of the believers. Evening services were as impressive as any this side of eternity. Many continued to pray and sing hymns far into the night. Laulewasika was among the last to roll up and sleep for a few hours before white dawn walked the rim of the horizon.

The following morning people were up brewing their tea or coffee, delicious breakfast aromas filling the camp. Laulewasika walked around, was invited to eat at several places though he did not understand the language until some food or drink was proffered. He was polite to all, partaking a little each time, then excusing himself in Shawnee and going on. He spied a group of Shemanese attired differently from all others and there he decided to stay when he was offered something to eat. They were dressed simply, the women in long white dresses covered by blue and white aprons, white muslin caps nearly covering their faces. The men wore blue and white pataloons, blue coats, and black waistcoats, wide-brimmed hats on their heads. All were dressed in uniform style.

"Good morrow, brother in the Lamb," people in this group said to Laulewasika as they took notice of him where he sat eating. He replied with the standard Shawnee greeting "Keewaukoomeelaa, I make my compliments to you." He noted there was no socializing between the men and women in this group.

When everyone had eaten the group of uniformed Shakers assembled and sang a hymn:

"'Tis the gift to be simple, 'tis the gift to be free,
'Tis the gift to come down where we ought to be,
And when we find ourselves in the place just right,
'Twill be in the valley of love and delight.

When true simplicity is gain'd,
To bow and to bend we shan't be ashamed.
To turn, turn will be our delight
Till by turning, turning we come round right.

Other people from the encampment began to gather as a venerable patriarch rose to speak:

"Brothers and sisters, when we assemble here to worship God, to sing His praises and hear His word, we will walk softly. We invite our brethren from the Outer Order to partake of our ceremony in praise of the Lord God. Often we are asked why we celebrate our love the way we do and this beautiful morning, gifted to us by the magnanimity of our Saviour, I will explain how we worship. Mother Ann advised us, 'Be joyful brethren and sisters! Be joyful! Joy away! Rejoice in the God of your salvation!' So we dance..."

The Shakers lined up for the wheel dance, four concentric circles, two composed of men, two of women, with no mixture of the sexes in any of the circles, men stamping in the opposite direction of the

230

women. "One foot up, the other down, tread the serpent to the ground!" sang out the men. "At Manchester in England this blessed fire began," sang the women after the men. "Awake my soul, arise and shake, no time to ever ponder, keep awake lest ye be rent asunder." The dancers in the exercise hardly looked at each other but their faces mirrored happiness and contentment. "Mother's love I want to feel, Father William's power, the innocence of Father James O heaven on me shower." Then all the dancers chorused together: "I love, I love the gifts of God, I love to be partaker, and I will labor day and night to be an honest Shaker!"

The exercise ended and the dancers went amongst the crowd answering questions posed them. Women talked only to women, men to men, and it was brought out that women were the equals of men in all Shaker communities. Except for the Quakers, no other denomination preached equality of the sexes. Indeed, Out Order society considered women to be property. Equality between men and women was little more than unheard of for it was men who made the rules of society. Laulewasika strained to understand bits and pieces of the conversations he heard. He would have enjoyed what he heard if he could have understood for the society from whence he emanated also elevated the position of women.

"We do not have pets like dogs or cats," explained one man, "because it is wastefulness to feed them while there are hungry people in the world..."

"Work as though you would live for a thousand years, work as though you would die tomorrow. Mother Ann instructed us, 'Hands to work, hearts to God.'"

"Gospel Order states: Ye shall come in and go out of this house with reverence and godly fear. All men shall come in and go out of the West doors and gates; all women at the East doors and gates. Men and women shall not intermix in this house or yard, nor sit together; neither shall there be any whispering or talking or laughing or unnecessary going out and in, during times of public worship."

"All your meeting houses are run that way?" asked a man of the Out Order.

"Yes, brother. Equality is as much our life as separation. All pervasive sinfulness comes from the flesh therefore marriage of the flesh is a covenant with death, an agreement with hell. If you wish to marry you may do so with the Lord Jesus Christ."

Laulewasika was planning on marrying Tukwaukee so perhaps it was just as well he could not understand this particular conversation.

"Things of the world have a corrupting influence. Once people begin to desire comforts greed is unleashed and overcomes the human personality. Soon there is no need to worship the Almighty and eternal damnation is assured. Therefore Shaker practice is as plain as possible. Frivolity is the handmaiden of vanity, which destroys dependence on the spiritual..."

"Dancing is basic to us because there are many references to it in the Old Testament: Jephtha's daughter danced, the daughters of Shiloh danced, King David danced before the Ark. Dancing is the holiest of exercise, not just an excuse to touch a member of the opposite sex..."

Laulewasika stayed close to the uniformed Shakers for the duration of the camp meeting revival. He believed they were sincere in their quest for oneness with the Great Spirit and he did his best to understand what they were saying. He resolved to attend as many revivals as possible for religious calling filled his heart. But the calling was not couched in the Shemanese language of the Shakers. In his heart it was the mellifluous, soaring, poetic language of the native people in the forests and prairies. His heart then was but a door, the door into the presence of the Great Spirit! *Had he, Laulewasika, who had been such a great sinner, been selected to lead the Indian people of this Great Island to salvation?!*

Episode 8: Teacher and Student

"Welcome, Mr. Tikomfa Chief," said Becky Galloway as Tecumseh rode up to the porch where the girl had been sitting reading a book. "Keewaukoomeelaa!" she said proudly, forcing a smile from Tecumseh's usually serious face. Becky knew now why the Shawnee was one of the handsomest men she had ever seen.

Tecumseh repeated the greeting and added "Good morning. I come to see your father."

"He is off a-hunting," said Rebecca as she pointed with her book toward the great forest. "I do not know when he is due to return. If you wish I can ask mother."

Tecumseh nodded his approval but he also said, "What do the talking leaves tell you this day?"

"What? Oh, yes. This is our Great Book, the Bible. It tells me many things. There are so many wonderful stories in it."

"So I have heard," commented Tecumseh.

"And which is your favorite?" asked Rebecca.

"Favrite?" stumbled the chief with the new word.

"Favorite. You know, which do you prefer best?"

"I must admit my education has been lacking when it comes to the Great Book."

"Some day, when you have time, I will read to you from it," suggested Rebecca.

"Why don't I wait for your father and you can read to me now?" said Tecumseh.

"All right. Tether your horse around that grass yonder?" The man did her bidding and returned shortly.

"Shall we begin... where would you like?" asked Rebecca. She had many favorite passages and stories in the Bible.

"You are the Grandfather," said Tecumseh as he sat down.

"I beg your pardon?"

"I am sorry, excuse me," chuckled Tecumseh as he noted Rebecca's perplexity. "Among my people teachers are mostly venerable grandfathers."

"I see," remarked Rebecca. "Would you prefer if I spoke in a grandmother's voice?" she asked in jest, smiling prettily.

"No, no, your own voice is fine."

"All right, let us begin with the Book of... Exodus," she said as she opened the Bible to wherever it fell.

With characteristic intensity, Tecumseh scrutinized the marks on the talking leaves.

"These are the names of the sons of Israel who went with Jacob to Egypt, each with his family..." read Becky, who stopped to explain the passages which Tecumseh might have difficulty in understanding, or words new to the Amerindian like "pharaoh," or "papyrus." Rebecca was a talented reader and the story of Moses and the Hebrews fascinated the young chief. The accounts of the nine plagues were vividly interpreted by Tecumseh's highly developed imagination but when Rebecca read about the parting of the sea the chief asked her to re-read it, such was his enthusiasm. She did so then asked, "What is it about this passage that appeals to you so much?"

"Because it is quite similar to what the Great Spirit did for us," replied Tecumseh, "though we have no Great Book to tell of it."

"Relate it to me," suggested Rebecca, always the serious student. "My voice is a little hoarse anyway."

"Our ancestors of a time out of mind in the misty long ago were living in lands far to the setting sun. The Great Spirit directed great animals to search out new territories for his red children, knowing the animals would be followed. But when the beasts got to the great seas there was no way to cross. So the Great Spirit willed that a land bridge rise over the waters so the people might cross in safety, opening up all these new territories for his red children. Thus we Amerindians believe these lands were the direct gift of the Great Spirit for He caused the land to rise out of the sea. This land is our birthright and the basis for our religion."

"I have been told some Indians believe the world is the back of a giant turtle," said Rebecca.

"You must understand our life is described with comparisons from nature," explained Tecumseh. "Perhaps there is a better word in She-manese?"

"Metaphor could be appropriate."

"My people speak in metaphors," continued Tecumseh. "This great island is shaped like the shell of a turtle, days pass like a turtle moves, slowly but steadily."

"I understand," said Rebecca. "Everything is metaphor and allegory."

"Allegory?"

"An allegory is when someone uses... the land or the animals to make a point about human beings."

"I see," commented Tecumseh. "Would that we had talking leaves to capture the beauty with which our people speak! But then perhaps our ears are strong enough to make our minds remember. Don't let me interupt, go ahead and tell me more. Or if you are tired perhaps you should rest and continue another day."

"I am a bit hoarse," she said as she cleared her throat. "I also want you to tell me about your religion."

"That is simple to do. Look around you and you see our Great Book. Every living thing, every object has a spirit of its own, therefore it must be respected. The earth is our mother and the sun our father."

"Who exactly is the Great Spirit?"

"The Ruler of Destinies is our omnipotent Grandmother, the life force of the universe," replied Tecumseh.

"A *grandmother?*" asked the girl in disbelief.

"Yes. Why does that appear to shock you?"

"I guess because I am not accustomed to thinking of God as a female. Among my people God is represented as male."

"There are male as well as female spirits," said Tecumseh, "but it is the Great Grandmother who will gather us up in the giant net *skemotah* which human beings weave with their good deeds so that we may be one with Her throughout eternity. Perhaps that is why women are so important in our nations."

"I see," commented Rebecca.

"Is it not so in your world?"

234

"Women are important, of course, but... we are not important in the nation."

"How could that be so?" Now it was Tecumseh's turn to be incredulous. "Women are the mothers of the great trees... I mean, the mothers of men who decide things, of chiefs, sachems, sagamores."

"Women in our society are not allowed to vote," said Rebecca. "Not many can read or write. Not one woman signed the Declaration of Independence, just men."

"We have women who are chiefs of villages," said Tecumseh thinking of Grenadier Squaw, the sister of Cornstalk. "Most councils are composed of men but delegates to councils are elected by the women and if these delegates don't vote as the women wish they can be removed."

"Really?" Rebecca was genuinely astonished. And these people were called savages?! Any society that honored its women and shared national power with them was quite civilized to say the least. And God... is a *woman?!* How unique!

"Yes, it is so," responded Tecumseh though he was slightly puzzled over Rebecca's reactions. "Women are pillars of the nation, just like men. I, a man, am no more important than my sister Tecumapease. Indeed, were I to speak honestly I would have to admit her superiority over me for she has been mother as well as sister."

"Perhaps there is much our two cultures can learn from each other," said Rebecca. "Of course, there has been much mixing already. I understand Daniel Boone was your foster brother."

"Yes, for a time," said Tecumseh, a strange expression of irony and puzzlement coming over his face.

Rebecca noticed immediately and commented: "Was he a good brother, to you and your people?"

Tecumseh was not sure if he should try to explain the enigma that was *Sheltowee,* Daniel Boone. But perhaps Rebecca would understand. She seemed quite mature and a strong student. "We have mixed feelings about Brother Boone," began Tecumseh. "I was little more than a child when I first met him. Black Fish, my father, was fascinated with him and I guess we were impressed with his forest skills. Boone came into Kentucky to hunt and was very successful. There were thousands of buffalo and deer so he made several camps. But our own hunters saw the results of his hunting prowess for he would take only the hides or choice parts of meat. The rest would be left to rot. Captain Will, one of our chiefs, succeeded in capturing him, if that could be said for he was not really a prisoner. The chief sternly demanded Boone take him and his warriors to all the hunting camps. One by one the camps were surprised, though

Boone tired to warn them. Everything in the camps was confiscated or destroyed. Then the Shawnees displayed real generosity, dismissing Boone and his men, presenting each with two pairs of moccasins, a doeskin for patch leather, a little trading gun, and a few loads of powder and shot so they might hunt for their needs during the way back to their settlements. Captain Will told Boone: 'Now, brother, go home and stay there. Don't come here any more for this is the Indians' hunting ground, and all the animals, skins, and furs are ours. If you are so foolish as to venture here again, you may be certain the wasps and yellow jackets will sting you severely, even to death. Go in peace and return only on the black path."

"You can easily see," continued Tecumseh,"how our people behaved with utmost restraint and generosity. A destructive party invaded our homeland, territories which have been ours since the Great Spirit provided us with the bridge on which to walk toward them, and slaughtered our animals in such a way as to assure total destruction of game within a short time. We are accused of being wasteful with land because we use it to hunt on but what of killing animals for their skins and letting the meat rot? That is sacriligeous! So we ordered the intruders out, without bloodshed, without drawing the scalping knife. Those who remember only the tales of battle cruelties, scalpings and torturing, should ponder how our people first treated the encroachers in Kentucky who were sent back to their villages well provided for by our people. What would have been our fate if we had gone into the Shemanese settlements and taken their stock?"

"I do not know," said Rebecca, "but I surmise it would not have been pleasant."

"You speak with wisdom," commented Tecumseh.

"I would fight also," agreed Rebecca, "especially if someone wanted my strawberry patch!"

Both laughed, a bit nervously perhaps. Neither wanted a confrontation.

"Ah, you too are a strawberry lover," said Tecumseh. "Our people have a beautiful story on how strawberries were first invented."

"Oh tell it to me, Mr. Tikomfa Chief!"

"All right, though I am not as good as the Grandfathers. My brother Sauwaseekau was a good story teller."

"Well you must bring him next time but now you must tell me. Please."

"Of course. Then I must go," said Tecumseh. "In the time out of mind in the misty long ago man chose his first mate and together they lived

236

very happily for a time until they began to quarrel because they did not understand how to adapt to each other. They got on one another's nerves. The man liked a diet of meat, the woman preferred vegetables so they argued even about that. At last the woman could suffer no longer so she packed a few possessions and fled toward the Sun Land in the east. She traveled many suns and many moons, not stopping even for food or drink.

The Watchful Sun maintained vigil over her and realized she must have food so he caused a patch of fine huckleberries to spring up along the trail in front of the weary woman but she passed them by without even noticing. Perhaps she preferred blackberries? Up ahead he caused a clump of large, juicy blackberries to sprout up, the Sun's rays dancing their invitation to succulent enjoyment. But still the unhappy traveller did not even notice.

The Watchful Sun now became seriously worried for the woman was losing the healthy summer bloom from her cheek and the redness from her lips. The gloss was fading from her beautiful raven hair and her eyes were no longer radiant. The woman's spirit waned without even realizing she was heart broken without her husband. Her eyes reflected her state best of all for they stared like cold sea shells in the dark.

Was there no hope for man and woman? The Watchful Sun turned toward the man to discover he too was so grief stricken he was following his wife's trail, calling her name. Try as he might he could not catch up with her and his skin suffered from exposure. 'Are you still angry with your wife?' asked the Sun.

'No, I am not angry and I will never be again if I can get her back,' said the repentant husband. 'I will do anything to heal all hurts between us. I will even give up my favorite meat dishes and eat more vegetables with her if that is what she wishes. Do you think... she has ever thought of me or missed me?'

'You let her go from you during a wintry hour. Her sigh tells me she wishes to die. Man's harshness kills if it is not curbed. You must solve your problem, if other human beings are to follow in your moccasin prints.'

The man looked at the Sun then pleaded, 'Help me find her, Brother, and I will fan the flame of love with cherishing thoughts instead of talking to her like vile thunder roaring through the canyons.'

The Great Apportioner took pity on him and his weakness. 'Look at me straight, with head high and eyes wide open. Now travel eastward and find your wife.'

The Watchful Sun now turned his attention to the woman. The

weakened and bewildered wife wanted to die, such was her heartbreak so she ignored the fruits and berries that had been put there for her benefit. She thought of her husband... why had she not learned to eat a little meat with him? She saw right in her path a tree full of black haws hanging in luscious bunches. Before they made her mouth water but now they only caused her sorrow and she walked by them. The Sun knew he had to do something spectacular if he was to save the woman so up in front of her a ways he caused a patch of strawberries to sprout, the first ever known. The woman noticed them and never having seen them before became intrigued for they were red as rose petals in the breeze. She sat wearily at the edge of the patch and heard little voices saying, 'Dear lady, let the frozen repose of your heart melt in the flavor of our kiss. We will wipe the tears from your heart...'

The woman gathered a few and ate the stange new fruit. She turned her face away from the Sun and gazed westward. The eternal cliffs, whose strength defied her heart and pride, bore silent record of her vanishing frown. The oak leaf breathed in mysterious relief as she thought of her husband. As she ate of the strawberries color returned to her lips and the memory of her love began to fill her heart. Suddenly she did not wish to continue her journey. 'Return,' chorused a bevy of small voices, 'return to your man and take us with you that your people may come to know the fruit of love.' The woman wept silently as she ate and the desire to see her husband and forgive him became stronger and stronger. She felt like melting ice drifting over a cold-blue ocean. Warm winds swept through her heart as she gathered bunches of the finest strawberry plants then started back along the path to find her spouse. She longed to give him the finest berries and her step was like the arrow's flight through vale and field.

The two quickly saw each other in the distance and raced into each other's open arms. Together they fanned the flame of love, promising never to think harshly of each other ever again. They ate the strawberries, smiled at each other lovingly, and ascended to the lands of their birthright where they planted strawberries which smiled from meadow to sandy shore, calming lovers who quarrel and roar like the sea.

"And thus it was that strawberries are the symbol of love among our people," finished Tecumseh.

"What a beautiful story!" sighed Rebecca. "You do not need talking leaves," she said wistfully.

Tecumseh smiled. He had not been so relaxed in many a moon. "The sun is high and I have kept you here all this time," he said apologetically. "I must let you get on before your mother comes out and beats me with a stick."

"You are always welcome here, Mr. Tikomfa Chief," said Rebecca, "and stay as long as you wish."

"I admire your hospitality," said Tecumseh as he got up and headed to fetch his horse, "and I especially appreciate you telling me what is in the talking leaves. Perhaps you will read to me again?"

"Of course."

Episode 9: The Model

Spybuck sat by the flickering fire, playing the flute softly, looking at Flaming Eagle of Delight as she opened the box. "I know you're going to like these," said Flame michievously yet calmly. That was one of her characteristics: she could be totally imprisoned by some passion and yet not show but a trace of the floodtide upon her. Spybuck had learned much about his woman since her return and perhaps even more about himself. It was truly amazing how he had missed her during her absence. He would never have thought it possible, living the way he had prior to Flame. Was it that he was getting old? Of course not. Passion became better with age. Before Flame, seducing women had been... a juvenile pastime, exciting and entertaining but of little significance. Using strong herbs to stir female passions was part of the game, titillating at first but ultimately boring as standard fare. Flame needed no such encouragement. She was the only woman who could wear him down... but not out. He could still give her all she could take.

"See?" asked Flame in her little girl's voice.

Spybuck looked at what appeared to be remnants of beautiful clothing. He stopped playing momentarily. "Yes. What's that?"

"Underwear, silly," replied Flame mirthfully. She took a pair of brilliantly colored panties and put them on Spybuck's head.

"Is that better than an eagle feather?" asked the man.

"Perhaps not but placed where they should go they will both soar," said Flame calmly. "I designed these myself," she continued, "just for you."

"Place them where they go," suggested Spybuck as he returned to his flute.

Red took the box and retreated to a dark corner of the cabin where she took off her clothing and put on the first of her creations, a sheer little jacket with matching panties. She walked lithely back to Spybuck, stood in front of him, turned this way and that as he played the flute and nodded his head approvingly. She went back into her corner and returned with another outfit which consisted of a sort of knit stockings that clung to the curves of her upper thighs, a G-string, and a sheer halter over her breasts. Flame remembered how her seamstress back in Philadelphia had been scandalized while she made these creations. "Whatever do you want such things for?" she had asked. Spybuck began to show signs of arousal as Flame moved rhythmically to the strains of the flute. Her curvaceous body moved easily, her flesh having moments of seemingly individualistic independence yet harmoniously seeking the ecstasy which guided her every move.

Spybuck put down the flute and stood up.

"Oh, don't stop playing," said Flame as she picked up the flute smoothly and handed it to him. His eyes told her the man wanted to press her to him but she stayed just slightly out of reach. He began to play again so she swayed to and fro, coming close enough to undo his breechclout, letting it fall to the floor. He just stood there playing, but next time Flame came close there would be no getting away.

The woman returned to the corner for another change of titillating apparel. When she was ready for Spybuck she was wearing gorgeous red slippers, shiny crimson panties that were oddly bulky down toward the kimbo, a scanty cup bra and a stunning headdress of the same material. She walked up to Spybuck and stood in front of him aggressively, hands on hips, feet slightly apart. He continued to play as if there was no vision of untrammeled passion in front of him. That is, except for his bod, which was anxious for some ecstatic probing. Flame looked at it, caressed it delicately with her hands then put it to herself as she opened her underwear at the bulky place. The cloth stayed open. Spybuck came closer, tantalized her caressingly at the open place but continued playing his flute.

Flame stepped back slightly but then came up to Spybuck, putting her arms around him as best she could but pressing her hips into his thigh and undulating softly, lovingly, passionately. Spybuck tried to turn to get her directly in front but the woman did not permit it. "Play, play," she whispered as she rubbed his body with her hands, "don't ever stop."

Spybuck was more than anxious to quell her obvious passion but he refused to let his own desire overpower him. After all, he was not a young buck under his first blanket. So he played the flute and watched his sensuous woman's titillations, wondering if she could hold out longer than he, vowing to blossom her passion flower when the moment came.

Flame retreated from her lover, quickly put a robe on the floor where the fire could flicker on her, then returned to stand close in front of Spybuck. She nudged herself to his bod, moving her hips rythmically from side to side, then with a soft hand encouraged penetration. Spybuck wanted to fling the flute away and pounce on her but he showed no emotion, beyond slight beads of perspiration on his forehead, and continued playing. When Flame began to make soft sounds from deep inside her throat, the rich crimson cloth beginning to obscure his bod, he decided to put the musical instrument away but suddenly Flame stepped back and lay perfectly flat on the robe by the small fire so he continued playing.

Flame looked at Spybuck, the fire light making his bod shine at the tip. She arched her back sensuously several times. This was something she particularly enjoyed about Spybuck: she could be openly aggressive in her desires and Spybuck would not become frightened. Some men did not like the woman to take sexual initiatives. As she lay flat again she wondered how long it would take for Spybuck to complete her. She put the greatest possible distance between her two feet, brought them back together, rubbed one leg with the other foot. But it was the little sounds she made deep in her throat that forced Spybuck to lay down the flute, bend over her premeditatedly to remove her scanty scarlets.

"You could leave them on," whispered Flame.

"I don't want them soiled," returned Spybuck as he placed everything to a side.

It was Spybuck who had put a stop to the foreplay but it was Flame who entered the first culmination of ecstasy almost immediately upon the two becoming one.

Episode 10: The Blue Jacket Mining Company

"He is here again," said Wabethe to her husband.

"Wife," replied Blue Jacket, "tell me what to do with that man. He is driving me insane with his importuning about the silver mines!" The chief was obviously sick to death of his Shemanese visitor.

"Perhaps you should tell him what he wants to know," suggested Wabethe.

"Precious wife," said Blue Jacket, "you just might have something there." He hugged the woman and went out to see his pertinacious visitor.

"Good morning, Chief Blue Jacket! How does this fine morning find you?"

"Keewaukoomeela," said Blue Jacket. He looked at the portly Shemanese. He was affable enough, but persistent as the flowing rivers.

"You know chief, I got to thinking," said Jonathan Loetking, "now that we are at peace we have to consider each other's welfare. Now we all know your people have done much for us and I'm the first one to admit it." Jonathan ran his fingers through his hair. "Why, in the old country they didn't even know what corn was before you folks taught us. And that maple syrup is a delicacy I couldn't live without, no sirree. So I got to thinking, how could we repay Blue Jacket's people? Now you know I've been hunting these here parts for a few moons. I've been treated well and I've seen you all need a little help here and there, don't you know. Ain't none of us perfect, we all need some help once in a while, eh?"

"Of course," intoned Blue Jacket, no expression on his face.

"Now I represent some business people," continued Jonathan, "as I've already told you. They're not the smartest crowd in the world, but they do know what they want. Now I'm going to make you an offer. It'll be a good offer, better than any other we've mentioned casually before." The man cleared his throat. "I'll get you horses, plenty horses, cloth, iron kettles, ploughs if you want them, different colored beads... You get what I mean? You tell me what you need and I will acquire it for you. All you have to do is tell me where your people have that silver mine. Fair is fair, trade for trade. You can still get some silver to make bracelets and earrings for your squaw. Nothing more generous than that, say what? We give you what you need for what we want."

"It is my duty to serve my people," said Blue Jacket seriously, "but I would have to undergo serious purification in order to obtain permission from the Earth Spirit to remove silver from her bosom." There was an expression of great consternation on his face now.

"The spirit will praise you, chief!" said Jonathan excitedly. This was the only glimmer of success he had seen throughout the months he had been with the Shawnee. "A leader must care for his people, now everybody knows that, including the spirit. You need steel axes? Save you a lot of work and sweat, hey? Why not trade some needed steel for silver? Now nothing could be more fair!"

"It is true we must clear land quite often in order to plant our fields and gardens," said Blue Jacket.

"Of course, of course. And you can't eat silver, now can you?" said Jonathan. "Now I'm gonna tell you something else," said he in a whispered confidential tone, "I've decided to recommend to my people that our business be called the Blue Jacket Mining Company. Now how about that, chief? And if we don't delay, I'll make you a full partner in the mine, right along with my backers. You know what that means, chief? Means you'll have an income as long as silver comes out of that there mine! Think of it! It's the chance of a *lifetime.*"

242

Blue Jacket's unruffled manner contrasted the Shemanese's enthusiasm. "Perhaps what you say is best for all concerned. But there must be many horses and trade goods exchanged if my people are to benefit from the loss of the mines."

"Just tell me what you want," said Jonathan, "and if it is reasonable," he added soberly, "we have a deal. You can trust me, I'm a serious business man."

"I hope my people do not depose me for telling you their secret, or shoot me some dark night."

"Out with that, they'll apppreciate you more, I guarantee it. Now tell me when you want to close the deal?"

"Well," said Blue Jacket reluctantly, "let us meet at the home of James Galloway within one moon. Bring the trade goods and I will show you the mine."

"Fair enough," said Jonathan, barely containing his eagerness and turning a bit redfaced with the effort. "Fair is fair! One month, uh moon. Best decision you ever made, chief. One moon! Now I'm gonna hightail it back to my people and get your trade goods together." He walked as calmly as he could toward his horse, mounted, and waved good-bye. "Peace, brother," he said as he rode into the forest. As soon as he was out of sight he lashed his horse into a full gallop. Lexington was a good distance away but he would cover it in record time for the path would be paved with silver!

True to his word, Blue Jacket was at the home of James Galloway within one moon, along with several tribal elders. Jonathan Loetking was there with a dozen other Kentuckians and a host of pack animals which carried all kinds of goods.

"Let us get to the business at hand," said Jonathan before Blue Jacket could take out his pipe and begin to invite everyone to smoke. "Now tell us what you want, chief. Like I told you, I'm a reasonable man."

Blue Jacket took two days to tell them what his people wanted in exchange for the mines. He would not be rushed and he needed time to learn what the Shemanese had brought. He was able to use the Kentuckian's eagerness to good advantage and when he finished he had all the trade goods, most of the horses, and a large amount of money, all of which he dispatched with the other Shawnee to the village where the entire nation would call for a share.

"Now," said Jonathan as all the Shemanese surrounded Blue Jacket, "now you can tell us where the mine is and take us there." The men quieted down and leaned toward the chief.

"The mines," began Blue Jacket slowly as if the information was painful to divulge, "the mines are not too far from here..."

"Yes... yes?"

"The mines are in the area of the Red River," said Blue Jacket.

"Red River?! In Kentucky?" gasped Jonathan.

"Yes. The Red River is a tributary of the Kentucky."

The Shemanese were stunned. Rumor and popular opinion held the Shawnee silver came from around Old Chillicothe, most likely the deep glen to the northeast a few miles from where they stood this very instant. But Jonathan and others had scoured the area to no avail.

"How many mines are there, chief?" asked one of the men.

"There are several in the area," conceded Blue Jacket.

In Kentucky, right there in their own back yard! And everybody had wasted their time searching in Ohio! But wait, it was better this way. While the competition was on a wild goose chase the Blue Jacket Mining Company would be staking claims and getting rich in Kentucky!

"Well, when do we start?" asked Jonathan.

"Would you mind if I took my wife on the journey with me?" asked Blue Jacket. "These old eyes of mine might never see the beauties of Kentucky again and I would like for her to enjoy the land with me."

"Why of course!" replied Jonathan. "Let's go collect her and we'll be on our way. Uh, you do remember exactly where they are?"

"I would never forget the sacred area, though I have not been there in a very long time. I think my old eyes are still dependable, though. But if you wish to be accompanied by a younger man, my son perhaps, I would not be offended."

"Of course not, my chief," said Jonathan, an injured tone in his voice. "We will follow you, no other. Now let's go pick up your wife and be off."

Wabethe was delighted to accompany her husband and the two were escorted in grand style to Kentucky. The couple were feted and feasted throughout the journey, nothing being too good for them. Wabethe especially enjoyed the outing for she had never spent much time in the Kentucky hunting grounds, first because they were for hunters then because the area was the scene of bloody conflict between the races. Hers was the poetic eye of her people and every scene evoked a poem. She chatted to him constantly, the Shemanese in the party genuinely surprised an Indian woman could be so loquacious. But she wore beautiful earrings, necklaces, and bracelets made of *silver,* a fact which only served to whet their appetites for future discoveries.

"That is the Red River over yonder," said Jonathan Loekting when the fairly large stream came into view.

"Yes," said Blue Jacket as he gazed at its beauty and put his arms up toward the heavens in thanksgiving. "The sacred area is a little further downstream. Why not make camp over there at the edge of the meadow? My wife and I will go into the sacredness alone. We must appease the Earth Spirit for permission to disclose the location of the mines."

"How you gonna do that, chief?"

"We must purify ourselves with praying and fasting."

"How long will you be gone?" asked Jonathan.

"Not long. A few days perhaps."

"All right. You go on ahead now and we'll be right here when you return."

The Indian couple were gone for nearly a week. When they returned Blue Jacket commented his purification had not been as complete as other times but it was the best he could do. So the search began in earnest, Wabethe remaining in camp while Blue Jacket led the Shemanese hither and yon.

"Perhaps the Earth Spirit has dimmed my eyes," said Blue Jacket toward the end of the day. Everyone else was perspiring and breathing heavily from so much walking and leading the pack animals loaded with digging tools. "I thought the mines should be right... yes, they begin right there on the side of that little hill. We have been favored! There they are!"

The Shemanese let out a shout for joy and raced toward the hill on foot, scaring the pack animals in the process. Sure enough, there was evidence of diggings, but with unsophisticated tools, it would appear.

"Let's get some of those picks and shovels over here!" yelled one of the men. Almost at the surface there was some rock that looked rather bluish. The pack animals were captured and the tools fetched. "That blue stuff... isn't that silver?"

"EEEEEEEEiiiiiooooooo!" yelled Jonathan, "it sure as hell is!" The man laughed uproariously. Blue Jacket looked on placidly. "We've done it!"

"If my eyes were not so dim I could show you others," commented Blue Jacket. "Perhaps I should return to Ohio and send my son. He knows where the others are."

"That sounds good to me, chiefie," said Jonathan. "We got enough digging to do until he gets here. Do you think you and your squaw can find your way back alone?"

"I think so."

"Well then you go right on ahead," said Jonathan as he shook Blue Jacket's hand, "and we thank you for all you've done. Well come on now men, we've got some work to do!"

245

It was truly amazing how the entire group fell into the enterprise as Blue Jacket returned to camp. "Let us return home, beloved wife. The Shemanese will be quite occupied for a time and no longer needs us."

The two packed their belongings and gifts on horses and headed toward the Ohio. The return trip was just as leisurely, the couple stopping to hunt, pick berries, or rest in the shade whenever they wished. They never heard of the Blue Jacket Mining Company again and within a short time all the Indian nations were convulsed with glee over the greatest pratical joke that had ever been played on the importunate Shemanese who did not know the difference between silver and galena.

Episode 11: The Suitor

James Galloway was aware Tecumseh would come visit whenever he was in the vicinity but he had no illusions as to who the young chief was visiting. He looked at the two sitting on the porch, Rebecca reading to him as always. Galloway himself was a highly literate man, especially for a frontier environment, but he was amazed how quickly Tecumseh could learn. He must have been endowed with a bear trap of a mind because if he heard something once he could repeat it word for word any time afterward. This day Tecumseh had arrived to see Rebecca with a present of a silver comb for her hair. Galloway pondered this momentarily: the young chief was acting something like a *suitor*. He usually brought some sort of gift for the family, a choice piece of meat from the hunt and the like, but he also brought expensive furs once and now this silver comb. Did Tecumseh have something else on his mind, in his heart? Rebecca showed no interest whatsoever in any young white men from the settlements. Was she taken with the young chief? It was obvious they thoroughly enjoyed each other's company. They could sit and talk all day long, exchanging stories and comments about one another's people... was it the prelude of romance or merely two intelligent people enjoying each other's education?

Galloway had to ask himself a question: what would he say or do if the two up and decided they were serious and wanted to marry? Rebecca was his only daughter. She was a happy, God-fearing child... no, not child, young woman. Hers was spirited charm, studious, a good conversationalist, a very talented homemaker. How did she feel about Tecumseh and his visits? Galloway had never thought of asking her, before now. As for Tecumseh, the young chief was easily one of the most intelligent men living in the Northwest, red or white. His activities dur-

246

ing war and peace had already made him famous. He never signed the Greenville Treaty. What would happen if war broke out between the races once more?

Galloway shook his head as if to curtail the ramblings of his mind. Ah well, such were the ways of a father. Let the future bring what it would. He was glad Rebecca and Tecumseh were friends. Galloway himself was attracted by the talented, intense, earnest young chief. Who wouldn't have been after hearing him orate at Urbana? He walked up to the two, pulled up a chair and listened to what Rebecca was reading:

"...Alexander's quick imagination could visualize its tremendous significance. This commonwealth of nations, once attempted, could be carried out on a scale to include all the western world. How much of this Alexander reasoned out for himself at this point, and how much he learned from hearing of the early Persian imperium of Kurush, may never be made clear. What is certain is that he visualized the possibility of a world state, a universe of men—in which women might share— that could preserve a balance of freedom within its parts..."

Neither heeded the addition of James Galloway to the study circle. Since he had read and re-read the history of Alexander the Great the father only half-listened as he saw what other books were on the stool next to Rebecca. He saw the Bible and *Shakespeare's Plays.* Not bad company for any pair of students. Perhaps Tecumseh would name his own horse *Bucephalus* in the future, thought Galloway mischievously. Wouldn't that wrinkle a few foreheads in these parts?!

"And when did all these events take place?" asked Tecumseh.

"Oh, at least... no, more than two thousand years ago," explained Rebecca, but immediately she realized she had not communicated the idea properly. "Let me see, long long before the grandfathers of the grandfathers were born."

"*Oalargoa,*" said the elder Galloway, which Rebecca didn't understand but to which Tecumseh nodded his head.

The young chief continuously marveled at the creation of the talking leaves! To relate the events of the misty long ago... even the Grandfathers would have been pleased. Rebecca continued with her reading, Tecumseh forcing her to pause with an occasional question or the young woman stopping to explain some word or concept. The elder Galloway finally wandered off to some chore or other, leaving the two to themselves.

During another visit Tecumseh asked Rebecca to read from her favorite work. "My favorite is Romeo and Juliet," she said. "I've read it

247

dozens of times and it still makes me cry. My ambition is to see it performed. You want me to read it?"

"Yes, of course, unless you wish to do something else."

"No, this is fine," said Rebecca and she began to read:
Two households, both alike in dignity, In fair Verona where
we lay our scene, From ancient grudge break to new mutiny,
Where civil blood makes civil hands unclean...

Rebecca had to make numerous explanations in her reading for the language of Shakespeare was difficult for Tecumseh to understand. But he thoroughly enjoyed the play, rightfully crediting Rebecca's perspicacious skills at translating.

"I fear I am making you labor too much with this kind of talking leaves," remarked Tecumseh after she finished the play.

"No, it isn't that," said the young woman in a throaty voice. "It's just..." and she tried to prevent the tears from filling her eyes.

"Yes, I understand," commented Tecumseh sympathetically as he took her hand to comfort her, "the story is tragic. And the basis of the tragedy is what the two never experienced. Their entire life was before them, everything was theirs, only to wind up in an early grave. But there is much beauty in their love if you understand that life without the other would have been little more than a living grave. My people understand such depth of feeling. I only wish we had someone who could record it for all time in the talking leaves. Perhaps then the world would come to know us as we really are."

"Tis a consummation devoutly to be wished," said Rebecca, now in control of her emotions.

"What?"

"That line is from another of Shakespeare's plays, the one called *Hamlet.*"

"And is that another sad love story?"

"It is tragic but it is more about a son who must avenge the death of his father," said Rebecca.

"Tecumseh, you will be the whirlwind and storm of your race until your enemies tremble at the mere mention of your name. You will live to scatter desolation and death among the Shemanese murderers who stalk the earth. You will be a fire spreading over hills and valleys until you and your warriors consume the race of treacherous murderers! See this bloody hand, Tecumseh?! It is your father's blood and his death! If you love your father, if you love me, it is you DUTY TO AVENGE!"

Methoataske's voice raced through Tecumseh, making him shudder involuntarily. He fully understood what it meant to have to avenge the death of a father.

"Mr. Tikomfa chief, what is wrong?" asked Rebecca.

"What? Oh nothing, nothing. I was just thinking of something that happened long ago when I was a child. I must be going now but next time would you read me *Hamlet?*"

Two months later when Tecumseh passed by the Galloway home the young chief's wish was fulfilled. He always liked everything Rebecca read to him but there was something extra special about Hamlet and he was to ask to have it read several times in the future. He had never heard of the kingdom of Denmark but somehow it thrilled him that there were people all over the world, people like Alexander out of the past, the warrior Romans, the poetic Greeks, the history of different peoples. At first Hamlet caused him great confusion but in time he appreciated enormously the philosophical lyrics and sheer poetry of the work. Tecumseh saw himself in the protagonist's role, with minor differences: he had never wished he was dead nor ever felt only evil thrived in the world. How he wished Methoataske could have heard some of Shekespeare's lines:

"Haste me to know't, that I, with wings as swift As meditation or the thoughts of love, May sweep to my revenge."

He was certain Shakespeare would have enjoyed the language of his people, especially as spoken by Methoataske and the orators of her race.

Tecumseh was disturbed by Hamlet's feelings of inadequacy. Were the duties of either too much for a solitary protagonist? But Tecumseh's role was not solitary: there were thousands and thousands of Amerindian brothers and sisters who wanted to retain the land which was their birthright.

"To be, or not to be: that is the question," read Rebbeca, "Whether 'tis nobler in the mind to suffer The slings and arrows of outrageous fortune, Or to take arms against a sea of troubles, And by opposing end them? To die: to sleep..."

Hamlet was so fearful of dying, thought Tecumseh. The two races approached death in such different ways. The tribes from across the great salt water seemed so unsure of the hereafter. Was it that way down deep they really did not believe in their God?!

"...To sleep: perchance to dream: ay, there's the rub: For in that sleep of death what dreams may come When we have shuffled off this mortal coil, Must give us pause..."

Yes, there it was right there! The Longknives really did not believe in the Great Spirit. The Amerindian is not afraid to die because he knows in his heart the Ruler of Destinies is waiting to gather him unto Her bosom. He does not pause to fear the unknown. Quite the contrary, he stands on his feet and sings his death song!

Every time Rebecca read Hamlet Tecumseh was able to observe something he had not discerned before. Perhaps that was why he requested it every so often. Rebecca was impressed with Tecumseh's acumen and quickly decided the chief could be as cultured and literate as any white man if he wished it. She believed if he were to move into a regular settlement he would be the equal of most, superior to many. She never wished to suggest such a thing, however, because the last thought in her mind was to offend her visitor friend. She found herself wishing he would come more often and when he did not show up regularly she would worry and wonder aboout him and his activities.

"It is time for you to be thinking of marriage," said Rebecca's mother one day as the two were working on some sewing.

"I did not know you wished to be rid of me," said Rebecca.

"Now be serious, daughter, you know that isn't what I mean, Becky. I just... why don't you pay attention to some of the young men hereabouts?"

"I don't know," answered Rebecca truthfully.

"Is there no one who has... caught your attention? The Armstrongs, Kyles, Greggs, Winters, McHattons, all those families are good stock and we see them as friends and neighbors."

Rebecca curtailed her work momentarily. "Am I to be auctioned off?"

"No child, now be serious with your mother. Few things are more blessed than a good marriage to a good man. I would not want you to miss out on one of the basic gifts of God."

"I guess I just haven't met the man yet," confessed Rebecca, "but perhaps I will before I am an old maid spinster. Forgive me, I do not mean to jest. I will marry I guess, everybody does, but as of right now there is no one in the horizon. I am happy with you and father and my Tikomfa Chief keeps me occupied and challenged."

Episode 12: Partnership

Tecumseh was in the small crowd gathered around Laulewasika for his oration. He had never heard his younger brother speak and he looked forward to it. Laulewasika's appearance was not the most impressive and the bright bandana around his head covering the missing eye gave him a negative aspect but more and more people kept arriving from the village of Anderson. "Brothers and sisters!" began Laulewasika with

250

hands dramatically upraised. "Hear my message for it will make you hearts filled with joy! I have been asked by many of our people why we have fallen into unhappy days. The lesson is clear if you will but listen. We all know the Master of Life is one of us. Why else would he have given us this great island and all its bounties? Yes, my brothers, the Ruler of Destinies put us here for a purpose. He created all people, but then we could also say 'She', could we not, for the Supreme Being is also a woman. The Shawnee were created from the brain of the Great Spirit and were the first people. Springing from His brain we were imbued with all knowledge. The Great Mysterious then parted the waters for the people to cross to this great island on dry land and other tribes were born as descendants. From His breast the Master of Life made the French, from His arms the English, from His feet the Dutch. The Longknives He made from His hands. All these inferior tribes he made pale, of varying colors, and put them on the other side of the big water.

"For many ages our people lived in harmony with the Ruler of Destinies and we were masters of all life. But then the people fell into sinful ways and earned the displeasure of the Master of Life. We were deprived of our learning and knowledge was transferred to the people beyond the ocean. Yet, in all His goodness, The Master promised us He would restore the precious knowledge to our people when they rose out of corruption and showed they deserved it back again. But many of our people did not believe and continued with their sinful ways. Time passed and one day the people saw a monstrous canoe come over the water, filled with the very people who had gotten the knowledge which had originaly belonged to the Shawnee and other Indian people. These newcomers were not satisfied with the knowledge of the Great Spirit. Now they wanted *the land.* They made great pretense at purchasing, but their dealings were based on fraud and duplicity. This was part of the test of the Great Spirit, to see if we could recognize the final danger which would devour us like ravenous beasts which roam the forests. Is this to say we must go fight the Longknives? NO! Fighting is not necessary. We must conquer OURSELVES! We must live as the Great Spirit intended us to live: we must hunt in the forests, we must use bows and arrows as did our ancestors, we must dress in skins. We must not eat the flesh of filthy hogs which wallow in the vilest refuse imaginable! We have been degraded by contact with the Shemanese. And above all we must worship the Great Spirit in our own way. We were not given the Great Book and it is not for our use. Never forget the massacre at Gnadenhutten! Our brothers, the Moravian Delaware Christians believed only in love but other Christians came and butchered them to the very last man, woman, and child! I believe Jesus Christ was a representation of the

251

Great Spirit but the people crucified him to death when He went to the lands across the great ocean. Yes, they killed Jesus Christ as they murdered the inoffensive Moravian Delaware! You cannot trust a people who come to you with the Great Book in one hand and a murderous weapon in the other.

"WE MUST STAND AWAY FROM THE WAYS AND METHODS OF SHEMANESE CIVILIZATION! That system of living is little more than violence against your brother, diseases which were unknown to us, and the degradation of firewater which makes us all as fools. This I know well from personal experience, my brothers," and here Laulewasika went on to tell about the horrors of his vision. When he described the scenes he noticed the crowd was one with him and he enjoyed the revelation. "We need people who will go to others of our tribes and speak as I am doing," he continued. "I am dedicating my life to spread the word of salvation in the next life and survival in the present. LOOK AT ME! I am poor, like you. I live under difficult conditions, like you, I am a refugee, like you. But the Great Spirit has seen fit to send me a vision which has changed my way of living. He has instructed me to disseminate this message and this mandate I shall obey to my dying day. *Seguoy.* Amen."

Tecumseh waited for the crowd to thin from around Laulewasika then he went up to him and shook his hand. "You have filled my heart with your oration and I would talk with you about it."

"Of course, elder brother," answered Laulewakika. "Let us go to my cabin." The two made their way to the wegiwa where wife Tukwaukee prepared a meal for the two.

"It is my desire for us to work together," began Tecumseh. "I have discussed the workings of my mind with no other person. Perhaps you can advise me."

"I shall do whatever I can," said Laulewasika.

"I want to form a country for all Amerindians," continued Tecumseh. "We must have a definite territory of our own, apart from the Shemanese, where we can live our lives as we wish and worship as we see fit."

"A country for all our people?" asked Laulewasika. "That would be a tremendous step for the tribes are accustomed to their independence."

"Yes," conceded Tecumseh, "it would be a very difficult but it must be done if we are to survive. The Shemanese can destroy us piecemeal but that would be impossible if we united. I believe our people have suffered enough to sober them and realize their annihilation is at hand if they do not take extraordinary measures for survival. You and I could go out amongst the tribes and carry the message. You have been given a

252

great vision and the people will respond to it. If my strategy is successful, and I believe it will because it is the path of wisdom, within a dozen years or so the various tribes will speak with one voice."

"We have tried confederations before," observed Laulewasika as he smoked. "Some were successful for a time. Eventually they fell apart."

"Yes, and do you know why? Because the leadership disintegrated, the union was never strong enough to overcome petty tribal jealousies, and there was no central force like your vision from the Great Spirit."

"I see," commented Laulewasika thoughtfully. "Our efforts would be political as well as religious..."

"Exactly!" said Tecumseh with intensity as his eyes brightened. "No longer shall we be tribes of Shawnee, Delaware, Wyandot, Creek, Cherokee, and the myriads of others. We shall be what we are: Amerindians faced with the common danger of cultural annihilation. There is peace now and we must do everything possible to maintain it, dishonorable though it might be, or we could be destroyed physically also. At this point in time I do not believe we could raise an army even for self defense."

"I would never preach war in any event," said Laulewasika.

"Nor would I, but deep in my heart I doubt the Shemanese will ever retreat across the Spay-lay-wi-theepi on their own. If I am forced into war I will defend myself but it would be a grave mistake to suggest we take up the hatchet. Our efforts must be directed toward making our people aware we all face the same danger of spiritual and possible physical annihilation because of our independent attitudes. Once we are united we could not be conquered militarily, and that is the cornerstone on which Shemanese civilization rests. Given equal arms and numbers no Shemanese force can conquer us. How many times have a mere handful of our people routed superior numbers of skulking encroachers? We have been defeated very few times, and then only because of weaponry and numbers. We cannot challenge cannon with tomahawks, this we all understand. Look how we turned Harmar back and sent him fleeing to safety. The force was larger than ours but we were better organized and own the victory. We slaughtered St. Clair's army with very little loss, their cannon notwithstanding. The brush with Blacksnake Wayne was insignificant militarily and lost because we relied too greatly on the perfidious British."

"But nevertheless we lost the Ohio country," observed the shrewd Laulewasika.

"Only because our chiefs sold us out," said Tecumseh heatedly. "We must develop new leadership from among younger warriors who have

253

not sold out to the Longknives and their annuities. That is the best way to make us forget to take care of ourselves. I see no other way out of the predicament our people are experiencing. We must return to the ways of our Grandfathers, as you spoke this afternoon. We must behave as one people, for we are all related, emanating from the first pioneers sent by the Great Spirit. Every bit of Indian land must be owned by all the tribes on this great island and should not be sold without the consent of all! This is crucial to our survival and our people must understand it."

"This is heady ideology," commented Laulewasika.

"Do you believe it is the path of wisdom?" asked Tecumseh.

"Yes. Will we be able to make our people recognize it as such?"

"Soon I will begin to speak to the tribes. Then we will see how they feel about amalgamation. My hope is we can draw our people into one Amerindian domain like the Sixteen Fires have done. In a way they are an excellent example for us. If the encroachers, all from a number of different countries, can become united into one, why can't we, who have many customs that are similar?"

Tecumseh's mind raced on with thoughts too rapid for words. To the northeast he would seek the Iroquois tribes, what was left of them. He felt certain the Mohawk, Oneida, Onondaga, Cayuga, and Seneca had suffered enough to force them to recognize what annihilating perils their people were in. Close by were the Delaware, Potawatomie, Wyandot, Miami, Tuscarora, Illinois, Kaskaskia, Shawnee. To the north were the Chippewa, Huron, Ottawa, and west of them the Fox, Winnebago, Sac, Menominee, Kickapoo, and further the numerous Dakota, Mandan, Cheyenne. There were tremendous untapped resources beyond the Grandfather of Waters: Pawnee, Iowa, Ponca, Omaha, Oto, Missouri, Osage, Kansas, Wichita. To the south there were Quapaw, Yazoo, Natchez, Caddo, Hasinais, Tawakonia, Kitchai, not to mention his friends the Creeks, Cherokees, Choctaw, Chickasaw, Alabama, Biloxi, Seminole, Santee, Catawba.

"This will *not* be done in one or two moons," said Tecumseh, "perhaps we will need a hundred. Some tribes will come around slowly, some not at all maybe. Some will swiftly strike the hatchet into the war post and circulate the war belts. These must be kept in check until there is no other choice but war."

"If we convince our people they must follow the religion of their ancestors..."

"Yes. You preach our religion and I will promote unity, my brother," said Tecumseh. "Together let us vow to dedicate our lives to our people."

254

"This I swear," said Laulewasika as the two shook hands warmly.
"Our father and mother would be most proud of you, my brother,"
said Tecumseh. He had found a staunch ally and he was grateful to the
Ruler of Destinies. On the sons of Puckeshinwa and Methoataske rode
the fate of an entire race of people.

Chapter 5

William Henry Harrison arrived at Vincennes early in January of 1801 to assume his duties as Governor of the Territory of Indiana. It was a vast wilderness region with a white population of about five thousand and only three settlements of note within its boundaries: Vincennes, Clark's Grant right opposite Louisville, and St. Louis. Indians were in great abundance and hunting parties roamed the territory, causing emotional discomfort if not outright disturbance for the People of the Eagle. President Jefferson was apprised of the situation in the new territory so he invested Harrison with extraordinary powers, civil as well as military. The governor could function as a legislature, appoint all civil officers as well as military personnel under the rank of general, he was commander-in-chief of the militia, could pardon any offense, the sole commissioner of treaties with the Indians, and had the power to confirm or deny all land grants, at his option.

A delegation of painted chiefs and headmen from the Wea, Piankeshaw, Kickapoo, Eel River, and Delaware villages came in to see Governor Harrison during the summer of 1802. They professed their friendship for the United States but also protested the ill-treatment perpetrated against them by individual citizens. They described acts of unprovoked murders, cruel deeds, and atrocities against their persons and properties, the validity of which Harrison did not doubt in the slightest. "Our people have been killed for no reason other than being natives of this great island," said one speaker. "Our lands, given to us by treaty, have been settled on, our game has been wantonly killed, our young men made drunk then cheated out of their peltries which were to be used to provide necessary clothing, rifles and ammunition to hunt with. Even worse, after trading away their skins and furs for whiskey, our people become so discontented they fight with each other, these combats often ending in death. Others awaken from their stupor, find themselves impoverished and without the means necessary to provide for themselves, they begin to break down fences and shoot livestock indiscriminately."

Harrison knew what the chief said was valid. One morning it had been reported to him that four Indians had been found dead in the streets of Vincennes. On another occassion it had been necessary to call out the militia in order to restore order after some Indians had wantonly destroyed property. Harrison had sent off a letter to President Jefferson, asking ..."Whether something ought not to be done to prevent the reproach which will attach to the American Character by the extermination of so many human beings, I beg leave most respectfully to submit to the consideration of the President. That this extirpation will happen no one can doubt..."

"My brothers," said the Governor to the Indians, "this very day I shall issue an edict prohibiting all white persons to hunt, settle, or survey on Indian land. I shall order that all trespassers must remove at once. The sale of liquor to Indians shall be forbidden in town and up to one mile outside of it. It shall be banned altogether on Sundays. Henceforth it shall be illegal for any white man to barter for an Indian's common necessities, espcially his clothes and hunting equipment. If any traders are found guilty of mishandling or cheating I shall personally revoke their license. I sincerely hope these edicts will alleviate the deplorable situations encountered in this Territory."

"The Sixteen Fires acknowledge you are independent nations," replied Harrison, "but when we threw the British on their backs all their claims became ours. We have jurisdiction until the great Father of Waters toward the setting sun."

"Our people have not been defeated out of their lands," said Coonahaw, "and they never belonged to the British king."

"We have acknowledged your occupation of the soil," said Harrison. "We do not condone tribal bloodshed, however, and we caution you to keep the peace. Your father, the President in Washington, has sent me a message on the talking leaves, advising you to consider the necessity of laying aside the bow and taking up the hoe as do the People of the Eagle. He wishes you to assemble your scattered warriors and form towns and

257

villages where the land is rich for cultivation. He will cause you to be furnished with horses, cattle, hogs, implements, and send someone to instruct you in their management. The game is rapidly diminishing and without agriculture you could face starvation. Serious farming has already been successful with others of your tribes. In the southlands the Cherokees and Creeks are raising large herds of cattle and harvesting bountiful crops. This has had a most happy effect on their population and their wigwams are filled with children.

"Your father the President also asks that in exchange for the help which we are offering you, livestock and implements must be paid for, obviously, we ask that you cede some land which will be sold—"

A definite murmur of disgust came up from most of the Indians present.

"Brothers," continued Harrison unperturbed, "there are no children present. Hear me out before you make any decisions."

"We have ceded land only to the French," said the minor chief Chiuxca. "We gave them small pieces of land for Vicennes and St. Louis. All else belongs to us."

"Yes," parried Harrison, "and I have here before me the original grant of land made to Monsieur St. Vincent, the first commandant at this post. You say only a small amount was ceded but this title shows an area seventy-two miles wide and two-hundred-ten miles long! According to this the cession to Monsieur Vincent extends far into the Illinois country. Yes, here it is, look for yourselves." The document was passed around to no avail because none of the Indians could read. But the men smouldered at the thought such a large expanse of land could be considered part of Vincennes. "Now I wish to be fair with you and it is also the command of our father in Washington. This cession seems quite large and I would be willing to reccommend a smaller piece of land, if you wish to discuss the matter. But right now let us adjourn and have some good food and drink which we have prepared for you..."

Governor Harrison wined and dined the Indians for five weeks and finally got them to sign a document for the cession of a strip of land thirty-six miles wide and seventy-two miles long, subject to approval and ratification of a later council of all the tribes which would meet at Fort Wayne at a future date. In the minds of the Amerindians there had been no transfer of territory but Governor Harrison now had a document on which to place a claim. He communicated the news of the council to President Jefferson, who was extremely concerned over the international situation of Spain yielding up the Louisiana territory to the Emperor Napoleon, ruler of a people whose friendship the Indians held in great reverence. Jefferson advised Harrison the occupation of New Orleans by French forces was "hourly expected and is already felt like a light breeze by the Indians." Should a French army be landed, should French influence become dominant once again, the tribes would probably stiffen and refuse to cede land. Jefferson was nothing if not practical in matters concerning land so he advised Harrison, as he had all other governors, "...whatever can now be obtained must be obtained quickly."

Not long after this missive President Jefferson sent Governor Harrison another letter, marked *"Unofficial and Private"* at the top, which contained a strategy for building up the area of Indiana Territory:

"Live in perpetual peace with the Indians. Cultivate an affectionate attachment for them. The decrease of game rendering their subsistence by hunting insufficient, we wish to draw them to agriculture, to spinning and weaving. When they withdraw themselves to the culture of a small piece of land they will perceive how useless to them are extensive forests and will be willing to pare them off from time to time in exchange for necessities for their farms and families. Should any tribe be foolhardy enough to take up the hatchet at any time, the seizing of the whole country of that tribe and driving them across the Mississippi as the only condition of peace would be an example to others and a furtherance of our final consolidation.

We must encourage them to change their views of the land. To promote this disposition to exchange lands we shall push our trading houses into their villages and be glad to see the good and influential among them run into debt. We observe that when these debts get beyond what the individuals can pay, they become willing to lop them off by a cession of lands..."

United States policy then was to purchase nothing less than all the territories east of the Mississippi River. Governor Harrison construed this as great magninimity for history was replete with instances of the stronger taking everything away from the weaker, the conqueror refusing to recognize the conquered as deserving of any rights or privileges whatsoever. Jefferson would most deservedly be remembered as an humanitarian for buying what could have been seized by force.

"I must repeat that this letter is to be considered private," concluded the President. "You will also perceive how sacredly it must be kept within your own breast, and how improper it would be if understood by the Indians."

259

Governor Harrison, very conscious of his role in the history of the Indiana Territory and that of the United States, also wanted to be considered a humanitarian and philanthropist by future generations. He recorded and communicated a wealth of material to his superiors in Washington. As he sat in his study at Grouseland, for such was the name of his estate, he searched for the address delivered by John Quincy Adams to the Congress. He found it and sat back to re-read it:

"It would appear to me that the Indian right of possession rests on questionable foundations. Granted the tribes are entitled to whatever they have annexed to themselves by personal labor but what is the right of the huntsman to the thousand miles over which he has accidentally ranged in quest of prey? Shall the liberal bounties of Providence to the race of man be monopolized by one or two thousand savages? Shall the exuberant bosom of the common mother, amply adequate to the nourishment of millions, be claimed exclusively by a few hundred of her offspring? No, generous philanthropists! Heaven has not been thus inconsistent in the work of its hands. Heaven has not thus placed at irreconcilable strife, its moral laws with its physical creation..."

Harrison sat back momentarily, sipped a bit of wine, and digested what Adams had written. It was the best ethical justification of American land policy he had come across. If it had a weakness perhaps it was Adams set himself up as the interpreter of Heaven... but then who was to assert it was fallacious. Certainly the Indians were unable to debate the issue. At any rate, the Indians were fortunate American leadership was willing to pay them for conquered land. He made plans to convene the representatives of the various tribes at Fort Wayne early in the spring as soon as the ice was gone from the Wabash.

Episode 2: The Vow

Chief Buckongahelas of the Delaware had been impressed with the young chief Tecumseh for many moons. That is why he invited the Shawnee to settle on Delaware territory and this evening Tecumseh would shortly rise to speak in council. The pipe was passed around, leisurely as always, then Buckongahelas informed the gathering Tecumseh had requested to speak to the wise and beloved men of the Delaware, grandfathers of the Shawnee. "Open you ears, my brothers, and listen with your hearts," he concluded as he nodded toward Tecumseh.

"Grandfathers of the Delaware," began the Shawnee slowly, "I

260

come to you with a message from all our people who yearn for the wisdom of our ancestors. I come to you in peace but the clouds do not shroud my eyes. Brothers: I long for the freedom of our ancestors. I wish to spend my life hunting our animals in our forests, fishing in our rivers and streams, making sugar from our maple trees. I want to spend my time dancing, I want to sit round a campfire and thrill to the exploits of our heroes, and yes, I would still listen to our wise and beloved Grandfathers recite the beautiful stories and legends of our people. It is my fervent wish the Walam Olum never be forgotten.

"But now I am informed by an alien people that I cannot live in the style of my ancestors. I am told I may not range over the land in search of game any longer and I have seen fences put up where I used to roam free. I am told I must devote myself to agriculture and live in one place only. Think of it, my brothers. We must till the land, the land which is owned by our women, and forget about hunting. We must live in one cabin for the rest of our days, on one plot of ground. Brothers: that way of living is but one step removed from *slavery*. We, who are accustomed to freedom, could not live as slaves. We who are accustomed to venison could not eat the flesh of hogs who wallow in filth!

"Or could we learn to do all these things? Shall we put on petticoats and throw our women off their land? Shall we grab the hoes out of their hands? Shall we bring in cattle and drive out the deer? Shall we fight among ourselves to see who owns the land on which to spread our blankets? Shall we sit down to eat pig? All these things I cannot and will not do. I will dress myself in tanned skins as our people have always done. I shall dance during the festival of the Three Maidens. I shall make syrup in the autumn. I shall worship our Great Spirit from under any tree, next to any stream, from the top of any hill. I will live my culture!

"I will sanction no treaty that denies me of my land. Those who sign such treaties are my enemies and the enemies of our race! Be they chiefs or headmen they have no right to dispose of the people's land without their approval being freely given without coercion. I believe as most of you do, that all Amerindians own all the land. Any of us can go into the north country and live off the land. It is the same in the south or anywhere else, so long as there is no war. Individuals do not have the power to sell what belongs to everyone. This is our country! Do not allow *anyone* to alienate it. No one has bought our rights to the land, not the Shemanese, not the British, not the French. Small parcels here and there have been sold by individual tribes, as you Delaware did with Brother Onas, but by and large treaties have been little more than a method to cloak the hand of the aggressive encroachers. Talk to any government official of the Sixteen Fires and they always have what they call "proof of purchase," even if it is false and a forgery.

"I ask you how to spread the word of our people: no Amerindian can sell land without the consent of *all* tribes. We all own the land and we have a share in it throughout this great island. Anyone who sells or tires to sell will have to bear severe judgment."

Tecumseh finished and waited for comments.

"We now live in peace," said one of the chiefs. "You say you come in peace yet you advocate militant ideas. Are not the two contrary?"

"I have not struck the tomahawk into the warpost," replied Tecumseh. "I will never become the aggressor and begin a war. But neither am I a fool who believes harm is impossible. If I am attacked militarily I will respond in kind if there is no other choice. Right now we are being threatened culturally and that is what I am combating, along with my brother Laulewasika and several of our villagers. I invite you all to go listen to him speak about the religion of our ancestors and the moral betterment of our people."

Buckongahelas listened quietly, nodding occassionally, fully aware Tecumseh was probably the best young war chief in the country. And he was also a stirring orator. "What would happen," asked the elderly chief, "if we were attacked? I don't mean your village or the Shawnee, I refer to the Delaware. What if the Delaware were attacked and we asked you to lead our warriors against the enemy?"

Tecumseh replied unhesitatingly by taking his warclub in hand and holding it at arm's length. "I vow that if any of our people are attacked by an aggressor I will join the war as leader or follower if I am asked to do so. I invite you all to touch this warclub if you can make the same vow. I also swear if I do not comply with this vow my life is forfeit to any who would take it. I invite you all to swear with me."

At first no one moved, Tecumseh's words and petitions not being trifling. Then Buckongahelas touched the warclub, age old weapon of the Amerindian. The others followed suit. "If the call ever goes out," said Buckongahelas calmly, as was the Indian way, "you shall lead us."

"Have no doubts," concluded Tecumseh as he held the warclub up high atop a fisted hand. "Like our Chief Logan there is no one who rejoices more than I at the beams of an honorable peace. But if we are forced into war my weapons will rain death and destruction on the enemy, even if it cost me my life."

Episode 3: Treaty refused.

It was late March by the time the ice was out of the Wabash River. Governor Harrison sent our runners to summon the Miami, Delaware, Shawnee, and Potawatomie to finalize the Vincennes Treaty as had been prearranged. He and his party ascended the Wabash by barge and when they arrived at Fort Wayne they waited for the chiefs to arrive. The Michigan country had been organized as Wayne County and integrated as part of Indiana. Detroit was the only settlement of any size but it was most important strategically. A ball was held in Harrison's honor and it was during these days that the Governor met William Wells, the Indian Agent at the fort. He learned Wells had been taken captive at the age of thirteen and lived with the Miami as a full-fleged citizen until General Wayne's army came into the area. Harrison did not remember the scout, though Wells had observed Wayne's aide-de-camp many times.

When the council fire was kindled Governor Harrison was aware of a certain defiance and unfriendliness emanating from the assembled chiefs. To a man the Indians maintained the Vincennes Treaty was invalid for it had not been approved or ratified by the tribes.

"But presents were offered and accepted," pointed out Harrison.

"Giving presents is protocol," replied a Miami. "This does not mean we have sold the land."

"I have a document signed by your representatives," said Harrison as he held it up.

"We all know it had to be ratified by all the tribes," said a Shawnee, "and it was signed solely on that premise."

"Your annuities could be withheld," observed William Wells, "if you do not stand by your word. Chief Little Turtle, my father-in-law, would not countenance such behavior."

"The Turtle is not here and neither did he sign the Vincennes paper," said Buckongahelas. "Nothing done at Vincennes is binding upon the tribes.

"You could all lose your annuities," repeated Wells. "Think of the suffering of the women and children."

"We are heirs to the original grant to Monsieur Vincent," said Harrison. "Even if we did not have it we would be owners because of the Greenville Treaty. It belongs to the government of the Sixteen Fires."

The chiefs became more voluble and the Shawnee delegation stood up and walked out of the meeting house.

"Brothers," began William Wells, "I see that some of you have been

263

to the British at Amherstburg. You have their clothes and your weapons are obviously British made. Do not allow yourselves to be led astray *again.* Listen to Governor Harrison. There is wisdom in his words."

Harrison prompted his surveyor to indicate the lines of the disputed cession on the floor with a bit of charcoal. "This is not a large piece of land, not nearly as large as the original cession to Monsieur Vincent, which in justice should be ours in its entirety."

"That is the land we discussed before," said a Potawatomie. "Your surveyor has drawn more land than what we talked about at Vincennes."

"Well then you draw it to your satisfaction," suggested Harrison. The Indian took the charcoal, erased a couple of lines, then drew new ones.

"That is unacceptable," said the Governor when the Potawatomie finished. He shook his head in disgust. "As of this moment all annuities will be withheld. This council is terminated."

The chiefs, sachems, sagamores, and warriors left the council house in leisurely fashion but highly irritated. They mounted their horses and rode to a spot in the woods where they had their own council. The Vincennes cession was totally repudiated. The Miami acknowledged Delaware rights to lands between the Ohio and the White River.

"Before the council fire is covered this day," said Buckongahelas, "I would suggest Chief Tecumseh be invited to speak and that we also listen to his brother Laulewasika who is preaching an Amerindian religion. Those of you who have not had the pleasure of hearing these two Shawnee brothers should do so as quickly as possible. But do not let Governor Harrison know about these activities...

As it turned out, William Wells became Harrison's confidant and right arm at Fort Wayne. Wells gathered a group of Indians, important people among the tribes, he told Harrison, and they signed a treaty agreeing to the boundaries defined at Vincennes. They also agreed to an additional cession of a salt spring upon the Saline River in the Illinois country. Harrison was elated with Captain Wells' work, restored annuities to all the tribes, and promised an extra annuity of 150 barrels of salt. When he reported to President Jefferson he wrote all matters were settled amicably.

Episode 4: Star of the Lake

Tecumseh rode up to the Galloway cabin one early evening leading a pack horse which bore the beautiful birchbark canoe. James Galloway

264

stepped out of his front door and greeted the chief pleasantly, which Tecumseh returned cordiallly. "And what might that be?" said Galloway in jest.

"A gift for your daughter," answered Tecumseh, "but perhaps she will allow her parents to use it during special times."

Galloway stepped forward to help untie the craft and was obviously impressed by it. The canoe had a beauty of line and color, pleasant grace which betokened poetry when spied on inland waters. Like so many things created by the Indian there was nothing European to compare with the birchbark canoe. It was totally a product of nature, easy to utilize, very light in weight. This particular canoe had painted on the prow a star over what appeared to be some water. "Beautiful," commented Galloway just as Rebecca was coming out of the cabin.

"Mr. Tikomfa Chief!" said the young woman as she appeared at the door with her mother.

"Beware of Greeks bearing gifts," intoned Tecumseh playfully, remembering a passage from one of Rebecca's readings, "but receive happily those from Indian friends."

"Oh, how beautiful!" exclaimed Rebecca. She paced around it excitedly, felt the texture of the leaf-brown bark with her hands.

"If you are not too busy I shall take you for a little ride in it," suggested Tecumseh. "I have already told your father perhaps you will allow your parents to use it once in a while and right here and now I want you to promise, Becky, that you will never use it alone, without someone watching."

"I promise!" said the girl without hesitation. "How do we take it to the river?"

"Just get in and paddle it," said her father, "any greenhorn knows that."

The canoe was lifted back unto the pack horse, lashed securely, then Tecumseh and Rebecca mounted the chief's horse and directed the two animals toward the nearby river. "Come back for supper," said Mrs. Galloway.

"Well, Bec," said Galloway to his wife as they watched the two retreating toward the river, "How do you feel about having Tecumseh as your daughter's suitor?"

"The thought has been on my mind for a long time," replied the woman. "I must admit I do not know what to think. I have known Tecumseh to be the best of men but... what if Rebecca... would she be safe if the chief became angered? This bothers me above all else."

"I trust the man," said Galloway.

"I do too, there is no question about it," said Bec, "but what of his people? There are those who say the Indians are discontented, that sooner or later there will be another war. I shudder at the thought of it. What would happen to Becky if she was living in an Indian village?"

"Perhaps we are being premature," said Galloway as he put his arm around Bec. "Let us trust in God and pray that He guide us unto the proper path."

When Tecumseh and Rebecca arrived at the river he unloaded the canoe and put it in the water, instructing the young woman how to step into it, how to walk along its length and where to sit. The sun had just set, the horizon ablaze in orange colored calm, an early moon beginning to splash silver as Tecumseh pushed the canoe into the water, took his seat, and began to paddle rythmically. Neither spoke, the moment being too beautiful and poetic.

The moon waxed full in a cloudless sky. "You seem very contented," remarked Tecumseh finally. The young woman looked quite beautiful and her natural subtle charms were enhanced by the canoe as it drifted in and out of the shadows of overhanging trees.

"I wish this moment could last forever," said Rebecca softly. "Life is so beautiful. Did you make this canoe yourself?"

"Yes."

"It is so artful, I should have guessed it."

"I even named it for you," said Tecumseh.

"The Rebecca?"

"No. The Star of the Lake. It is a name that befits you well. I do not know what Rebecca means, I am sure it must be beautiful."

"I do not know either," admitted Rebecca.

"You are the Star of the Lake to me," said Tecumseh. "Your smile is the glow of the stars, your person is the lake that reflects your goodness and intelligence. When you ride in this your canoe perhaps you will think of me, occassionally, for I am your true friend."

"You have become... very important to me," said Rebecca softly.

"How so?"

"I... value your friendship. You have made me think and learn. I am a better person for having met you. I mean, who else would gift me with a canoe like this?"

Tecumseh chuckled. "Any Indian. It is I who must be appreciative. Very few could have read to me as you have done, instructing me and filling my mind in a way I had never thought possible." A weed became entangled in the maple paddle but Tecumseh turned it deftly and let the current pull it away. Rebecca put her hand in the water, bending slightly. "Careful you do not tip over," cautioned Tecumseh. "One must remain upright in a canoe."

"And what is wrong with a bath?" asked Rebecca in jest. This was something Tecumseh particularly liked about the girl: she could be serious about important facets of life but she had a good sense of humor as well.

"Should we change the name to 'Beaver of the Lake?'"

Rebecca giggled slightly. She had come to know Tecumseh as an intense personality with not much that was humorous but no one could deny he was witty. "Is it hard to paddle?"

"No, not at all," replied Tecumseh. "Look at that bird overhead."

"I do believe it's following us."

"Must think we are a new variety of large fish," said Tecumseh. He looked at Rebecca and asked, "What do your parents say of me?"

"What do you mean?"

"How do they feel about me, really? I have spent much time with you... and we are worlds apart."

"What are you driving at?" asked Rebecca. "You know my father is very proud of the friendship you accord us. He sincerely admires you, as you well know. Says you are the best hunter in the territory. This from a professional hunter, mind you. Mother is... well, you know mothers."

"What do you mean?"

"Well, she is very solicitous as to what I think and feel. I guess she thinks I should be married by now. I don't know, maybe I should be. But, nobody wants me I guess."

"I am sure that's not true," chided Tecumseh. "Perhaps it is you who wants no one?" He looked intensely at Rebecca.

"No, not at all," she said. "I have been to Chillicothe and talked to your sister."

"Oh?" The non-sequitor caught him off guard. "And what did you learn?"

"What a wonderful person your sister is... and how much she loves you."

"She has been very good to her younger brother," said Tecumseh. "I wish there was a way to repay her."

"In her mind I think you already have, by treating people the way you do. I asked her to tell me about you so I could get to know you better."

"You have never asked me."

"I guess I find that rather difficult to do," confessed Rebecca.

"I understand," said Tecumseh supportively, "but you can ask me whatever you wish and I will answer."

"I shall remember that. Why aren't you married?" she asked candidly.

Tecumseh smiled. "I guess nobody wants me." Rebecca laughed quietly.

"No, seriously," she said.

"I guess I feel more blessed in the single state," Tecumseh answered sincerely. "I am not against marriage, I was married for a short while before."

"Tecumapease did not mention that."

"It is not important," said Tecumseh. He told her about Manete, his young son Pugeshenshewa, and how unhappy he had been during the brief marriage. "But I am myself again now. Many moons have passed since then."

"I understand how things can happen," said Rebecca.

"Perhaps we should be getting back?" asked Tecumseh. "I would not want your parents to worry about you."

"No, it's all right, for my part. Unless you wish to return."

"No, I am in no hurry."

"Then tell me one of your legends," suggested Rebecca. "I love hearing them. I wish someone would put them into a book so I could go over them."

"I cannot make a book, as you say, but I can tell you a little story I heard when I was in the south country," began Tecumseh as he paddled the canoe over the placid river waters. "A brave and fearless warrior named Skegon lived beside the beautiful, winding Susquehanna River. He loved Nunga and together they would stroll through laurel and fern. One day Skegon carried his bow and quiver full of arrows as the two walked until the edge of the forest. Nunga then bid her lover farewell until he should return from the hunt.

Nunga's hair was black and shone like obsidian. She was graceful as a fawn, beautiful as a shining star. Her entire personality was like the fragrance and beauty of forest life. Her most highly prized jewels were the modest flowers gathered by her warrior hunter as he ranged throughout his forays. Nunga, the bride to be, was always happy with the sweet blossoms. While she waited she would weave fine baskets or make the best of moccasins, trimming them with colored quills. She also liked to sit by the river's edge, communing with the stars, keeping a heartfelt watch, waiting for her beloved.

One evening a mournful sun went over the hill to sleep. Nunga felt the air was heavy. Dark clouds gathered and thunder roared angrily. Nunga sat fearful. Her brilliant eyes searched the deep forest. Where was the footstep of her returning hunter? Suddenly she felt a gentle tap on her shoulder. Nunga jumped nervously and saw her mother at her side.

"My daughter," began the woman in a serious way, "I come as friend and comforter. Word has just reached the village... Skegon... ambush...

268

an arrow has pierced his warrior's heart. His lifeless body is in the village, ready to join his ancestors in rest. My daughter, I am sorry to bring such news..."

Nunga walked bravely into the village to claim her beloved. She chose for his grave the spot where she had been sitting when her mother came to inform her of Skegon's death. When the burial rites were over and her warrior was sleeping forever in the glade Nunga's eyes grew dim from weeping, her heart breaking anew each day. Her only consolation was to be near his resting place. She built a lodge near by and lived in it alone. The women of the village tried to console Nunga for she had been greatly admired for her forest beauty and charm but they understood only time could heal.

Many suns crossed the sky. Nunga watched the small flowers come with the freshness that is spring, saw them grow to their fullest summer bloom, watched autumn's changing colors shed their splendor on the woodland tomb. The flowers were the only life the poor woman had for she would see no one, shrinking within her silent lodge even from the light of day. It was when the shades of evening fell, darkening the hue of leaf and flower that Nunga walked outside, the light of her star friends in the far-off sky her only company on her solitary path. She came to her destination, knelt by the sacred grave, and wept until the frowning sky itself lifted its dark blanket of night, leaving only the imprint of dew. Nunga even fell to ignoring the beautiful river for it did not seem to concern itself with her, always hurrying on its course. When the earth was wrapped in its wintry shroud and all the trees and bushes were grim and bare like Nunga's heart, the woman came like a wounded fawn. Grief was her only haunt. She lay prostrate on her lover's grave, her long black tresses spread out like a shroud, and during the cold night the hand of death touched poor Nunga. Where her eyes had shed her last tears there sprang from the earth some star-shaped flowers, meekly looking at the sky. But the cold winds blew and snow wrapped Nunga's body in a heavy blanket of white which hid her from sight. The wild geese had long since taken their southward flight, flashing like bits of bronze against the sky, fleeing the earth where trees now stood denuded, solitary, forbidding. The great round moon reached fullness and lurched over, peering into the deep river. Even the little stars, who had kept faithful watch over Nunga, looked wane and sad.

When spring came the villagers went to Nunga's lodge but could find not a trace of her. It was as if her star friends had taken her with them. The air was filled with beautiful fragrances once more and the earth put on her gayest robes and greeted a host of flowers that were curiously starshaped on Nunga's tear watered grave. Never before had such blossoms been found on banks of the Susquehanna. The villagers thought it to be a message for all hearts that loved too overpoweringly as had Nunga and Skegon and the star flowers bloom to this day by the blue waters of the Susquehanna, the ancient trees staring at them, considering them a gift from the stars in the far-off sky.

"And mothers," finished Tecumseh, "being mothers, as you say, tell their daughters the story of the star flowers when they find they are hopelessly in love, reproaching the hearts which love too well."

"Is there such a thing?" asked Rebecca, who wanted to cover up the fact that the story had made her want to cry. "Can a heart love too well?"

"Yes, among our people it is possible," replied Tecumseh. "I don't know how it is with yours."

"I believe we hide our feelings more on some matters," reflected the girl.

"Perhaps we should be getting back," suggested Tecumseh. "Your parents will begin to worry."

"Or your men out in the forest will begin to wonder if I have abducted you," said Rebecca as the canoe was directed toward shore. "Why are Indian legends so sad?"

"I do not know if I would say they are sad," reflected Tecumseh. "Perhaps they are governed by the laws of nature and since we accept nature as being what it is... death is merely the final experience in this life. This is not sadness to us."

"All right, but the next story you tell me I want you to make me laugh, not cry."

Tecumseh thought of the stories the Grandfathers had told him. How many had been humorous? Right at this moment he could not think of any but there had to be some funny ones. "I will make you laugh when next we meet," said Tecumseh as the canoe came to shore. He jumped out and helped Rebecca, then pulled the canoe onto dry land. "I will get the horses," he said, whistled for them and saw them munching on grass a ways up river, fetching them quickly.

"Here, I'll help you load the canoe," said Rebecca. "My how light it is. It is hard to imagine how something like this can carry our weight so easily."

The canoe was lashed securely to the pack horse then Tecumseh lifted Rebecca atop the mount which was to carry them back home. "I am too heavy," she protested but with a little spring and Tecumseh's strong arms there was no difficulty mounting. Then the chief sprang up, side-saddle fashion, Rebecca endeavoring to help, pulling just enough to make Tecumseh lose his balance and causing both to tumble down the other side of the horse. "Ooomph!" said Tecumseh as he hit the ground, Rebecca landing on his chest, thus breaking her fall, screaming just a bit then laughing uproariously.

"I said I would make you laugh *next* time," said Tecumseh, "but you could not wait, impatient paleface." He also began to laugh good naturedly.

"Mr. Tikomfa Chief, I had never heard you laugh before,"giggled Rebecca. She got up quickly then grabbed Tecumseh's hands and helped him to his feet. "Are you hurt?"

"No, no, do not worry. Are you all right?"

"Of course, silly. I landed on you, softie. Here, let me brush off the sand from your shoulder. My parents will think you were wrestling a bear or something." She dusted off the muscular shoulders as best she could then suddenly she became aware of Tecumseh's closeness. "I..." He put an arm around the beautiful young woman and kissed her tenderly on the cheek, then the lips. Rebecca put her arms around him and returned the affection that was now so obvious to both. When the kiss was over they just stood gazing into each other's eyes, aware that much meaning had been communicated.

"Come, we must be getting back," said Tecumseh softly.

They walked to the horse and once more the chief put the young woman on top of the animal. He sprang up behind, put his arm around her, then directed the horse toward the Galloway cabin.

Episode 5: The Prophet

People who had known Laulewasika in previous years could hardly believe the transformation they now saw. The youngest son of Puckeshinwa and Methoataske displayed indefatigable energy in preaching his new religion. First efforts were directed at the Shawnee but in conjunction with his brother he began visiting as many tribes as possible for all needed helped against the foes of corruption, degradation, and imminent loss of land. People began to refer to Laulewasika as a reincarnation of Manabozho, the Algonquian tribes' first doer and teacher who also had to contend with extremely difficult conditions of that early day. At first Laulewasika attracted attention because his regeneration had been so complete then because he learned to speak with such great emotional fevor, alternately weeping as he pleaded for the tibes to return to the traditons of their ancestors then growing stern in his admonitions to those who refused to heed the ominous signs of impending doom.

271

Laulewasika would often go by himself into the forest, fasting and praying, communing with the Great Spirit. It was during these times he evolved the basic tenets of his religion: witchcraft and magic were evil because they wrought great harm on innocent people; all lands were owned collectively by all Amerindian tribes and could not be sold except by the consent of all; men should not beat their wives for not having children; fidelity in marriage was sacred and parents had to be responsible for their children; Indian women must not marry or take up with Shemanese men for it lead to the transmission of horrible diseases; Amerindians must dress in skins like their ancestors, not cloth like the Shemanese; the tribes must not fight with each other but instead should live like brothers, which is what they were.

Once Laulewasika went into a trance that lasted all day and all night. Some thought he had died but his wife would not allow anyone to touch him. When at last he awoke he was famished and extremely thirsty but he had a message from the Master of Life, a message he himself did not quite understand. As he ate slowly he told his wife how he had visited the spirit world, seen the drunkards who spewed molten lead from their mouths, "... but then the Ruler of Destinies advised me I must do more than just lift the moral standard of our people for I was to be the new prophet."

"The new prophet?" asked Tukwautu in awe. She had always believed in her husband and his destiny but ths indeed was immortal greatness. Laulewasika was to lead the Indian people! Her very own husband!

"That is what I was told," said Laulewasika, "though my feeble mortal character tells me Change of Feathers is the acknowledged Shawnee prophet.

"No part of you is feeble, my husband," admonished Tukwautu gently. "You have the mantle of greatness upon you. Your vision will come true."

It was several days before Laulewasika could carry on his typical duties preaching. He related his latest vision to his listeners and within one moon it was learned Change of Feathers, who had been residing in one of the Auglaize river villages, had died precisely on the day Laulewasika had gone into his trance. Tukwautu began to refer to her husband as *The Prophet* and within six moons everyone referred to him by that name. He also changed his name from Laulewasika to *Tenskwautawa*, the "Open Door," a term he adopted from the saying of Jesus, "I am the door."

The Prophet began to attract attention from religious as well as governmental authorities from the Sixteen Fires. William Wells, the

Indian Agent at Fort Wayne, relayed to Governor Harrison that large numbers of Indians were passing through the area, rendezvousing at the White River villages. He advised that the scattered villages be consolidated in some way in order to better keep apprised of any goings on, particularly if the British were involved. In time he learned there was a religious movement among the Indians and the agent's suspicions of the British were allayed for the time being. Wells did communicate to the governor he might expect some kind of mythological miracle, for he knew the Indians well from having lived with them so long. There were stories about a mammoth bull jumping over the Great Lakes, a grapevine carrying an entire tribe across the Mississippi, an eagle's wing producing thunder while its eyes flashed lightning, men stepping on invisible stairs up the blue arch of the sky, a rainbow made into baldric, a little boy catching sunbeams in a snare, hawks rescuing shipwrecked mariners from an angry ocean and carrying them in leather bags up a steep mountain... "These and the events of yesterday are related by chiefs with equal gravity, expecting to claim the same credulity for both," wrote Wells. "It is difficult to decipher where mythology and allegory give way to fact..."

The Prophet did not concern himself with Agent Wells, although Tecumseh did not like the man, for he was completely occupied with his work. He proved himself shrewd and sagacious, handling his disciples with expertise worthy of any statesman. He was totally commited to his code and was not happy that two of his sisters had married white men. When he learned Tecumseh was often in the company of a white girl when he visited Ohio the younger brother did not know how to handle this delicate situation. Certainly Tecumseh could not be serious about her! But then the injunction was about Indian women marrying white men, not men marrying white women. The Prophet realized this was shaky ground bordering on the hypocritical but he could conjure up no better solution. Perhaps the woman wanted to become an Indian. It had happened many times before. Spybuck and his woman were a case in point. So perhaps it was permissible. Still, the primary leader of an Indian confederation should marry from among his own. Certainly Tecumseh could have his pick of maidens... Ah well, it was no great problem either way.

The Prophet finished preaching one day and decided to walk alone into the forest, deep in thought. His followers were asking that he send out representatives to inform the many who could not come in person to hear him speak. After walking far into the forest he came to a slight clearing, raised his hands to the heavens and implored aloud, "O Great Spirit of the Universe, give me guidance in my weakness and ignorance. Tell me how to raise our people as the tall trees that yearn to touch your face." The Prophet looked straight into the Sun Father and was quickly overcome by its power, falling to the ground.

"My son, my son," murmured a voice through the trees. *"You must send your words to all my children."*

The Prophet could hardly believe what he heard! Was someone in the forest?!

"Have faith in your work as you have faith in me," continued the voice sweet as honey, gentle as a leaf falling to earth, cool as an autumn breeze.

"Take pity on me," moaned The Prophet.

"I will teach you," continued the voice. *"As you return home you will find a bowl in which there will be strings of beans. Those who touch the beans will shake your hand. Gaze into the bowl often for it will show you what will transpire."*

"Where will I find it in this great forest, Master?" asked The Prophet.

"Manabozho has put a flaming torch by the bowl. You and all Believers must keep this sacred fire alive at all times. No household must let the fire die for it is the path to eternity. Tend it carefully and live the Way. My red children have lost much pride and independence, thinking the warpath was the Way. Friendship and peace are the Way."

"Grandmother," said The Prophet weakly, "sometimes... I feel the task is too great for a creature as pitiable as I."

"Do not doubt yourself. Heed your innermost thoughts and the leadership of Tecumseh. I love you as I did Hiawatha and Dekanawida, Pontiac and Wagomend. Your mission is the greatest of all..."

The Prophet began to weep and shake uncontrollably. It was as if his entire being was imbued with greater faith, resolution, dedication, driving out all insecurities. When the trauma abated he closed his eyes and rested, his body fatigued to an extraordinary degree. He slept peacefully and awoke to find the spreading wings of night casting their shadows over the forest. "The torch!" he said aloud, "I must find the sacred fire!" But what direction should he take?! Then he grew calm, as if an invisible hand plucked away the agitaiton. He walked in the direction of the village, meditating over the messages he had been given. As he walked he noticed some kind of fire up ahead... yes, it was so. A torch was stuck in the ground. Next to it was a bowl, bright on the outside. He picked it up, inclined it toward the torchlight and saw strings of beans inside it. He plucked up the torch and continued toward the village.

Episode 6: Black Hawk

Black Hawk's love of his tribal lands was typical of his people, the Sauk-Fox. Perhaps it was the contrasts which appealed to the noted warrior: in the center were plains that stretched interminably with billowing prairie grass on which fed buffalo, deer, elk. To the south of Saukenuk, his native village, there were rich, almost impenetrable forests of cypress accustomed to the gentle climate. Far to the north there were deep forests of oak, birch, tamarack, ash, maple, that denied penetration of sunbeams. Stately tamaracks and elegant cypress were basic to the domain of Black Hawk and the Sauk-Fox people. They loved the animals as much as the land itself. The forests which edged the plains of central Illinois were filled with wild turkey, bear, fox, wolf. Geese in formation blared their way across the sky and hundreds of thousands of ducks sped south for the winter or north for the summer as directed by the great instincts of nature. The norhtern forests blazed with variegated autumnal hues in their season and spring brought forth the magic blanket of wild flowers which covered so much of the dark, rich earth.

Black Hawk had been so named because at the age of thirteen he had shot a black sparrow hawk out of the air with his bow and arrow, dressed it out, dried it and hung it on his belt where he always wore it as his talisman. Pyesa, Black Hawk's father, had educated the boy to the hunt and the traditions of the Sauk-Fox. The father held an important position in the tribe for he was Guardian of the Medicine. Along with learning about herbal medicine Black Hawk learned to hate the Osage tribe, traditional enemies of the Sauk-Fox, on whom he led a successful raid at the age of seventeen.

Black Hawk's first experience with the People of the Eagle came when he talked to a young lieutenant named Zebulon Pike in 1804. Pike and a small squad of soldiers had been ordered to scout the area and had been watched by Sauk-Fox warriors for several days as the keelboat forced its way up the Mississippi. The entire party could have easily been destroyed but the braves allowed it to penetrate their territory until it landed at a place called Rock River where the young lieutenant came ashore with his interpreter. Black Hawk extended his hand in friendship and Pike spoke to the assembled Indians:

"Brothers, I bring you greetings from the great white father in Washington. We wish to live in peace and prosperity with our brothers of this beautiful country. We Americans intend to treat you well and the great white father sends you fine presents. I am certain you know this great land is now part of the United States of America. The French and the Spanish no longer have authority here." He saw the Union Jack waving from a tall pole. "Neither do the British. Know that we come in peace. The People of the Eagle are promoters of peace and we hope you will follow the example. Nothing causes more hardship than war: good men die, women and children suffer from cold and hunger, wailing like the winter wind through the trees. Live in peace with your neighbors. Do not take the warpath to the Osage villages but stay on the white path of happiness. I give you now the symbol of our country, the American flag." Pike handed the Stars and Stripes to Black Hawk, who unfurled it and showed it to the other men and chiefs in attendance. "Now my brothers, before we distribute other gifts," continued Lt. Pike, "I would like you to haul down the British flag now that you have the proper one. I notice also that you have British medals around your necks. I request also that you give them to me so I can bring you more proper ones."

When the interpreter translated this part of the message the Indians did not react overtly but medals were very important to the Amerindian, something young Pike did not understand.

"Thank you for your gift," replied Black Hawk after a brief council with the Sauk-Fox, "but we will keep the items you mentioned, brothers, as friendship is most important to us. We welcome you to our country and I will send a runner up ahead to our village so the people can welcome you properly."

Pike scrutinized the warrior who spoke, noting his confidence and friendly manner. They would not give up the British flag and medals? This would be noted in his report to President Jefferson. "Let us distribute more presents," said Pike amiably as he led everyone toward the keelboat. The first item was a small barrel of whiskey which was distributed by the drink among the Indians. Spirits immediately rose and as the other trade goods were passed around Pike brought up the subject of the Sauk warrior who had killed an American settler near St. Louis. "As you know," said Lt. Pike, "the Treaty of Greenville says anyone accused of killing an American must be brought to justice according to American law. The murderer must be given up for trial."

"It was a case of self-defense," said one of the chiefs standing next to Black Hawk. "the paleface demanded Mequapa's daughter go with him to his cabin. He had been drinking whiskey and when the girl refused the man became rude and threatened her with his knife. She ran to her father for protection, who confronted the paleface. Mequapa advised the man to put away his knife and leave his daughter alone but he would not listen, persisting in his rudeness. He tried to stab Mequapa whereupon the

276

warrior drew his tomahawk and killed the paleface. It was a case of self defense. Mequapa tells the truth. His heart is good."

"The man will be given a trial by jury," said Pike, "and if he is found to be innocent he will be set free. But he must be given up as the law says. Rest assured our system of law protects the innocent. If the accused is not given up this could cause our soldiers to come take him forcefully, causing bloodshed unnecessarily."

"The matter will be taken up in council," said Black Hawk calmly. The answer seemed to satisfy Lt. Pike and the rest of his visit was marked by amity and cordiality on both sides.

Mequapa sat in on the council that was to decide his fate, though he had already decided what he would do. The chiefs discussed the matter thoroughly, reviewing all options carefully and minutely. They were a proud group and extremely hesitant to give up one of their own to aliens but neither were they unaware a grave situation could develop if their country was invaded. Before any vote was taken Mequapa stood up to speak:

"Wise and beloved men, allow me to state that I will go to St. Louis to refute the charges against me. I have murdered no one, for self defense is not murder. Even among the Longknives there are fathers who would protect their daughters. I volunteer to go and I ask that our warchief Black Hawk accompany me until I am in the hands of the American authorities in St. Louis."

The council was relieved that Mequapa was willing to insure tribal bloodshed would be avoided. Black Hawk was asked to accompany him to St. Louis and he consented, though he did not personally approve of handing Mequapa to the Longknives. He was, after all, a warchief, and he thought as a warrior. But he took two other men with him and escorted Mequapa the long way to St. Louis.

The four Amerindians were impressed with the town of about 200 houses, many of them built of stone. There were many Indians around and Black Hawk had no trouble finding the headquarters of the military commandant, to whom Mequapa was surrendered.

"Do you wish me to stay until the trial is over?" asked Black Hawk.

"It does not matter," replied Mequapa, "I won't need an escort back." Black Hawk mentioned his other two companions were going to see some relatives in Cahokia across the river. He would return to Saukenuk and the other two would check in on him for his release. "That will be fine," said Mequapa.

So Black Hawk left the man and returned to his native village, hoping Mequapa would follow shortly. The two companions visited in Cahokia but weeks later when they returned to Saukenuk Mequapa was not with them. They informed the council that immediately upon surrender Mequapa had been thrown into a dark dungeon. There had been no trial of any kind. Plans were being made to hang him for murder. All this information had been obtained from reliable Indians who knew their way around St. Louis. When Black Hawk heard the news he seethed vengeance, chagrined by the duplicity of young Lt. Pike. The council decided to send four minor chiefs to St. Louis to make reparations for the killing and thus obtain Mequapa's release. Black Hawk was not asked to go this time. They young men assigned to the mission prepared themselves quickly and were off. Black Hawk was one of the many who came out to bid the delegation farewell. Later he noted Mequapa's relatives had blackened their faces and were fasting, praying all the while the man would return safely to his wife and children.

The Sauk delegation was under the informal leadership of Quashme. The quartet made a hurried journey in an effort to avoid Mequapa's being executed. When they arrived in St. Louis they saw emissaries of their enemies the Osage and learned Governor Harrison was in town, that they could present their case directly to the white chief himself. Harrison granted the four an audience, heard all they had to say through an interpreter. "I shall investigate this situation further, gentlemen. If what you say is true I shall return the man forthwith. In the meantime, I shall entrust your care to Monsieur Auguste Chouteau, a trader who perhaps you already know." Chouteau stood up from where he had been sitting and shook hands warmly with the four Sauks. "Perhaps he will assign someone to show you the town so you may tell your people about it. We will distribute presents for your return trip. I am pleased you have informed me of this matter and it will be resolved in short order. Monsieur Chouteau?"

"Oui, Monsieur Guveneur; comment allez-vous, mon amis?" The Indians just looked at the Frenchmen. "Je parle francais, et vous? Oui, le francais est une belle langue." Chauteau looked at the Indians then pointed to Governor Harrison and said, "Cet homme est l'honnetete meme. Tel est mon avis." He looked at Quashme then mumbled, "Ce garcon agit moins poliment que l'autres," as he motioned for the Sauks to walk out with him.

The Sauk's followed Chouteau, made it known they needed an interpreter, obtained one, and were shown to their quarters, a large room in a building used as a warehouse. They were taken out to eat and though unaccustomed to some of the food they ate heartily and drank their fill of wine. Quashme made efforts to see the Governor in a few days but was not successful, the white chief being in conference with the Osage delegation. He tried to learn about Mequapa but could discover nothing except he had not been executed. In the meantime, Pierre and Auguste Chauteau lavished fine coats, medals, and all the whiskey the Sauk's could drink. The two brothers knew how to keep Indians happy and the Sauk's made daily rounds of the grog shops in St. Louis, expensive food being catered to them at supper time when they could no longer walk. After a month of this Quashme pleaded with the Chouteau brothers to obtain an interview with Governor Harrison.

"The Governor has empowered me to make a treaty with your tribe," responded Auguste Chouteau. "He assured me your man in prison will be released for a slight consideration."

"What do you mean?" asked Quashme. His head hurt from so much drinking the previous day. The other three were in even worse condition.

"We have extended to you the large sum of $2,234 in credit," said Pierre as he held a pile of papers on which were written some numbers which none of the Sauk's understood.

"In return for that debt, and for the release of your warrior, we wish you to touch the pen for a land cession," continued Auguste.

"Why must we do this once more?" asked Pierre. "Ce travoil devient de plus em plus difficile."

"Rul travoil n'est trop difficile." replied Auguste.

"What are you talking about?" asked an ever more confused Quashme.

"Well, monsieur, all four of you touched the pen last night when we met for supper," said Pierre. "Don't you remember? Surely you could not forget so quickly."

The Sauk's looked at each other in disbelief at the translator's words.

"The Governor will see you this very afternoon after his regular business is finished," said Auguste. "He is a very busy man but he always has time for his Indian children. We have been here more than one moon but the results will be very gratifying to him, I assure you. Your man will be released this very day. Your people will be grateful for such a successful mission."

Quashme struggled to gather his thoughts. Mequapa would be set free? Perhaps it would be worth a bit of land. "Let us go to the governor," he said.

Late that afternoon the Chouteau brothers and the four Sauk's were ushered into the Governor's temporary office, a richly furnished room in the Chouteau business headquarters.

"I am glad to inform Monsieur le Guveneur that our brothers have agreed to the treaty and have already touched the pen," said Pierre Chouteau. "Once the papers are delivered everything will be, how you say, legalite?"

"Yes my friend, wonderful," replied Harrison. "The papers are all ready. We have copies for your people, if you will make your marks right here. Yes, all four of you, if you please. See, my signature is right here, and these are your four benefactors, the monsieurs Chouteau."

"When will Mequapa be released?" asked Quashme.

"This very evening, my brothers," replied Harrison. "I have written to President Jefferson requesting a full pardon and I am certain the great white father will be motivated by mercy when he understands the particulars. Touch the pen and all is settled."

The four Sauks made totem marks on the documents.

"Fine, thank you. This is your copy," said Harrison. "Let us honor this treaty and keep it faithfully."

"What parcel of land has been exchanged?" asked Quashme.

The interpreter read from the Sauk's document: "The Sauk and Fox cession extends as far as the Wisconsin River in Wisconsin territory on the northwest side. It extends seventy (70) miles at the extreme north into Wisconsin, thirty-five (35) miles from the mouth of the Wisconsin River then down to the junction of the Fox River and Lake Sakaegan in Illinois..."

"But that is the most important part of our country!" exclaimed Quashme.

"The people will fill us with arrows, and rightly so," said one of the other Sauks.

"You and all your people will have the protection of the United States," remarked Harrison, "and you will have an annuity of $1,000 a year."

"Where does it say that?" asked Quashme.

"Right here," interpreted the translator. "And this says the Spanish grants in Upper Louisiana heretofore claimed by the Sauk-Fox nation are ceded to the Chouteau brothers."

"We came only to buy Mequapa's release," said Quashme.

"Brothers, I must leave you now to prepare for certain festivities this evening," concluded Harrison. "If you will repair to headquarters of the military commandant he will see to the release of your kinsman." He shook hands with the Sauks, then with the Chouteau brothers as the Indians exited. It had been a most impressive treaty: 15,000,000 acres had been added to the territory of the United States, including a rich mineral region in the north.

280

Mequapa was in a desperate emotional state in prison. More than a month he had waited for the trial that never came and all he ever heard were contemptible epithets which he understood only by the tone of voice of the various speakers. The food was bad, moreso because he was unaccustomed to it. Evening was unfolding its shadowy wings in the prison compound as Mequapa lay on his bunk. He heard the rattle of keys in his cell door. If he was not liberated soon he would die! How he longed for the freedom of prairies and great forests! His very soul was drying up inside him. What a fool he had been to give himself up! *Better to have died like a warrior!* He happened to look up and saw his cell door was slightly ajar. Was he finally insane? Had his incarceration finally killed his senses?! He got up slowly and walked to the door, pushed it gently, heard it creak open. Yes, it was open! Mequapa began to perspire freely. What was the meaning of it all? He looked out into the yard and saw four Sauk's at the other end of the yard, walking in his direction! Could it be?! It was not Black Hawk, but they were definitely Sauks! Mequapa walked out into the moonlit dusk and yelled, "BROTHERS!"

Quashme and the others stopped dead in their tracks, such was their elation. They saw Mequapa running toward them then a rifle boomed out and Mequapa fell heavily to the ground.

"Jailbreak!" hollered someone and quickly the yard was full of heavily armed sentries who pointed their weapons at the Indians. They did not move.

"This one's a goner," said a uniformed sentry as he turned Mequapa over with his booted foot.

"Trying to escape," said another man.

"Now the score is even."

Quashme and the others felt their own lives were in great jeopardy so they did nothing. Even had they been armed they would not have had a chance. They were detained until an interpreter came with orders to set the Sauks free. They packed their gear and left St. Louis that very night.

The four took a long time to return to their village for their hearts were heavy with bad news which they must communicate to their tribesmen. Quashme dreaded the wrath of his warchief Black Hawk. When the men got to the vicinity of Saukenuk they camped a short distance from the village, put on their fine coats and medals, and waited until the next day when they entered the town and were escorted by Black Hawk and others to council with the chiefs. The tragic story came out piece by piece: the land had been ceded, Mequapa had been shot to death at the moment of his release, the Longknives would be coming to build homes.

Black Hawk had never fought the Longknives but he was smouldering at the infamy of what had transpired in St. Louis. The chiefs were all angry but they could do nothing except assert the four messengers had not had the power to sign away any lands. This did not stop the Longknives for within a very short time a large group of them came in keelboats to a point just above the Des Moines Rapids and began to cut much timber. The news spread rapidly among the Sauk-Fox and more councils were held. It was also learned the Longknives brought big guns with them and Black Hawk decided to take a group of tribesmen and see for himself what was happening at the rapids of the Des Moines.

When the Amerindians arrived at the site it was quite evident a fort was being built, not merely homes or trading houses. The numerous soldiers had their guns ready, even while they were cutting lumber. Black Hawk knew a war party when he saw it. He parleyed with the officers, saying "This is our land and we do not understand why you visit us with so many guns."

"We, like you, are hunters," replied the officer, "and we must be prepared in case we see game."

"What is it you are building?" asked Black Hawk.

"Some trading houses for our traders. They will come with many fine goods for the betterment of your people."

"Then why do you come with so many soldiers?" asked Black Hawk.

"Our traders like the company," replied the officer. "Our young men volunteered to come into this country and keep the trader company."

At this moment some youths, who had crept behind the soldiers on the logging detail, let out blood-curdling warcries. The soldiers became terror stricken and scampered for their weapons and any available cover, believing an ambush was being sprung on them. Black Hawk and the chiefs did not move. They could have easily been shot by the frightened soldiers had not the mischievous youngsters burst out laughing raucously. Why, the soldiers had scurried about like confused field mice! But the war whoops had been heard at the fort and soldiers began to pour out in the direction of the logging detail. Black Hawk saw several men pulling a cannon into place and one soldier was running toward it with fire in his hand. "Into the forest and return home," said the warchief calmly. Everyone melted out of sight immediately.

Episode 7: The Debate

The Prophet began a mission at the village of Anderson then a bit later he was asked to do the same at Greenville. His movement was growing stronger with the passage of time and his fame was an ever growing phenomena. Tecumseh remained in the background and observed how effective The Prophet had become in his plan of building a country for all Amerindians. Insiders compared the brothers continuously as they labored toward the confederation. Both of Puckeshinwa's sons were proud. Tecumseh's pride gave him dignity and set him apart as a leader of stature and magnetism. The Prophet felt divinely called. Perhaps that is why he was intolerant of those who might cavil or refuse to recognize the importance of salvation. He thoroughly enjoyed the power he exerted over people. His brand of evangelism was flambuoyant. His mysticism and exhibitionism stimulated the emotions of his listeners, aroused enthusiasm, and attracted great crowds to White River, Anderson, and finally Greenville. No one could harague a crowd better than The Prophet, no one was a better showman. Tecumseh's oratory was forthright, well reasoned, full of native poetry and imagery yet laced with incontrovertible fact and logic.

Both brothers now had a retinue of hard core followers who could be depended on to help in any endeavor. Jainai, for example, was a former Christian until he was converted by The Prophet at Anderson. He had studied the Shemanese religion seriously and whenever The Prophet needed information about it he turned to Jainai with confidence. One day when a couple of missionaries came to Greenville and began to preach Christianity to followers of The Prophet the men were invited to meet and discuss religious matters in front of anyone who cared to listen. The missionaries accepted with alacrity and on the appointed day The Prophet and Jainai sat informally with the two, a large crowd gathering for the occassion.

"Brothers in Christ," began one of the missionaries as his assistant, an Indian, translated into Shawnee, "my name is Brother Lawrence and this is Brother Frank. We thank you this day for taking time out to listen to the word of God. All races of men would do well to listen." A black man held the horses for the missionaries.

"How many races of men are there?" asked Jainai.

"Only one race," replied Brother Lawrence, "for all are descendants of Adam."

"How was it then, if all came of one man, that some men are black?"

"That is a difficult question to answer. Noah had three sons, Shem, Ham, and Japhet. *Ham* signifies black, so I suppose his posterity must be negros, although he himself was of the same complexion as his brothers, as they had the same parents.

"If he was white," persisted Jainai, "how did his posterity become black?"

"Noah was said to be a good man," said Brother Frank, "but he drank too much wine on a certain occasion and became drunk. Ham made sport of him and when he sobered up he found out, became angry with and cursed him by telling him 'Blessed be the Lord God of Shem and Japhet, cursed be Canaan, a servant of servants shall be to his brethren.'

"Canaan was Ham's son," responded Jainai. "Why should it be that Canaan was cursed for what his father had done and not all of Ham's children? The Christnan God is a Being of love and forgiveness, we have been taught. And if Canaan and his posterity were cursed with servitude why was it they also became black?"

"That is a difficult question," conceded Brother Lawrence, "yet we think they were black from the fact that Ham signifies black. We are satisfied to have it so anyhow as Ham's people were in Africa."

"Is that the reason you make slaves of the blacks?" asked The Prophet.

The two missionaries looked at each other quizzically. "That is the best reason we can give you," said Brother Frank.

"Well, that happened many many years ago," continued Jainai. "Since then Jesus Christ came into the world to bring about a change in the order of things. Did he not come to end such injustice and to establish righteousness, peace, love and do away with ideas like one race of men being punished for the sins of another?"

"Yes, he did. And the Testament says to put an end to sin, and finish transgression. This we all confess."

"If He came for that purpose," said Jainai, "and fulfilled his mission, how does it happen sin yet abounds in the world?"

"Because bad people do not keep his commandments."

"How does it happen," asked The Prophet, "that good missionaries hold black slaves? I don't understand it and since you are here to teach the Indians I want you to explain it. I think it is wrong, even when missionaries do it. I am very anxious for you to answer."

"I hardly know how to explain this to Indians," conceded Brother Lawrence. "I can scarcely understand it myself sometimes. I have heard our best men say the blacks are much enlightened by being with us, even in bondage, because they see so much light from us by our godly worth before them. And they will, after they are set free in a few more generations, know better how to appreciate freedom as well as Christianity."

"Would slavery not then help us to become likewise more appreciative?" asked The Prophet. "Would you recommend Amerindians be enslaved in order to appreciate Christianity?"

"I cannot answer such a question," said Brother Lawrence, struggling to maintain his composure.

"As each generation of blacks is born in a state of bondage," continued Jainai, "they remain slaves as long as they live and die so. How is the following generation to get any light, more light than his parents?"

"I cannot explain that so ignorant people can understand," said Brother Lawrence. "All I can say is as we progress in the right path and our lights shine with more brilliance than our fathers' did, so it will illuminate their path better, as they follow us in the ways of religion and truth."

"Then you believe," said The Prophet, "that good can come out of evil? Do you own slaves?"

"We expect to bring good out of it at last, by enlightening our slaves," said Brother Frank.

"Do you believe it is good for people to take Indian land even if laws like the Treaty of Greenville say these are our territories?" asked Tecumseh from the first row of the assembled crowd.

"I am not going to discuss politics," said Brother Frank.

"Must we continue to do evil, that good may come of it?" asked Jainai. "Must we sin, that grace may abound? I want that explained."

"I cannot explain so Indians can understand," replied Brother Frank.

"The Prophet exhorts us to loose the bonds of wickedness, to break every yoke until the oppressed go free," said Tecumseh. "Would you tell us the same?"

"That would be difficult for me to explain to you, being an Indian, so as to satisfy you. It seems a contradiction how we can be keeping such a fast as that, while we have slaves, and I would rather not have much to say about that to avoid confusion." Brother Frank wiped the sweat from his brow.

"Why don't you teach the blacks to read the Testament?" asked Jainai. "You tell the Indians it is the Lord's Book. You could teach them to read it and understand it on the Lord's Day so it does not interfere with their labor.

"I don't like to discuss such things with Indians," said Brother Lawrence, "because it really doesn't concern them."

"Do any of your slaves belong to your church?" asked Jainai of Brother Frank.

"Yes, some of them do."

"Are they a part in full fellowship, with you and your Indian members at the communion table?"

"No, we never do. Such a course would not do."

"When Jesus commands us," continued Jainai, "to do unto others as we would have others do unto us, does he mean this to include blacks and others?"

"I suppose He does mean them too," answered Brother Frank as he shook his head in exasperation.

"Would any of you missionaries wish to be slaves?"

"I suppose not," said Brother Frank as he stood up, "and now I have answered you so much I hope you will excuse me." Brother Lawrence also got to his feet.

"I see you are tired of answering my questions," concluded Jainai, "but I thought you were here to teach us a knowledge of the Scriptures by explaining them to us and clarifying our duty. Other missionaries have come among us and told us slavery and oppression are wrong. They tell us it is contrary to the Bible to oppress anyone and since you have the same kind of Bible I want to know the reason why you don't agree with them."

"I hope not to have to explain such things because it would be hard for me to make ignorant people understand it," said Brother Frank. "Good day to you."

The two missionaries walked away from the crowd, which remained silent, mounted their horses and rode out of the village, the black man behind them.

"My friends," began Tecumseh from where he sat, "you have seen for yourself the hypocrisy masquerading as belief in the minds of these officious men who come, according to them, to promote our welfare. There is much hypocrisy among the Shemanese, so much it appears to be part of their character and institutions. When the Longknives threw their British fathers on their backs and began their own country they wrote about all men being created equal. That idea was basic, they said, that all are equal. But the people who wrote this owned black slaves and cheated the Amerindian tribes out of their land at every opportunity. They preach love as basic but when Captain Williamson got the upper hand at Ghnadenhutten he butchered the Moravian Christians despite their religion. Christianity meant nothing to Williamson and Crawford and you have had an indication of what it means to the two missionaries who came to visit this day. That is what we can expect at the hands of the people who crucified Jesus Christ."

"Are all Shemanese bad and evil?" asked one man.

"No, they are not," replied Tecumseh, "there are many good and noble Shemanese. But many among us have observed the good do not control a situation, they never seem to be in command, they do not become chiefs. I do not understand why this is so."

"Perhaps Christianity makes a person soft," observed The Prophet, "perhaps it makes a woman out of a man. The Moravian Delawares did not even resist their cruel fate."

"Lambs to the slaughter," remarked Jainai.

"What would happen to us if we became Christians?" asked Tecumseh.

"We would be as the Shemanese," said The Prophet, "hypocrites."

"We would never be accepted among them," remarked Jainai, who spoke from personal experience. "I was seldom considered a Christian when I lived with the Shemanese. Most often I was just an Indian, inferior by nature. The Shemanese can unite against a common enemy but when there is no outsider they turn on themselves and separate into disagreeing factions."

"I wonder if our people are any better," said Tecumseh. "Look at how jealous we all are of our independence, refusing to join with our brothers in order to survive. We do not see the danger until it is too late. We can live as our ancestors lived but we must learn to unite, even with tribes we considered enemies before. Will our people be able to see that?"

"It is our duty," remarked The Prophet, "to enable our people to realize truth. For that reason," he said as he pulled something out from under the blanket draped over his shoulders, "I have prepared this Sacred Slab, given to me during a vision while I gazed into the Forest Bowl."

The slab appeared to be carved of red cedar wood, slightly more than a foot long and perhaps half an inch thick, one side of which was inscribed with various symbols. "This we shall give to the nations which join us in our national crusade," continued The Prophet. "Only the sincere will own a Sacred Slab to put in a war bundle and if ever the time comes when it is ignored or not kept secret it will be the end of the world."

The Sacred Slab created quite a stir among the assembled Amerindians. Everyone was interested in the great Beyond and how to get there. Surely The Prophet knew the way if anyone did. It was obvious the irritated missionaries did not have sacred knowledge for they could not answer questions put to them. "The Sacred Slab begins here at the bottom with the family," explained The Prophet as he stood up so everyone could see clearly. "These three lines represent not only our individual families but all Amerindian people on this Great Island for we are all one family. This circular symbol above the lines represents Earth Mother on whom we depend for our existence. The line across the circle is the path which we must follow if we are to live in happiness and contentment with the Great Spirit. Next is the line which symbolizes pure, clear water which we find throughout the land. Above that is the lightning and other elements which come into our world from beyond, adding to our lives even if we cannot always understand the message flashed to us. These elements all nourish the trees in our great forests, the next symbol, which are so much a part of our lives. The four directions are represented next, along with the weather that comes from each. Above that is the symbol for corn, the principal base for our civilization. Next we have the birds of the air and the animals of the earth, all of which are gifts from the Great Spirit. This represents all plant life, in which our people are so rich. Our great father the sun makes all life possible, and above the symbol for the sun is that for the eternal sky where lives our father. Next to the top is the sign for the Gate Keepers of Heaven and at the very top is the Great Beyond itself. This my brothers," said The Prophet forcefully, "is the representation of our life, our civilization, our religion, no matter which tribe produced us. We are one large family living under one sun, one sky. Those of you who will be chosen to go speak to our brothers in distant lands will be provided with a Sacred Slab."

There was much commotion among the Amerindians to gaze at the slab up close and fortunate were those who could touch it. It appeared many individuals wanted to go out as emissaries and preach. The Prophet was pleased.

Episode 8: The Dilemma

When the meal was finished Rebecca grasped the canoe paddle from its rack on the wall and said, "Come on, Mr. Tikomfa Chief, I want to show you how I have practiced in managing your canoe. There is a beautiful tree about a mile down river and some strange flowers the like of which I have never seen. Perhaps we could transplant some in the flower bed."

Tecumseh looked at his hosts, James Galloway and his wife Bec, as if to ask permission to go with Rebecca. The Galloways nodded slightly and Tecumseh said, "We shall return in a while... if we don't drown," he added playfully.

"You might be pleasantly surprised," said Bec Galloway, "I know I was when she gave me a ride."

Tecumseh and Rebecca left the cabin, took the canoe to the river, placed it in the water, and sailed. "Is the tree near the bank of the river," asked Tecumseh, "or at the second bend above?"

"Near the bank," said Rebecca as she paddled expertly. "You seem to know something about it, and I was going to surprise you. Whatever made you ask about its location?" Tecumseh was impressed with the young woman's handling of the paddle and canoe. "Mr. Tikomfa Chief, you have to tell me about it when we get there, all about it, now mind, not half around, please, like you Indians do when you don't want the palefaces to know your secrets."

"Oh, and you have gotten to know us so well, have you?" He gazed at her as if to read her thoughts.

"Not all, just some," conceded Rebecca. "I have talked much with Tecumapease. What a beautiful person, that sister of yours!" She paddled toward the magnificent sycamore, whose branches far overspread the river bank, a strong thick root streched into the water serving as a pier, the canoe nestling alongside so its occupants could step easily onto it. "Come," said Rebecca, "the tree is just around the hill yonder and the flowers are there too. Maybe you'll know what they are. I certainly don't. There is nothing like them that I can find in the woods."

Tecumseh appeared concerned to the point of worry as the two walked hand in hand.

"Here they are," exclaimed Rebecca as she ran ahead a little. "See the blossoms on the tree, how bright and beautiful they are? And the flowers there, what are they?" She stooped over and picked up a couple. "They look good enough to eat and I believe I'll try one. Want one?"

Tecumseh bounded to her side with the celerity of a springing panther, grabbing her wrist tenderly but firmly. "Come, let us sit on that big rock and I will tell you about those flowers. You cannot eat them, inviting though they look. Yes, come on, sit. There, that's better. I guess I never expected you to find that tree and those flowers. They are in no other place around here. I should have destroyed them when I first saw them. But before I tell you about them you must vow never to repeat what I will say. Will you listen, then forget completely?"

Rebecca looked into Tecumseh's earnest face. Such power and determination she had rarely seen in a human countenance. His was an irresistible force. She nodded her head slowly.

"The tree and the flowers shall be destroyed," said Tecumseh. "You and your family are under my care and no harm may come to you. It is our pact of peace."

"What is it?" asked Rebecca a bit nervously. "What do you mean? What kind of tree is it? Are the flowers poison? Tell me, please!"

In an authoritarian voice she had never heard him use before Tecumseh asked once again, "Will this I tell you be for you and you only? No one else must know, not even your parents or family."

"Yes, if it is your wish, and it will be for my ears only, unless you consent to allow me to share this knowledge with one of my descendants whom I consider worthy, before I die."

Tecumseh nodded his consent and said, "That is good." He took a flower from where Rebecca had dropped it. "This is a secret of our people. The Amerindian suffers pain like anyone else. The warrior fears the wound, the torn arm, the disabled leg, but this little flower you have found, if prepared properly, quiets all pain, no matter how searing. The medicine man takes the powder from the flowers and leaves, or from the fruit this tree will bear, gives it to the warrior to take into battle with him. If the bullet bites or the arrow pierces the potion quiets the pain. If the warrior falls in battle this eases his path to the Great Beyond. What you had in you hand is the best. With a small dose of it the torture of the stake is as nothing. With it a wounded warrior can be removed to a place of safety without pain. It is more powerful than your opium but without the harm. No paleface knows its power. It is our secret. If the Indians loves, he speaks the truth; if he does not, he is silent."

Was this Tecumseh's affirmation of love? Rebecca hoped it was as she took his hand "My good and special friend," she said, "I would ask you a question that might be difficult to answer. We of our religious belief do not like war. Do you think it might ever break out again, between your people and mine?"

"Speaking for my people," answered Tecumseh, "war would be the very last resort." He did not wish to give a political speech to Rebecca but he could not help but continue: "War has always been forced upon us. We have fought only in defense of our land."

Rebecca did not know what to say so she said nothing, though she did squeeze his hand just a trifle, as if hanging on.

"If the ultimate calamity should befall us," said Tecumseh, "you and your family would not be harmed, I have seen to that."

"I see you so seldom," said Rebecca. "Could you not move back and live closer... I know Tecumapease and Wasegoboah would like it too."

"I love the Ohio country," said Tecumseh. "Perhaps someday I could live here again in peace and contentment."

"I... love you," confessed Rebecca.

"I have the same feeling deep in my heart," said Tecumseh tenderly, no longer the leading war chief in all North America, but merely a man in love with a beautiful woman. "I do not know how this came to be but I no longer care why. I know you fill my heart with all that is good." Gently he pulled her to him and kissed her. He forgot all misdeeds committed on his people, dismissed all warfare of the past, and even the confederacy was out of his mind. His every thought was Rebecca, the intelligent, radiant Rebecca!

290

"I do not want you to leave, ever!" whispered Rebecca. "You are so unlike anyone I have ever met."

Tecumseh regained his composure quickly. For a fleeting moment he had forgotten everything. A little orphan with a mission in life could not afford such luxuries! But strong forces pulled at him now. "Is it that I am an Indian?" he asked.

"You will always be my Mr. Tikomfa Chief," said Rebecca, "but I do not think of you as an Indian. You have become my special, my dearest... I do not have proper words. I have never been in love before."

Tecumseh, the accomplished orator, appeared not to have appropriate words either for he said nothing.

"We are so different," said Rebecca, "and yet I am so comfortable in your company, no matter what we are doing. Perhaps we are more alike than I am aware. We seem to like the same things."

"You are a good woman. I think about you and miss you when I am away from you. You bring out the finer sentiments." He kissed her once more.

"Perhaps we should be getting back," said Rebecca. Tecumseh nodded and both walked in silence to the canoe, stepped in, the man doing the paddling this time. The silence was not heavy, both lovers contented as the breath of spring, yet neither added to the feelings they had expressed. Perhaps neither was sure of the other's courting habits but there was no problem because of it.

Upon their return to the Galloway cabin Tecumseh was asked to stay for supper but he declined saying he must return to his men who were camped down river. He bid everyone farewell and Rebecca marvelled at how inscrutable was his face when he said goodbye to her.

"When will you return?" she asked.

"Very soon, I hope," he said as he mounted his horse and rode away. He touched his heart then waved in silence. Nothing else needed to be said. Rebecca stood and watched until he was out of sight.

As Tecumseh rode at a leisurely pace his mind began to work in a way not usual for him. More than once he had been told he should leave all border troubles and live his life in peace. If he loved Rebecca why did he not ask her to marry him? Was he ready for such a step? What would happen to the confederacy, to his people? Surely there were other leaders who could guide the tribes to security... what had the Amerindians done to promote their own weaknesses? What were the weaknesses of the tribes on this great island? He had spent so much time studying with the Grandfathers and now his mature mentality began to dredge up observations made by his many excellent teachers.

From the beginning the tribes failed to recognize their interests as one people. To this day many Amerindians did not realize they were confronting a clear, unmistakeable danger. Their homeland was being overrun by invaders but the brothers felt no urgent impulse to combine their forces in common defense. What was it about Amerindians that prevented them from doing so? Had they known too much freedom, experienced too much liberty? Everyone was so afraid of losing sovereignty at the hands of his brother but few were willing to recognize the loss of their tribal lands to aliens from across the salt water.

It was not that the Amerindian did not know battle. War was a favorite pastime, the principal way to gain fame. But the preoccupation was to make war on each other, not the invader. Quite the contrary, one tribe would ask the invader to help exterminate the other tribe. Whenever a tribe obtained firearms from the aliens that tribe would use them on another that didn't have them! This fratricidal psychology enabled the early invaders to exist all along the sea coasts. A united resistance would have destroyed them immediately.

How could the Amerindian be taught to de-emphasize making war? Tecumseh asked himself. War-making was as integeral a part of personality as hunting. It was the basic method to show courage. It was the national sport. But with firearms warfare became deadly. Deaths were frequent now and they left huge gaps in the national as well as personal life. His own father was a case in point. His death had been the greatest trauma in Tecumseh's life and the ruination of his mother. Cheeseekau had lived the path of vengeance. Sauwaseekau had also been killed. Tecumseh, the fifth born, was now the oldest surviving male in the family... how many others were like him? How many other families had been destroyed? But there was a difference with Puckeshinwa's family: the men had died at the hands of the Shemanese, they had never fought against other Indians. Why had this been so? Perhaps the family had never craved Shemanese tools, utensils, and weapons as some others did. Tecumseh had observed some Indians to be consumed by a desire to own these foreign things, as avariciously as any Shemanese. The compulsion was also accompanied by the desire to deny trade goods to other tribes in order to augment their own power and profits. Intertribal war was no longer merely a hazardous sport but instead a struggle for material advantage, a monopoly of trade routes, or the exaction of tribute. The Iroquois were an excellent example. They had all but exterminated their rivals, the Huron, Erie, Mohican, Susquehannock, in the merciless conquests needed to establish their trading empire. In the south country the Yamassee, Catawba, and others were destroyed, the

Shawnee and Tuscarora driven north into exile, dissipating the energies of powerful tribes like the Cherokee, Creek, Chickasaw, Choctaw. If the tribes had used their power to attack the invaders! It would have been so simple to destroy the intruders while they were still weak!

Tecumseh made a conscious effort to stop dwelling on what might have been as he rode, the only sounds in the forest being the hooves of his horse, birds chirping, running water occassionally. But the facts hurt! Why did the tribes not see the omnipresent danger?! Perhaps it was asking too much. How could the Grandfathers possibly know of the untold hordes of people living across the salt water? They could not. But there were other factors: the Iroquois were instrumental in barring the French advance into the upper Ohio Valley. If the French had become dominant instead of the English the Indian culture would have been maintained, along with Indian independence. It was the English who came to seize the land and dispossess the Amerindian, to exterminate him as Amherst had tried to do with diseases like smallpox. The northern tribes had supported the French, excepting the Iroquois. The Cherokee had also fought for the English, thus making the two most powerful tribes enemies of the French, who were, as it turned out, the Amerindians' best friend! The Iroquois and Cherokee were enabling the English to win the war, assuring these same English would survive to seize the land and exterminate the native populations. It was a dilemma worthy of Hamlet!

Tecumseh shook his head in consternation. How would his efforts be different from those of the leaders who had gone before? Pontiac had captured every English fort in the west except Pittsburg and Detroit. Many tribes joined him but there were others who demanded normal trade relations be resumed with the English. The materialistic civilization of the intruders had already become part of the Amerindian character. The English drew a line at the Appalachian Mountains, stating all lands to the west were Indian territories, but this did not hold back the encroachers. Any tribe was willing to sign away the land of the other if they were offered trade goods for it. The Iroquois and the Cherokee were guilty of this when they sold Shawnee land in Kentucky and Tennessee, thus opening it to the Shemanese.

There had been only one glimmer of hope Tecumseh was familiar with: when the Shemanese revolted against the English both northern and southern Indians warred against the Shemanese. For years the tribes were able to halt the advance of the People of the Eagle until Fallen Timbers in 1794. The Amerindians were told they were whipped but it was not true. Fallen Timbers had been an insignificant skirmish militarily. It was the chiefs who sold out the people at the Treaty of Greenville. The Amerindians were unconquered and if the British would supply firearms... but that would be the last resort, Tecumseh did not want war. There was still much land on which the tribes could live in peace. There had to be formed a country for Amerindians! No more territory could be given up by chiefs or anybody else!

Things were different in the south country. The tribes still owned much land but all of it was encircled by Shemanese settlements. There was no room for retreat or maneuver as in the north. This could be a more difficult situation.

After thinking out everything as thoroughly as possible, which was the way his mind worked, Tecumseh concluded the confederacy was the only way to meet the approaching crisis. The Prophet would be of immense assistance if he could spread the religion of Amerindian ancestors. There would be two fronts: political and religious. Former leaders like Pontiac and Joseph Brant had worked only on the political. Dependence on Shemanese trade goods must be broken or at least de-emphasized as greatly as possible. Still, firearms could not be gotten rid of. There were weaknesses in The Prophet's religion but there were also great strengths: the prohibition of whiskey was among the most important. The people must react very unfavorably to any selling of land without the consent of *all the tribes.* Perhaps it should be made a crime punishable by death to sell the land. Yes, it had to be so or there would be no land on which to build a country for Amerindians. And what about the injunction against intermarriage with the Shemanese? Tecumseh had not come to grips with this tenet before now. What if he married Rebecca? Would that make a hypocrite of him? No, she could become a good Shawnee. She would be a worthwhile addition to any group of people. Actually the push was to prevent Indian women from marrying Shemanese, for they often moved away from the tribe and tried to live as Shemanese. It was also aimed at preventing disease, which so many Shemanese transmited to women. But what of his own two sisters? One had married a Britisher, another a Frenchman. The French were still highly thought of among the northern tribes, and the British were allies. Tecumseh was the only one interested in a Shemanese! He was unable to work his way out of his dilemma before he rode into camp.

Episode 9: The Purge

The Prophet held no doubt whatever as to where he stood on the issues. He had power and was unafraid to use it. For example Buckongahelos had died more than a year ago and there were those who murmured it had not been of natural causes. The great Delaware had been one of the principal chiefs in the destruction of St. Clair and he had invited Tecumseh to live at White River. He had been a true warrior and leader of his race. Teteboxti, the new chief of the Delaware, had aroused the suspicion of friends of Buckongahelos for they believed the great chief had not died of natural causes. Had Teteboxti used poison or some kind of witchcraft to remove his rival from the chieftainship? These and other rumors reached The Prophet in Greenville so he called a council of his ablest lieutenants and discussed the matter.

"I want to know the facts," began The Prophet, "and what course of action we should pursue. It is enough of a condemnation to know that Teteboxti signed a land treaty with Governor Harrison but perhaps there is something in his favor of which I am unaware. Speak."

"I myself took the word to Chief Teteboxti," began Jainai as he took a puff from his pipe. "He was unreceptive to say the least. The mud of ignorance is in his ears. He will never render homage to our efforts."

"Think you it would change if I talked to him personally?" asked The Prophet.

"Perhaps," said Jainai, "but I did not feel encouraged. He would not stroke the beans."

"We must crack the shell of the tortoise," said Arawaee. "We need an example for the rest of the tribes."

"The Delawares are being hit by an epidemic of bilious fever," said another man. "If we could put a stop to it we would do much good and attract much attention."

"There is talk of canceling the Corn Harvest Festival," said Jainai, "if the epidemic continues to rage."

"The first thing we should do," said The Prophet, "is take the people the proper medicine..." He would check quickly with Spybuck for the proper herbs. "Then we shall take part in the festival and observe Teteboxti. We can put him to the question about Buckongahelos death. How is he responding to the Moravian missionaries?"

"I saw no signs that he was friendly or ready to embrace Christianity," said Jainai. "Perhaps that is something in his favor."

"Neither has he embraced our native religion," observed Arawaee.

"He shall have that opportunity," concluded The Prophet. "Let us be ready to travel within three sleeps."

"What if Teteboxti cannot answer the questions?" asked Jaimai.

"The penalty for witchcraft and sorcery is death," said The Prophet, "the penalty for ceding lands without consent of all the tribes is death, or should be."

Had the death penalty already been passed on Teteboxti? Was The Prophet serious? The chief of the Delaware tribe would be executed?! Was the power of the native religion that strong already or would everyone be killed in reprisal? No one knew but none were afraid to find out.

The Prophet went to see the medicine man Spybuck that very afternoon. The older man greeted him cordially and the two sat down to visit, chatting about this and that. The Prophet saw the woman, Flame, though she paid no attention to him beyond common courtesy. From the beginning Laulewasika had been curious about the red-haired female. There was some kind of mysterious quality about her. Since he had become The Prophet he had seen how awed people were of him, sometimes, but that was not the case this afternoon. Spybuck and Flame were not awed. If anything it was the other way around. The Prophet was curious about Flaming Eagle of Delight and he was hesistant about Spybuck and his reputation as a juggler. He had seen the pair in the crowds listening to him or Tecumseh but he really did not know where they stood with regard to his religious leadership.

The Prophet finally got around to asking Spybuck's help in stamping out the bilious fever raging among the Delaware in the vicinity of Anderson village. Spybuck asked Flame to bring him a certain herb that was in a leather pouch. "Perhaps this is what you need," said Spybuck. "Boil this until the water is strongly colored then let the afflicted drink."

"I will need as much as you can spare," said The Prophet.

Flame looked at the younger man out of the corner of her eye. There was something sinister about him. She thoroughly liked his brother, Tecumseh, but this Prophet was different... ruthless, cruel or was it mostly negative vibrations he always put out when she was around? His wife seemed to be all right, though quite pushy, even for an Indian female.

"This should do quite well for it is very potent," said Spybuck. "Boil it well. Drink it before you start ministering to the sick that you may be protected."

"Thank you brother," said The Prophet, "now I must be on my way."

"I am glad to help the people," said Spybuck. "It is good you came today for it is possible I will be going north."

"Oh," said The Prophet, "a little hunting trip?"

"No, my wife purchased some smallpox medicine several moons ago," said Spybuck from behind his inscrutable face. Flame had learned smallpox was the only disease in the world Spybuck feared so she had gone to the military commander at the fort and paid to have some vac-

296

cine brought in from the east. She had learned how to vaccinate many years ago so she vaccinated Spybuck against the dread disease after puncturing her own arm with it first. "I heard there have been a case or two and I sent a runner to see if they need help. I should not be gone long."

"It is good to tend our people," said The Prophet as he exited. It was foutunate he did not have to combat smallpox for then the Corn Festival certainly would have been canceled.

The Prophet and his men made their way to Anderson and learned many were ill indeed. Immediately he and his men invited everyone to come drink of their cure and within a few days people were getting better. Word spread that The Prophet was healing the sick in miraculous fashion so Chief Teteboxti went to meet him and shake his hand. "We appreciate your efforts in behalf of your Delaware grandfathers," said the old chief, emphasizing the rank which his tribe held among the various nations.

"You are most welcome," said The Prophet. "Perhaps later we will have time to talk, when the people are well."

"Of course," said Teteboxti, "and I would like to invite you to stay for the festival. Many people are already beginning to arrive. With your medicine the feast may be held at the appointed time."

"Of course."

The Prophet either cured the epidemic or coincidentally began ministering to it when its virulence had been spent because most people got well before homage was paid to great Mother Corn.

The Moravian missionaries looked askance at the Corn Festival, considering it a typical outburst of savage heathenism. But they were powerless to stop it and Amerindians came from all directions across the flatlands. Large numbers of deer and bear were brought in for food. The Prophet was as irritated at the missionaries when he saw the number of barrels of whiskey which would be consumed during the festival. How he wished he could have given one of his orations but out of respect to Corn and its significance he chose not to interfere with the proceedings.

The Corn Festival began with a procession solemnly winding its way around the village of Anderson. Teteboxti led it, carrying a beautifully worked basket in which were several ears of corn. The drum beat rhythmically and the people started to chant as they had since time out of mind: "Mother Corn, open your way! O hear us as we draw near. Let our souls touch you while we pray. Mother Corn, hear!"

Teteboxti arrived at the Council house and handed the basket of corn to a small group of elders. One of the venerables took out the whitest ear and from a round bowl painted its tip blue to represent the sky, the dwelling place of the spirits, and four blue equidistant lines running halfway down the ear, to symbolize the four paths along which the spirits descend to minister to men and women. As the other corn was being painted the venerables took up a chant:

"Mighty one, standing we wait thy bidding.
Mother Corn awaiting stands,
Waits to serve you here.
Mighty one, we in thy dwelling stand.
Mother Corn is leader here,
We your children follow.
Mighty one, the downward path we take.
Mother Corn with power leads,
We her symbol bear...

Thus was symbolized the journey of the Great Mother from the vault of heaven, where the Sky Father dwells, to earth. Having arrived in the land corn lead the wonderful procession which was to bring peace and goodwill to all. The ears of corn thus represented supernatural powers that dwell on earth, which brought forth food that sustained all human creatures so the people chanted "Mother breathing forth the life!" The power in the earth which enabled it to bring forth sustenance emanated from above, therefore the corn was painted blue. The wooden bowl was round like the dome shape of the sky.

The procession began again amidst chanting from the people:

"Mother Corn, O hear! Open our way
Over hills, over streams, over forests
making our way...

The Prophet and his men were in the procession, chanting with the rest. He saw the Moravian missionaries looking on with stony expressions. He knew immediately they understood nothing of what was happening. The entire ceremony was a prayer that the people might increase and be strong, that everyone may have long life and enjoy the gifts of the Great Spirit, that all may live in happiness and peace, that children may be born to the people...

"Mother Corn, O hear! Our heads we bow,
Our souls touch thine,
Children give to us...

298

The ceremony was an effort to balance the warrior society which was Amerindian life. Only by such festivals could the people save their souls. While the Delaware tribe held the celebration, people from many different nations attended so (through the years) it had become a pan-Indian festival. This suited The Prophet for he and Tecumseh were promoting the idea that all Indians were part of one family who had to live in peace if they were to survive.

"Mother Corn, O hear! our journey's end is near.
We look on strange land,
Seeking children there...

Teteboxti handed the bowl of corn to another and was given in return a sacred bundle. The Prophet stopped in his tracks. Medicine bundles were forbidden by the new religion for all too often they were used for sorcery and incantations. He dropped out of the procession, his disciples following suit, though he did not wish to mar the festivities. The Prophet was in something of a quandry: he wished to promote Amerindian festivals of all kinds but he could not be a part of anything which smacked of witchcraft. The basic way to neutralize a sorcerer was to deprive him of his medicine bundle, thus rendering him harmless.

"Mother Corn, oh hear! At her touch comes a dream.
A bird calls, 'My son!'
While his soul responds. Mother Corn, hear!

The procession made its winding course through the village then ended where it had begun. The Prophet's eyes were now as stony as those of the Moravians but few seemed to care for there was much singing, dancing, eating, and the whiskey barrels were opened. The Prophet and his men refused to participate further.

"Perhaps if you preached to them," suggested Jainai.

"We shall return after the festival," said The Prophet imperiously.

Nothing was more disgusting than to see Amerindians drinking themselves into a stupor, obliterating the path to salvation. "Let us get our horses and make camp a ways from the village. We can do nothing at this point. I would like to know who brought the whiskey into the village," he said as he walked with determination toward the horse compound, "and I would like to see what is in Teteboxti's medicine bundle. I thought we had made more progress with our Delaware brethren. Judging from what we have just seen our religion has made no impression whatever on our neighbors! It is time for drastic action," he concluded ominously.

The Prophet kept his people in camp for nine days then rode back into Anderson. The village looked as if a storm had swept all kinds of debris into it but it was only the festival and perhaps the after effects of men on a drunken spree. Amerindians were not moderate drinkers; they imbibed until the whiskey was totally used up or until they could no longer remain awake. "We wish to confer with Teteboxti!" demanded The Prophet of an older Indian sitting in front of the Council House.

"He is not in the village," said the man. Numerous people had seen The Prophet's encampment. Had the chief been warned to flee?

"Father," said Jainai, "can you tell us where he might be found?"

"I do not know," came the reply, "perhaps at the Christian mission."

The Prophet considered this to be a rather insolent remark but he said nothing as he reigned his horse around and rode to the mission.

"That is Brother Joshua," said Jainai who was the quickest to catch the zeal of his leader, "a Christian pointed out by two people as being a sorcerer when last I was here."

"Bring him to me," commanded The Prophet, "we will put him to the question." He counted on the fact that few would come to the aid of a Christian being interrogated by The Prophet himself. Two of his followers jumped off their horses, walked up to Brother Joshua, boldly seized him by each arm and informed him The Prophet wanted to talk with him. Perforce, he complied.

"I do not want you to be frightened, Brother Joshua," began The Prophet. "We need some information from you, at this point. Know that I can look into your heart. Tell me the truth or you will suffer the consequences, I assure you. Now tell me, where is Teteboxti?"

"I heard he was going to Muncie," said Brother Joshua, unafraid. "Perhaps that is where he is, though I cannot verify it."

"You should know where your chief is," said The Prophet.

"Teteboxti has denounced the Moravian mission," replied Brother Joshua. "He probably does not consider me one of his people, since I am a Christian."

"And do Christians believe in sorcery and witchcraft?" thundered The Prophet. "How long should a man live, Brother Joshua?"

"I do not understand," replied the man.

"It is a simple question. How long should a man live?"

"I do not know," answered a confused Joshua.

"A man should live until his teeth are worn out," said The Prophet, "until his hair is white or his eyes are dim. That is what we believe. But we find that some die before these signs are apparent. Why would this be so, Joshua?"

"I do not know," said the man.

"Could it be sorcery?" asked The Prophet. "Could they be victims of witchcraft? Does Teteboxti own a medicine bundle? Brother Joshua, do you own a medicine bundle? ANSWER ME!"

"No, I do not," said Brother Joshua, becoming unnerved for the first time. "I am a Christian, I have no need of such things."

"What do you know of the death of your great chief Buckongohelas?" continued The Prophet. "Did he die a natural death?"

"I suppose he did, I do not know," said Joshua.

"Would Teteboxti know?"

"I can speak for no one but myself. Why am I being questioned about such things? I am innocent of any wrongdoing."

The Prophet seemed satisfied. "You are to stay in this village and not leave or we shall hunt you down like a beast in the forest. We might want to question you again. Tell no one of this if you value your life. Be gone."

Brother Joshua hurried away as The Prophet talked to his men. "I wish six of you to blacken your faces and go get Teteboxti in Muncie. Make a camp and keep him there until I arrive."

"Do you wish us to question him?" asked Jainai.

"Yes," answered The Prophet. "Find out if he has a medicine bag and what he has in it. I will confer with Coltan, who is friendly to our movement and would be in line to become chief of the Delaware. Now go."

The six, headed by Jainai, quickly made their way to the Muncie village, spied Teteboxti, the eighty year old sachem, and overpowered him easily. He was taken to a place where camp was made and Jainai became the interrogator: "Do you own a medicine bag? Tell me, Chief Teteboxti, that your life might be spared."

"What are you talking about?" asked Teteboxti. He knew the men in painted black faces represented death but he was perfectly calm and dignified.

"Where is your medicine bag?" slashed Jainai verbally. "You stand accused of sorcery, witchcraft, even treason!"

"That is preposterous. Most of our peorple own medicine bags. Why should I be different? I am not a sorcerer."

"Then tell us where you have hid your medicine bundle so we may look at its contents and set you free," said Jainai.

"You well understand a bundle is the most personal of possessions," replied Teteboxti. "You have no right to defile it."

"We have heard you have tobacco and human bones in it," said Jainai. "Some of your tribe have accused you of having Buckongahelos poisoned. Prove they are wrong and you will be set free."

"I am Chief of the Delaware nation," said Teteboxti, "and you can expect retribution if you break our law."

"The Ruler of Destinies can decide our fate," said Jainai. "Let us inspect your medicine bundle and if you are innocent you will be pardoned. If you do not we will put you to the fire."

These maniacs are serious! thought Teteboxti to himself. *The Prophet and his machinations! He is worse than the Christians! What is this world coming to?!*

"You signed away the people's land," accused Arawaee. "That is punishable by death according to the people."

"Admit where we can find your medicine bundle," counselled Jainai. "We do not want to harm you. Give it up."

Teteboxti reflected on his chances. The Prophet and his brother Tecumseh were madmen who believed they could stem the Shemanese tide which was engulfing the land. What lunacy! The Indian people had to strive for co-existence, it was their only way to survival. The chief had scorned the Prophet's religion because it was impossible to return to the past. It was a wild goose chase that would end in dust. And to make war on the Shemanese as Buckongahelos had implied when Tecumseh visited was the path of annihilation. Teteboxti needed time to get help to extricate himself from this predicament. "All right," he said, "I will tell you where to find the medicine bundle because there is nothing in it which you seek. May the Great Spirit forgive you if you defile its contents. It is behind a large rock by the fork in the stream that runs through the village"

Jainai dispatched Arawaee to fetch the bundle. Teteboxti hoped his absence would be missed and a search party sent out but help did not arrive by the time Arawaee returned that afternoon with news the bundle was no where to be found.

"You have lied," said Jainai, "despite our promises of mercy. Build a fire," he said to the others, "we will smoke it out of him."

A blaze was quickly built and Teteboxti tied close to it where heat and smoke would affect him greatly. Even this drastic measure did not loosen the old chief's tongue so he was stretched between two poles above the fire. He hung there until he could endure no longer:

"All right, I will tell you, I will tell," said Teteboxti, his joints ready to break.

"Tell me and I shall cut you down," said Jainai.

"It is in Brother Joshua's house!" said Teteboxti.

The man was cut down immediately and Jainai instructed Arawaee to go fetch Brother Joshua and inform The Prophet of what was happening.

Within four days the leader arrived at the camp, accompanied by a contingent of ten men along with Brother Joshua. No time was lost in hearing the case against Teteboxti: a circle was formed and several of the Delaware who had arrived with The Prophet gave testimony against the old chief. He was accused of engineering the death of Buckongahelos, of using charms and incantations, of selling Delaware lands to Governor Harrison.

"What have you to say on your behalf?" asked The Prophet of Teteboxti. "You have heard the charges. Speak."

"Everything is untrue, except about the land!" replied Teteboxti.

"You have no right to sell the land!" thundered The Prophet. "For that you must die. But we shall be merciful and make it quick, a simple execution with tomahawks. Let this be an example to all of your kind who believe they have more power than the people of this great island. I can look into your heart: you believe we are stupid, wicked people. Evil exists in your soul because you have aligned yourselves with the Shemanese, the Shemanese who would ursurp all our land despite their own treaties to the contrary. Take him away, he is no more!"

The men with blackened faces walked the old chief out of camp. When the execution party came to a clearing in the forest Teteboxti was instructed to dig his own grave with the shovel handed to him. The man did as he was told, working calmly and steadily. An observer would never have believed he was helping to carry out his death sentence, such was his stoicism. When he finished he knelt calmly by the shallow grave and sang his death song until Jainai's hatchet cleaved his skull from behind. His body fell into the grave and the black faced executioners began covering it up before it had stopped twitching.

Episode 10: Flame is accused.

Caritas was an older woman known as Ann Charity to the Moravian missionaries at Anderson village. She had lived with the Christians since childhood but she still clung to certain traditions of her native people. An informer, of which there were many in the various tribes now that The Prophet had been able to execute the chief of the Delawares and get away with it, reported her as owning a medicine bundle and using it for evil purposes. The Prophet ordered she be executed by fire so she was apprehended by men with blackened faces, which people now began to dread for good reason, taken to a secluded spot in the forest and tortured by fire in an effort to make her tell where she had hidden her medicine bundle. The old woman proved exceptionally obdurate. It

303

took four days of roasting her over the fire before she admitted her grandson had the bundle in his possession.

"Where is your grandson?"

"Out hunting," sighed the tortured woman.

"Where?"

"By the big bend in the river."

Jainai pulled out his tomahawk and struck her a death blow on the head, ending her misery forever.

A party went out in search of the grandson and luckily found his hunting camp. The five men walked into the camp and addressed Walkos by name, telling him, "You must give up your grandmother's medicine bundle, Walkos, and come with us or we shall carry out The Prophet's command right here on the spot!"

Walkos was an adequate hunter but when he saw the black faced men he knew he could not fight his way out of danger so his nimble mind began to work quickly.

"Your grandmother has been executed for witchcraft," said one of the men, the black paint on his face giving him an ominous countenance, "and your life is in peril if you are guilty of such crimes."

"Where is the medicine bundle?" asked another of the executioners.

"It is back in my cabin," confessed Walkos.

"Have you seen its contents?"

"Of course," said Walkos, "I have even used a charm or two from it."

What?! The executioners were taken aback. He admitted to using charms? All they had heard up to now from everyone else were denials.

"Yes," continued the young hunter, "I used the most powerful charm during one of my flights."

"Your flights?!" asked one of the executioners, intrigued. "You mean, in the air?"

"Where else? One night, between sundown and sunset, I flew over Kentucky and saw for myself how the Shemanese have taken over our hunting grounds of old. I swooped down on their settlements and could have torn at them like the eagle if I had had claws but I did not think of weapons beforehand. I flew back on high then, up around the clouds bathed in moonlight. I went through one just to see what it was like and I came out on the other side totally wet so I flew lower in order to dry out. Hawks and birds came up to greet me but they could not keep up, such was my speed. I began to get thirsty and the strongest desire came over me to drink from the Father of Waters so I headed west. Halfway there I ran into a rain storm but quickly I flew up above the rain cloud and didn't

304

get wet. Along about midnight I got to the banks of the Mississippi and landed softly. The water was too muddy so I walked in the night in search of a sweet water spring but could find none so I took to the air and from a high vantage point located some sparkling water and drank. The river was so beautiful from the air I journeyed above it for a time then I turned and headed for home to our praires and forests. I was in my bed just before the sun began to walk the rim of the sky."

The executioners were totally enraptured by Walkos story. What an incredible adventure! What fantastic power that medicine bundle must have! "Wait here," said one of the black faced men as he motioned for the other executioners to follow him. A council was held on the spot: Should Walkos be executed? No! The Prophet could probably use such a fellow! The young hunter was allowed to go free on the promise he would report to The Prophet when he was done hunting.

The purge continued and became more sanguinary: Brother Joshua and a halfblood chief named Billy Patterson were executed by order of The Prophet. An old Delaware chief named Hackinkpomska, who had been among the first to welcome the Moravians to Indiana, was denounced to The Prophet and his execution was ordered but he escaped the hatchet men with black painted faces. Myriads of Prophet imitators sprang up among the tribes and certain ruthless, ambitious leaders cleared their paths of political rivals by accusing them of sorcery and having them assassinated. The Prophet visited the Wyandot at Sandusky and accused four leading Wyandot women of being witches. He appointed a party of warriors to execute them but the women hid in the cellar of Reverend Joseph Badger's house on the appointed night then were able to make good their escape. Because of incidents like these word reached the Shemanese a bloodbath was taking place among the Indians. It seems purges were occuring as far north as Hudson Bay and to the westward as touched the Missouri River tribes. In one notable witch hunt in New Madrid, Missouri, there were *fifty* Shawnee and Delaware Indians executed by men whose faces were painted black.

In Greenville the Prophet held trials a distance outside the village and one day he noticed that Spybuck's woman, Flaming Eagle of Delight, stood among the group accused, her hands tied behind her back. This put The Prophet in a very precarious sistuation: Spybuck was Tecumseh's very good friend and his own mentor. Moreover, Spybuck was perhaps the only person in the country whom The Prophet was in awe of. He inquired as to who had brought the woman in and made the accusation. Jainai. That was even worse! Jainai, the former Christian, had become The Prophet's right arm due to his zeal. And he was the most able of the executioners. No one ever escaped Jainai once a death sentence was given for him to carry out. How could he move to smooth things out?

The first person put to the question that afternoon was a Kickapoo who had refused to surrender his medicine bundle. The Prophet ordered he be burned and he was taken away. Flame now was brought forward, her glance steady yet serious for she knew her life was at stake.

"What are the charges against this female?" asked The Prophet, trying to sound as impartial as possible.

Jainai spoke up: "Witchcraft. And I would presume she has been a practicing Christian in former years. Among other things."

Flame looked at Jainai. For a fleeting moment he was vaguely familiar... somewhere in the past... somewhere.

"Does she have a medicine bundle?" asked The Prophet.

"Not exactly," answered Jainai. "She has caused the people to come down with the smallpox."

"What?" gasped The Prophet. This was a grave offense, punishable by death! How could Spybuck's woman be guilty of such a thing?! The Prophet scrutinized her... attractive as ever, in her ineffable way... uncowed... perhaps she did not realize the predicament she was in... there, that quick gesture, a bit of fright, perhaps she did realize... "What have you to say in your defense?" asked The Prophet. "Did you infect people with smallpox?"

"Yes and no," said Flame.

"You must not answer in riddles, woman," said The Prophet menacingly.

Suddenly a magnificently garbed Amerindian made his way into the gathering, tossed something into the small fire that had been kindled and a gigantic puff of smoke filled the air. "You want witchcraft I will give you more than you dreamed possible!" thundered Spybuck as he strode up to Flame, cutting the bonds from her wrists. No one moved to stop the yellow spider magician.

When the smoke cleared and The Prophet stopped coughing he was ready to demand immediate punishment until he looked up and saw Spybuck standing in front of him, Tecumseh at his side.

"I have heard many stories and rumors," said Tecumseh to his brother. Now he knew they were all true. "This reign of terror is ended here and now forever!"

"The woman was being put to the question," said The Prophet, not losing his composure.

"I will answer any questions," said Flame.

"No!" thundered Spybuck.

"It is my wish," said Flame calmly. "I have been accused of bringing smallpox to the people. This is nominally so. While you were away," she said to Spybuck, "some villagers came to me and said they wanted to be protected against the smallpox. I told them you were away so they asked me to vaccinate them because they had seen people die of the hideous sickness. So I vaccinated them a few days ago from the vaccine left for our people here. Then this morning some men with black faces came to our cabin and forced me here with them, saying I had been accused of being a witch. I am guilty of helping our people, nothing more."

"And you would have been declared innocent after stating the facts," said The Prophet, "and I do so declare." He looked at the other prisoners who were awaiting trial. "Let us proceed."

"I would talk with you, brother," said Tecumseh.

"As soon as I am done," said The Prophet.

"I would council with you and your men now, brother," he said in a tone of voice that ordered compliance. "The rest of your are free to go," he said to the prisoners. The men with the painted faces were confused but they were certain Tecumseh would not be thwarted.

"Go," said The Prophet to the liberated prisoners, "but heed my words and see to it you live by religion, not sorcery." Everyone disappeared immediately except Tecumseh, The Prophet, and his men.

"You are never to paint your faces black again," ordered Tecumseh of the executioners. "Black is only for the warpath, not the spread of religion."

"Then how do you wish us to handle witches and wizards?" asked The Prophet. "We have seen people disguise themselves as owls, foxes, wolverines... this pestilence cannot go unchecked."

Tecumseh did not believe what his brother said for he had worked his way out of superstition many years ago. He had never seen such phenomena himself. "We must find suitable ways to deal with opposition," said the chief. "I will not encourage fanaticism that could lead to civil war."

The Prophet wrinkled his forehead in disbelief. "Have we not made great progress in ridding ourselves of chiefs who signed away the land?"

"We have made progress, yes," said Tecumseh.

"Do we not have leaders now who look to us for advice and counsel?"

"Yes, that is true," admitted Tecumseh. "Your work has been most effective, my brother."

The Prophet was mollified. "I have been formulating another plan," he continued. "Let us have a big feast... let us invite all hostile chiefs to assemble for the festivities... let it be known many rich presents will be distributed... when they are in the midst of feasting my hatchet men will fall upon them and execute all enemies!"

"NO!" thundered Tecumseh in a voice that carried as it had in the fields of battle. He took his knife and raised it over his head: "This knife shall not be drawn against any Amerindian except in self defense. Everyone here is enjoined to do the same, by our law. If any would cut down his misguided brother, let him face Tecumseh first!" He resheathed the gleaming blade and looked at each man present. There was no doubting his sincerity. "My brothers," he said calmly, "we do not have to be sanguinary. We can use subtle means to depose the misguided chiefs. We do not even have to depose them but rather undermine their authority. If the people do not follow them they are chiefs in name only. My only intent is to reduce them to a private capacity. Let them live out their lives in peace. Violence must be the last, the ultimate recourse. We can say any chief who sells land of his own accord will be executed but first let us work to convince the people that no chief has the power to alienate their land and the chief will heed the people."

"What if he still refuses?" asked The Prophet.

"Then, my brother, and only then, will the chief forfeit his life."

Episode 11: The Challenge

Governor Harrison re-read the report of William Wells. It was difficult to believe so much blood was being shed among the Indians. And someone named a *prophet* was the cause of it all? Teteboxti had been executed? This could be serious, according to Agent Wells, for the chief was amendable to American demands... at any rate a witchhunt was dangerous to the peace of the frontier... perhaps this prophet could be removed from Greenville... but could it be done without starting a war? His influence had to be neutralized... Wells had the annuities for leverage... perhaps they could be curtailed among the Indians with sinister motives... but first he would use his own personal influence with the Delawares.

No one was more erudite than Governor Harrison and few could communicate better with Indians. He collected his thoughts and composed an adroit message to the Delaware people:

"My children: my heart is heavy with sorrow and my eyes drown in tears at the news which has reached me. You O Delaware, have been acknowledged for your wisdom above all the tribes of red people who

308

inhabit this great island. Your fame as warriors has spread to the furthest of nations and the wisdom of your chiefs has gained you the title of *Grandfathers* from all the neighboring tribes. Why then, have you departed from the wise counsels of your fathers to walk the path of shame?

"My children: tread back the steps you have taken and regain the white road which you have abandoned. The dark, crooked, and thorny path which you are now pursuing will certainly lead you to misery. Who is this pretended prophet who dares to speak in the name of the Great Spirit? Examine him closely in your councils. Is he more wise and virtuous than you are yourselves, that he should be selected to convey to you the orders of your God? Demand of him some proofs at least of his being the messenger of the Deity. If God has really empowered him, He has doubtless authorized him to perform miracles that he may be known and received as a prophet. If he is really a prophet, ask him to cause the sun to stand still, the moon to alter its course, the rivers to cease to flow, or the dead to rise from their graves. If he does these things you may believe that he has been sent from God. He tells you that the Great Spirit commands you to punish with death those who deal in magic, and that he is authorized to point them out. Wretched delusion! Is then the Master of Life obliged to employ mortal man to punish those who offend Him? Has He not the thunder and the power of all nature at His command? And could he not sweep away from the earth a whole nation with one motion of his arm?

"My children: do not believe the great and good Creator of mankind has directed you to destroy your own flesh. Furthermore, do not doubt that if you pursue this abominable wickedness His vengeance will overtake you and crush you.

"The above is addressed to you in the name of the Seventeen Fires. I now speak to you for myself, as your friend who wishes nothing more sincerely than to see you prosperous and happy. Sweep the mist from your eyes, I beseech you. Do not be imposed upon by the artifice of an imposter. Drive him from your towns and let peace and harmony prevail amongst you. Let your poor old men and women sleep in quietness and banish from their minds the dreadful danger of being burnt alive by their own friends and countrymen. I charge you to stop your bloody career if you value the friendship of your great father, the President. If you wish to preserve the good opinion of the Seventeen Fires, let me hear by the return of the bearer that you have determined to follow my advice.

Your friend and advisor,
William Henry Harrison
Governor, Indiana territory

Governor Harrison sent the letter to William Wells who in turn sent Anthony Shane, a well known halfbreed, to deliver it to the Delaware. The chiefs heard the challenge and in a short time word spread throughout the Indian country that the white chief governor had declared The Prophet to be an imposter unless he produced some sort of miracle. The burden was directly on The Prophet and his power. Many Amerindians had accepted the new religion but most had remained watchfully uncommitted. Perhaps they too were waiting for some incontrovertible sign. All agreed this would be the time to produce unassailable proof.

Tecumseh happened to stop at Greenville when The Prophet heard of the challenge. The two brothers sat and smoked, discussed their strategy, and within one day of conferencing knew exactly what they would do. The Prophet addressed his most loyal followers, and anybody else who cared to listen, telling them he would produce a miracle just for the white chief. "Ours is a world of miracles," said The Prophet to his eager listeners, "but this is the only time I will ever take up a challenge for my powers are not at the beck and call of encroachers and aliens like the Shemanese. The people from across the great water do not understand religion. To them it is superstition. We, the children of the Great Spirit, see the workings of our Creator when the wind whispers through the pines, when the muskrat grows a heavy coat, when the whippoorwill calls from a different place in the night. We see the Great Spirit on a moonbeam, on a rainbow, for all are His workings. Then animals of the forest are as much his creations as we human beings, but the Shemanese does not understand because he has no real faith. Governor Harrison wants a miracle? I shall give him one, one that even he will have to notice. HEAR ME NOW, O PEOPLE OF THIS GREAT ISLAND! Never again will I accept a challenge but I now tell you that fifty sleeps from this day, when our father the sun is at the highest point in the sky, I shall beg the Great Spirit to darken his face so the veils of night will cover our entire country. The night stars will shine, the birds will roost, and the nocturnal creatures will stir about their haunts. The day shall become night on my command! Then there will be no doubt if your Prophet is sent by the Ruler of Destinies or if he is an imposter as Shemanese Harrison would have you believe. Spread this story, all of you. Tell all the tribes who live on this great island, tell the British, tell the Shemanese. I welcome their scrutiny and if I have lied cast me out of the race of human beings!"

The challenge was taken up with as much vigor as the chiefs of old striking the war post in a declaration of war. The news spread like wild fire on dry prairie grass and Amerindians everywhere waited expectantly, some believing the sun would be blotted out, others scoffing derisively, but all immensely interested. Gamblers among the tribesmen even laid down bets as to what would happen on June 16, 1806.

Episode 12: Snow on the roof.

Spybuck looked at Flaming Eagle of Delight as the two sat eating their supper. Things just hadn't been right since the woman's near brush with death but Spybuck didn't know what to do. Even her passion was not as strong, he mused to himself as the two ate in silence, but somehow that was not overly important. He wanted her to be happy... he did not wish to risk losing her again, permanently, as he thought had happened before when she returned to her people.

"What do you think of The Prophet's latest antics?" asked Spybuck. He knew what the answer would be.

"That farce!" said Flame. "I wish the sun would fall on him. I don't even want to talk about him."

"I would like you to talk about him," said Spybuck. "I feel you are distant to me because of him."

"Dearest," said Flame as she stopped eating, "that is not true. You are the only man I have ever loved. You are the sun and the moon in my life. But The Prophet is the serpent in the garden. If it had not been for Tecumseh..."

"I would have saved you, woman, or lost my life with you."

"He preys upon the people, strutting about like some great tree of the race. I've never trusted him, even before he turned religious."

"I do not believe he would have hurt you," counselled Spybuck. "His cronies were the ones who made you a prisoner and accused you."

"But would The Prophet have stopped them?" asked Flame.

"I think so," said Spybuck calmly.

"He will be the ruination of the people," said Flame, "mark my word. He will undo all of Tecumseh's good work. When the sun continues to shine everyone will see him for the imposter he is. I feel sorry for Tecumseh. His brother's shame will carry over to him."

"What if he is successful?" asked Spybuck.

"Don't be ridiculous," said Flame contemptupusly. She looked hard at the man sitting in front of her. For once she saw an Indian, a silly, superstitious Indian. It shocked her for a moment because Spybuck had been a man to her almost from the beginning, her lover, her husband, the best imaginable. She had tried to help her adopted people, turning her back on her own, following the dictates of the inner recesses of her being.

311

Now that charlatan of a Prophet had attacked all the happiness she had known during the past years. Life could not hang from such a slender thread! Any whim from that madman would cause someone to die. But then another remembrance penetrated her consciousness: when she was a child that little old lady was accused of being a witch... strange that she thought of it now... whatever happened to her? The Prophet was not the only charlatan in the world, not by a long shot. Could she and Spybuck go back and live among the whites? She could not live with the Indians if her life was going to be threatened. Perhaps it was as Spybuck said: The Prophet's henchmen had been responsible for her peril. One had accused her of being a Christian, she didn't remember his name, where had she seen him?

"Well?" repeated Spybuck.

"I'm sorry, dearest, I didn't hear what you said. My mind was wandering."

"I said we could go far into the north country and leave all this behind. Or we could go west, if you preferred. We do not have to stay here if you are unhappy."

"Why not east or south?"

"The Longknives are in the east," said Spybuck, "and there is much war in the south. Our people are hemmed in by the Longknives there, it is not like here in the Ohio country. I want to take you where you will be safe."

"How could you leave your practice?" asked Flame impishly. "After all you are the master juggler and everyone holds you in awe."

"I can practice any where and the only awe I want is yours. Close up and deep. You have been so upset of late..."

"You dirty old man," she whispered. "Aren't you ever going to put out that fire of yours? Here you are talking like a young buck. Why, even your hair is beginning to turn white." She moved up close to him and caressed his hair tenderly.

"Snow on the roof means a fire inside," said Spybuck. "I will kill any one who tries to hurt you again," he whispered seriously. "Without you I would not wish to continue living. If you want to leave this country, we will."

"You will never... finish your supper," Flame said as she pulled Spybuck toward her. He came willingly.

"Tell me if you want to leave."

"Not right now," whispered Flame.

Episode 13: The Miracle

June 16 of 1806 chanced to be clear and beautiful, nary a cloud in the sky. The Prophet and his wife Tukwautu peeked out of the wegiwa at the hundreds of people who were waiting for his miracle. This was it: henceforth The Prophet would be a demigod or he would be cast out of society for all time.

Tukwautu worked on her husband's costume, showing as much confidence as possible. "Master, soon you shall be among the immortals. I am so very proud of you, husband."

"Thank you, dear wife," responded The Prophet. He fidgeted with his headdress, his robe.

"Do not be nervous, my husband," advised Tukwautu, "you will be magnificent. The people will know you are a true Prophet and your word will be law. I too am your servant."

The Prophet looked at his wife. She had indeed been good. It had been she who helped him when the whiskey urge was upon him. It was she who bolstered him now that his confidence ebbed. What if the sun did not darken?! He could be killed for being an imposter! What would they do to his wife, his brother, to all the workers who helped him?!

"Believe in yourself as I do, husband," ordered Tukwautu. "I saw the stamp of greatness upon you from the beginning and now you shall be among the immortals! You are ready now. Go, beg the Master of Life to give us all a sign! Go!"

The Prophet took a deep breath as if to collect himself then stepped out of his wegiwa and strode majestically to the center of a large circle of Amerindians. The only person he really saw was his brother Tecumseh sitting among the chiefs. The Prophet looked calm, totally in command yet strangely humble, as if this portentous day would introduce him to the Almighty Power of the Universe. He was a large, powerfully built man and his costume this day was splendiforous: his headdress was capped by a pair of outstretched raven's wings which made him look a foot taller than he actually was. A black silk handkerchief was tied around his head in order to cover his mutilated eye but his face was still capable of remarkable expression. His former life of drunkenness had left telltale signs on his countenance and he looked older than his years. Indeed, Tecumseh, who was seven summers older, looked younger than The Prophet. There was a necklace around his neck, gleaming gold, and his dark flowing robe would have been the envy of any medieval magician. His entire coustume had been the creation of his wife Tukwautu and the impression he made was worth all the labor it had required.

The Prophet stood in the center of the huge circle, erect, gazing toward the heavens, praying silently. He begged the Great Spirit to take pity on him and give him the sign he so fervently prayed for. All Indians throughout the great island were depending on the Goodness to allow them to live in their lands as they had since the time of the first dawn of humanity. But they needed the hand of the Great Spirit to boost their life force against the onslaught of pressures which could annihilate them into nothingness. The People had to have incontrovertible proof that the Master of Destinies had not abandoned them to a cruel fate of extinction. The Prophet asked forgiveness for his weaknesses, past and present, asked forgiveness for his vaulting ego which occassionally proved an obstacle to his missionizing efforts. He begged for pity and understanding, promising to devote all energies to the betterment of Amerindians everywhere. Suddenly he put his arms up as if to reach the heavens, the loose robe falling far enough to display a bracelet on each wrist, one of gold the other of silver, both glistening in the sun.

The Prophet's face also glistened, with small beads of perspiration, as he spoke aloud for the first time: "O Great and Good Spirit of the Universe, Grandmother of the Heavens, let us see your presence, if it is your will. Show the believers and the unbelievers alike The Prophet speaks truth! Give us FAITH in your infinite powers. Pardon us for asking, for making such requests, for doubting, but take pity on your children in their ignorance. We, your creations, implore you to give us a sign." Everyone looked to the sky as The Prophet began to chant a song, his upraised arms beseeching the heavens.

The sun continued in its brilliance, forcing people to look away. Several minutes went by and The Prophet lowered his arms, his face glistening in the sun. He stood silently now, his isolation complete. Was he defeated? Was Harrison's challenge too much for him?!! Suddenly The Prophet raised his hand, said, "Hear the voice of your servant, Almighty Spirit of the Universe: cover the life of this world," and pointed to the sun. Slowly the sun began to grow dark as if a mouse was eating it away. *Bit by bit it was darkening.* The Amerindians were engulfed in amazement! The sun was being covered up! Many gazed at The Prophet in utter disbelief... how could this be?! No one could cover the sun yet The Prophet was doing it! They looked at each other and saw an earthly hue color the faces of their friends and neighbors. It looked like the end of the world! Women in the crowd began to moan and then clamor arose for The Prophet to order the sun be uncovered but he stood as if transfixed, rooted to Mother Earth as he pointed upward majestically.

314

The sun was almost totally covered now and just before its darkness a tongue of fire was seen around the edge of the sun as if it was fighting to stay alive. Throughout the entire Ohio country birds in the air sought a resting place for the night and cows lay down in their pastures. The night stars shone brilliantly and nocturnal animals began to stir. Many people were frightened, even warriors who would not admit it, and groans turned into wails from the women and children in attendance.

"Thank you, Great Spirit!" intoned The Prophet. "We are believers in your power. Grant us the gift of life! Return to us the light of our father the sun! This I beg of You in all humility!" The world remained dark a few moments longer than a tongue of fire was visible again. Gradually the sun began to light up the world once more, much to the relief of the Amerindians present.

When the world was normal again everyone sought to congratulate The Prophet, shake his hand, touch his robe. The white chief Harrison had asked for a miracle and gotten it! The challenge had been met! Was there any doubt as to The Prophet's power?! Only a crazy person would scoff at the new religion! WHAT A MARVEL WAS THIS PROPHET OF THE AMERINDIAN PEOPLE!!

Tecumseh wanted to shake his brother's hand but he could not get through the crowd. Laulewasika had indeed put on a masterful performance. But why call him by his family name? He was indisputably *The Prophet* now and forever. Tecumseh hoped his brother would use his influence wisely, no more witchhunts, no more miracles. Harrison would have to hide his face as the sun had! Methoataske, with her flair for the dramatic, would have been so proud of her youngest offspring. Puckeshinwa, who had never known him, must have been gazing at him from the heavens. Tecumseh's eyes glistened then he caught sight of his sister Tecumapease among the crowd. Her eyes were full of tears.

Chapter 6

Blue Warrior had lived with the Descendants of the Blue Wolf since infancy when he was captured during a raid in the south country. He had grown to love his domain of snow with its long winters and short summers and now he was a respected member of society in the land called Saskatchewan. Blue Warrior heard emissaries of The Prophet would be brought to visit this day and he, along with most of the villagers, waited expectantly. Rumors had travelled far ahead of the emissaries: The Prophet had caused the face of the sun to be covered and uncovered; he was producing ears of corn large enough to feed twelve men each; his pumpkins were bigger than the largest kettles; The Prophet could cause huge hailstorms to rain down on the Longknives, thus forcing them to leave the country to its rightful owners. Soon he would command the return of the rapidly disappearing game and all native people everywhere would enjoy life in peace and contentment.

A beating of drums summoned the people to congregate at the council house. Blue Warrior and most of the villagers gathered there quickly and saw two young Indians standing in the midst of the people who stared curiously. They were far from home but the two were not ill at ease. Before anyone spoke the young men began to sing a chant, wordless but smooth and effortless. Then one began to beat on the drum in front of him, rhythmically adding to the voices which somehow invited the Descendants of the Blue Wolf to participate. After a while the other young man waved at the crowd to join in. The villagers hesitated at first but then the principal singer of the tribe united their voices to those of their guests and slowly the people added their efforts in song.

The chanting ended when one of the emissaries commenced to beat furiously on the drum. "Brothers and sisters! Descendants of the Blue Wolf, I bring you tidings from The Prophet and his brother Tecumseh, natives of this great island, citizens and brothers who wish to preserve your peace, well being, and contentment. Those of you here assembled today who wish to strive for these goals are readily taken unto our hearts and spirits..." The young man informed the crowd as to the tenets of The Prophet's religion, emphasizing the prohibition of firewater, the injunction against selling land to the Longknives, unity among the tribes. "Throw away your medicine bundles and devote yourselves to caring for the sacred fire. Here, in this vessel," he said as he uncovered an oddly shaped bowl, "is the eternal fire from The Prophet's own wegiwa. Light your fire sticks from it and kindle the sacred fire in your homes. Gaze at the eternal fire and think of the Master of Life often during the day.

"Know that The Prophet loves you and cares about your welfare. He spends his energy visiting the many tribes of our brothers and sisters. Since he cannot go in person everywhere we will leave you this," said the other young man as he uncovered a straw man created in the image of The Prophet right down to the kerchief over the missing eye, "if you will build a cabin for it where the sacred fire will never be allowed to die out. The fire is from a torch presented to The Prophet by Manabozho and I cannot emphasize too much how important it is to maintain this spark of life in your homes and village. It will light the way to peace and contentment in this life, eternal happiness in the Great Beyond. Do you wish the figure and the fire to remain? Let us hear your decision."

The religion seemed to be worthwhile and certainly it was time someone did something about the poisonous firewater that lead to untold suffering. Yes, the people wanted to embrace the creed.

"Good!" said one of the emissaries. "The first thing you must do if you are sincere is go to your lodges and bring your medicine bags. We shall place them in a pile and burn them with the flame of the sacred fire."

This was a real test for one's medicine bundle was a very personal and highly prized possession, though it usually contained more herbs than anything else. But it was also an accepted fact that if an evil person was deprived of the paraphernalia of sorcery he was rendered harmless so

The Prophet had instructed all his emissaries that all converts had to begin anew by throwing their bundles into the fire.

Many villagers walked to their cabins while a fire was begun by the two emissaries. When the blaze was high they picked up the straw figure and carried it around the fire, chanting as they danced, the figure appearing to dance the rhythm also. "Throw your bundles in the fire when you are ready to embrace The Prophet and the religion of your ancestors," said one of the young men as the other continued to chant. "Then you can join us and sing for peace!"

One bundle flew into the blaze and the owner fell in behind the two singers. Others now began to do the same and in a short while most of the people were singing and dancing, harmonizing with Earth Mother, absolved from any predilection toward doing harm.

One of the emissaries now handed the straw figure to the other and went to his leathern pouch from where he took a short belt of sacred beans. "My brothers and sisters!" said the young man, "everyone is to run this belt through your hands as The Prophet has done in order to shake his hand now that you are one with us and the ancestors. Touching the beans is a promise to follow The Prophet or Tecumseh when they issue a call. Everyone, shake hands with The Prophet."

The emmissaries stayed in the village of the Descendants of the Blue Wolf for a few days, answering questions and encouraging the people to embrace the new religion. By the time they left their work had been well received by men like Blue Warrior and many of his neighbors.

Episode 2: Springfield Council

Tecumseh knew all too well how vulnerable life was on the frontier when Shemanese were lurking about. Stories reached his ears and disturbed him because he knew what it was to lose loved ones who died when they had never provoked a fight. He was informed by visitors to Greenville that three Shemanese were fed and well treated by an Indian family one evening, even putting them up for the night. The Shemanese repaid the Amerindians by murdering all of them, down to the last child, while they slept, and stealing everything of value. He was told of a Wyandot and a Shemanese who argued while drinking, a friend taking the Wyandot away to sober him up. The Shemanese followed them and bashed out the brains of the man who had argued with him. He was apprehended by the authorities and it took only a few minutes for the jury to decide he was not guilty of murder.

It was not part of Tecumseh's character to accept such injustice. He

318

was on the white road of peace and committed to it but he would not turn the other cheek as the Christians taught. The military man was always at beck and call within him and few were more talented or daring when it came to war. Secretly did he long for the war path? Probably not, due to the influence of his sister Tecumapease and Rebecca. But if ever he was to confront danger while hunting, as his father had, if ever he went to the Shemanese's stronghouse and they tried to imprison him as they had done with Cornstalk, that day he would sell his life dearly. It rankled deep within him that by treaty law all disputes had to be settled in Shemanese courts. The Treaty had not stated a double standard of justice would be maintained but the chiefs should have known... well, maybe they could not have... they were not accustomed to such duplicity, such hypocrisy. He remembered how he felt when Daniel Boone fled Old Chillicothe after convincing everyone he was perfectly content living with his "Indian brothers." Soon after he was just as contented trying to kill them. But were all Shemanese that way? No. Rebecca was not. The Galloways were not. Big Fish was not... but then Stephen Ruddell was really an Indian... how he missed his friend! He wondered where he was and what he was up to.

"Tecumseh my chief, someone is here to council with you," said his elderly housekeeper as he sat deep in thought. The chief rose from where he had been sitting and went outside his wegiwa to find three Shemanese surrounded by an ever increasing number of Amerindians.

"Keewaukoomeela," said Tecumseh to the three.

"Hello, chief," said one of the three, "we'd like to talk to you if you would favor us."

"The matter is quite pressing, Chief Shooting Star," said another of the Shemanese, "and your assistance is urgently needed."

"If you have time, sir," finished the third man.

"Of course, gentlemen," said Tecumseh in English. "There is a comfortable log under yonder tree."

While many Amerindians had gathered only Tecumseh and the three Shemanese went and sat on the log, though Tecumseh's men hung around the area to safeguard their chief. "What can I do for you gentlemen?" asked Tecumseh. He did not wish to offer the usual amenities. Shemanese were always conscious of how much time something took.

"Perhaps you have heard, sir," began the Shemanese who seemed to be the leader of trio, "that a white man named Myers has been murdered by an Indian just west of Urbana. They say the Indian was a Potawatomi who fled here and that a general attack is forthcoming."

Tecumseh shook his head incredulously.

"Now I know this might be far fetched but there is always someone to start a war, seems like," continued the Shemanese. "All I can say is the settlers are preparing for an outbreak and arming themselves. If some trigger happy hothead starts shooting and there's retaliation... you know how it goes. Sir, do you have any knowledge of the Potawatomie who purportedly took refuge in this village?"

"Not at all," replied Tecumseh. "I had not even heard of the incident."

"Murder is more than an incident," murmured another Shemanese.

"Yes, my friend," said Tecumseh calmly, "it is when a white man is killed but not when an Indian is the victim. When one of your people kills one of us your jury sets him free immediately but if we kill one of you your people demand an Indian be turned over for hanging. This you refer to as justice."

"Chief, we do not mean to offend," said the Shemanese leader, "our efforts here are strictly to promote peace and calm everyone. Militia companies have been called out, at great expense, and a great furor is raging throughout the white settlements. We are in your village and I would afffirm this instant if an attack is coming on the settlements it is not springing from here. Give us your word this is true and I will stand beside you before my people."

Tecumseh was impressed with the man's apparent sincerity. And it took more than a little courage to ride unannounced into a village that might be preparing for war, as the Shemanese thought was possible. "I give you my word that no one in this village is making any kind of military plans and furthermore such plans are not being effected in any village with which I have dealings."

"We accept the word of honorable men, chief," said the Shemanese. "Would you be willing to speak to some of our leaders and give them the same assurances? I know you have done this on previous occasions."

Tecumseh did not answer immediately then suddenly said, "Of course."

"Good!" said the Shemanese. "A number of other chiefs have been invited also and will attend. The council will be held at Springfield, a new town close to the site of Old Piqua, your former home."

"You seem to know something about me," said Tecumseh.

"Everyone has heard about Shooting Star," said the man, "and I am no exception."

"Who will preside over the council?" asked the chief.

"General Simon Kenton and Colonel Robert Patterson," was the reply. "Some militia officers will serve as commissioners..." The rest of

320

the details were communicated and met with Tecumseh's approval. When the talks were finished the chief invited the Shemanese to spent the rest of the day in the village and to rest comfortably in a cabin that would be supplied for their use that night. The offer was accepted and later the three reported they encountered nothing but hospitality at Greenville.

When the council fire was kindled at Springfield the old Indian fighter Simon Kenton looked for signs of trickery but found none as groups of Indians straggled in to the Indian encampment outside of town. The old Wyandot chief Crane from Upper Sandusky lead his delegation. Chief Roundhead lead the Wyandots from the Detroit area. There were a number of Indians from the Fort Wayne area, though no major chief accompained them. Tecumseh came in with his contingent of smartly dressed warriors, all heavily armed. All together Kenton thought there were about three hundred redmen in camp. He shook hands with a number of Indians as he and Patterson walked through the camp. He instructed his interpreter to inform the redmen that when the council started no arms would be allowed on the premisies.

On the day of the council Tecumseh led his men, all armed with knives and tomahawks, to the meeting site. They carried no firearms but the chief would never forget how Cornstalk met his treacherous end so native weapons hung on Amerindian hips.

"That group of Shawnee," indicated Simon Kenton as he surveyed the group, "is armed." Robert Patterson nodded his awareness and the two men walked in the direction of the armed warriors. "Who is the chief here?" asked Simon Kenton.

"I am," replied Tecumseh.

"This is General Simon Kenton, and I am Colonel Robert Patterson. The rules agreed upon for this council were that all participants would be unarmed." By now everyone was looking at the two Shemanese and Tecumseh.

"I was invited here as a guest," said Tecumseh calmly, "and I do not travel without my tomahawk. Besides, it is also a peace pipe, see?" he said as he displayed it to the pair. So this was the Kenton he had out fought years ago... Tecumseh almost smiled. "I might want to smoke during the ceremonies as is the custom among our people."

"Give your hatchet to the presiding officers," said an officious, lanky Pennsylvanian as he handed Tecumseh a clay pipe, "and you can smoke this one." Tecumseh looked at the dirty little thing then shot the Pennsylvanian such a scornful glare the man scurried away into the crowd. The crude pipe would not have been considered fit for any ceremony anywhere and Tecumseh tossed it away.

"All about you are men unarmed," said Kenton.

"Arms do not kill people," replied Tecumseh, "men do. A warrior cannot be separated from his equipment. I was invited here as a guest and I will be responsible for my contingent of warriors. They will cause no trouble. Neither will they be ambushed."

"This council is to promote the peace," said General Kenton. "You have my word your men are safe without arms."

"Are we safe with them?" asked Tecumseh.

"Well, yes," admitted Kenton, "but—"

"Then we will keep them," concluded Tecumseh. "Your people are in less danger than we."

Kenton and Patterson walked away to confer: they could order the group to leave but that might cripple the entire council. There probably was no real danger from the savages. Besides, the armed guard could be called immediately from its secret hiding place and the Indians had no firearms. So the council was begun.

The calumet was passed around to all principals of the council, each taking a puff or two as was necessary to establish amity. General Kenton and Colonel Patterson made preliminary remarks of welcome and after other ritualized comments the council got down to business. Testimony was heard that Myers had been killed by a certain Potawatomie. Kenton demanded the murderer be turned over to the commissioners immediately.

Now it was time for the Indians to give an answer. The Crane stood up and made a short address, emphasizing how the two races had been at peace during the past years. An Ottawa chief followed and said much the same thing. Then it was Tecumseh's turn so he got to his feet and walked gracefully to the center of the circle, completely at ease yet his countenance set with determination. He looked tall and lithe, in excellent physical condition. His clothes were of tanned buckskin and his appearance impressive. "BROTHERS!" he began in a booming voice which snapped everyone to attention. "You who believe in justice are gathered to behave as you believe. Does it bother you that you no longer have the right to dispense justice if a Shemanese commits a crime on you or your loved ones? We, the most independent and freedom loving people, can no longer defend ourselves if our attacker is a Shemanese!"

What was this?! The gathering was a peaceful one to smooth ruffled feathers, not brighten the hatchet! Some of the Amerindians began to fret over what Tecumseh might say.

"According to the law, which is the Shemanese treaty, everything must be decided by the Shemanese council which they call a court. Tell me, my brothers, when is the last time a Shemanese was punished for killing one of us? To my knowledge there has been no 'last time' because there is yet to be a *first time!* My tongue is not forked, you all know my words are truth. Yet the Greenville Treaty says we must deliver up anyone accused by a Shemanese.

"My brothers: we are a people who live by the law. Yet we have no jails, no prisons, no locks on our doors. We value the law so in the past we have lived by it. But now... must we live by Shemanese law? Do the Shemanese live up to the treaties they themselves create? I say NO. I will show you this day how they violated their own laws almost before we even touched the quill to them. Let us go back to when our ancestors first saw the newcomers when they landed on the seacoasts. Jamestown was their first settlement, Plymouth their second. Our ancestors could have destroyed them utterly at this time but instead the strangers were met cordially and given food which kept them alive. More and more people arrived from across the great salt water and in time the foreigners became strong enough to challenge our ancestors with death dealing weapons. Powhatan in the south country went to Jamestown and addressed their council, asking why the foreigners wanted to take by force what they could obtain by love. His words live on in the mouths of the Grandfathers and the ears of our people: 'Why will you destroy us who supply you with food? What can you get by war? We are unarmed but willing to give you what you need if you come as friends. I am not so simple as not to understand it is better to eat good meat, sleep comfortably, live quietly with our families, laugh and be merry with our friends, than to eat like a bird on the bough, watch our women always looking over their shoulders, and running from strangers. Take away your guns and swords or you may die in the same manner...'

"In the north Chief Massasoit of the Wampanoag took the new comers to his heart. All was peace and tranquility while he lived. But then the foreigners multiplied in such great numbers they no longer needed the friendship of our people and theyu trampled on Amerindian rights. Metacom, the second son of Massasoit, they tried to unite the native people against the encroachers and for a time he succeeded. Then the war went badly because various tribes sided against Metacom's warriors and the chief was killed, his head paraded on a spear for all to see. If you could but read the accounts of the war you would find it difficult to understand how a patriot like Metacom could be portrayed as fiend and devil. Not only have we been mistreated on our own soil but for generations to come people will read in the talking leaves how fiendish were our ancestors. Massasoit, friend and benefactor of the newcomers, is por-

323

trayed as a true man. His son Metacom, the first patriot of our people, is described as a devil from the alien's hellfire. Metacom's son, the grandson of Massasoit, is not spoken of at all except that he was sold into slavery far to the south, never to tread the soil of his homeland. He who should have been chief of the Wampanoag fell into the clutches of slavery, perishing forever along with his tribesmen who have since disappeared.

"Brothers: is this our fate? Will we vanish from the face of our Earth Mother? Yes, this sounds ridiculous! But there are those among us who see our lands are being taken piecemeal. Soon, they say, we will have no land on which to spread our skins and blankets. THEY SPEAK TRUTH! Why are we losing land? Very little has been won honorably in war. The land is being swept away by *treaty*. Yes, my brothers and sisters, it is touching the quill that is now our greatest danger. Of what worth have treaties been with the Longknives? Have we been protected by these laws? My fellows, I don't have to answer for you know yourselves our lands and our persons are not protected. It has been so from the very beginning..." Tecumseh now spoke about every major treaty between the Amerindians and the Longknives, beginning with that which the Delaware made with the revered Brother Onas, William Penn, in 1682. He explained what each treaty contained then cited in detail how each had been broken, violated, or tatally ignored by the people from across the great salt water.

The Longknives present were awed by Tecumseh's wealth of information as the interpreter translated each point as clearly as possible into English. The three hundred Amerindians were deeply moved by Tecumseh's courage and the power with which he spoke. This council fire was supposedly to make the Indians produce a murderer but instead Tecumseh had directed it in favor of native people everywhere. Kenton and Patterson realized the tables had been turned on them as they saw how the warriors' eyes flashed, ready to spring to the attack if Tecumseh directed. Even the most aged of the savages, many of whom had been smoking leisurely, displayed excitement at the panorama which Tecumseh brought to life with such poignant imagery.

"...since the treaty making with Governor St. Clair had been a rump fiasco the Longknives had to send General Harmar and his army to make it legal. He was thrown back by the patriotic arms of fighting warriors who would not abide with having their lands stolen. Harmar suffered many losses but this did not stop the Longknives from sending another army under St. Clair, which was totally annihilated. Some of us here present were at the scene of the carnage and the Great Spirit must have wept bloody tears that day. But our lands remained ours, for the moment. The Longknives were not yet done in their efforts to legalize on the battlefield what they could not accomplish at the council fire. The Black Snake was sent against us with the largest of all armies to be seen in the Ohio country. There was little more than a skirmish but this resulted in the Greenville Treaty which took away much of the Ohio country. 'Oh but you were paid for the land', we are told, 'it was not just taken by military might'. My brothers, war was forced upon us just as the settlement was. Do you know how much we were finally paid for the Ohio lands? We received one-sixth of one cent for each acre taken by the People of the Eagle. YES! One-sixth of one cent per acre! I have no word but truth. And did you receive your share, brothers, your pittance? It was probably taken by the dishonorable individuals who touched the quill, if you did not get your share. One thing is certain, the land is no longer under our jurisdiction. If you even walk on it you might get shot or killed, or both! This is how much the law protects you and me.

"Brothers: do we condone murder? Certainly not. A murderer is an evil person and causes untold harm in any society. But we citizens of this great island are accustomed to having the law enforced on all. Why is the Indian killed with impunity without the Shemanese law doing anything about it? This has occurred too many times for me to go into detail about it. Now we are asked to produce someone of our people who is accused of murdering a Shemanese. If we do it is certain death for the accused. But it is the law, according to the treaty.

"How were these treaties effected, my brothers? We all know the Amerindian way: everything is discussed minutely and everyone speaks until he is finished. How do the Shemanese accomplish their treaties? The Greenville document was created and signed with guns pointed at our heads. The Black Snake informed the chiefs they must touch the quill or be driven into the sea. This was perhaps the most honorable of all the treaties of recent times. Other treaties were made after the whiskey cask was opened, its poison robbing men of their senses. Then it was easy for one tribe to sign away the lands of another. The tribes were set at variance with this technique and it was always simple to induce some drunken sot to touch the quill. Why have the Shemanese gone to such lengths to make these treaties? They were worthless then and are so now. I will tell you why, my brothers: the Shemanese and other peoples from across the great water have talking leaves in which they record the events of history. If the aggressors simply come into our country and steal it the Shemanese will be judged harshly by others across the water. This they do not want. With a treaty they can write in their talking leaves that the land was fairly paid for and the war which followed was proof of

Indian savagery because the savages, as they call us, would not abide by their own treaty. The war was therefore justified, they will write, and readers will believe they behaved properly.

"I SAY TO YOU most treaties are little more than specious documents intended to cloak the bloody hand of the aggressor! Most of the time our people would not sell the land so an incident was manufactured in order to send in soldiers. The Shemanese leaders have been masters of deceit and hypocrisy,causing untold bloodshed among their people and our own! Look at the Greenville Treaty, my brothers: the Shemanese bought every sixty acres of land for *ten cents!* They now control most of the Ohio country and have paid next to nothing for it but they can tell the world it was paid for at the Harmar Treaty, conquered militarily, then paid for *again* at Greenville! See how magnanimous are the People of the Eagle! They do not publicize the fact that all payments together amounted to ten cents for every sixty acres!

"But we Amerindians know the truth. My brothers, we know how we have died in defense of our freedom and our way of passing through this world. Is their goal to exterminate us? Will we vanish as the snow melts before the sunbeam? We are told we must become civilized if we are to survive. We must become like the Shemanese if our race is to endure, they say... this to an entirely independent race of men and women, as independent as any race that ever lived. Is it we who must reconcile ourselves to this onerous task? We, the undaunted men of the forest, from the time of the first dawn when all was green and fruitful, have been the independent keepers of the soil, or Earth Mother. We have been the undisputed keepers of this sacred earth which the Longknives now call America. Before the Longknives ever saw our noble, beautiful homeland our ancestors roamed over it, ate its fruits, filled it with our race of people. Wherever we set our foot there was our home, the eternal gift of the Great Spritit. Our ancestors were on their own soil. No tyrant could disinherit them, order them away, or make any law to imprison them or take away their freedoms. No voyages of discovery troubled their imaginations for they had already been gifted with their legacy from the Master of Life. They conquered this great island as they conquered themselves right here, where they were led by the huge game animals and they were contented. All they needed was food to eat, clothes to put on, and time to enjoy the fruits of life. They never believed they were superior to the other creations of the Great Spirit so they lived in harmony with the Sun Father, the Earth Mother, the water spirits of the lakes and rivers, our cousins the animals. We knew freedom to the fullest, its ecstasies and its sorrows.

"Now we are told we are an ignorant people, unworthy of noble sentiments, inferior to men who would oppress us! Our ancestors were told by the newcomers they were fleeing evil men who would oppress them so our fathers gave them land on which to survive. Now we are told by their descendants that we, the native people, have no rights to the land! And who says these evil thing to our ears? The Longknives! They demand we change our maner of living. Yes, we must adopt the lifestyles of our oppressors and make our minds as theirs if we are to progress! They call themselves *civilized*. What do they mean? What is *civilization?* Is it love as the Christian missionaries say? Then where is the love among the Paxton murderers who slew the Christian Conestoga Indians? Where is the love of Colonel Williamson and his men who massacred the unarmed men, women, and children at Ghnadenhuten? These Delaware were Moravian Christians. Blackfish, our beloved chieftain and father, put the fate of Daniel Boone and his men to the vote. The so-called *savages* voted for mercy and the men lived! Perhaps our *naturism* is superior to their form of civilization?

"Brothers: I can tell you what the Shemanese mean by *civilization*. It has little to do with conditions of the mind or heart. Civilization is the broadaxe with which to cut down every forest on this great island. Civilization is a thunder stick which belches fire and death from a great distance so the user is in little danger. Civilization means using the land and the water to produce wealth for the few. Civilization is slaughtering animals for their skins and furs, leaving the meat to rot. Civilizaton is disease and sickness, hypocrisy and speciosity, anything goes so long as it acquires what you desire to have. This is *progress!*

"Brothers! Is it progress to forget our heritage? Is it progress to forget our religion and take on a strange, alien one, one in which there are so many variatons and competitors? Is it progress to cut down the forests, scar the breast of our Earth Mother, then watch the wind and rain destroy the fertile land of the Great Spirit?

"Has there ever been a race as mistreated as ours? Are we too not sensitive, intelligent creations of the Great Spirit? Is there no love in our hearts for our parents, our grandfathers, our wives and children? Do we not care for each other, are we not tender and kind to our loved ones, do we not concern ourselves with our totems and clansmen? Yes, we are. YES, WE ARE! We also have laws which must be obeyed and we do not suffer splendid villains if daring wickedness to triumph over helpless innocence. We are warriors who love the land but will not be enslaved to it for the Ruler of Destiny provided for us amply. We will not abandon our heritage! We are human beings with rights and privileges invested in us by our society. We respect differing lifestyles but we will not abandon our own. There are good people among the Shemanese and to these our hand is extended in friendship. In every group there is always a force for evil but this I say: let no man, red or white, approach me or my people with vile schemes for I am descended from warriors. My father Puckeshinwa, was a warrior, and so have been his sons. I know nothing of the Indian who is said to have killed a Shemanese named Myers. My hand is extended in friendship. The hatchet was buried at Greenville. There was planted in the same place the tree of peace, to be carefully perserved. HEAR ME! Take care for the future that loss of Indian lands do not choke the peace tree. It will be a great loss, if after it has so easily taken root you should stop its growth and prevent its covering your country and ours with its branches. Our warriors wish to dance to the calumet of peace under its leaves and remain contented on their mats, refusing to dig up their hatchets. We have murdered no one. We live in poverty at our village but we do not complain. There are no murderers amongst us. I have come here to speak truth and I have spoken it."

As Tecumseh finished his oration he stood for a moment until the interpreter finished, facing the Shemanese. Then he turned on his heels and walked gracefully to the outer edge of the circle and took his seat among the young men of his escort. The defiance, the wrath, the bitter indignation of his speech vanished as he sat and looked forward to the rest of the council. It was difficult to follow such an oration and other Indian speakers quickly finished their talks. Tecumseh had conquered everyone with his boldness, his sincerity, his dynamism, and especially his wealth of information on interracial matters. His oration would soon be discussed by everyone in Springfield and soon by most of the Shemanese in Ohio. *Sixty acres for ten CENTS!* One-sixth of one cent per acre! Could such a thing be true?!

The Shemanese concluded the murder of Myers was the act of a single unknown Indian. No tribe could be held accoutable on such evidence and the matter was grudgingly dropped. So all matters were reconciled, the council adjourned in friendly spirits and the Amerindians remained in their encampment for three days engaging in various frontier sports as suggested by Chief Crane of the Wyandot.

The Shemanese were not invited to participate but onlookers were welcomed if they went by the camp. The first contest was rapid loading and firing at a target which contained three marks. The winner was Tecumseh.

The second contest was loading on the run and firing at a target with a single mark on it. The winner was Tecumseh, who informed everyone

Daniel Boone had taught him how to do it.

The third contest was throwing the tomahawk at a target the size of a man's head. Tecumseh and another warrior tied for first place.

The fourth contest was throwing a knife: Tecumseh came in second.

The fifth contest was what all Indians prided themselves in: wrestling. A large, powerful warrior was beating everyone until Tecumseh stepped into the circle and with herculean effort managed to throw him to the ground.

So it went those three days at Springfield. Tecumseh had shown how magical words could be during his oration. The translator had grown shaky and fearful in his efforts to render the chief's words into English because, he said later, parts of it were so grand, lofty, and powerful he had not the words in English. Others he was afraid to pass on to Kenton and Patterson, the words were so full of wrath and defiance. Tecumseh had shown himself a master orator in a race of orators and then on the field he had proven none was a better athlete, this in a race of athletes. After the three days he invited all to visit his village, an invitation which many Amerindians decided to honor.

Episode 3: British designs?

William Wells, the Indian agent at Fort Wayne who also held the rank of Captain in the military, was suspicious of The Prophet and his brother Tecumseh. The former he considered a charlatan and mountebank, the latter a trouble maker. Was it possible these savage brothers were spies for the British? This disturbing idea gnawed away at him from time to time... but what would the British gain from stirring up the tribes? Wells had done his best to neutralize British influence with them. How could the Indian brothers, for such he considered Amerindians, fall for English propaganda after being deserted at Fallen Timber? The tribes had to align themselves with the Americans. If they were to survive. Would it be possible to bring the Prophet into the American fold? No. Captain Wells was certain of it. Several missionaries had reported how unfriendly he was toward Christianity and the Americans. What a hold he had on the superstitious brothers! He himself had seen hundreds of Indians on their way to and from Greenville. Sure, they came in for handouts but after they had visited with The Prophet there was something ineffable in their faces, something akin to hope or defiance, Wells couldn't quite put his finger on it. He knew councils were being held constantly and that many of the Indians represented nations from remote regions. His spies informed him messengers were being sent from tribe to tribe, carrying pipes, belts and strings of wampum... everything done as clandestine as possible, as if the Americans and chiefs friendly to them were not supposed to discover what was taking place. There were about eight hundred Indians living at Tecumseh's Greenville, he had been informed... none of the wampum belts were black, so war was not imminent... except for The Prophet there was no trouble on the horizon... Governor Harrison had really made him a famous rogue by challenging him to perform a miracle... and the weasel actually performed one! The British must have informed him ahead of time. Those infernal Britishers! They would ruin the tribes for their own ends. A lot they cared about the Indians.

Wells stepped outside his office, leaned against the wall and got an impulse to get on his horse and ride. He had no where to go but every once in a while he gave in to just going, chalking it up to his life among the Indians, the freest people in the world. They did what they pleased and took their chances every day of living. So he had his horse saddled and rode out of Fort Wayne, his rifle in its rawhide carrying case just in case he saw something. But he knew most of the game had been scared away by the influx of settlers.

Captain Wells rode in a southeasterly direction and chanced upon a small Indian encampment in the woods. He did not know the Indians although he could tell they were Winnebagos. "*Notha*," he said to the oldest of the three men who were evidently resting from their journey. All had the aspect of venerable elders. If Wells had been dressed in Miami garb he would have blended perfectly with the scene for he was as dark as any of them. "May I join you, my chiefs?" asked Wells. "I come in peace and my heart is clear as the blue skies."

"Join us, my captain," said Pakesemou, the Evening Twilight. "We have some kinnikinnick for all."

William Wells searched his memory for Pakesemou but he could not remember meeting him before. Perhaps it would come with conversation so he dismounted and sat with the older men. Pakesemou filled his pipe with the mixture of tobacco and herbs, lighted it, puffed to get it going, then passed it around. "How goes it at Fort Wayne?" asked Pakesemou of Captain Wells.

"Everything quiet," replied Wells. "And your journey?"

"Very disturbing," said Pakesemou. "We have been to Greenville to visit The Prophet and his brother. We had some very disturbing questions on our minds. Unfortunately they have been answered."

"I do not understand, ne-kah-noh," said Wells.

"My friends are like me, chiefs of their people," began Pakesemou slowly as he gestured with his right hand. "We have seen countless summers come and go. We have witnessed birth and death, good times when the kettle was high and bad times when the spoon came up empty. Now, in our old age when our hair is white and our mouths toothless, now that we should be respected for our wisdom we find ourselves chiefs in name only."

"That is hard to believe," soothed Captain Wells. "Perhaps the black clouds are merely temporary."

"No, I wish it were. Everywhere tribal affairs are in the hands of young warriors. We older chiefs have been undermined without us even knowing."

"But how could that be so?" asked Wells.

"I and my companions have pondered over the same question," said Pakesemou. "It is The Prophet and his brother who have undone us. The young people of our tribe look to them for leadership, not their own proper chiefs. Granted The Prophet is a great man, some say his is the voice of the Great Spirit but I doubt it. The Ruler of Destinies would never favor us being deposed and reduced to a private capacity. We are the trees of our people! We have worked our whole lifetime for their benefit! We who should be the beloved men are now toothless old ones waiting to die." Tears formed in the old man's eyes. "With the warriors in control there will be war sooner or later. Destruction and death will follow our moccasins. The younger generation does not know how to co-exist with the Longknives. They think they can decide their own destiny and The Prophet encourages that attitude. I have seen that war leads only to death or impoverishment. The young warriors have not seen, do not understand. Their hearts are filled with false hope."

Wells was touched by Pakesemou's dilemma. "Father, you do not think the young men are being led to war? Where would they get gun powder and lead, the British?"

"No one says it," responded one of the other two Indians who had been quietly stoic all this time, "but where else would supplies come from? The French are long gone."

"At one time the people thought the French king would return with his young men and take control again," said the third Indian. "Dreams and delusions, they have become the soul of our people since the first strangers came from across the big water."

"Does The Prophet talk of war?" asked Wells. He really didn't believe that a preacher, even with a large following, could take the Indians to war.

"Not to my knowledge," replied Pakesemou, "and not while we were in Greenville. It is the young bloods who seem to yearn for the warpath. With a little encouragement they would lift the hatchet for they do not listen to leaders of wisdom and experience."

331

"We must neutralize the British influence," suggested Wells, "and let them recognize their true friends, the Americans. It is with the People of the Eagle with whom they must live. Here is some tobacco for my fathers," he said as he gave Pakesemou a small pouch filled with the aromatic stuff. "I will be on my way. Come by Fort Wayne where presents await you from the People of the Eagle. Tell all my brothers the hand of friendship awaits them. Do not be deceived by the British who speak with forked tongues. Fallen Timbers is proof enough. Farewell until we meet again."

The Indians put up a hand but said nothing as Wells mounted up and rode away. Could The Prophet be a British agent used to rile the tribes? But what could they possibly hope to gain by it? They could never hope to control the fur trade on American territory, they needed trading houses and forts for that. Maybe they wanted to lure the trappers to go trade in Canada... some might even make the trek if American prices were not competitive. What if... no, that was pure nonsense. But the thought kept forcing its way into his brain: *what if the British still had designs on the land and wanted to reconquer North America?!*

Episode 4: Shakers visit.

"That is the village up ahead," said George Blue Jacket, interpreter for the three Shakers who had been selected to visit The Prophet to observe the character of the reform work being done at Greenville and to determine whether financial help and evangelical assisitance would further its progress. The three were Benjamin S. Young, David Darrow, and the well educated Presbyterian minister turned Shaker, Richard McNemar. First to catch the visitors attention was the large meeting-house, considerably more than a hundred feet long. Cabins spread out in evey direction and though it was a cold March day people were about their business. George Blue Jacket asked for The Prophet and Tecumseh and learned they were out in the forest making maple sugar. A man volunteered to take them to the site, which he said was not far off so the Shakers decided to go meet them immediately.

"What is that big house for?" asked David Darrow.

"To worship the Great Spirit."

"How do you worship?" asked Benjamin Young as the group headed out of the village.

"Mostly in speaking."

"Who is your chief speaker?"

"The Prophet. He converses with the Great Spirit and instructs us how to be good."

332

"Do all that live here believe in The Prophet?" asked Richard McNemar.

"Yes, we all believe. He can dream to God."

The sugar camp was about four miles away from Greenville Village. There were thirty or forty Indians working the sugar but The Prophet was ill, confined to his tent. George Blue Jacket suggested the guide inform The Prophet of their presence, which he did, entering the tent, coming out directly with a message:

"The Prophet will be unable to talk to you today. He is ill and anyway ministers of the Longknives never believe anything he says, considering everything foolish and laughable. He has a bad pain in his head and is very sick."

"Tell the holy man we are not such ministers," said Richard McNemar. "There are many who make light of our Shaker worship also. Tell him we are Shakers."

The guide reentered the tent, the Shakers waiting patiently. Within five minutes The Prophet emerged, obviously ill but interested in talking with the men. He shook hands with the visitors and suggested all sit around the fire. Tecumseh took his place but said nothing beyond introducing himself. When all were seated The Prophet looked at everyone--all were silent, every countenance grave and solemn--then asked the Shakers: "Do you believe a person can have true knowledge of the Great Spirit, in his heart, without going to school and learning to read?"

"We believe they can," said Richard McNemar, "and consider that the best kind of knowledge."

"Years past," began The Prophet, "I was a very wicked man..." He related about his visions, explaining them as he went until he summed up "...from which the Great Spirit told me to go and warn the people of their danger, and call upon them to put away their sins and live good lives. I began to speak to them and when I did I always felt great distress, weeping and trembling. Some believed and were greatly alarmed. They began to confess their sins, forsaking them, and set out to live good lives. This spread the word and brought many others from different tribes to see and hear the word. They became affected in like manner."

"Some of the chiefs proved very wicked and refused to believe. They made great effort to keep the people from believing, encouraging them in their former wicked ways. The Great Spirit told me to separate from those wicked chiefs and their people. He indicated where I should live, by the big ford where the peace was concluded with the Longknives. There I must make provision to receive and instruct all from the tribes which were willing to lead good lives. Many came and settled with me, and a great many more come to hear. We always expect great numbers, seldom being disappointed. We are told some white people are afraid, seeing so many Indians, but that is foolishness. We are here to do the work of God. We cannot hurt anyone."

The Prophet paused as if he had finished speaking. The Shakers were itching to ask him questions:

"Do you believe mankind is going away from the Good Spirit because of wicked works?"

"Yes," replied The Prophet. "We believe that about all people, Indian as well as Shemanese. And I feel great pity for all."

"Do you believe the Great Spirit once made himself known to the world by a man called Jesus Christ?"

"Yes, and the Good Spirit has made revelations to me, what has been in previous generations. I would like to discuss these things with you."

"What sins do you speak out against?"

"Witchcraft, poisoning people, fighting, murdering, drinking whiskey, beating wives because they will not have children. All who are guilty of these die to a bad Eternity. We also consider fornication to be bad."

"What do those people do who have been wicked, when they believe The Prophet?"

"They confess all."

"To whom do they confess?"

"To me and four chiefs."

"Do they confess all the bad things they ever did?"

"All from the time of age seven. And they cry and tremble when they confess."

"How did you learn this? The Roman Catholics confess their sins."

"Some Wyandots joined the Roman Catholics at Detroit. Now they believe in our Naturism religion. Roman Catholics confess their sins but go and do bad again. Our people forsake their badness when they have confessed, never entering it again." The Prophet appeared to have thrown off his pains and now asked, "Do your people drink whiskey?"

"We never touch that pernicious liquor," said Richard McNemar. The Indians seemed happy to hear such news, hoping the sentiment would spread among the Shemanese. "How are you fixed for provisions?"

"Not very well," said The Prophet. "So many people come to hear us. They eat up everything. But we share with a happy heart. Come, let us all partake from the kettle. You might be hungry from your journey."

334

The Shakers were served first to what was a kind of turkey stew. It was portioned out among everyone. Benjamin Young gave them ten dollars with which to buy corn. Another conversation ensued in the afternoon and toward evening the determination was to return to the village so the visiting delegation mounted horses and bid everyone farewell. It was beautiful evening dusk, the full moon just rising above the horizon. An Indian speaker stood up from where he had been sitting and with great solemnity spoke for fifteen minutes, the sincerity being heightened at every pause with a loud *Seguoy!* Amen! from the surrounding believers. Richard MeNemar thought of Jacob when he cried out "How dreadful is this place! Surely the Lord is in this place! And the world knew it not." With these impressions in their hearts the Shakers returned to Greenville.

Next morning, as soon as dawn walked the rim of the sky, a speaker got up on a log near the southeast corner of the village and began the morning service in a loud, reverent voice, paying homage and expressing thanksgiving to the Great Spirit. He spoke for an hour, though all remained in their dwellings. The Shakers could hear the man distinctly, as could the Indians for from time to time they uttered a loud, solemn, SEGUOY! as the speaker paused.

"Do you know," said David Darrow to his companions as they took in the view from the end of the meeting house which was on rising ground from where they could see the surrounding cabins, the vast open prairie to the south and east, overlooking the big American fort toward the north, "I feel as if we are among the tribes of Israel on their march to Canaan. Their simplicity and unaffected zeal for the increase of the work of the Great Spirit, their ardent desires for the salvation of their unbelieving kindred, along with the rest of mankind, their willingness to undergo hunger, fatigue, hard labor and sufferings, all for the sake of those who come to learn the way of righteousness! What faith, what high expectations of the multitudes flocking to hear The Prophet. How truly affecting! And the man outside, even if he were alone, hailing the opening day with loud aspirations of gratitude to the Great Spirit, encouraging the obedient followers of Divine light to persevere! What marvelous people these are!"

The Shakers walked around the village, interviewing everyone who would talk. They were shown letters of friendship from the Governor of Ohio and others proving many Americans considered them peaceable and brotherly. They watched how the Indians, with great industry, prepared timber for larger buildings. Some busied themselves with agricultural pursuits. McNemar wrote in his Journal, "From all we could gather, from their account of the work and of their faith and practice--what we heard and felt in their evening and morning worship--their peaceable dispositions and attention to industry, we were induced to believe that God, in every deed, was mightily at work among them..."

When it was time for the Shakers to return home they invited The Prophet to come visit and worship with them at Turtle Creek.

"I appreciate your graciousness, brother. Perhaps I will send a few of my men to reciprocate."

The Shakers discussed the possibility of sending a missionary among the Indians but all three men felt it would be a waste of time. The Prophet was already leading his people on the proper road. It would be better to help the Indians than to compete with them for converts.

The following month a delegation from Greenville arrived at Turtle Creek, twenty in all, The Prophet not among them. They held services every day at their encampment and on the Sabbath attended the meeting of the Shakers, displaying reverence and utmost decorum. They were treated royally by the Believers and when they left for home they led twenty-seven horses loaded with provisoins for the impoverished followers of The Prophet.

This act of Christian charity did not escape censure from among some of the Longknives. A delegation came to Turtle Creek, demanding to know why the Shakers were encouraging the Indians to war, or at least to contend for the land on which they were settled.

Richard McNemar was on the committee chosen to hear out the delegation. He wondered how all the rumors had gotten started: that a number of Indians had joined the Shakers and many more were coming on; that an Indian offered to confess his sins but the Shakers could not understand him; that the Indians considered the Believers nothing more than deceivers; and so on ad nauseum. McNemar and the others laid all rumors to rest and that evening the preacher wrote in his Journal: "Although these poor Shawnees have had no particular instruction but what they received by the outpouring of the Spirit, yet in point of real light and understanding, as well as behavior, they shame the Christian world. Therefore, of that Spirit which hath wrought so great a change, the Believers at Turtle Creek are not ashamed. Yet they are far from wishing them to turn to the right or to the left, to form an external union with them or any other people. We are willing that God should carry on His work among them without interruption, as He thinks proper."

Episode 5: Harrison and Wells

Governor Harrison refused to admit it publicly but he was very concerned over The Prophet's activities at Greenville. He sent a communique of warning to Governor Thomas Kirker of Ohio for Greenville was under Ohio, not Indiana, jurisdiction. Then Harrison instructed William Wells at Fort Wayne to do his utmost to break up The Prophet's center at Greenville. It simply would not do to have a British sphere of influence anywhere in United States territory, for such was his suspicion of the fraudulent prophet: the Shawnee charlatan was being duped into British service. Harrison wasn't certain what British intent was but no chance could be given them to grab hold anywhere.

Harrison felt something about The Prophet, something akin to fascination convoluted with sinister showmanship. He, a literary man with few peers, could hardly evoke words to express his sentiments. The Governor had never in his life felt such chagrin when the mountebank performed his "miracle," the miracle which Harrison himself had challenged him to effect. The savages could not have known about the eclipse ahead of time, it had to have been the British. Was there any wonder he suspected the British of having close ties with the Indians? If the Governor of Indiana Territory did not have foreknowledge of a solar eclipse and savages did this was proof relations were quite strong and intimate with a foreign power.

"Sir," interrupted the Governor's secretary, "Mr. Prince has returned and wishes an audience with you."

"Yes, of course, show him in," said Harrison. William Prince was the Irishman he had sent out to reconnoiter the prairie country villages and report firsthand what was happening among the tribes. Harrison was nothing if not thorough. "Good morning," said the Governor as he shook Prince's hand vigorously. "Sit down and make yourself comfortable."

The red-faced Irishman did Harrison's bidding and said, "Thank you, sir. I wanted to make a report as quickly as possible," he began.

"Yes, I appreciate that, my friend. How did it go?"

"Chief Reynard, our best friend among the Kickapoos, has been deposed," said Prince directly. Harrison wrinkled his forehead in disbelief. "Yes, the Kickapoo now owe their allegiance to The Prophet and will follow the Shawnee wherever they will lead."

"How was this done? Has Reynard been hurt? Assassinated?"

"No sir, he is as healthy as ever," commented Prince. "It is merely that he has no authority, the people will not follow him. You know the savages sir, there is no law to make anyone do anything. Reynard is considered too friendly with the whites, too willing to sell land or form an alliance with them, I was told."

"And the other tribes?"

"The Potawatomi and the Delaware are walking the same path," said Prince, "their allegiance is to The Prophet and his new religion. I am truly amazed at the zeal with which his disciples have done their work. I mean, so quickly have they spread their teachings."

"This Prophet, does he wander out among the villages?" asked Harrison pensively.

"Constantly, as does his brother."

"What would happen if this prophet were to be taken in to custody?"

"I don't know, sir."

"Do you think," asked Harrison, "the tribes would arm themselves and attack?"

"I have not considered such an eventuality, sir. Their missionizing is peaceful, I saw no evidence of preparing for war, certainly not offensive. The savages are always armed, of course, but they are living in more peace than I have ever seen on any frontier. There is a great feeling of amity between tribes."

"Which of the tribes is most disposed toward us?"

"I could not rightly say."

"If you were to hazard a guess?" persisted Harrison.

"I would say none of them, sir," answered Prince honestly. "It would take many presents to acquire another Reynard and at this time I could not even suggest where to begin. But in the past it has not been difficult to set the redmen at variance with each other. This pattern is ingrained in their character so I am certain there will be openings in the future."

"I see," commented Harrison. "Did you see any British agents while you were in the prairie country?"

"No sir, none. I would wager they're about, though."

"Yes, well thank you William," said Governor Harrison as he stood up, shook Prince's hand, and showed the man out. "I'll be in touch with you soon and your stipend is with my secretary. Good job."

"Thank you, sir."

Governor Harrison went back to his desk and wrote out a quick letter to Captain Wells at Ft. Wayne: The Prophet must be dislodged from Greenville and made to move as far away as possible.

When Captain Wells received Harrison's communique it was glad tidings for he was certain The Prophet was a British tool. It did not bother him in the slightest that Greenville was in the state of Ohio where Harrison had no jurisdiction. Annuities were dispersed at Ft. Wayne and that was jurisdiction enough. So Wells called in the halfbreed Anthony Shane and gave him a message to deliver to The Prophet and his brother, summoning them to Ft. Wayne as quickly as possible.

Shane made the journey to Greenville and when he arrived at the village he let it be known he carried an important message. A council was called immediately and Shane was asked to state his message in the presence of everyone, which he did: "This is from Captain Wells, Agent at Ft. Wayne, to The Prophet and his brother. 'You are to repair to this fort at your earliest convenience in order to receive urgent news from the government of the Seventeen Fires'."

Tecumseh rose to his feet immediately and said to Shane, "Go back to Ft. Wayne and inform Captain Wells that my fire is kindled on the spot appointed by the Great Spirit above. If he has anything to communicate to me he must come here. I shall expect him in six days from this time."

Tecumseh's contempt for Wells was thinly veiled. Nothing could be more preposterous than Tecumseh doing Wells' bidding. As if a patriot would obey the imperious summons of a deserter! Anthony Shane, whose mother was Shawnee, looked helplessly at The Prophet but no one said a word because Tecumseh had covered the council fire. Shane had supposed The Prophet was the leader at Greenville. Now he had an inkling it was Tecumseh who pulled the reins. But the revelation was not important at the moment. He returned to Ft. Wayne and within six days reappeared at Greenville. This time he had a letter from Secretary of War Henry Dearborn so another council was convened quickly: the Indians were to vacate the Greenville mission with all possible speed. The message ended with an omnious note: there would be no other warning.

Tecumseh was already irritated because Wells had not come himself, sending the half-blood Shane again in direct contradiction of the chief's wishes. Now he sprang to his feet angrily and said, "Enough with these vile messages! We will hear no more of them! These lands are ours! No one has the moral right to remove us because we are the first owners of the land! The Great Spirit above has appointed this place for us therefore here we light our fires and here we will remain. Boundaries? The Great Spirit gave us oceans for boundaries and his people do not acknowledge any other. Who are the Shemanese to talk about boundaries?! They must not have eyes, they are so blind when they come to boundaries. How many times have they crossed the Greenville line and upsurped Amerindian land? I say this in the ears of all here present for you know it is truth. We must observe boundaries but not the Shemanese! They cut down the trees of peace whenever and wherever it suits them! But what do they tell us when they wish us to touch the quill? 'Those lands shall be yours so long as rivers flow and grasses grow.' But before we are safely back in our cabins the Shemanese are overrunning our land once more. Being warriors we defend what is ours then the Shemanese raise huge armies and send them against us, forcing us to cede more land in order to restore the peace. They give us presents intended to cover the bodies of the dead but we are sensible that the land is everlasting and the few goods we receive for it are soon worn out and gone. Now the black clouds hang heavy over us because we realize soon we will have no land on which to spread our blankets or bury our dead!

"Our people have fallen upon such evil days! Now we cannot even live in peace where we wish! Must we finish out our lives as refugees and displaced persons?! We have tried to brighten the chain of friendship, preserving it from all stains. Now we are ordered to leave! Perhaps that is our destiny: to live under the red sun, our path full of thorns and brambles, the clouds black, the waters troubled and stained with our blood. Perhaps our women must endure soul felt tears, constantly weeping over the loss of loved ones, not daring even to go off in search of firewood with which to prepare meals. Our children will cry in fright whenever they hear any noise in what used to be our forest. Our cabins will be abandoned and our fields will lay fallow. We will have empty stomachs and drawn faces. Game will flee from us and snakes will hiss and bare their fangs as we pass. And birds perched in trees will sing only songs of death... THIS I WILL NOT TOLERATE WHILE THERE IS BREATH IN MY BODY!!" Tecumseh turned to Anthony Shane as he finished his impromptu oration and declared, "If the President of the Seventeen Fires has anything more to say to me he must send a man of honor as his messenger. I will have no further correspondence with Captain Wells. I have spoken."

Shane returned to Ft. Wayne and delivered all information to William Wells, who became angry and responded by writing to Governor Harrison that very large crowds of unfriendly Indians were continuing to journey through his post headed for Greenville. In a succeeding letter to the Governor at Vincennes he stated The Prophet and Tecumseh had 800 armed men living at Greenville. By the third letter he was remarking that various informants had advised him the British were behind The Prophet, that their machinations boded ill.

Governor Harrison was directly responsible for the safety of his far-flung Indiana territory so it was only natural to fret over a possible British threat to American security in its western fringe. When one of his spies informed him the Shawnee were circulating war belts to the other tribes and that traders were alarmed over the possibility of a general war against the United States he alerted the Secretary of War immediately, who in turn contacted other governors in the general area.

Episode 6: Jainai

Jainai had become very powerful in the movement and there were some who said he was second only to The Prophet himself in authority. Of all the disciples Jainai was the only one who was bilingual and bicultural in English and Shawnee. He had not used much English the past few years but he had lived with the whites, as they liked to call themselves, and learned the language quite well, observing closely and astutely their "civilization," as again they liked to describe their way of living. Jainai had become a sincere Christian, been victimized by the insincere varieties, and almost everywhere he was ostracized from society for being an Indian, his Christianty not withstanding. At length he concluded most Christians were little more than hypocrites, professing ideas which they did not believe for they did not live by them. Indeed, their basic commitment was to themselves and their desires fair or foul, it mattered not which. The ordinary Christian, he finally concluded, knew nothing of love and cared less if any religious tenet stood in the way of desire, ambition, or greed. This was not learned from one incident or one group of people. Jainai had travelled widely from Virginia to Massachusetts, doing the most menial of labor, being paid little when anything at all, begging when there was no other means of keeping body and soul together, getting beaten and run out of town all too often. One thing he never did: he never drank liqour of any kind, no matter what the circumstance. Something he always did, during the *civilized* part of his life as he was wont to refer to it, was read the Bible every day after he had learned the skill from dedicated missionaries in Boston. The Good Book was his constant, usually his only, companion and consolation. He believed that if people lived by it they would benefit greatly but few cared about their immortal souls as much as mundane items like flesh, land, money, whiskey, and the rest. He still kept a Bible hidden in his cabin, pulling it out to read occassionally. He really didn't have to be so clandestine about it but his loyalty was now to The Prophet so he did not wish to be discovered reading the Christian Bible. It just wouldn't do.

This day was drawing to a close so Jainai decided to walk out into the village cornfield and enjoy the sunset in wordless contemplation, communing with the Great Spirit as He showered the land with glow. As he walked he saw Spybuck and his devil wife riding by the Council House. They did not see him as they rode the same horse, she with an arm around the juggler. That either of them lived was a regret to Jainai. If anyone was an evil influence on the people it was that witch Flame. Flaming Eagle of Delight indeed! He had known her in Boston when her name was Dawn, a pay woman working in a brothel! No, she did not remember Jainai, he was just a miserable Indian cleaning up after the customers had spent their *love*. Love indeed! Christian lust. And paying for it besides! How ludicrous. And Dawn had been the most popular of all. Droves of men were always after her, she going with the highest bidder only. Jainai had looked at her often, marvelled at her stamina, wondered how such a beautiful woman could live such a life. But Dawn never once looked at him. Why should she, all he ever had was a Bible! The Prophet should have let him execute her as he wanted to during the purge. If anyone deserved an evil end she did. But that part of the movement was over, by orders of Tecumseh. What a pity!

Jainai shot an ominous glance at the couple on horseback and turned away toward the cornfield, walking quickly, much in contrast to his usual manner. As he walked into the tall corn he struggled to rid his thoughts of the vile woman, succeeding when he was almost at the other end of the beautiful Corn Maiden's handiwork. He sat down and cleansed his mind with beauty. Never was the earth so lovely nor the sunset so bold. Jainai let his mind wander to the river, so calm, so free from rocks, so safe for the canoes of the people. Never had the corn--suddenly a woman's sultry giggle broke Jainai's concentration, forcing him to look around for the intruder. There, a few paces away, were the evil woman and her juggler. He might have yelled at them but he had been in deep meditation so he decided against it, squinting at them through the cornstalks and their foliage. They were undressing! No, she was already undressed and undressing him. What in the world... an occassional beam of sunset squeezed through the corn and danced off their nudity, the woman taking on a redish tint, the man looking like bronze. She laughed throatily, its quality disturbing Jainai, tantalizing him, forcing him to watch as if... expectantly. *He had witnessed scenes like this before in Boston. At times Jainai had desired Dawn with an all consuming passion.* The woman pressed herself against the man, her arms around his neck, kissing him on the mouth, cheek, ear, both her legs wrapped round him.

Jainai saw the man wrap his arms around the woman, grab her with his hands,lifting her until her head was above the corn. It was as if Flame had come out of a ocean for she looked around then reentered the privacy of the enveloping greenery. Spybuck made her incline backward as he grasped her legs, placing her calves around his neck and shoulders, trying to raise her up for cunnilingus but Flame gently struggled against it. Jainai then saw the painting immediately above the hirsute area as Flame dangled upside down: it appeared to be a representation of flames leaping up... or was it multicolored wings? Jainai was not sure. He had a vague impulse to get up and leave the animals to their lust but he was fascinated by such reckless abandon, a symbiosis he could not command. The flaming wings fluttered as Flame continued to prevent Spybuck's goal and Jainai understood why the girl he had known as Dawn was the most popular of the pay women in Boston town. The vile wretch, leading men to perdition! Of course, Spybuck had earned his place in everlasting hellfire long before meeting the woman, if what Jainai heard was true. And now he didn't doubt a word of it.

Jainai's scrutinous eyes resembled those of a hawk spying its prey as he looked at Flame a dozen feet away. Spybuck didn't grow irritated even if he was not allowed to have his way. Instead he put the woman back on her feet and took a breast in his mouth for a few moments until he turned her around, following her spinal cord with his tongue all the way down to her sacral dimples situated toward the top of her voluptuous, curvaceous pompis. Jainai saw the woman shuddering in ecstasy, endeavoring to turn around and face Spybuck headon but he would not allow it, holding her thighs firmly. It was obvious Flame could not take much more when she began to pull on Spybuck's hair so he freed her and allowed her to turn at him but immediately he set his mouth to her belly, flicking his tongue lightly along the navel muscles. This was not as highly erogenous as the sacral dimples but within a short while the woman began to move with urgency, pressing his face into her abdomen, pulling his shoulders toward her, all the while making deep little sounds which disturbed Jainai as much as anything he saw. But Spybuck was not done yet: he brought his mouth up to her breast, lingered there a few minutes then went to a little bump she had on her clavicle, rubbing it strongly with his tongue until Flame once more was losing control over her desire, resulting in violent passionate struggle which Spybuck cut short by easing her gently onto the blanket on the ground, penetrating her gently then strongly as both lovers climaxed almost immediately.

Jainai could not stand it any more so he got to his feet and stalked away through the cornfield, Spybuck and Flame totally oblivious to the rest of the world. Jainai shook his head in a combination of disgust and overpowering frustration. Something had to be done with that woman! He had never witnessed such a carnal spectacle, even when he had worked in the Boston brothel. Such things should never be allowed to happen. It was the work of the devil! The man was just as guilty as the woman. Something had to be done! The executioner was ready.

Episode 7: Reunion

Thomas Worthington and Duncan McArthur were Governor Kirker's personal choices for making an eye-witness report over the activities at Greenville. Secretary of War Dearborn had instructed Kirker to be on the lookout for Indian troubles and Governor Harrison of Indiana had alerted him months ago so he felt pressed to do so, especially since Greenville was under Ohio jurisdiction. Worthington had been one of Ohio's first two Senators and McArthur, who fought under Harmar, had laid out the state capital of Chillicothe, among many other accomplishments. The two picked up an interpreter who was supposed to have lived with the Indians for many years and all three were anxious about their reception at Greenville as their journey wore on.

"You say you lived with the Shawnee, Reverend Ruddell?" asked McArthur.

"Yes sir," replied Stephen Ruddell, now a Baptist minister serving as a missionary among the Auglaize River Shawnee, "for many years. I'd be with them still if it had not been for Fallen Timbers, I guess."

"You seem to have enjoyed it right well," observed Worthington.

"Those were probably the best years of my life," said Ruddell wistfully. "The Shawnee are a wonderful people."

"Ever run across this chief of theirs, Tecumseh?" asked McArthur.

"He was my best friend during those years. We did everything together, hunted, fished, went on the warpath. There could not be a more loyal friend than Tecumseh. You gentlemen will appreciate him once you meet him."

"Is he capable of breaking the peace with a sneak attack?" asked Thomas Worthington. "I hear the tribes all look to him for leadership, along with his brother The Prophet."

"Tecumseh was always honorable and straight-forward," said Ruddell. "I doubt very seriously he has changed. We will soon see for ourselves. There is the village up ahead. The runner I sent before us will have them ready to greet us."

"When did you see him last?" asked Duncan McArthur as the trio spurred their horses.

"Not since 1794, better than a dozen years," said Ruddell. "I am anxious to see my old friend, gentlemen." Worthington and McArthur noted the shine on Ruddell's face. With the slightest encouragement he would have forced his horse into a full gallop.

The entire village came out to meet the three men. Stephen Ruddell spied his foster brother among the village dignitaries and guests, jumped off his horse and bolted grinning toward Tecumseh. The usually reser-

344

ved chief was every bit as eager as he made his way toward Ruddell.

"Sinnamantha!" exclaimed Tecumseh.

"My brother!" said an elated Stephen Ruddell. "Keewaukoomee-laa!"

The two men embraced each other in their happiness, a rare thing indeed among the Shawnee for such emotions were generally considered effeminate.

"Welcome!" said Tecumseh. "My heart is filled!" Then he remembered there were other men with Sinnamantha. "Welcome, my friends, welcome to our village. You see before you our people who have come to make you feel at home. The sounds you hear are the testimony of their happy hearts. We extend to you the chain of friendship. This day no high wind will blow over the land, no heavy clouds will put out the ancient council fire for it is renewed. Some dry wood is thrown upon it so the blaze will ascend to the clouds. It is our desire we and you should be as of one heart, one mind, one body, thus becoming one people, entertaining a mutual regard and love for each other, to be preserved firm and entire, not only between you and us, but between your children and our children, to all succeeding generations."

Tecumseh led everyone to the large Council House where festivities were convened to honor the visiting dignitaries. Stephen Ruddel translated Governor' Kirker's letter of friendship into Shawnee, Potawatomi, and Chippewa. McArthur and Worthington each made little talks in which they emphasized the People of the Eagle and their government wanted peace with all Indian nations. Tecumseh told the visitors various chiefs would address them tomorrow but now was the time for feasting, that the people had prepared them quantities of food, would they like to go outside and partake?

Of course they would, so everyone exited and was served generous helpings of venison, turkey, bear, hominy, beans, and various other dishes basic to Amerindian cuisine. Tecumseh sat with the visitors and carried on a lively spate of reminiscences with Steve, incidents and stories of growing up in the woods. Worthington and McArthur listened attentively in order to acquaint themselves with the charismatic chief of Greenville. The man seemed to be exactly as Ruddell had described him.

After everyone ate Tecumseh invited his guests to walk around the village that they might become familiar with it. It was an excellent opportunity for Worthington and McArthur to see whether or not marItial preparations were being made. After close examination the two decided there was nothing military about Greenville. The only weapons they saw were those necessary in the chase and hunt.

345

The following day the council fire was rekindled. Blue Jacket, principal chief of the Shawnee nation, spoke first, emphasizing that all Amerindians wanted to live in perpetual peace with all tribes and with the Shemanese. The Prophet spoke next, recounting the story of his conversion, telling of his preaching to the tribes, emphasizing his sense of mission: "...did not move to Greenville because it was such a pretty locale or because it was so valuable for it was neither. We came here because it was revealed to me in a vision this was the proper place to establish our doctrines. We live by our beliefs for they were not given to us by men but rather by the Supreme Ruler of the Universe. Stay among us and you shall see the sincerity of the Believers."

McArthur and Worthington were favorably impressed. They decided the Indians at Greenville posed no military threat, that The Prophet was sincere in his religious activities, that a delegation of chiefs should accompany them to Chillicothe so Governor Kirker could see for himself. Tecumseh immediately accepted the invitation, especially when it was learned Ruddell would go as interpreter. Blue Jacket then volunteered to go, as did Roundhead and the Panther.

Before beginning the return trip to Chillicothe Thomas Worthington noticed a white woman with flaming red hair riding horseback with an Indian man. He asked Ruddell, "Are there... there aren't any captives in Greenville are there?"

"I am certain there aren't," replied Ruddell as he followed Worthington's glance to the white woman. "All were freed. I myself am proof of it."

"I am sure you are correct," commented Worthington. "Could you call those people over here for a minute?"

Ruddell walked over quickly, called the woman in English but she did not turn around until he called in Shawnee. Flame and Spybuck reined in their horses, heard what Ruddell had to say, returned to where the two Shemanese were standing but did not get off their horses.

Worthington introduced himself and his compainions then asked the woman how she came to be in Greenville. A crowd began to gather, including The Prophet and Jainai. Flame did not answer until Ruddell put the question into Shawnee.

"She likes our cornfields," said Jainai, though it was loud enough for only those immediately around him to hear. None understood what was meant.

"I live with my husband," said Flame in Shawnee as she nodded toward Spybuck. "Does not your wife live with you?"

"Yes, of course, dear lady," said Worthington, "forgive my curiosity. It sometimes gets the best of me."

346

"She is free to live where she pleases," said Spybuck calmly.

Flame shot him a questioning glance. Was he trying to say he didn't care where she lived? No, he hadn't meant it that way.

"I am certain she would be a credit to any town or village," said Duncan McArthur.

Jainai smiled ruefully. Dawn was not one for credit, it was always cash in hand or a wave of the hand. He cringed inwardly. She had been so close to execution. The vile woman should have met her tragic end. She so deserved it!

McArthur and Worthington took leave of The Prophet and the village of Greenville with very good impressions. They made absolutely certain they were not being duped, that The Prophet wasn't simply staging a theater for their benefit. He was sincerely religious, wasn't preaching war, and there were no military activities taking place in the area. His followers were from many tribes, most were dirt poor but the village was self-sustaining through agriculture and hunting. Fur trading was not a major activity at Greenville.

The horseback journey to Chillicothe was uneventful but once there Governor Kirker gave the visiting chiefs the treatment their status deserved, calling together important state officers and other influential citizens for a council over which Kirker himself presided. The Shemanese wanted one of the chiefs to address the assembly. The men deferred to the youngest of the party, Tecumseh, who took on the responsibility even though the building in which the council was being held filled with curious citizens when word got out Governor Kirker had four chieftains in council at City Hall.

"Brothers of the Seventeen Fires," began Tecumseh, "we of the Amerindian tribes here represented speak with one voice. We, the people who were born free on this great island, wish to live with you as brothers as long as the sun and moon shine in the sky. We recognize we have a broad path to walk and we welcome it. It is with an open heart that we receive your hands. Friendship stretches ours to yours, uniting them together. I tell you now that we native people do not have war on our minds. Bad birds may fly over our heads with crow mischief. Their flesh will be poor, their voice weak. They will hush and fly away when hearing the word of our fathers. While there is always great difficulty in controlling individuals, we with ours and you with yours, rest assured no nation is contemplating an offensive war. It would be sheer folly to declare war on the Seventeen Fires. If my people are to fight they are too few, if they are to die they are too many. We have smoked the black pipe in remembrance of the dead. Now we smoke the white pipe and the sky is cleared.

"Brothers of this beautiful Ohio country! Let me speak this day on other related matters. We are now holding tightly the chain of friendship. Our people are accustomed to facing the future standing straight and tall. I have but one word and that is truth so consider what I am about to say." Tecumseh looked at Governor Kirker directly as he did those personages in council and several individuals in the audience, measuring them or what he was to verbalize. "In the time before we knew the Shemanese our wants and needs were fewer than they are now. Our desires were always within our control. At that time we had never seen anything we could not acquire. Before contacts with Europeans, who have caused such destruction in our game, we could go to sleep and when we awoke we would find game animals feeding around our camp. But now many of our people who have not heard the word of The Prophet are killing them for their skins and feeding the wolves with their flesh. Our future children will cry over their bones. My brothers and I came from Greenville, as you know, and during the journey I received shock after shock over how the land has changed. In conversations with many friends I have been told civilization is taming the wilderness. Concepts like *civilization* and *wilderness* do not exist exactly in Shawnee but I have the impression one is the adversary of the other. Is this true, my friends, is wilderness the adversary of the *pioneer,* as you call the person who comes into Amerindians land? I can understand how a ferocious bear or panther can be dangerous but what about a tree? Why must whole forests be cut away from Earth Mother, especially when the wood is merely piled up and burned to no purpose? Little saplings are like children standing next to their parents, tender as a blade of grass. A tree is a living creature, showing its years with circular rings of growth, spring wood and summer wood, giving it age. When times are good the rings are wide, when bad, narrow. We people of the great lakes love our trees and their endless varieties. Did I say endless? Whole forests are not where they used to be.

"Brothers, the chain of friendship is bright between us. The Treaty of Greenville says so. We have ever wished it. When there was war it was strictly self defense on our part, was it not? Never in my studies with the Grandfathers did I ever hear that *we* began hostilities. War, always defensive war, was forced upon us by encroachers who would not respect Amerindian rights to the land. If we were to be guided by law would we not all, everyone here present, have to admit the Greenville Treaty is invalid?!" There was a noticeable stirring among the Shemanese. "If we were to be guided by law there could have been no Shemanese settlements north or west of the Ohio!" Tecumseh now reviewed all the treaties made with the Ohio country tribes, related in his bold, commanding manner how minor chiefs or sachems had been duped into signing treaties which were misrepresented by interpreters, how the whiskey barrel had been used to confuse issues, how one tribe had been bribed to sell the land of others. His words came rapidly, vehemence rearing up here and there, his gestures almost violent. "These pretented treaties and pacts are worthless if they are not supported by military might! They are monuments to the art of speciosity and hypocrisy! But the tomahawk is buried. The council fire burns brightly.

"Brothers: we know the treaties have been mere devices to wrest the land from us. I am certain I could find among you various individuals who would sell me New York or Virginia or Pennsyvania if all you had to do was touch the quill. This pretended sale would be invalid, would it not? Of course. If I went to those lands and told the people there they must move back across the great salt water they would answer with a battle cry, would they not? Then, if I had enough warriors, we would attack and vanquish the resistors in battle. It would be another example of a strong, numerous people taking advantage of a smaller nation. The final treaty of peace, forced upon the vanquished, would then be law which the victims must abide with but if the victors choose not to or if they want more land they can begin the vicious circle all over again. The weaker nation will resist until they are vanquished again and again unto extermination! THIS HAS BEEN THE HISTORY OF AMERINDIANS AT THE HANDS OF THE SEVENTEEN FIRES! The Greenville Treaty and all others before it have been invalid because they were effected clandestinely in many cases, with the few instead of all the people, military force necessary to support these pretended treaties.

"Brothers! We must be accorded our share of human dignity. Our way of living is different from yours but it is as dear to us as yours is to you. We must be allowed to live securely on our land. We cannot live like birds on the bough, scattering with the slightest provocation. There never would have been war if we had been respected in possession of our lands north of the Ohio. Are we going to keep our remaining lands or are we going to be pushed off this great island? It has been only a short while since we were told to vacate our village at Greenville! The treaty states we may live wherever we wish so long as we are peaceful but we have been ordered to get out by the Secretary of War for the Seventeen Fires! Is this law based on justice?!! No, it is the law of the knife and our people are targets once again, birds on the bough of a treaty which is not respected by the very people who forced it on us."

Tecumseh now felt a close rapport with his listeners. He had made his points and driven them home in his own style. It was time to sum up. "Brothers, a liar is unworthy for consideration as a man. I have spoken truth this day and I entrust my spoken words to the rising smoke. They will reach the Ruler of Destinies. We have wiped away the tears from our eyes, the dust from our faces. We have cleansed our hearts and covered the bones of those killed in battle. No one is singing for war. Take our hand in friendship and let us live in peace and contentment for such is the path of wisdom."

The assembled Shemanese gave Tecumseh an extremely warm round of applause as he finished his oration. Several individuals came up to shake his hand, led by Governor Kirker himself.

"Do you remember me?" asked a man of Tecumseh as he shook the chief's hand. "Think way back."

Tecumseh looked at the individual. There was something quite familiar about him then he saw it and said, "Benjamin Kelly! Is that you?!"

"Sure is, my brother!" said Kelly who had also been adopted by Black Fish many years ago. "Our father would have been proud of your oration." Benjamin Kelly had been quite moved by Tecumseh's speech. The years spent with the Shawnee, now gilded by time, had turned out to be some of the best of his life. When Tecumseh spoke Kelly saw the workings of a brilliant mind, indicative of the genius of native people on this great island. Why had he chosen repatriation? Kelly had often asked himself that question.

The two promised to meet and talk at the earliest opportunity then bid each other farewell. Others made their way to Tecumseh's side, making congratulatory remarks then stepping aside for the next individual. Governor Kirker finally rescued Tecumseh by suggesting all four chiefs accompany him on a tour of the state capital and enviorns. The offer was promptly accepted and all stepped into a large carriage which took them around the area. Stephen Ruddell continued to accompany the group as interpreter and Governor Kirker had him relate to the chiefs the people's fear and unrest over possible Indian hostilities had been laid to rest. He expressed an interest in The Prophet's religious work, which Tecumseh assured him was a labor of love, that it should continue to prosper and teach how to handle the realistic conditions brought about by the Treaty of Greenville.

There had been a large multitude at the council but evidently they were a small part of the citizens of Chillicothe for everywhere there were busy, hustling, bustling people going this way and that. Tecumseh shook his head slowly as he gazed at everything. The Shawnee could never declare war on the People of the Eagle and hope to win! Sheer numbers would destroy the tribe. He sincerely hoped the Shemanese would keep peace.

The day before the chiefs were to return to their villages a sumptuous banquet was held in their honor at the home of Mr. and Mrs. Worthington, a magnificent estate called Adena. The banquet turned out to be quite a social event, most state officials and influential citizens in attendance.

Adena was located in the commanding range of hills west of Chillicothe, looking across to Mount Logan almost like a sentinel facing the beautiful Scioto Valley. As Tecumseh gazed at the sight he remembered being told by the Grandfathers the Mound Builders had been the first pioneers in this picturesque terrain, the handiwork of the Great Spirit. How he loved the entire Ohio country! Why had the Secretary of War ordered his tribesmen to abandon their village? Where would they go? Perhaps outside the Greenville Treaty boundaries. There they could live in peace and not be ordered about.

"Sir, come in," said Miss Worthington, the daughter of the host, "we will be eating and cannot start without you." She looked at Stephen Ruddell to translate the message to Tecumseh but it was not necessary for Tecumseh said, "Thank you."

The young lady was rather surprised the man could speak English but she showed no emotion outwardly. Everyone at Adena had been coached beforehand not to take notice of any eccentricity displayed by any of the visiting chieftains. No sign of displeasure at any accident would be tolerated. The chiefs were to be given whatever they wished or asked for. They must be treated exactly as any other elegant white diplomat. Consequently everyone servicing the banquet in any way concentrated on evey act performed, every detail of every assignment.

The table was shaped like a circle in the large Adena dining room. It was a beautiful sight and heaped bountifully with delicious foods. The chiefs were perfectly at ease as they sampled the elaborate dishes. Coffee was served to Blue Jacket and Tecumseh but then the server ran out of the steaming liquid, having to return to the kitchen for more. A different waiter then came out and served the Panther, neglecting to see that Roundhead, a very noted Wyandot chief, had not been served his coffee. It was no great problem, though Roundhead liked his coffee. The chief merely took the cup and saucer in hand as he turned toward the waiter who, concentrating on his pouring, turned his back on Roundhead as he went down the line.

Miss Worthington saw the slight and turned a bit pale. Others, including her mother, grew tense that Roundhead might consider the incident an intended affront. Mercy! How could that impossible waiter have missed a guest of honor! Everyone tried so hard to please and now something like this had to ruin everything! The other Indians noticed the slight and began talking among themselves. Lord, what if they all stood up and stalked out in a body!! Wars had been fought for less!

It happened that Roundhead was the only chief present of the *msaywaywilandi* Umsoma. Tecumseh and the Panther belonged to the *patakuthidaywi-landi* division and Blue Jacket to the *palawi-landi* so the three recognized it was fair game to make light of Roundhead's attendant spirit for such was the Amerindian way at all social gatherings.

"It appears that Roundhead's good genius cannot obtain for him even a cup of coffee," began Tecumseh in mock seriousness.

"I have always known it," said the Panther. "Msaywaywi-landi have no power. Who would choose such a representative for a guiding spirit?"

"Only those who will have no coffee," said Blue Jacket.

It was Roundhead's duty to defend his Umsoma against all disparagement and he did so in his typically manly way. The chief displayed no emotion as he defended all of his Umsoma for such would have brought disgrace to his division but he returned like for like, providing great jollity to the Amerindians banqueting at Adena.

The Worthingtons and some of the other guests, aware of the "coffeeless chief," grew more and more tense as the Indians continued to speak solemnly among themselves. Tecumseh was the first to become aware of the charged emotional atmosphere when he happened to notice how nervous was Mrs. Worthington.

"Forgive me, please," said Tecumseh to Mrs. Worthington to her immense relief, "our friend not getting any coffee opened up exactly the opportunity which our people revel in." He explained that Roundhead belonged to a different Umsoma, which Tecumseh translated as a club with a mascot considered a guiding spirit or genius, from the other chiefs, whose duty it was to tease as it was Roundhead's to defend.

Mrs. Worthington's embarassment faded but nervertheless she got up from her chair of honor and poured Roundhead a cup of coffee with her own hands, a service she performed every time the cup was even halfway empty.

"Our brother chief," remarked the Panther, "will soon have his eyes turning yellow." The comment was in his own language, uninteligible to everyone except the Amerindian delegation. Only the many years practice of strict emotional control kept the chiefs from rolling on the floor in laughter.

Episode 8: Flowers

Rebecca helped her mother clear the table and wash the dishes before she joined the group of visitors, which included Tecumseh, in her father's cabin this day. She cast side glances at her Mr. Tikomfa Chief, the only Indian in the group of half a dozen men, but he did not appear to be ill at ease in the slightest. Rebecca was completely relaxed with Tecumapease but she had to admit in a large crowd of Indian women and she the only white, she grew a bit nervous sometimes. It was not Tecumapease's fault by any means for Tecumseh's sister was as grand and noble as her illustrious brother. Still, there were times when she felt a tinge of nervousness. She asked herself how it would be if she were to live in an Indian village.

The men's conversation centered around the second Fort Stanwix Treaty, the document which provided the legal basis for the United States takeover of land north of the Ohio.

"The treaty was signed," asked good naturedly a man named Johnson, good friend of James Galloway who smoked his pipe leisurely, "by representatives of the tribes, was it not?" The question was posed for Tecumseh to answer.

"No, not representatives, just members of the tribe," replied the chief.

"I do not see the difference clearly," commented a gentleman named Crenshaw.

"It is very simple," began Tecumseh. "Suppose some of our people called all of you here present to a treaty signing. And let us suppose you went because you were offered presents. So you sign the treaty in order to receive gifts. You do not really care what you are signing because you are a private individual. The document is worthless because you represent or can speak for no one but yourself. But you touch the quill to acquire presents. Now my people can go into your land and take it, pointing to the treaty as proof the land has changed ownership. Would the People of the Eagle acknowledge validity of the treaty because you signed it? Of course not. You had no authority to sign away your country. The Indians at the second Fort Stanwix in 1784 were not representatives, just individuals, sharpers who were there to receive presents. They would have signed away the moon and stars if they had been asked to."

"I did not know it had been achieved in that fashion," said Galloway.

"But the lands have been paid for time and again with good money," said another man named Allison.

353

"That is another popular delusion," replied Tecumseh. "Have you any idea how much the Blacksnake paid for the land?"

"Blacksnake?"

"Excuse me," said Tecumseh. "To us the snake is not a vile creature. The Blacksnake is a courageous animal to us. I should have said General Wayne at the Treaty of Greenville. Do you know how much was paid for each acre of land taken?"

"I do not know," conceded Allison.

"I heard it was a marvelous treasure," said another individual, named Dunway.

"One sixth of one cent for each acre!" said Tecumseh.

"No!" exclaimed Johnson in disbelief.

"Yes," said Tecumseh calmly. "This is common information among my people. I cannot but wonder why it is not among yours."

"Perhaps we must include," said Allison, "the cost of the war. Harmar, St. Clair, Wayne. Those campaigns, all campaigns, are expensive."

"It is the price the aggressor must pay," said Tecumseh pensively, "but I find it strange you do not first value the many lives which were lost."

"That goes without saying, of course."

"Perhaps it is worth it to win a rich country," said Tecumseh. "It must be or surely the President would not authorize the aggression in the first place. We love our land as much as it is coveted so there must be war, I guess."

"No one is for war," said Johnson.

"I have heard that so many times," commented Tecumseh, "yet it is difficult to understand why everyone is so proud of his weapons. I understand it is part of your law that anyone can own any weapon of his choice. This is the law, I am told. Such an instinct for war and aggression this displays, yet everyone talks for peace."

"We are all hunters," observed Dunway, "same as you and your people."

"Not quite like Tecumseh," said Galloway, knowing of the chief's great prowess.

"Mr. Tikomfa Chief," said Rebecca quickly, "come with me and help me if you would?"

"Of course. Gentlemen, if you will excuse me." Everyone nodded their assent as Tecumseh stood up and walked outside after Rebecca. "What do you need done?" asked the chief.

"I want you to help me go pick some flowers," replied Rebecca, "for transplanting. They are not too far away, we can walk." She took his hand as they walked. "I do not like talk about war."

"I will help you with your flowers, little pumpkin, but you must always remember I am a warrior like the rest of my race."

"You could be anything you wished," said the young woman.

"My heart is happy that you have such confidence in me. What would you have me be?"

"I want you to do what you wish and what you must," said Rebecca, "nothing else. I would never wish you to change if you do not want to. I love you the way you are."

Tecumseh gathered her in his arms and kissed her. Rebecca had always been a wonderful person to him. Yes, a person, not only a woman, for a long time. Tecumseh had not been attracted to her blue eyes, blond hair, fair complexion, her very feminine body. These characteristics took time to de-emphasize. It was Rebecca's ability as a student that kept him interested in her company. She could remember things as well as he, she was enthusiastic about knowledge even if she had only dry books from which to garner wisdom. There were always women wherever he went but none had ever taught him to read the talking leaves or write his name. No one else could have prepared him better for dealing with the Shemanese. He often forgot *she* was a Shemanese. Now her blue eyes were part of the universal sky, her hair like strands of sunbeams at daybreak. Now she was a woman to him, as well as a valued companion. She could be closer to him only as a wife.

"Come," said Rebecca, "help me with the flowers."

"You are blossom enough in my life," he said as they resumed walking.

"See, look yonder! How beautiful!"

Tecumseh thought of his mother when the two would walk in the forest. Rebecca would have loved her!

"I forgot to bring my little spade," said Rebecca in disappointment.

Tecumseh drew his knife and said it was no problem to cut the soil away, asking which flowers she wanted.

"These here, and those. I'll carry them in my apron." Quickly the garment was full and the couple made its way back to the cabin where the flowers were transplanted then watered immediately.

"And when you marry," asked Tecumseh, "will you take our flowers with you?" There was an unusually serious tone in the chief's voice, quite unlike the rest of the small talk.

"I have never thought of that," said Rebecca, "since no one seems interested in marrying me."

"That could not be," chided Tecumseh. "I am certain you have numerous suitors."

"Only one that I am interested in."

"And he? What must he be like?"

"He must be a chief," said Rebecca, "trying to help his people." At first she had wanted to make a joke out of it but failed. "And I would love him even if he were not a chief."

"Chiefs are often weighed down with the problems of many, many people. They must travel around much and be gone from home too often."

"Perhaps I could convince him to take me with him."

"I do not doubt it."

At that moment James Galloway's guests exited from the cabin and saw the country's greatest war chief, on his knees, next to Rebecca, transplanting flowers!

"Good evening," chorused the group of men in farewell. Johnson wanted to add, "Mr. Tikomfa Chief," but he thought better of it.

"Good night, do come again," said Rebecca.

"Farewell," said Tecumseh as he got to his feet and helped Rebecca up. In a short while it was time for him to say good night and when Rebecca came back into the cabin she had something to tell her parents.

"I believe Tecumseh is going to ask me to marry him," she said. "I don't know when, but I think he will."

"That is wonderful, my dear," said her mother, "if that is what you want. Only you know your heart." Rebecca was the youngest of her children and perhaps she had hung on to her daughter for too long. Nevertheless, tears welled up in the woman's eyes. "If he does, what will be your answer?"

"Somehow I feel a little uncomfortable," confessed Rebecca. "I guess I have loved the man for quite some time. Everyone else is so dull in comparison. But if I said no, what would happen... to all of us?"

"Child," said her father, "do not concern yourself that way. Tecumseh is a man of honor. We would not be endangered by your refusal."

"No, I don't think we would," continued Rebecca. But everyone had heard Tecumseh speak. The storm of war could break out in the Northwest at any time. He had pointed out the injustice of tribal treatment by the United States, the refusal of the national government to allow the Indians to sell their lands to whomever they wished, the disregard for overlapping tribal interests, the ever-increasing wave of settlers encroaching on Indian land guaranteed by solemn treaty. Treaties were indeed the cloak which camouflaged the hand of aggression. How long could Tecumseh control his people before they went on the warpath to save their land, their dignity, their honor? This could be done only through confederation of all the tribes. And the master of this impending storm of unrest and uncertainty was the suitor of Rebecca Galloway!

Did Rebecca feel that prescience by which some women have sensed the events of the future? Something told her this man she had come to love bore within him an all encompassing power, dangerous and fateful. What if she married Tecumseh, could she keep him on the white road of peace? Was she really in love with him or was it overpowering fascination? No, it had to be love for she had never felt like this before.

"Come," said her father, "let us submit this great question to the altar of our Saviour." He took his daughter and wife by the hand, went to the family altar and led his family in supplication: "O Jesus Christ, interpret for us Thy divine will. Give us direction in all moments of confusion or puzzlement. Sweet Jesus, extend to us your hand in guidance, especially to her who must tread a difficult way. A great and good man of Ohio also needs your divine favor. He is not a Christian, Lord God, yet he is your child and renders homage in his own fashion, the way of his people. Extend your hand, your wisdom to him that sincere patriot of the Ohio country, that he and his people may live in peace and contentment. Hear us, O Lord God!"

Episode 9: Harrison's letter.

William Wells was absolutely convinced The Prophet continued to be inspired by the British in Canada and he constantly urged that force be used to halt his activities. His spies reported on The Prophet's every speaking tour and if anything suspicious turned up he would write Governor Harrison messages which ended with "...the British are behind this," or "...nothing would have a better effect on the tribes than an immediate show of resentment on our part at their endeavoring to form unfriendly combinations toward us..."

Governor Harrison was not overly impressed with The Prophet. What could he really accomplish? Anyone who claimed the power to perform miracles was more a joke than a threat. Furthermore, the Shawnee under The Prophet owned no land to speak of, not even their handful of ground where they lived at Greenville. It was the landed tribes who received the Governor's attention and even his political enemies had to admit he had proven himself a master at handling the Indians and extinguishing their land titles. In 1802-03 he had extended the title to

Vincennes village into a veritable fiefdom. In 1803 his diplomacy was immensely successful with the weakened Kaskaskias, who he described as "...the most servile, contemptible creatures on the face of the earth," extinguishing their title to half of Illinois. In 1804 he purchased most of the land of the Sauk and Fox tribe, probably the most important coup of his ambitious career. People began to describe him as presidential timber after that. In 1805 he obtained the Piankeshaw tract in one treaty and a large area above Clark's Grant, the document for which was signed on Harrison's estate and therefore called the Treaty of Grouseland.

The last couple of years he had been laying the groundwork for his greatest effort of all, the lands north of Vincennes all the way into Michigan. This was not an impossibility for the Sauk and Fox had ceded land from the Missouri River north to the Wisconsin River. It could be done... it would be done! The growing United States needed the land for its enterprising, industrious people. The Indians would be well taken care of and treated justly. Roaming through miles and miles of wilderness in quest of food for one's family was much too wasteful. A fraction of land under proper cultivation was immensely more rewarding to individuals as well as society in general, Indian or white.

Harrison wrote to Wells asking if there was any possibility of winning The Prophet over to the Americans. If he exerted the infulence over the savages that everyone said he did he could be most valuable. The Indian Agent wrote back there was no likelihood of this, that he wanted to dislodge The Prophet from Greenville, working through discontented branches of the Delaware and Shawnee. As of late August, 1807, Wells admitted he had been unable to get anything going against the impostor.

The Governor wrote to Secretary of War Dearborn that if the self-styled prophet continued to excite disturbances among the Indians he should be threatened with the vengeance of the United States. In Harrison's voluminous correspondence was also a letter sent to the Shawnee on the Auglaize, denouncing The Prophet's "dark and bloody councils," which read in part: "My children, this business must be stopped. I will no longer suffer it and I cannot understand what has happened to your ancient wisdom. You have called in a number of men from the most distant tribes to listen to a fool who speaks not the words of the Great Spirit but those of the devil and British agents..."

Then Governor Harrison heard of the fateful Leopard-Chesapeak affair off the Virginia Capes. He did not publicize the matter but it made him very conscious of British aggression: six Americans had been killed, nineteen wounded, several others impressed into British service. Perhaps

Wells was more correct than anyone had supposed? What would happen if war between the United States and Britain were to break out? The frontiers, of which Indiana Territory was the first, would be ravaged! If the prophet was indeed a British tool... nothing could be more dangerous. The British would have to march their soldiers into Indiana but the savages were already there.

In his office Governor Harrison searched for Wells' letter of June, the same month as the Leopard-Chesapeake business, though no one in the West heard about it till much later. Something had to be done about communications. He should have been informed about the solar eclipse of a few years ago and he should have been told of the goings-on at sea! Ah, here it was... "The Indians have continued to flock to Greenville, which increases the fears of our frontiers... They are deaf to everything I say. The Prophet tells them the Great Spirit will in a few years destroy every white man in America..." When the Governor finished reading the letter he was thoroughly convinced Wells had been correct all along. The Prophet must be gotten out of Greenville at all costs. If military force was necessary, well and good. He and his people must be pushed north into Canada since they preferred the British to the Americans. If Kirker didn't do it he would be glad to lead his Indiana militia and do the job himself.

Harrison now began interpreting signs of British activity in the West. There was no paucity of signs but the most disturbing of all came when he learned Thomas McKee, the son of Colonel Alexander McKee, who had been killed by his pet deer during Fallen Timbers and whom the Indians loved so much, was a British agent like his father and visiting The Prophet in Greenville. When he also learned from a Chicago trader the Michigan tribes were planning an attack on the settlements and traders along the Mississippi he promptly warned the Indiana legislature that war could break out at any time.

The Chesapeake affair was enough to sting the legislators into immediate action but when the Governor spoke to them with oratory like, "We are peculiarly interested in the contest which is likely to ensue for who does not know that the tomahawk and scalping knife are always employed as instruments of British vengeance?" The militia was immediately called out for training and Harrison found himself in the multiple roles of Commander-in-Chief, Adjutant, and even drill corporal. He reported to the Secretary of War that military preparedness was disgracefully deficient. Although the militia were required by law to equip themselves Harrison felt they could not be depended upon to do so. He found cavalry without swords, light infantry without bayonets or cartridge boxes, and battalions armed with a combination of rifles, fowling pieces, broken muskets, even sticks! To a regular army man like Harrison this was truly shocking and he urged Secretary Dearborn to make deposits of arms at Vicennes and other points along the frontier.

Governor Harrison received another urgent communique from William Wells, suggesting the prophet and his brother should be imprisoned as quickly as possible, that American provisions should no longer be distributed to the Shawnee and other uncooperative tribes. Harrison valued his Indian Agent at Fort Wayne but arresting the Shawnee brothers might bring on a frontier war and if provisions were not given out the Indians would go to the British for aid. Indiana was not ready for war. He ordered Wells to feed the Indians from public stores so long as they were peaceful and he wrote another letter to be read to the tribes:

"My children: Listen to me, I speak in the name of your father, the great chief of the Seventeen Fires. My children, it is now more than a dozen years since the tomahawk, which you had raised by the advice of your father, the king of Britain, was buried at Greenville, in the presence of that great warrior, General Wayne.

"My children you then promised, and the Great Spirit heard it, that you would in future live in peace and friendship with your brothers, the Americans. You made a treaty with your father, and one that contained a number of good things, equally beneficial to all the tribes of red people.

"My children, you promised in that treaty to acknowledge no other father than the chief of the Seventeen Fires; and never to listen to the proposition of any foreign nation. You promised never to lift up the hatchet against any of your father's children and to give him notice of any other tribe that intended it. Your father also promised to do something for you, particularly to deliver to you, every year, a certain quantity of goods; to prevent any white man from settling on your lands without your consent, or to do you any personal injury. He promised to run a line between your land and his so that you might know your own, and you were to be permitted to live and hunt upon your father's land, as long as you behaved yourselves well.

"My children, which of these articles has your father broken? You know he had observed them all with the utmost good faith. But, my children, have you done so? Have you not always had your ears open to receive bad advice from the white people beyond the lakes?

360

"My children, let us look back to times that are past. It has been a long time since you called the king of Great Britain *father*. You know it is the duty of a father to watch over his children, to give them good advice, to do everything in his power to make them happy. What has this father of yours done for you, during the long time that you have looked up to him for protection and advice? Are you wiser and happier than you were before you knew him? Is your nation stronger or more respectable?

No, my children he took you by the hand when you were a powerful people. You held him fast, supposing he was your friend, and he conducted you through paths filled with thorns and briers which tore your flesh and shed your blood. Your strength was exhausted and you no longer follow him. Did he stay by you in your distress and assist and comfort you? No, he led you into danger then abandoned you! He saw your blood flowing and he wouldn't even give you a bandage to tie up your wounds. This was the conduct of the man who called himself your father.

"The Great Spirit opened your eyes. You heard the voice of the chief of the Seventeen Fires, speaking the words of peace. He called to you to follow him. You came to him and he once more put you on the right way, on the broad, smooth road that would have led to happiness. But the voice of your deceiver is again heard and forgetful of your former sufferings, you are again listening to him.

"My children, shut your ears and mind him not or he will lead you to final ruin and misery.

"My children, I have heard bad news. The sacred spot where the great council fire was kindled, around which the Seventeen Fires and ten tribes of their children smoked the pipe of peace--that very spot where the Great Spirit saw his red and white children encircle themselves with the bright chain of friendship--that place has been selected for dark and bloody councils.

"My children, this business must be stopped. You have called in a number of men from the most distant tribes, to listen to a fool, who speaks not the words of the Great Spirit but those of the devil and British agents.

"My children, your conduct has much alarmed the white settlers near you. They desire that you send away those people and if they wish to have the impostor with them they can carry him. Let him go to the lakes. There he can hear the British more distinctly.

"My children: HEED MY WORDS!"

The head chiefs were absent from Greenville when Harrison's message arrived but The Prophet heard it patiently then asked the interpreter to write his answer immediately for the Governor:

"Father, I am very sorry you listen to the advice of bad birds. You have impeached me with having correspondence with the British and with calling and sending for Indians from the most distant part of the country, 'to listen to a fool that speaks not the words of the Great Spirit but the words of the devil.'

"Father, those impeachments I deny and say they are not true. I never had a word with the British and I never sent for any Indians. They came here themselves to listen, and hear the words of the Great Spirit.

"Father, I wish you would not listen any more to the voice of bad birds. You may rest assured we have no idea of making disturbances, that we will rather try to stop any such proceedings than encourage them. The happiness of the Amerindians is the object of our labors. We want to lead more virtuous lives, retain our lands, and do what the Seventeen Fires say they want for their children, extend friendly union of all tribes. Others of your people have come to inspect our activities and have laid to rest their fears.

"Father, I wish you not to listen to bad birds anymore. If it is your desire I will come speak to you in person. Soon my people and I will leave this village in accordance with the wishes of the Seventeen Fires in order to prove our good faith."

Harrison read the message, judged it to be as cautious and artful as it was pacific. Perhaps a meeting with this Prophet would be worthwhile. That is, if war did not break out. He would continue to train the militia and store materiel, just in case.

Episode 10: The Partisans

Tecumseh and The Prophet made their way overland to the tract on the west bank of the Tippecanoe River where Prophet's Town was built. The area extended to the confluence with the Wabash River and the spa-

362

cious bottom lands could have produced enough corn to feed all the tribes of the Northwest. Eighty followers and their families went with the Shawnee brothers and all set about building wegiwas and finally a huge mission building. When the work was accomplished pilgrims began arriving to hear The Prophet speak. Extreme poverty was endured and would be rampant until crops could be planted and harvested but no one complained. The work was reward enough.

A delegation of Miamis and Delawares arrived at Prophet's Town but their motives were not conversion or alliance. Tecumseh met the group and extended a cordial invitation to all. "I shall call The Prophet from his wegiwa."

"Our message is for all of you, not just The Prophet," said Peketelemund, third in command of the Delaware nation. His stony countenance and cold manner had already informed Tecumseh the meeting would be a confrontation. There were some warriors in the delegation but no one of extraordinary distinction.

"We wish to know," said Reynt, a Miami leader, "by whose authority you have taken possession of this land."

"By the authority of the Great Spirit, my brother," said The Prophet as he approached the group. Other residents began gathering but the delegation did not flinch. They were heavily armed.

"The Great Spirit gave these Wasbash lands," said Peketelemund, "to the Miami and Delaware."

"The Kickapoo and Potawatomi gave us permission to settle here, brother," said The Prophet. "You are welcome to live here also if you wish."

"This land belongs to us," said Reynt, "and we do not countenance your possession of it."

"Brothers," said Tecumseh, "the last village on this spot was inhabited by Shawnee, until a Shemanese expedition from Kentucky destroyed it. We are not an enemy. Kinsmen we are. The Ruler of Destinies has brought us here. Take our hand in friendship. We were told to leave Greenville though we had done no harm to anyone. In order to keep the peace and to be outside the treaty line, we moved here voluntarily. We might need your help to survive. Someday you might have cause for us to reciprocate." Tecumseh reflected quickly and asked, "Who is your agent?"

"Captain Wells," replied Pimoacan.

Tecumseh wrinkled his forehead. "This land belongs to all of us," he said, "not one tribe in particular. In truth, it does not belong to the Potawatomi or Kickapoo. Neither does it give exclusive rights to the

Delaware or Miami. Any Amerindian may live wherever he wishes so long as someone is not living there already and working the land. All tribes own all the land on this great island."

"We can fight to protect our interests," said Peketelemund.

"Grandfather, I am Tecumseh. If I must walk the warpath I do not wish it to be against my brothers. I have made a vow never to spill Amerindian blood because I recognize it as my own. But I am not a fool. Fire upon me without provocation, you or anyone of your people, and I shall defend myself as a warrior. You are welcome here as friends. All of us own all lands in common. We will not depart." He turned on his heels and walked away in perfect tranquility.

The Prophet talked to the delegation and wound up asking the visitors to share in what little food was available. It was obvious to the Miami and Delaware that wretched poverty would probably destroy Prophet's Town before anything else. The delegates returned to their villages, impressed with Tecumseh's courage and The Prophet's religiosity. Some individuals vowed to send provisions when they could.

Tecumseh realized he must soon start mustering the tribes to the idea of a giant confederacy in which every tribe on the North American continent would have representatives. He was not certain as to who would be most difficult, the Shemanese or his far flung kinsmen. The Amerindians must be made to comprehend that without union they were a lost race. The People of the Eagle would gobble up the land and crush piecemeal resistance. He would soon be forty summers old, going into the prime of his life, a life full of experience, on and off the warpath. No one could deny he was a charismatic leader. Many knew him as a man or warmth and charm, with soft hazel eyes and flashing white teeth. He was a delight to converse with. As an orator he had few peers. But he could also listen for he had been educated by the most accomplished and intelligent Grandfathers as well as varied personalities like Methoataske, Cheeseekau, Blackfish, Cornstalk, Daniel Boone, Stephen Ruddell, and so many others.

Tecumseh felt confident as fighter or orator. Now he had to prove himself a statesmen if he was to achieve his grand dream of confederacy. That is why he had ordered the abandonment of the Greenville mission, though it had been so laboriously built by The Prophet and his followers. But it had to be let go for the mission was too close to Shemanese settlements. Nothing could take place at Greenville that was not reported by informers, usually exaggerated alarms, to Governor Harrison of Indiana Territory. Tecumseh did not really understand why Harrison was so worried about his countrymen when other leaders like Governor

Kirker of Ohio demonstrated little more than passing concern. Perhaps Harrison was "ambitious." The Shemanese liked that word. So many wanted "opportunity." Perhaps a war forced on the Indians is what Harrison wanted. But what would he gain from it? The land, of course. And after that? Tecumseh was not sure. Loss of life was no simple matter for a warchief to live down but then the Shemanese were different. There were so many of them that human life was of little concern, a concept of "civilization" which he found quite distasteful.

Prophet's Town was vastly superior to Greenville. Game had not been exhausted by so-called civilization. Cornlands were available in abundance. The many pilgrims coming to listen to The Prophet had to be fed. Incantations would not replace meat and bread.

Tecumseh decided to make a speaking tour of the Mississinewa towns in hopes of attracting converts and allies so he left Prophet's Town a few days after the irate delegation had spoken its piece.

A week later the village received another unfriendly visit. This time it was led by Captain William Wells himself and included a trader named John Conner and a half dozen heavily armed Indian warriors. The Prophet welcomed them though he knew they did not come looking for religion.

"We have been informed some stolen horses might be wandering around this area," said Wells. "Governor Harrison has sent us to reconnoiter." He looked around clandestinely. "Do you mind if we inspect the horse compound?"

"Of course not," said The Prophet.

At the enclosure John Conner spoke for the first time: "That piebald over there is one of the stolen animals. So is the black with the white stocking."

"We will have to take those horses," said Captain Wells.

The Prophet shrugged his shoulders and Wells took it as acceptance so he ordered the Indians to go in and get the horses. When they were roped Tall Bear and Bo-nah reacted to the taking of the animals for they owned them.

"We have had those animals for a long time," said Bo-nah, warrior and follower of Tecumseh. "You will not take my property."

The Prophet raised his hand in peace and said in Shawnee, "The animal will be replaced. There will be no fighting in this village." Secretly he was glad Tecumseh was absent for his older brother detested William Wells. Tall Bear uttered no dissent for he was a follower of The Prophet.

"Take the animals and go in peace, brothers," said The Prophet.

365

John Conner, a confidant of Governor Harrison and most observant man, noted The Prophet had about forty Shawnee followers in the village, and perhaps fewer than a hundred from other tribes. Certainly these scant numbers offered no threat to Harrison or the People of the Eagle. Indeed, the Miami and Delaware could come in and wipe out the village any day they wished. He could not understand what prevented the two tribes from running off the motley crowd immediately.

The horses were taken without incident, though Bo-nah's stare after Wells and Conner as they left the village, horses in tow, was a portent of furture strife.

Tecumseh returned from the Mississinewa towns with a new follower, a man named Billy Caldwell. He had been fathered by William Caldwell of a Shawnee woman. Called "Straight Tree" in his youth because of his strong, sinewy, erect physique, in manhood he was called *Sauganash,* "The Britisher," though his father was Irish. Billy Caldwell had the deepest respect and admiration for Tecumseh, whom he regarded an extraordinary warrior and leader. His estimate was no doubt formed from his own military experience and close observation of British and American fighting men, including officers, in the western armies.

The chief was not informed of the Captain Wells' visit by order of The Prophet. Tecumseh had returned with a new idea: he wanted a group of partisans, hard core followers to travel with him. Some of the people could be unfriendly and if there was difficulty there had to be enough men with him for a proper defense. Billy Caldwell had given him the idea and volunteered to be his first recruit, following him to the ends of the earth if need be. Tecumseh sent a rider for Wasegoboah, Tecumapease's husband, asking him to join the group, which he did.

The Prophet was the fourth man and together with a few attendants the entourage, mounted on ponies, travelled as warrior knights across the central plains, hunting the deer and buffalo, gathering berries, grapes, plums, and pawpaws. Tecumseh made certain to invite Spybuck to serve as doctor for the group, remembering the broken leg he had suffered years ago. Spybuck had not been enthusiastic about going, not wishing to be separated from his Flaming Eagle of Delight but he could never refuse Tecumseh anything.

They made their way across northern Indiana and came to the Potawatomi village along the upper Illinois River where the elderly Topinabee was chief. The delegation was received with the greatest amity for it was festival time and the visitors were invited to participate.

Topinabee was a great admirer of Tecumseh. "Come," he said to the younger chief, "let us go watch the wrestling contests. Perhaps you would like to wrestle one of our champions."

366

"I came not prepared to compete," admitted Tecumseh. He wanted to talk, not wrestle. But he went with Topinabee to where a great crowd encircled two wrestlers, one of which was physically as fine a specimen a man as Tecumseh had ever seen. His shoulders were huge, his arms bulged as he put a bear hug on his opponent, paralyzing him just long enough to lift him off his feet and throw him to the ground for another victory.

"That is our tribal champion," said Topinabee amid the noise. There was a little smile on his face, a glint of mischief in his eyes. "I have heard you are a champion also."

"Father," said Tecumseh, "if your champion can wrestle as strong as he looks I would not have a chance." But the Shawnee realized if he wrestled and gave a good accounting of himself it would do much to attract attention to his mission. "I will wrestle, if it pleases you, father."

"Brothers and sisters," said the elderly Topinabee to the crowd, "we have among us another challenger, the Shawnee chieftain Tecumseh! Give him room to prepare!"

There was much hooting and hollering to welcome the new challenger as Teucmseh stripped to the waist and limbered up. His opponent was ready so he eyed Tecumseh steadily. The Shawnee looked up and was impressed with his antagonist's face for its lack of viciousness. It showed more great strength of character and goodness of heart than the killer instinct. Teucmseh sized him up quickly: tall, straight as an arrow, immensely powerful, stronger than himself so he would have to move quickly. He hoped the man was tired from previous exertions because speed would be his only salvation. "I am ready," said Tecumseh.

"Let the contest begin," said Topinabee.

His antagonist began to circle cautiously so Tecumseh immediately feinted to his left and threw himself to the other side with the speed of lightning, managing to encircle the muscle man's waist and lift him off his feet. But the antagonist was able to clamp an arm around Tecumseh's throat and both fell heavily to the ground, Tecumseh on top.

"Release and begin anew," said a self-styled referee, "no fall."

The two heeded the bidding, got back on their feet quickly. Each now knew what to expect. Tecumseh had hoped for a quick fall but it would be difficult now that the element of surprise was lost. They locked arms, the antagonist surprised at how immensely strong was his opponent. Tecumseh slipped an arm but somehow found himself off balance so his antagonist lifted him off his feet and flung him to the ground. With panther-like agility Tecumseh turned a great sommersault in the air and landed on his feet. Immediately he attacked once more, throwing him-

367

self at his antagonist. Once more the powerful arms were around him, this time in a bear hug which would momentarily crush his upper ribs but Tecumseh exhaled every bit of air in his lungs, slipped down at precisely the right moment, then slipped his arm under the man's crotch, grabbed his leather pants from the waist and pulled up with every bit of strength at his command. The antagonist hit the ground back first.

"Fall!" said the Amerindian who was obviously enjoying his role as arbiter.

"Two out of three, two out of three!" began to chant several spectators as Tecumseh went to his antagonist and pulled him to his feet.

"Brother," said the chief, "I was lucky and I admit it. There will be no more wrestling for me this day." He was sweating copiously, as was the other man. He took Tecumseh's right wrist and raised it up high. Tecumseh did the same with his opponent's free wrist and the crowd thundered its approval.

"Come, my sons," said Topinabee, great pleasure expressing itself on his face, "let us get you cleaned up so you may enjoy the festival. Chief Tecumseh, I want you to meet my son-in-law, Shabbona."

"Your crafty father-in-law did not inform me who I was wrestling," said Tecumseh as he shook hands.

"It would have made no difference," said Shabbona agreeably. "You move like the panther."

"I would not want to wrestle you when you are fresh," admitted Tecumseh.

The men went to the river to bathe and Topinabee saw to it that fresh clothes were brought to them after which they enjoyed the festival. That night around the fire Tecumseh rose to speak:

"My brothers, I am most fortunate to be here sharing this wonderful festival with you. The Potawatomi and the Shawnee have always enjoyed the bright chain of friendship. The road between this place and our nation has always been open and clear. I am here to keep it free of all obstacles and incumbrances.

"Brothers, it is good that I, and you, should do so, for all we citizens of this great island have much in common. We Amerindians live in the open, responsive to sun, wind, rain, snow, all the elements. We know our lands, our country: every marsh, glade, hilltop, rock, spring, creek, as only hunters can know them. We love our land. We are as much a part of it as the rocks and trees, animals and birds. Our homeland is holy ground, sanctified by the bones of our ancestors. It is the shrine of our religion. Our waterfalls, clouds, mists, our ridges, glens, meadows, all hold spirits of their own which help us in our endeavors. This land, be it forest and lake or prairie and grass, is our very soul.

"Brothers of the Potawatomi, our land is in great danger. The People of the Eagle are taking it away from us in treaty after treaty. WE MUST STOP SELLING THE BONES OF OUR ANCESTORS! Next we will be asked to sell the air which surrounds us! This is my message and mission this evening. We must not sell any more land! I call upon you to carry this message to all the nations of our people wherever found. We are one people for the Great Spirit formed us all and bequeathed this beautiful land to us. No one has the power to sell without the consent of all. If this is allowed to continue soon there will be no ground on which to spread our blankets!

"Brothers, I love our people for they always make me welcome with the best they have. We are people who are honest without written laws or people paid to enforce them. In our lands there are no jails or poor houses. We need no Great Book with which to worship. You can not but love a people who do not steal from each other, who never raise a hand against you when there is no law to punish either."

"Brothers, we must preserve our way of life. The Grandfathers of old, founders of our society, whisper this to us from the Spirit Land. The voices of my ancestors cry out to me in a voice of love. Give ear, my people, for there is no evil in my heart. My song is the song of peace. We have thrown away all our war songs. I invite any of you who wish it to join me to carry this message to all of our nations."

Tecumseh finished speaking and Chief Topinabee asked, "What if we are attacked? Are we to turn the other cheek?"

"By no means," replied the Shawnee. "Once we form the confederacy to attack one is to attack all. It will be a gigantic deterrent for any enemy. I am a warrior. Send me a message for help and I will come like a squirrel running over a smooth log. So will my men. Do I have your promise if you hear *my* call?"

"YES!!" chorused what must have been every male voice in the large assembly. The Potawatomi thus became the first members of the Amerindian League.

The following day Shabbona sought out Tecumseh and said, "My chieftain, it is my wish to ride at your side in this good work. Your heart is good. You speak sincerely. If I may be of service I will never be more than an arrow's flight away."

"My brother," said Tecumseh as he took Shabbona's hand, "of all the many fine warriors here you would have been my first choice to accompany me. It is with an open heart that we receive your hands. Friendship stretches ours to yours and unites them together. Welcome to our brotherhood, my Partisan."

So it was that Shabbona joined Tecumseh's warrior knights and set out in quest of Amerindian union. He bought himself a splendid mount, paid his respects to his chief and father-in-law, bid farewell to his tearful wife and took his place by Tecumseh's side.

As the growing brotherhood rode toward the Wisconsin country to confer with the Sauk and Fox, Tecumseh grew to like Shabbona. It turned out he was not a Potawatomi at all but Ottawa like the great Pontiac. His father had been a nephew of the great leader, fighting in his war for independence from British tyranny. Shabbona proved himself to be a generous, hositable, compassionate man of frank words and inflexible integrity. Like Tecumseh, he was temperate in eating and never drank firewater. He was thirty-two summers old and probably the strongest, speaking physically, member of the Brotherhood. (But then Tecumseh had beaten Shabbona in wrestling. No one knew exactly how strong the leader was.)

The first stop was at the Sauk and Fox village where White Cedar was chief. The Prophet asked the chief to gather the chiefs and headmen that he might speak to them before Tecumseh addressed everyone. White Cedar did as requested but there was something intransigent about the chief. When The Prophet addressed the group he told them of his dreams and trances in which he conversed with the Great Spirit. He told them of miraculous occurences and emphasized that medicine bundles were merely signs of superstition which had no power at all.

Chief White Cedar stood and marched up to The Prophet saying, "You wish to impose your thoughts and beliefs on us. Our medicine bundles have not lost their virtue. In our time of need we apply to them, generally with success. Nothing is successful in all cases, except perhaps you, but our bundles are in most instances."

"WHAT IMPUDENCE IS THIS?" thundered The Prophet. "Certainly you are familiar with basic manners of protocol. HAVE YOUR SAY, BUT WAIT TILL I AM FINISHED or do not let me speak at all until you are done!"

"I will not stand by and be insulted!" returned White Cedar. "If that is your intent you are not welcome here. My warriors-"

Tecumseh stepped up to the two men and put a hand on White Cedar's shoulder. "Brother," he said, "we are not here to cause trouble. Neither will we tolerate any. Sit down and let The Prophet finish or risk the wrath of my men."

"DO NOT TOUCH ME!" yelled White Cedar at Tecumseh, who removed his hand and let it rest on the warclub that dangled at his side. "Have your say but realize I will not be insulted," he said to The Prophet and returned to his seat. Tecumseh also returned to his place and things resumed normally.

"Brothers," said The Prophet, "it is not my mission to insult. I speak with an open heart. All I have said I have proven before. I am not the Ruler of Destinies who can perform miracles whenever He wishes. I am merely his disciple instructed to bring truth to our people." He was visibly angry so he terminated his talk at that point.

Tecumseh stood up, visibly annoyed by White Cedar's outburst. "Brothers of the Sauk and Fox, you do not need me to explain what a refugee is. You have recently lost most of your tribal lands to the machinations of the Longknives. They took even your capital Saukenauk! Soon they will come and take this one. If you want to avoid that we offer you membership in a grand Amerindian League of our people. Do you think your medicine bundles will protect your land? If that is your belief then do not bother to unite with your brothers. Did your bundles protect your vast lands now in illegal possession of the Shemanese? OF COURSE NOT! Do not be foolish any longer. Do not listen to evil reports and the whistling of bad birds. You say you will defend your remaining pittance of land? If you are to fight you are too few. If you are to die you are too many. JOIN WITH US IN DEFENSE OF AMERINDIAN LAND EVERYWHERE! That is our only salvation. You lose nothing by joining the Confederacy. If you send out a call I will come with my men. If I call you will send yours. Weigh and consider what I say. No one knows better than you and I what it is never to leave your moccasin prints on the ground of your native village. The place where I was born is now overrun with Shemanese. It is the same with Saukenuk. Join with us for the common good. I have spoken."

Due to the affront by White Cedar Tecumseh refused to speak again except informally to those who gathered round him the next day. One of those was the staunch warrior Black Hawk, implacable foe of the Longknives. He took Tecumseh aside, told him how many warriors had no confidence in the national chief appointed by the Longknives, Keokuck, because he would do whatever they ordered.

"That is one of our basic dilemmas," asserted Tecumseh. "It is that kind of chief who sells away our lands. And he does it without tribal consent. Those men must be gotten rid of."

"What do you mean?" asked Black Hawk.

"Power must be plucked from their hands like feathers from a bird's wing. It is the duty of the people for it is their children who will suffer the greatest loss, never having known what is to be an Amerindian proud and free."

"You can count on me and my warrior followers," said Black Hawk. "Only through confederacy can we cope with invasion."

"True," said Tecumseh. "Our immediate goal is to end the shower of treaties which pluck away our best lands. Talk to your men. Have them spread the message that no further land can be sold without everyone's consent. Ride with us, brother, and welcome."

"If I leave Keokuck will sell the rest of our lands," said Black Hawk. "I must remain to form the opposition to appeasement. But when you call, that day my warriors and I will ride to join my brothers."

"Then we shall consider you one of the Partisans," said an elated Tecumseh as he shook Black Hawk's hand. "Welcome to the Brotherhood."

The group moved north across the land to Green Bay where they visited the Winnebago and Menominee of northern Wisconsin. Both tribes joined the League. The head chief and sub-chief of the Winnebago, Naw Kaw and Four Legs, became travelling members of the Partisans.

At Green Bay the elderly Menominee chief Tomah held a big council and Tecumseh was introduced as a representative from the tribes to the southeast, an emissary with an important message. Tecumseh reviewed the major incidents of his life, emphasizing how the Shemanese had been a major force in the more tragic incidents concerning his father Puckeshinwa, Cornstalk, Black Fish, and Cheeseekau, the famous Shawnee Warrior. Then he reviewed how some of the Amerindian people were taking the clouds from their eyes and joining the Confederacy to prevent future tragedies. He declared that only through union could their lives and lands be preserved.

The younger warriors heard him with excitement rising in their hearts. "We shall destroy the Longknives!" yelled one muscular warrior as he lifted a tomahawk over his head.

Chief Tomah stood up and lifted both arms. "My children, these hands are unstained by human blood!"

"I do not advocate war, father," said Tecumseh to the old chieftain, "unless we are attacked. We desire strength through unity. Then we will not be attacked."

"I will personally enter into no war," said Tomah, "but I do recognize the encroachments of the Longknives as totally illegal. Each person here is free to follow this noble Shawnee chieftain if you so desire." The people were ready for Tecumseh's call.

Tecumseh now went in a southwesterly direction across Wisconsin, visiting villages at every opportunity. He came to the Mississippi River at La Crosse then moved down the east bank to Rock Island in the Illinois country. He journeyed to lands of the Kickapoo where a grand council was held under a giant oak tree and the tribe pledged its undying allegiance to the Shawnee leader in his efforts to check further encroachment into Amerindian lands.

The tour had thus far been a resounding success. The first real snag was enountered in the Mississinewa towns of the Miami. Little Turtle, father-in-law of William Wells, still exercised a negative influence on his people as far as confederacy was concerned.

So the Partisans moved on to what was left of the Ottawa nation. Though just a remnant of their former numbers, they responded positively to Tecumseh, pledging their allegiance. In fact, two hundred warriors left their villages and trudged their way from the lower Maumee Valley to live in Prophet's Town, women and children included. This was proof of Tecumseh's leadership qualities for before he was forty years old the Ottawa tribe, where the Shawnee was little more than a stranger, looked to him as its head chief, Ottawa chieftains voluntarily subordinating themselves to him and his goals.

Tecumseh now turned his attention to the Wyandot nation. A great council was called to meet at Lower Sandusky. The Wyandot were a branch of the Iroquois family and numbered about 4,000 people living in northwestern Ohio, southwestern Ontario, and the Detroit area. Unknown to Tecumseh, the Crane, venerable chief of the Wyandot and one of the first to sign the Treaty of Greenville, was unremitting in his efforts to denigrate ideas of joining any league. When Tecumseh rose to speak from the midst of his entourage, which by now was dressed in gorgeous costumes of the nations they represented, he did not burden them with a recounting of Shemanese encroachments. They were as fully knowledgeable as he "...so I will not waste your time and mine. My intent is to extend our league of confederacy to your numerous people. This invitation holds for you and your Seneca kinsmen. Let us concentrate our power and interests at Tippecanoe. There is much game to live as we are accustomed. Corn lands are rich and abundant. Prophet's Town is remote from Shemanese settlements while now your vilages are becoming roads for the People of the Eagle, especially along the southern shore of Lake Erie." He explained why the League was necessary and many nodded their enthusiastic agreement.

The conciliatory, aged Crane rose to speak: "My children, let us not react to haste or adventure. Time will let us know if Tecumseh and his followers at Tippecanoe are intent on good purpose at their headquarters. Let us wait a few summers to ascertain our brothers at Prophet's

373

Town are happy living away from their ancestral homes. There is always ample time to move toward the setting sun.''

But the majority of the Wyandot tribe aligned itself with Tecumseh and his goals. It was a sad defeat for the Crane that a Shawnee could come into council and sway away the more spirited members of the nation. *At least,* he thought later in his cabin, *the people did not pick up and migrate to Prophet's Town as the Ottawa did. But they would heed Tecumseh's call when he summoned.* He would have to inform the agent, William Wells.

Tecumseh now decided to give his Partisans a rest by encouraging them to spend time in their respective vilages. All had been gone a long while. He was elated over his success but he too needed rest... before he made a trip to the south country to gauge the temper of the southern nations. He would give everyone time to rest. And he wanted to see Rebecca in order to ask her a very important question.

Chapter 7

Governor Harrison was looking forward to meeting with The Prophet tomorrow but today he was addressing the Indiana legislature: "...We do not wish to wage an eternal war with the numerous and warlike tribes of aborigines that surround us, and perhaps forced to the dreadful alternative of exterminating them from the earth.

"By cutting off their communication with every foreign power, and forcing them to procure from ourselves the arms and ammunition and such of the European manufacturers as habit has to them rendered necessary, we have not only secured their entire dependence, but the means of ameliorating their condition, and of devoting to some useful and beneficial purpose the ardor and energy of mind which are now devoted to war and destruction. The policy of the United States with regard to the savages within their territories forms a striking contrast with the conduct of other civilized nations. The measures of the latter appear to have been well calculated for the effect which has produced the entire extirpation of the unhappy people whose country they have usurped. It is in the United States alone that safety and protection from every species of injury, and considerable sums of money have been appropriated, and agents employed to humanize their minds and instruct them in such arts of civilized life as they are capable of receiving.

"To provide a substitute for the chase, from which they derive their support, and which from the extension of our settlements is daily becoming more precarious, has been considered a sacred duty. The humane

375

and benevolent intentions of the government, however, will forever be defeated, unless effectual measures be devised to prevent the sale of ardent spirits to those unfortunate people. The law which has been passed by Congress for that purpose has been found entirely ineffectual, because its operation has been construed to relate to the Indian country exclusively. In calling your atterntion to this subject, gentlemen, I am persuaded that it is unnecessary to remind you that the article of compact makes it your duty to attend to it. The interest of your constitutents, the interest of the miserable Indians, and your own feelings, will urge you to take it into your most serious consideration and provide the remedy which is to save thousands of our fellow creatures. So destructive has been the progress of intemperance, that whole villages have been swept away. A miserable remnant is all that remains to mark the names and situation of many numerous and warlike tribes.

"In the energetic language of one of their orators, it is a dreadful conflagration which spreads misery and desolation through their country, and threatens the annihilation of the whole race. Is it then to be admitted as a political axiom that the neighborhood of a civilized nation is incompatible with the existence of savages? Are the blessings of our republican government only to be felt by ourselves? And are the natives of north America to experience the same fate with their brethren of the southern continent? It is with you, gentlemen, to divert from these children of nature the fate that hangs over them. Nor can I consider that the time will be considered misspent, which is devoted to an object which is so consistent with the spirit of christianity, and with the principles of republicanism..."

In other matters addressed that day by the Governor was a bill for supplies with which to fete delegations of Indians. When Harrison was done speaking several individuals congratulated him for his humanity but expressed concern that supplies for aborigines were rather expensive. "I never knew an Indian that was not more grateful for having his belly filled than for any other service," responded the Governor and the matter was dispensed with.

The following day The Prophet came into Vincennes with forty of his disciples. Harrison was summoned immediatley and the two leaders finally met face to face while food was brought out for the Amerindians.

"I have been most anxious to confer with you, sir," said Governor Harrison as the two sat at a table under the shade of a tall maple. I have heard many disturbing reports concerning you and your activities. Today we can discuss them." The interpreter put them into Shawnee and Billy Caldwell was at The Prophet's side to assure veracity.

"Father, I too have heard many rumors but I give them little credence. Tell me what you have heard and I will speak from the heart."

"Perhaps the worst chirping is that you are under the influence of the British, that you are a British tool used for stirring up strife among the Indian nations. What have you to say about this charge?"

"Father, the message I bear is from the Master of Life, not the British," said The Prophet with characteristic plausibility. "My brethren need guidance from the Creator in order to reclaim them from the degrading vices to which they have been addicted. My mission is to cultivate in them a spirit of peace and friendship, not only with the Longknives but with our many nations as well."

"How could such a rumor have gotten started?" asked the Governor.

"Father, that I do not know. If I was doing the British work, doing their bidding, would I not be espousing the beliefs of their religion? Our religion is ours, not of the British. The Great Spirit has called me to this sacred work and I have dedicated my life to it. Look at me, do you see a rich man before you? Scrutinize my followers. They could not be described even as well fed. It is unfortunate we do not have enough provisions for ourselves but we share what we have with the many pilgrims who come visit. They come to listen and hear the word. They return richer in spirit than before."

"How long have you been communicating with the Great Spirit?"

"Father, it is a few years since I began the system of religion which we now practice. The Longknives and some of the Amerindians were against me at times but I had no other intention but to introduce among us those good principles of religion which your people profess. I was reproached by some. Brother, even you called me a fool."

"I must recant that hasty word," said Governor Harrison. "Bad birds were flying everywhere at that time."

"I defy anyone to say I have lead the people astray. Talk to my people over there and learn for yourself of their motives."

"What of all these miracles attributed to you?" asked Harrison.

"Father, you too are a leader of people," said The Prophet in a more confidential tone. "You realize as well as anyone how much showmanship goes into statesmanship. Have there not been times when you allowed your people to think what they wanted in order to better them? I am an instrument of the Master of Life because I bring people to him. I too am merely mortal but my work can be described as miraculous if it brings people to the happiness which your prayer chiefs call 'God.' "

It was apparent to Harrison this prophet, self-styled or otherwise, was a man of decided talents, of great tact, admirably qualified to play successfully the role he had assumed.

"Father, I was told you intended to hang me if I came into Vincennes!"

"What?" exclaimed the Governor. "That's preposterous! Have I hung you or any of your people? Do you see any of my soldiers?"

"When I heard the evil bird chirping I remembered it only so I could repeat it when I came to see my father and relate to him the truth. I was also told, when I settled on the Wabash, that the People of the Eagle had declared all land between Vincennes and Fort Wayne to be property of the Seventeen Fires. I also heard, my father, that you wanted to know whether I was God or man and that if I was God I should not steal horses. I heard this from Captain Wells."

"I have never uttered such a thing," said Harrison. "Perhaps it originated with himself." The Governor suddenly found himself on the defensive. "I know you are a very talented man, not a god. But tell me about your system."

"The Great Spirit told me to tell the Indians that He had made them and made their world for them, that He had placed them in it to do good, not evil. I told them the way they were living was not good, that they ought to abandon it. My message was that we ought to consider ourselves as one man, though living agreeably to our several customs, the Indians after their mode, the Longknives after theirs. In particular the Amerindians should not drink whiskey for it was not made for them. The white people alone knew how to use it properly and that is the cause of all mischief which the Indians must suffer in the end. The tribes must always follow the directions of the Great Spirit as it was She who made us—"

"*She?*" exclaimed Harrison in sudden surprise.

"Yes, father, the Great Spirit is a female force."

"But how can one know that?" asked the incredulous Governor.

"Is it not the female that causes life to spring forth?"

"But the male must... take part."

"Yes, that is the Sun, our father."

"I see," acknowledged Harrison. The conversation continued well into the afternoon when the Governor invited The Prophet to sup with him.

"Thank you, my father, but I must see to my people and conduct their prayers as is our custom."

"As you wish," said Harrison. "Tomorrow perhaps I and my friends can converse with your men in order to get to know them?"

"Of course," replied The Prophet. "I shall speak to them as I always do. Invite your interpreter to come listen so he may translate for your people."

378

The following day Harrison and several Longknives began discussing various topics with The Prophet's men. After getting to know them fairly well in succeeding days the whites commenced to drinking, inviting the Indians to partake. For some unexplained reason the water casks were completly empty, liquour being the only available liquid. But the Indians would not touch a drop under any circumstance.

Harrison marveled at The Prophet's control of his people. He would listen to the holy man's harangue and wished such power could be turned to advantage in ameliorating the condition of the Indians, which had long engaged his own attention. He decided the cause of humanity would be benefited by sustaining rather than trying to weaken the influence of the preacher.

At the end of the two week visit The Prophet assured Harrison: "Father, we are determined to listen to nothing that is bad. We will not take up the tomahawk should it be offered by the British or the Long-knives. We wish to mind our own business, cultivate our land that our women and children will have enough to sustain them.

"My father, I have informed you what we mean to do and I call the Great Spirit to witness the truth of my declaration. The religion which I have established these last years has been attended to by the different tribes of Indians in this part of the world. Those Amerindians were once different people. They are now but one. They are all determined to prac-tice what I have communicated to them, which has come immediatley from the Great Spirit through me.

"Brother, I now speak to you as a warrior. You are one and we know it. Let us lay aside this character and attend to the care of our children, that they may live in comfort and peace. We desire that you join us for the preservation of both red and white people. Years past, when we lived in ignorance, we were foolish. But now we listen to the voice of the Great Spirit and we are happy.

"I have listened to what you have said. You have promised to assist us. I now request you, in behalf of all Amerindians, to use your exertions to prevent the sale of liquor to us. We are all well pleased to hear you say you will endeavor to promote our happiness. We give you every assurance that we will follow the dicatates of the Master of Life.

"We are all well pleased with the attention you have showed us and the good intentions of our father, the President. If you give us a few articles, such as needles, flints, hoes, powder and the like, we will take the animals that afford us meat, with powder and ball."

The Amerindians returned to Tippecanoe with a handsome supply of provisions.

Episode 2: Indiana treaty.

Governor Harrison confided a long-contemplated project to William Eustis, Secretary of War under new President James Madison, successor to Jefferson. The Governor pointed out how the Indian boundary was just twenty-one miles north of Vincennes. Below it the land was sunken and wet while to the west the country was mostly prairie "...and not of such quality as to be settled for many years." However, if tracts above Vincennes could be acquired further growth would be assured and the Territory would advance toward statehood. Would Washington give him authority to negotiate a treaty with the Indian tribes living on the desired lands? It would also be a good move militarily. At high water Indain canoes from Prophet's Town could descend the Wabash faster than a man could ride on horseback.

President Madison mulled over the idea for six weeks and decided to authorize the cessions, advising Harrison to "...take advantage of the most favorable moment..." and to restrict payment to "... the rate heretofore given."

Harrison immediately informed the Fort Wayne Indian agent, John Johnston, successor to William Wells who had been removed from that post. Runners were sent in all directions to summon chiefs and sachems to the grand council while the Governor got men and supplies together. He received a letter from Secretary of War Eustis which echoed in part what Captain Wells had suggested a year or two ago:

"It has indeed occured to me that the surest means of securing
the good behavior from this conspicuous personage and his
brother, would be to make them prisoners, but at this time
more particularly, it is desireable, that peace with all the
Indian tribes should be preserved, and I am instructed by the
President to express to your excellency his expectations and
confidence that in all your arrangements, this may be considered a primary object with you...

The Governor arrived at Fort Wayne on September 15, greeting Agent Johnston and the commanding officer cordially, asking immediately if all preparations were accomplished without mishap.

"Yessir," replied Johnston, "the Indians are beginning to come in."

Within a few days Chief Winamac arrived with his delegation of Potawatomi, Peccon, the Miami chieftain, came along with The Owl, Silver Heels, and Osage. Blackhoof, grand chief of the Shawnee, arrived next, then Charley of the Eel River Miami, and several Delaware. Harrison was not satisfied so he sent out more runners to invite other

380

chiefs, headmen, and warriors. He sent out a special runner to invite once more the great Little Turtle. The messenger returned saying the gout-ridden Little Turtle was on his way but could not move faster due to ill-health.

Harrison whiled away the time by visiting each of the Indian encampments, approaching them informally on what he wanted to accomplish with the treaty. A friendly Mohican chief informed Harrison that British agents at Malden had warned the tribesmen never to entertain another proposition to sell their lands. The Governor also learned many other bits of information: Five Medals, a Potawatomie, refused to attend when he learned the Indians were going to be asked to sell land for the benefit of Harrison and his friends. He was given the names of chiefs who were at Fort Amherstburg receiving British bounty. But he also learned the Delaware and Potawatomi were in favor of the land cession. The Miami contingents, which included William Wells, vowed not to sell a pinch of ground. At every encampment there were Indians asking for whiskey and such was their insistence Harrison relented by issuing two quarts per contingent.

The Governor had begun with good intentions, ordering the whiskey casks be locked up safely inside the fort. He was intent on getting things done and had thought to use firewater as a reward for speedy conclusion of the treaty rather than endeavoring to inspire good will in advance. He didn't prefer the whiskey in any way for he had seen that if used beforehand the Indians grew befuddled, if held back they paid little attention to details. Perhaps he could pursue a middle of the road policy.

The council fire was lit on September 22. The nations represented were the Delaware, Miami, Potawatomi, and Eel River Miami. Black Hoof represented the Ohio Shawnee. The Wea and the Kickapoo residents on the land which Harrison wanted ceded, were not present. All realized the most influential voice in this part of the world was The Prophet and behind him stood the commanding figure of his brother, Tecumseh. The Amerindians were aware of an ominous scepter hanging over the council. *What would Tecumseh do if in his absence and with no Shawnee, Wea, or Kickapoo present, the chiefs sold away the Wabash lands?*

William Wells, Joseph Barron, John Conner, and Abraham Ash were sworn in as official interpreters. A company of Regulars leaned on their rifles and watched the proceedings as Governor Harrison rose to speak:

"My brothers, listen to me. I speak to you about matters of importance, both to yourselves and the white people. Open your ears and attend to what I shall say.

"The Seventeen Fires are crowding with people, a strong hardy people who plant the land in order to live with security. It is the ideal way to live for it gives us surplus of life's necessities. We wish to share these ways with you, as your former father Thomas Jefferson advised many years ago. You have received annuities from the People of the Eagle. They have improved your life and made it more secure.

"Brothers, game has much diminished north of Vincennes. Even if there was a super-abundance of animals the price of pelts has greatly decreased due to embargoes among the warring powers in Europe. No one can deny your women and children suffer hunger and privation. This is not due to encroachment so much as it is to the influence of British traders who tell you to kill for skins alone. Your children shall cry over their bones if it is not halted."

"Brothers, farming is a good way of life. Your women have done it for centuries. Your father in Washington will send you hogs and cattle to raise so you can dispense with the uncertainties of the chase. Besides, farm animals require but little labor for such a certain resource."

"Brothers, look at your nations. The Wea tribe, invited but refusing to attend, is poor and miserable, habitually spending all hunting proceeds for whiskey. The branches of the Miami nation are so spread around the country. If they were to assemble in one area they would be once more quite formidable and respectable. I have caused to be prepared a map of the land desired by your father in Washington." He passed around a large sketch of the territory he wanted.

"Contemplate what I ask, brothers. We are willing to make handsome presents for the land, of which you have more than enough already. I know you will discuss this matter fully as is your fine custom. When you come to me with your answer we will open the casks for your refreshment."

A Miami chief, The Owl, responded briefly and promised an answer from the tribes. The next day the Amerindians met by themselves in the woods, the Delaware and Potawatomi doing most of the talking, the Miami listening sullenly.

"The Longknife chief is correct," said a Delaware, "game is scarce and we need the annuities to survive. The old ways must change."

"Of what use is so much land?" harangued a Potawatomi.

"You would feel differently if it was your tribal land instead of someone else's!" exclaimed a Miami.

"Brother, what do you mean? The Prophet says all tribes own all the land!"

"You notice he is not here, nor is Tecumseh. Where are they?"

"They were probably not invited."

"There is no need to invite them!" stormed Black Hoof, chief of all Shawnee. "Neither one of them is a chief! One is an impostor, the other a trouble maker who will abide by no one's law but his own. I say we sell the land!"

The Maimi refused to budge. "Brothers, you speak as if you are ready to hang the kettle against us," said The Owl. "Annuities take care of you in a way that makes you forget to take care of yourself."

"Let us not allow bad birds to fly over this council with crow mischief," said one sachem of the Delaware in an attempt to pacify everyone.

"Let us sell the land and get our pittance for it," said a Potawatomi "or the Longknives will take it whether we sell it or not! Such is the way things are."

The council continued far into the night but nothing was resolved when the Amerindians met with Harrison next morning.

"Father," began a Potawatomi, "we are agreed to sell, if the presents are fair, except for the Miami nation. They are thick headed and refuse to recognize the wisdom of your words! They are blind, they have no eyes!" There were ugly rumblings from the crowd, 1100 strong.

Such was the bitterness Harrison was afraid serious trouble would ensue. "Miamis, be not he offended with your brothers the Potawatomi. If they have discovered too much eagerness to comply with the wishes of their Father, comprehend that their women and children are exposed to wind, rain, the snows of bitter winters. Great ones of the Potawatomi, do not suffer your own distresses to make you angry with your brothers. I wish to hear you speak with one voice. Consult together once more." He turned on his heels and left the council house to the Indians.

Little Turtle followed Harrison outside as inobtrusively as possible, hailing the Governor and saying, "I would have a private word with you."

"Of course. Let us sit under yonder tree. What's on your mind?" Harrison had to slow down for the old chief could not walk very well. "Tell me honestly, man to man. Do you believe I have made a fair offer?"

Little Turtle had not heard any specifics but that was not what was on his mind. "I wanted to ask first... why my son-in-law, Captain Wells, was removed from his employment of Agent here."

"Oh," said Harrison, a bit disappointed. "There are accusations that money has been lost. Captain Wells is a friend of mine but there were too many mistakes on the books."

"I see," commented Little Turtle, earrings dangling all the way to his shoulders. "The Eel River people have not received a sum of $350 since Captain Wells was removed. The money belongs to them as their just due."

"I shall look into the matter after this treaty business, I give you my word on it."

"I hope," said The Turtle, "my standing with the United States is not impaired because of Captain Wells."

"Of course not," said Harrison, "the People of the Eagle do not function that way. Futhermore, I personally would be quite grateful if you could make your people see the wisdom of the presents we offer. You are the most noted, the most accomplished warchief in the history of North America. When you speak the great Father in Washington listens. Your people should pay you the same courtesy."

"Do you think you can get us that annuity money... immediately?"

"I vow to do so."

"Then let me try to talk with my people. I will take the whole Miami contingent to you tomorrow evening. Perhaps you can unlock one of the whiskey casks?"

"I will honor my guests," replied Harrison.

"Until tomorrow evening then," said the Turtle as he hobbled away.

Harrison watched him for a few minutes. What a sharper! The Eel River Indians were just another branch of the Miami nation but back at Greenville the Turtle managed to fool General Wayne, thereby getting double provisions and annuities for his nation. They had been receiving them all these years until Harrison himself cut them off. Now they would have to be reinstated. If the treaty was successful.

More tribesmen arrived next day, loaded with gifts from the British, it was believed by Harrison's people, for these latecomers remonstrated against selling any land whatsoever. Some of the Miami chiefs had begun to waiver in their resolve but when these newcomers, from the Mississinewa towns in the interior, began to speak, the waivering chiefs were intimidated, refusing to sell the land.

The Potawatomi agitated against the newcomers whereupon the Mississinewa tribesmen declared they no longer considered the Potawatomi as brothers, that the chain which united them would be broken by the tomahawk. An answering shout of defiance went up and Harrison had to walk in to avoid bloodletting:

"Brothers, my young men are waiting and will fight at my signal if you dare stain this place with human blood! My friends, once more we are threatened by British intrigue! We can work out our differences until the

British come upon the scene. Can you not see for yourselves how the Redcoats delight in embroiling every situation they touch? When was there ever a war that the British did not seek to interpose Indians between themselves and the Americans? My brothers, recognize your friends. If there should be war, and the British have already invited it with their actions on the high seas and elsewhere, they would be unable to defend Canada themselves. They do not have enough soldiers. That is the simple truth. Do not fall into their trap again for they will desert you as they did at Fallen Timbers."

Harrison talked for two hours, driving home every plausible argument he was capable of.

That evening the Miami visited privately with the Governor in his quarters. A small quantity of whiskey was passed around. A spokesman suggested to Harrison the Miami would accept the treaty if the government paid two dollars an acre. This took him by complete surprise. Someone had been coaching them! "If the government buys the land at that price," countered Harrison, "it would take only what was good, leaving many useless, scattered tracts." More whiskey was passed around and The Owl declared toward the end of the evening that perhaps a small tract should be ceded so the Governor would not return home empty handed.

The proceedings wore on and Governor Harrison was staring into the face of defeat, a defeat which would mean an unhappy loss of prestige. People would begin to ask, especially his political enemies, if the government's commissioner was unable to handle a group of unlettered savages. He decided to send his interpreters and some friendly chiefs into the Miami contingent and learn the real cause of their obstinacy, which he did, but once again he came up with nothing. The army officers at the fort began to say the recalcitrants would never sign.

But Harrison would not admit defeat. The following morning as white dawn walked the rim of the sky, stretching far into the blue deepness of departing night, he and interpreter Baron entered the Miami camp and asked to meet with the chiefs not as a Governor but as their friend. When all were gathered in Chief Peccon's tent he said, "I am now ready to listen to your complaints. Speak from your heart. My ears are open."

Charley, son of Little Turtle, produced from his shirt a copy of the Treaty of Grouseland and said, "Father, here are your own words. You promised you would consider the Miamis as owners of the Wabash lands. Why then are you about to purchase it from others?"

"The Miami are the sole owner of this land," said Peccon.

Everything fell immediately into place for Harrison as he nodded. "I agree the land belongs to the Maimi. I invited allied tribes in order not to offend your friends and neighbors. If you wish, I shall draw up a treaty that shows the Delaware and Potawatomi participating only as allies of the Miami, not having any direct right to the land."

"Do that and we will meet you in the council house," said Peccon.

"My friends, everything shall be attended to." Harrison left the Miami camp, barely able to contain his great enthusiasm. He ordered the whiskey casks be brought to the vicinity of the council house and dispensed the firewater by the drink.

The treaty was executed without further delay. Harrison was forced to shade his original demands for land along the Wabash until the Kickapoo consented. In addition to the twelve mile strip west of Dearborn County he secured a broad tract bordering the original Vincennes cession, and a long narrow strip west of the Wabash was ceded on the condition the consent of the Wea be obtained. If the Kickapoo could be induced to yield still another tract higher up along the Vermillion River, said to contain a rich copper mine, $700 in additional annuities was to be granted them. Annuities promised for the principal cessions totaled $1,750. Goods totaling $5,200 were delivered on the spot. The Miami received $1,500 worth of domestic animals in order to satisfy their exclusive claim of ownership. A few weeks later Chiefs Lapoussier, Little Eyes, and other Wea tribesmen readily agreed to terms and were awarded $1,500 in goods and $400 in additional annuities.

A gathering of citizens and a public dinner awaited Governor Harrison upon his return to Vincennes. Toasts were drunk to the treaty. Statehood was predicted within five years. The Indiana Legislature and the militia officers of Knox County adopted resolutions recommending his appointment for a fourth term as governor "...not only because of his superior military talents but also his integrity, patriotism, and firm attachment to the general government." President James Madison in Washington signed the commission for another renewal in office. And well he should have for Governor Harrison had added about 3,000,000 acres of land to his country with an expenditure of $10,350, which came to about 290 acres for each dollar spent. The government could now sell the land and make not less than $6,000,000, excluding revenues from mining operations, for a profit of $5,989,650.

Episode 3: Worn out traitors.

Tecumseh was returning from an unsuccessful attempt to enlist the Mohawk Valley Iroquois tribes into his League when runners from Prophet's Town located him and informed him of the Treaty of Fort Wayne. Billy Caldwell, who had been trained and educated in Jesuit schools, did some quick figuring on the ground and informed his chief that each dollar paid by Harrison had bought 290 acres!

Tecumseh seethed with anger as he mounted his horse and quickened the pace toward home. Governor Harrison had shown utter contempt for the Shawnee! The treaty making had been done so covertly and quickly, before the chief even heard about the proceedings! If only he could have been there! The Shawnee had hunted over the Wabash lands for generations. Now they were lost forever, and for a pittance! No one from Prophet's Town had been invited. The Eel River Indians had received a share of the annuities?! They had not the remotest connection with the land, except through the principle of common ownership. At least Harrison had indirectly acknowledged the principle. But then the governor had proven time and again he was not concerned with who owned the land, so long as it was signed over to the People of the Eagle! He gave them whiskey, after vowing to The Prophet he would prevent it entering Indian country, and got their marks on the treaty!

Upon his arrival at Prophet's Town he rested a couple of days and assembled the Partisans for an informal council. "It is my feeling," he said to his lieutenants, "that we have no choice but to break with the Longknives or punish the irresponsible chiefs who touched the quill. I would like to speak with Harrison myself. Perhaps I can get him to annul the evil work. Otherwise the executions will stain his hands."

"My brother, I suggested long ago that we rid ourselves of these worthless elements," admonished The Prophet.

"Perhaps you were more sagacious than I," conceded Tecumseh.

"Father," began Billy Caldwell, "in a confrontation with Harrison you will be at a distinct disadvantage?"

"How so?"

"Your direct mind compels you to tell the truth. You scorn trickery and falsehood. You believe in 'quaint' principles like justice. You speak your mind openly and freely under all conditions. Civilized men cannot get on in their world if they are handicapped with those virtues. The Longknives are masters of deceit and deception. Already I am certain Harrison is preparing for the whirlwind he started by blaming us for making trouble. He will bring many ignorant people to his side, people who will go out and die for freedom when in fact they are dying because of speciousness which veils evil as good."

"I understand what you say," replied Tecumseh. "I will kill the treaty-making chiefs. Spread this among the Northwest tribes at every opportunity. If Harrison does not abrogate, the worn-out traitors will die!"

387

The news spread like wildfire. It was no joke in the Northwest for everyone had vivid memories of The Prophet's purge.

Tecumseh was far from being alone in his feelings. Immediately warriors began descending on Prophet's Town, stating they had no intention of having their country slip through their fingers merely because some toothless old chiefs were befuddled out of their minds with presents and whiskey! Instead of the 80 poverty stricken men and their families who had followed The Prophet from Greenville in 1808 by the early spring of 1810 there were living in the Tippecanoe area a force numbering 1,000 warriors! Had there been more provisions the number would have been greater. It was typically commented that the most spirited Amerindians from all the tribes had cast their lot with Tecumseh and The Prophet.

There was always much activity at Prophet's Town. Greater acreage for corn was always being cleared. Agriculture was the people's mainstay. Ceremonies from the various tribes were encouraged to promote Amerindian amity, age old enmities neutralized. Games and athletic contests were stimulated and given a military turn. Arrows were made by the thousands. Tecumseh never spoke of waging an aggressive war. His goal was to intimidate Harrison's forces away from Indian land. The chief knew he was being spied upon by an assortment of "visitors" and traders enlisted by Harrison to report all goings-on at Prophet's Town. He welcomed them, recognized them for what they were, and hoped their reporting of his strength would deter war. The Amerindians had been forced to yield Ohio and now the Longknives wanted to expand to the Wabash, the last Northwest barrier that would leave the people any territory worth mentioning east of the Mississippi and south of the Great Lakes. If a stand had to be made it would be right here.

Harrison sent two French traders, Joseph Brouillette and Touissant Dubois, to Prophet's Town to observe first hand what was taking place. The Governor had been bombarded with rumors... or were they facts? Winamac, the friendly Potawatomi who had been so valuable an ally at Fort Wayne, came with the news that the Prophet was planning to attack Vincennes, then Fort Wayne, Fort Dearborn, and St. Louis. Grosble, a Piankeshaw chief who had helped Harrison with the treaty of 1805, issued warnings of great danger to a Frenchman then came to the Governor begging that his little band of tribesmen be removed across the Mississippi to escape the coming war. "The Prophet," said Grosble, "is planning to enter Vincennes under the guise of friendship. Then he will give the signal for a general massacre." Excellent student of history that he was, Harrison remembered the infamous Pontiac who, in 1763, annihilated the British garrison at Michilimackinac by such a ruse.

Upon their return, Brouillette and Dubois reported that warrior numbers at Prophet's Town fluctuated greatly as hunters went out and new delegations arrived either to visit or stay.

"I see no danger of an offensive war," commented Dubois. "There is much talk of former glories, much friendship and activity, but the tribesmen are not likely to descend on any white settlement."

"How were you treated?" asked Harrison.

"I do not believe they considered us anything but traders out hustling," said Brouillette. "Tecumseh and The Prophet stated the recently ceded lands would never be surveyed. He wishes to talk with your excellency, with his warriors, I believe."

"I already conferred with him."

"No sir, I mean Tecumseh."

"How are they provisioned," continued Harrison, "the British?"

"There is much activity to be self-sufficient," said Brouillette. "I did not see any Britishers in the area. I am sure they are skulking around, however, they always are."

"Do you believe I should call out the militia?" asked Harrison.

Both Frenchmen smiled for the militia were more a joke than anything else. "It might be a good political move," said Dubois.

The Govenor thanked the men and dismissed them. He understood perfectly so long as rumors floated about, immigration to Indiana would be curtailed, if not checked completely. Without white families the territory would not become a state. People were frightened so easily by hostile savages. Perhaps the Prophet was only being theatrical? A military confrontation would extirpate his people from the face of the earth, certainly he recognized that fact. The Prophet was a master of guile and deception. Perhaps he was merely endeavoring to intimidate? Time would tell.

In June of 1810 the salt which the U.S. government was treaty-bound to deliver to the Indian tribes was brought up the Wabash and dropped off at the various villages. The barrels of salt were refused by the Kickapoo so they were dropped off at Prophet's Town.

"What do you want me to do with them?" asked the head boatman of an Indian standing by the shore at Prophet's Town.

"We will not accept them. Do what you will with them."

The boatmen, all of them young Frenchmen, rolled the barrels off the boat and continued upriver for the rest of their deliveries. When they returned down the Tippecanoe the barrels were still where they had been left, untouched. Tecumseh and The Prophet, along with many other Indians, stood behind the barrels. Tecumseh waved them onto shore.

The head boatman gave the order to comply and momentarily he walked up to Tecumseh and issued a friendly greeting.

Tecumseh sprang at the boatman, grabbed him by the hair and shook him violently as a child would a rag doll. "Are you an American dog?" demanded the chief.

"Non, non, monsieur, je suis francais!" pleaded the boatman. He was let go (and later he stated his death was narrowly averted by his ancestry).

"Come here!" said Tecumseh as he pushed the man roughly. "Do you think this salt is worth our country?" he demanded.

"No sir, of course not!" said the young man. Tecumseh could see the fellow was quite confused.

"What is your part in this?"

"Monsieur, I do not understand. I am hired to deliver goods. I make a living for my wife and children. I just deliver what I am told."

"Let me explain to you," said Tecumseh, not angry as before. "Some vile people of ours traded our country away for a few trinkets, pigs, and salt! We who live here were not even invited to the treaty making. We do not accept the treaty as valid therefore we cannot take the salt. The chiefs who signed the treaty will be punished. I cannot punish them and at the same time take the salt, now can I?"

"Monsieur Chief, I do not know. I merely deliver what is given me. Everyone always takes what I deliver without questions."

"Return to your home," instructed Tecumseh, "and do not bring me anything related to that treaty, even if it is not your fault. Now begone!" Tecumseh reflected quickly. "No, wait. Have your men put the barrels back on the boat."

The Frenchman did as he was ordered and pushed away from shore as quickly as possible. Some of the Indians made obscene gestures at the crew.

Brouillette's trading house was stripped of all trade goods and provisions for the Amerindians knew he was Harrison's spy.

Back at Vincennes the boatmen reported the incident and the alarm quickly sounded throughout the frontier. Harrison sent out more scouts and called for a public meeting in which he urged preparedness. Many advocated callng out the militia and the Governor stated he would take that step if it was so advised by the people he had sent out to observe the situation first hand. He was slightly surprised so many people could become so frightened right here in the middle of Vincennes. "Do not worry," he soothed at the end of the meeting, "bodies of undisciplined savages, wherever collected, are often subject to unaccountable paroxysms of terror, scattering at the first sight of disciplined soldiers." The crowd gave him a huge ovation.

The following day Harrison called in his most trusted interpreter, Joseph Barron, and wrote out a speech directed at The Prophet and the Tippecanoe chiefs:

"Brothers, listen to this message! This is the third year that all the white people in this country have been alarmed at your proceedings. You threaten us with war. You invite all the tribes to the north and west to join against us.

"Brothers, your warriors who have lately been here deny this but I have received information from every direction. The tribes on the Mississippi have sent me word that you intended to murder me, and then to commence a war upon our people. I have also received the speech you sent to the Potawatomis and others, to join you for that purpose. But if I had no other evidence of your hostility to us, your seizing the salt I lately sent up the Wabash, is sufficient.

"Brothers, our citizens are alarmed and my warriors are preparing themselves, not to strike you but to defend themselves and their women and children. You shall not surprise us as you expect to do. You are about to undertake a very rash act. As a friend I advise you to consider well of it. A little reflection may save us a great deal of trouble and prevent much mischief. It is not too late.

"Brothers, what can be inducement for you to undertake an enterprise when there is so little probability of success? Do you really think that the handful of men that you have about you are able to contend with the Seventeen Fires, or even that the whole of the tribes united, could contend with the Kentucky Fire alone?

"Brothers, I am myself of the Longknife fire. As soon as they hear my voice you will see them pouring forth their swarms of hunting shirt men, as numerous as the mosquitoes on the shores of the Wabash. Brothers, take care of their stings.

"Brothers, it is not our wish to hurt you. If we did we certainly have the power to do it. Look at the number of our warriors to the east of you, to the south, on both sides of the Ohio, and below you also. You are brave men but what could you do against such a multitude? But we wish to live in peace and happiness.

"Brothers, the citizens of this country are alarmed. They must be satisfied that you have no design to do them mischief or they will not lay aside their arms. You have also insulted the government of the United States by seizing the salt intended for other tribes. Satisfaction must be given for that also.

391

"Brothers, you talk of coming to see me, attended by all your young men. This however, must not be so. If your intentions are good, you have no need to bring but a few of your young men with you. I must be plain with you. I will not suffer you to come into our settlements with force.

"Brothers, if you wish to satisfy us that your intentions are good, follow the advice that I have given you before. That is, that one or both of you should visit the President of the United States and lay your grievances before him. He will treat you well, listen to what you say, and if you can show him that you have been injured, you will receive justice. If you will follow my advice in this respect, it will convince the citizens of this country and myself that you have no design to attack them.

"Brothers, with respect to the lands that were purchased last fall, I can enter into no negotiations with you on that subject. The affair is in the hands of the President. If you wish to go see him I will supply you with the means.

"Brothers, the person who delivers this is one of my war officers. He is a man in whom I have entire confidence. Whatever he says to you, although it may not be contained in this paper, you may believe comes from me."

"My friend Tecumseh! The bearer is a good man and a brave warrior. I hope you will treat him well. You are yourself a warrior and all such have esteem for each other."

Joseph Barron took the letter and set out immediately. The voyage was uneventful but when he landed at Tippecanoe and identified himself he was taken before The Prophet, who was seated on a dais his followers had built for him. Barron thought it appeared much like a throne. His escort promptly fell away from him.

The Prophet looked at Barron for a long while without speaking a greeting or any other sign of recongnition. Finally the mystic spoke: "For what purpose do you come here? Brouillette was here, *he* was a spy. Dubois was here, *he* was a spy. Now *you* have come. You too are a *spy!* Over there is your grave. Look at it!"

Barron gazed to where The Prophet pointed. He did not doubt the mystic's veracity, he knew Brouillette and Debois had been spies! At that moment Tecumseh stepped out of a nearby cabin and from the moment of his saving appearance he was in charge of the situation.

"Your life is in no danger," said Tecumseh coldly. "What is the purpose of your mission?"

He stated he had a speech from Governor Harrison so Tecumseh had him deliver it on the spot.

"I will go confer with Governor Harrison myself," said Tecumseh.

"Come with me." He took Barron to his cabin, ordering food for both of them. "You will be safe in here," he said as the two sat down. "A short generation ago messengers were slaughtered for their efforts but in this village we realize the privileged status an envoy should be accorded."

Barron looked around the cabin. It reflected the poverty of the entire village. Stew was brought for the two men to eat and they talked frankly and openly.

"...I do not intend to make war," said Tecumseh, "but the People of the Eagle must cease extending their settlements into Indian land if we are to remain friendly. They must recognize the remaining lands as common property of all remaining tribes. The Great Spirit said he gave this great island to his red children. He placed the Shemanese on the other side of the big water. They were not contented with their own but came to take ours from us. They have driven us from the sea to the lakes. We can go no further. They have taken upon themselves to say this tract belongs to the Miami, this to the Delaware, and so on when in reality it is the common property of all tribes. It has ever been so, except during war time. NO land can be sold without the consent of all. Our father tells us we have no business on the Wabash, that the land belongs to other tribes. Who brought us here if not the Great Spirit, way back from the time of the earth's dawn, when all was young and green? This great island is our home and here we shall remain."

The two conversed into the evening and when Tecumseh left the cabin to find a place to sleep he realized Barron was still in danger from the women. Tukwautu, The Prophet's wife, dominated most of them, with a few independent exceptions like Flame, Spybuck's wife, who now approached him.

"Father," she said, "the women of Tukwautu are planning to kill the messenger while he sleeps."

"Are you certain?"

"Beyond a doubt. Spybuck sent me to inform you. If the man dies it would not go well for our village."

"Thank you, dear lady," said Tecumseh. Rebecca would soon be a part of village life, he hoped, like Flame. "Leave everything else to me." Quickly he communicated with Shabbona and Wasegoboah then went back to his cabin.

"Mr. Barron, come, we must away this evening in order to keep you safe," said Tecumseh. He could have stationed himself outside the cabin for the rest of the night but he did not want to engage in controversy the women who followed The Prophet and Tukwautu with so much zeal. Tecumseh personally escorted Barron from the village to a wooded ravine near the Wabash where he made a wild turkey call. It was answered from a distance and within minutes Shabbona and Wasegoboah appeared leading Barron's horses and two others.

"My men will escort you until you are close to your people," said Tecumseh. "Remember, tell your Chief I will be with him in eighteen days."

Barron saluted and, followed by two members of the Partisans, disappeared into the night.

Episode 4: Tecumseh meets Harrison

"We need some of our people to go into Vincennes and obtain information about Harrison and his intentions," said The Prophet to the Brotherhood. "It cannot be a large group or it will arouse suspicion."

"You speak with wisdom, my brother," said Tecumseh. "Billy, what would you say to putting on white man's clothes?"

"I do not prefer them but I will," said Caldwell.

"Jainai also speaks English well," said The Prophet. "I shall send him also."

"If we could send a family it would not arouse suspicion," observed Tecumseh. "We need a woman..."

"There is only one woman who can handle English."

"Yes. Flame."

When the woman was approached with the idea it was Spybuck who objected. "You will go nowhere with that dog Jainai! You are certainly going nowhere without me!"

"Oh?" said Flame, not particularly intent on going until Spybuck let his feelings be known. "You can leave me for weeks at a time, riding all over the country but I cannot step outside the village? You forget that women have rights in this society! Wasegoboah," she said to the Partisan's envoy, "tell our father I will begin whenever he orders."

And that was that. Proper clothes were found for Flame, Jainai, and Billy Caldwell. The journey was begun without hesitation for information had to be returned quickly. Tecumseh's meeting with Harrison was hardly two weeks away. Spybuck said nothing to Flame as she strode out of the village. He glared at Jainai as everyone got in the boat.

The journey to Vincennes was relatively quick. The three did not know each other well so they did not converse much except when necessary. When they got to Vincennes they were able to walk around without anyone paying them undue attention.

"Well, where do we start?" asked Caldwell.

"I would think the largest pub would be the best place," suggested Flame. All conversation was perforce in English.

"Good thinking, woman," said Jainai.

"By the way, what shall we call you?"

"*Red* is--" Flame said but then stopped abruptly, Jainai giving her a hard glance. "Call me *Dawn.*"

"All right, Dawn. Sounds like this place over here is loud enough. Now remember," said Caldwell, "you're my wife and Chief here is our servant."

"And remember, I don't drink," said Jainai.

They went into the whiskey house, sat down inobtrusively, ordered two drinks. The large room was filled with men, a few women.

"We're not going to learn much sitting here," said Flame. "I'm going to walk around." She got up and walked away, spoke to one or two of the women and within a short while brought a host of people over to her original table. Caldwell bought drinks for the group and encouraged politics as a topic of conversation. Posing as new settlers, Caldwell and Dawn asked about the Governor's ability.

"Old Harrison, huh? He'll do anything for a poor man, except be seen with one!"

"Yeah, you gotta be from Virginia to be on the in with him..."

It took the Shawnees three days to glean what information they learned: Harrison's father Benjamin had been a signer of the Declaration of Independence. His family was very wealthy, owning many slaves on their Virginia plantation. He was educated by private tutors. He inherited 3,000 acres of land in Virginia. A relative got him his commission in the army, serving under General Wayne at Fallen Timbers. Married Ana Tuthill Symmes, who had so far given him seven children. Ana was the daughter of the wealthy Col. Symmes, who did not much care for his son-in-law at first. Harrison was too ambitious for Army life so he resigned his commission and wound up in politics. At twenty-eight he was appointed Territorial Governor for Indiana, the youngest ever. His greatest triumphs had come in treating with the savages for land. But the tide was turning now that Indiana had been divided up. Or perhaps it would just push Harrison on higher. He was the ambitious type. Some said he would someday be President of the United States. He had favored legalizing slavery in Indiana but the people voted it down. His handpicked choice for delegate to Congress had been defeated a couple of years ago. He was concerned that war might come out of Prophet's Town, calling out the militia a couple of times. The British were behind the Prophet for sure. The British wouldn't learn a lesson until the

Americans whipped them a second time. Canada should be part of the United States anyway.

The return trip to Prophet's Town was effected as quickly as possible. Jainai kept silent unless spoken to, though he stole glances at Flame at every opportunity. Caldwell felt there was something amiss between the two but he didn't let on. Once at the village all intelligence was reported to Tecumseh and afterward Flame hurried to find Spybuck. She had not enjoyed being away from her husband. The Prophet sent a couple more men to Vincennes in order to keep apprised of anything happening in the town.

On August 11, 1810, Captain George Rogers Clark Floyd was summoned by a sentry when Tecumseh's flotilla of eighty canoes, "filled with warriors painted in the most terrific manner," and several pirogues came into view of Fort Knox three miles north of Vincennes. Floyd had the canoes halted for inspection, which Tecumseh allowed without opposition. His warriors were well armed. The Captain wrote in a letter that night, "They were headed by the brother of the Prophet, who is one of the finest looking men I ever saw, about six feet tall, straight, with large, fine features and altogether a daring, bold-looking fellow." He estimated there were between three-to four-hundred Indians with Tecumseh.

The flotilla arrived at Vincennes later the same day and Tecumseh was escorted with thirty warriors to Grouseland where Harrison happened to be sitting on the porch, reading and smoking. The Governor got to his feet to meet an unusually handsome chief... *so this was the Moses of the family, the really efficient one! No wonder he is described by all as a bold, active fellow, daring in the extreme and capable of any undertaking...* Harrison noted the chief's deep-set eyes and their hazel color, his nose somewhat aquiline, a cheerful, friendly expression on his face. He was dressed in tanned buckskin, his small arms--a silver moun ted tomahawk, a hunting knife in a neat leather case--on his hip.

"Welcome to my home," said Governor Harrison as he extended his right hand, which Tecumseh shook with enthusiasm. "I am glad you have come to partake of our hospitality. Your room is ready for occupancy."

"Thank you sir," replied Tecumseh through his interpreter Billy Caldwell, not wanting the Governor to know he could speak English, "with your permission, we children of nature are comfortable out of doors. If I may pitch my tent under yon elm tree I will be quite satisfied."

"As you wish, sir," replied Harrison.

"Tonight I shall spend with my men in their encampment," said Tecumseh. "Perhaps we should agree on any outstanding details," he suggested. "Will you be accompanied by armed men?"

"I will leave that to your decision, being the visitor," said Harrison graciously.

"Thank you. I believe sidearms would be acceptable."

"That is fine with me. I have been informed you have brought a large force with you."

"Only thirty picked men will attend the council," interrupted Tecumseh. "The others will stay in camp. I understand your militia is in Vincennes."

Tecumseh did his utmost to remember Harrison but he could not since the only opportunity he would have had to see him close up would have been during the Treaty of Greenville, which Tecumseh refused to attend. Remaining details were agreed upon then Harrison said, "All right, let us council day after tomorrow."

Tecumseh bowed slightly, turned on his heels and returned with his men to the Amerindian encampment situated near the river one mile north of town. The Chief saw to his defenses by posting sentries and deciding who would do what in case of surprise attack. When all was arranged Tecumseh went aside by himself to prepare his oration.

He did not go meet Harrison on Monday so Tuesday morning Joseph Barron dropped by to inquire about the delay. Tecumseh was not one to have his schedule arranged by antagonists. Besides, if a trap was in the offing the delay would keep it off balance. "Tell the Governor I will be there this afternoon."

Tecumseh approached Grouseland accompanied by thirty lithe warriors armed with tomahawks and wearing clean, neatly fashioned deerskin breeches. Their faces and bodies were decorated with brilliant vermillion paint, their heads shaved closely except for the scalp lock. Tecumseh wore his usual tanned buckskin but in his jet-black hair was thrust a lone eagle feather, emblem of his rank, held by a red handkerchief encircling his head.

Grouseland was reminiscent of the main house in a southern plantation. On the southwest side was a veranda with an arbor over which the Governor had placed a canopy. Beneath it were a number of chairs for the dignitaries who had come to observe the proceedings. The ranking officers of Indiana Territory were present, as were Supreme Court jus tices, a company of ladies, and a number of distinguished male citizens. Behind them were posted an honor guard, a platoon with their sergeant, pistols in their belts. Tecumseh saw them immediately and thought

Harrison had purposely deviated from their agreement. To the Chief sidearms meant swords. To the Governor it had obviously meant pistols! Intelligence from Vincennes had come to Tecumseh that the town was bristling with soldiers and bayonets.

Harrison was taking no chances with four hundred savages camped on his doorstep. Not far from the main house, ready for instant action was hidden a troop of dragoons under full arms. In the outskirts of Vincennes, stationed strategically during the night and ready to intervene should Tecumseh call for reenforcements, were another calvalry detachment and two companies of infantry. If that was not enough, the entire town was ready to pick up rifles and strike a blow for freedom.

Tecumseh looked at the assembled Longknives. He did not know where the soldiers were but he, and all his men, surmised they were in the vicinity. Such was the way of civilized men. Tecumseh put up his hand and his men stopped in their tracks. He was displeased. He affected a suspicion of treachery and refused to approach further, standing there with all his men.

Harrison sent Barron to discover what was the problem.

"I am accustomed to speaking from a circle," Tecumseh informed the interpreter. "It is the democratic way of my people, putting everyone at the same level. The way your Governor has things set up it will make the speaker appear to be pleading. I am no supplicant. Let us rearrange the seating under that shady tree over there."

"It will be quite troublesome for so many chairs to be moved," said Barron.

"Move only the chairs for the Governor's people," suggested Tecumseh. "Houses were made for Longknives and their councils. Amerindians hold theirs in the open air."

Barron returned to Harrison and informed him. He walked back to the Shawnee and said, "Your father requests you to sit by his side."

Tecumseh looked at the man then his piercing eyes took in the entire scene. He raised his very muscular right arm, pointed to the sky overhead and in a most sonorous voice that carried to everyone's ears, said in a tone laden with contempt, "My father! The Master of Life is my father! The Sun is my father! The Earth is my Mother and on her bosom will her son recline!" He went to the shade of the tree and sat down, followed by his warriors.

There was no other choice for the Longknives but to take their chairs to the grove, which they did, and the council was begun. Harrison spoke first about Indian-white relations but clouds gathered and dropped rain which halted all proceedings. The following day both Harrison and

Tecumseh spoke briefly but it was not until August 20, nine day after his arrival, that Tecumseh delivered his oration. He was still escorted only by thirty warriors, even after he learned 100 militiamen were hiding inside the main house.

Harrison and Tecumseh had now had time to measure each other and were face to face: the Virginia aristocrat and the unlettered chieftain tutored by nature, the college educated soldier of distinguished lineage which had witnessed the birth of the United States and the warrior tutored by Grandfathers.

Tecumseh listened as Harrison made preliminary remarks regarding a visit to the great father in Washington but his mind wandered off to a session with his Shawnee Grandfathers:

"What is more important," asked the Grandfather, "something which you value and desire, or the method you use to obtain it?"

Tecumseh reflected quickly. "I wanted an arrowhead a few days ago," he confessed. "It was beautifully fashioned and I wanted desperately to have it for my own. I challenged its owner to a wrestling match, putting up three of my arrowheads against his one."

"Was the other boy a talented wrestler?" asked the Grandfather.

"He is good enough I suppose."

"Did you feel you could throw him?"

"Yes, Grandfather."

"Then you really were not risking anything, were you? Remember, my Tecumseh, the deep forests and wide prairies teach us humaneness and charity for they add to the values of living. A cause worthy to be pursued with all one's heart will lose its greatness if it is won by craft or cruelty. Wilful deception poisons the heart and human beings so afflicted degenerate into agressive beasts bent on destruction of the world around them, including themselves..."

When Tecumseh stood up to speak he asked Governor Harrison to listen very carefully for he was going to summarize ages past. He began by reviewing how the French had come into Algonquian territory, adopting them as their children, giving presents and expecting very little in return, asking only for a patch of ground to live on. "...Our people gave them what they asked for the French came and kissed us. They lived with us like brothers in the same lodge. They never mocked our ceremonies and they never molested our dead. After a time the British arrived and quarreled with the French, throwing them on their backs. Even in defeat the French promised to think of the Indians as their children and serve them whenever they could.

"The Indians were forced upon in their change of fathers. The British were quite different from the French: they took us into war against the People of the Eagle, resulting in many young men killed, then abandoning them at Fallen Timbers. The tomahawk was buried at Greenville and the Amerindians had new fathers, the Americans, telling us they would treat us well, not like the British, who merely gave us a small piece of pork each day. The Americans made us many promises but the most repeated was that the land would belong to us as long as rivers flow and grasses grow. The nations wanted to believe your words. You recall the time when the Delaware lived near the Americans and put confidence in their promises of friendship? They thought they were secure, yet one of the Christian towns, Ghadenhutten, was surprised by Colonel Williamson and his men, murdering every man, woman, and child. Crawford also burned innocents in their Christian Church."

"These same promises were given the Shawnee, it is no isolated example. Flags were presented to my people and they were told they were now children of the Americans. 'These flags will be security for you,' we were told. 'If the white people intend to harm you, hold up your flags. You will be safe from all danger.' This we were told and in our good faith we believed it. What happened? At the very first sign of danger the person carrying the American flag was murdered! So also were others in our village. Now, my brother, after such bitter experiences can you blame me for placing little confidence in the promises of our officious fathers, the Americans?

"Since peace was made at Greenville the Americans have been guilty of unprovoked murders of Shawnee, Miami, Winnebago, Delaware that I know of personally. In return for Kickapoo land the Americans gave that tribe tainted food which killed many. Other gifts caused smallpox, which killed many more. You are a military man. Do you have pity for defenseless women and children dying of poisoned food or horrifying disease?

"We are always hearing demands for land. The People of the Eagle are numerous, we know that, but they have not filled up the land already obtained from the tribes in previous deals. What is the reason for demanding more? Do you not respect our needs for our land? Surely you recognize we must live too. Are we not also creations of the Great Spirit, with needs like all other human beings?

"When we tell you we do not wish to sell, how do you react? You foment discord, do you not, turning brother against brother, tribe against tribe? You push us to commit some mischief so that you can call your armies to take what you could not obtain legally. You, Governor Harrison, are doing your utmost to destroy Indian unity. You endeavor to make distinctions. You endeavor to prevent the Indians from doing what we, their leaders, know is best for them, unite and consider their land common property of all. You do not wish this because it will be more difficult for you to take it away from them. You wish to deal with tribes individually and advise them not to join the League.

"Are not the Seventeen Fires one country? Have not the separate fires joined in union for the welfare of all? Why do you refuse to believe we have the same right to such freedom and security? Your law says you believe all men are created equal. Brother, are not women equal? Are not the blackfaces men and women? Are we, citizens of this great island, not human beings? Of course we are. It is wrong for you to make distinctions for our people by assigning certain lands to specific tribes. The land belongs to all in common. I have the right to go anywhere and work my plot of land or hunt in any wilderness.

"It is true I am a Shawnee. My forefathers were warriors. Their son is a warrior. From them I take only my existence. From my tribe I take nothing and it owes me nothing. I am the maker of my own fortune. Oh that I could make the fortunes of my people and my country as great as the conceptions of my mind! I marvel when I think of the Great Spirit who rules this universe! I would not then come to Governor Harrison and ask him to tear up the treaty and obliterate its boundaries. Instead I would say to him, 'Sir, you have permission to return to your own country.' The being within me, communing with past ages, tells me that once, and until lately, there were no white men on all this island, that it then belonged to the native people, children of the same parents, placed on it by the Great Spirit that made them to keep it, to traverse it, to enjoy its benefits, and to fill it with the same race. Once they were happy people. Now they are made miserable by a race of encroachers who are never contented.

"The way, the only way, to check and stop this evil is for all redmen to unite in claiming a common and equal right in the land. That is how it was at first and should be still, for the land was never divided but belongs to all, for the use of every one. No group among us has a right to sell, even to one another, much less to strangers who want all and will not do with less. SELL A COUNTRY! WHY NOT SELL THE AIR, THE CLOUDS, AND THE GREAT SEA AS WELL AS THE EARTH? The Great Spirit made them all for use of his children. Governor Harrison, could you sell the United States? If I brought you all the precious gold and silver your people covet would you be able to sell me your country? Of course not! You might exchange it for the parcels of land you have under your personal jurisdiction but you could not sell your country. Neither can the individuals in our society.

"If we are to survive as a race of people the tribal nations must heed our message. Since reaching Tippecanoe we have endeavored to level all distincitions. The village chiefs who permit our ruination must be set aside. Power must reside with the people. It is the warriors who finally must pay the ultimate price for patriotism.

"Brother, I was glad to hear your speech. You said if we could show that the land was sold by persons who had no right to sell, you would restore it. I trust this was said in good faith. Those who sold the land did not own it. I speak for the owners—the people. The chiefs who sold it could set up only the claim of owning as much as anyone else. By listening to them you directly condoned or approved of our beliefs. All of the people were not consulted therefore the sale is void. The tribes who have heard my message will not agree to sell. If the land is not returned to us, you will see how things are resolved. We shall have a great council at which all the tribes will be present. Then we will show those who sold they had no right to do so and we will decide what shall be done with those chiefs. I am not alone in this. It is the determination of all the warriors and citizens who follow me.

"Brother, this is very important. If you do not rescind the treaty of Fort Wayne it will appear as if you wished me to execute all the chiefs who sold you the land. I assure you I am authorized by the tribes to do so, just as you authorize your hangman to execute evildoers among your people. I am the warrior of the people. All warriors will meet together in two or three moons from now. We will call for the chiefs who sold you the land and shall know what to do with them. If you do not restore our land your hand will be killing them.

"There is pity in our hearts for our people. We recognize the Wea, for example, were induced to give their consent because of their small numbers. The Treaty of Fort Wayne is the vile work of evil dogs like Winamac, your friend who sits beside you at this very moment. Winamac is a beast that makes lies and spreads them, causing hate between redmen and white! Your days are numbered, evildoer! You have forfeited your life!"

Winamac brought out a pistol from under his hunting shirt, laid it before him, prepared to acquit himself well if the Shawnee should become violent.

"Come now," said Harrison, "we must show faith in each other." The interpreter translated the aside into Shawnee.

"How can we have confidence in the Longknives?" asked Tecumseh. "When Jesus Christ came upon the earth you killed Him, nailing him to a cross! You thought he was dead but you were mistaken. You have

402

Shakers among you and you make light of their worship." Harrison's face displayed obvious anger.

"Brother, everything I have said to you is truth. My people ask nothing but to be left alone in the enjoyment of what is theirs. The Seventeen Fires have set the example for union, an example *they* took from our cousins the Iroquois, begun by Hiawatha and Deganawidah. We did not castigate you for it. Why should we be censured for following it? I would now like for you to make a statement on your intention of rescinding the treaty. I will be glad to know immediately your determination about the land." Tecumseh returned to his place among his warriors and sat down.

Unperturbed, Harrison sat for a few minutes, formulating his reply. The savage had already put him on the defensive but it would not do to react to the Shawnee's insolent, arrogant pretensions.

"My brother, it is my understanding your tribe of Shawnee are native to the country we call Georgia. You could have no legitimate claims to lands on the Wabash which have been occupied by the Miami since beyond the memory of man." Harrison paused for the interpreter.

Tecumseh shook his head irritably. This was no more than a feeble evasion of his demand. Surely the Governor knew the United States had accepted the theory of common Indian ownership of the land at the insistence of Joseph Brant. It had been reiterated and prevailed at the Treaty of Greenville in which Harrison had taken part! Furthermore, Tecumseh laid claim to the land as an Indian, not a Shawnee. And was Harrison the supreme authority on this issue, did he not have to refer it to his grand council at Washington?

"The chiefs were not induced or coerced to sign the treaty. We offered them a substantial amount of money, more than has ever been paid before, as a matter of fact. From the beginning the United States has endeavored to rule by justice. Any other people would merely have confiscated the land they wanted and submitted the aborigines to genocide."

Tecumseh was becoming further irritated with Harrison's double-talk. Smooth, artful speciousness was a product of civilization and its degeneracy.

"Your people have always been treated fairly," continued Harrison.

"HE LIES!" shouted Tecumseh violently as he sprang to his feet even before Barron finished the translation. "WHAT HE SAYS IS FALSE! YOU ARE A LIAR! Tell him," he said to Barron, "tell him exactly!"

The interpreter hesitated. He did not wish to translate word for word, fearing the consequences. The council scene became one of confusion for Tecumseh's wrath was evident to all. Secretary Gibson, standing next to the Governor, understood Shawnee, drew his pistol and called for Lt. Jennings to rush up the guard. Twelve riflemen ran up to the crowd and held their rifles at the ready. Harrison unsheathed his sword and stepped toward Tecumseh. Major Floyd, recently arrived from Fort Knox, drew a knife. Winamac lay in the grass and readied his pistol. Women rushed toward the house and one man grabbed a rifle and stationed himself gallantly at the door in order to defend the women from attack. Tecumseh's thirty warriors had leaped to their feet, drawn their tomahawks and knives when they saw the riflemen racing up. All they needed was Tecumseh's signal. Silence now reigned supreme, each side waiting for the other to make a move.

"This council fire is covered," said Governor Harrison. "I did not invite anyone here to be insulting. There will be no more discussion today." He stalked toward the house, his guests trailing after him, looking back every few steps.

Tecumseh, still furious, turned and led his warriors to their camp.

When the excitement died down at Grouseland everyone praised Harrison's courage in facing a horde of savages with nothing but a sword. The Governor accepted the compliments graciously but secretly he marvelled at the savage's boldness: to confront armed men so arrogantly with nothing but tomahawks and knives! What supreme confidence! He no longer misjudged this Tecumseh. Certainly he knew armed men were secreted everywhere. And Vincennes was an armed camp! Still, with a handful of men, he dared insult the leader of every soldier in the vicinity! What daring. It bordered on insanity, this fanaticism! And he had not yielded an inch nor withdrawn the insult. *This man was dangerous.*

The following day interpreter Barron was sent to make contact with the Indian camp. Harrison didn't say so but he wanted to converse with his antagonist.

"Keewaukoomeela!" said Tecumseh when he saw Barron. His anger had cooled quickly and he knew he was to blame because he could not control his temper. "My heart is glad you came to see us. I wish to make my apologies to Governor Harrison. It is not my desire to give offense in a personal way over a difference of opinion in philosophy."

"Speaking for myself," said Barron, "I believe the Governor would continue the council if I communicated your message to him."

"By all means do so," said Tecumseh with enthusiasm. "He may

404

even come here, in perfect security, if he wishes. I will personally be responsible for his safety."

Barron returned to Grouseland, communicated the missive, and Harrison accepted it with such good graces he visited the Indian camp that very afternoon.

Tecumseh appreciated Harrison's effort and as the two sat on a bench he became quite loquacious. He talked about the many treaties made between the two races and as he spoke he sidled up close to the Governor. Harrison became uncomfortable due to the proximity so he moved a bit away. Tecumseh continued as if nothing had happened then he moved himself up closer once more. The Governor listened as attentively as he could, moving away again. In a short while Tecumseh moved closer, crowding Harrison to the edge.

"Sir, excuse me, but shortly you will be throwing me off this bench."

Tecumseh chuckled happily. "Governor, how would you enjoy being pushed off?"

Harrison suspected treachery for the fleetest moment. But no, the man was in a playful, waggish mood. "I would not like it."

"Think of the Indians who are constantly being crowded by encroaching Longknives. Soon we will be pushed completely away from our country. The Seventeen Fires' policy of taking the land, either by treaty or unjust war, is a mighty water which threatens my people like a dangerous flood which will destroy a whole race. To stop this deluge I am trying to form a dam. Every sale opens new channels for the approaching deluge and in a little time will overflow the whole country."

The council was reconvened formally on August 22, Tecumseh addressing the assembled crowd, much larger than before. He spoke that some Shemanese had come to Prophet's Town saying many People of the Eagle did not like the Fort Wayne Treaty, that within two years another man would be Governor, more friendly to the Indians. Meantime the goal was to drive the Indians off their land. He pointed out once more that lands between Vincennes and the Ohio were extremely sparse regarding settlements so new acquisition of territory could not be justified.

"When we send surveyors," asked Harrison, "to map the land recently obtained, will they be interfered with? I desire your answer explicitly. And will the Kickapoos receive their annuity payment for the land they sold?"

Tecumseh answered: "Brother, when you speak to me of annuities, I look at the land and pity the women and children. I can state in no uncertain terms the Kickapoo will not receive the annuities. We must save their small piece of land. We do not want you to take it. It is little enough, why bother yourself with it? If you do take it, you must blame yourself as the cause of trouble between us and the tribes who sold it illegally to you. I want the present boundary line to endure. Should you cross it I assure you the consequences will be bad."

The council ended on that ominous note. The Indians went to break camp and Harrison retired to his study to make his report to Secretary of War Eustis. The letter he penned reflected a modicum of the admiration he had acquired for Tecumseh but the Governor's mind was uncertain as to the Shawnee's preparedness for war. He quoted a number of Tecumseh's statements, how the Indians would not be pushed into the lakes yet they did not intend to go to war. He agreed that much of what Tecumseh said regarding frontiersmen treatment of the Indians was all too true in most cases. He asked for clarification on the Government's stand on the Fort Wayne Treaty.

Episode 5: Richard McNemar

Richard McNemar was in Vincennes just before Tecumseh and his men came into town. Needing a brief rest from his missionizing, he decided to rent a room and renew his acquaintance with The Prophet and Tecumseh. As he always did, he kept a written record of his activities. As he walked through Vincennes the day of the Indians arrival he made efforts to engage various people in conversation but the only topic on everyone's mind was the horde of savages descending the Wabash. Even friendly Indians who had been known well around town were considered suspicious. Perhaps they had been spies all along? Maybe they had already decided who would be scalped?

McNemar could not believe the terror people displayed, alternating with moments of bravado. But it was a fact settlers in outlaying areas moved into town for the duration of the savage visit and he was informed many had gone into area forts. The Shaker did not believe he was in grave danger and to prove it he walked to the Indian encampment. He talked to The Prophet and Tecumseh, who remembered him well. The rest of the Indians looked hungry, not hostile. There were many women and some children with them, performing camp chores. Come evening time they would sing and dance in honor of the Great Spirit. McNemar considered them all peaceable for they showed everyone nothing but hospitality, drank no whiskey, and stole absolutely nothing.

"All we want is peace and friendship in our country," a man told him when McNemar spoke with a group of Amerindians. "Look at the women and children with us," he continued as he pointed. The Shaker spied a red-haired woman ladling food out of a kettle. "Does this make us a war party? Why will the Longknives not believe us? It grieves us that we are looked on as wild beasts. We came here only because the Governor invited us. We wish to be friends. Why are the people so fearful?"

McNemar felt like saying, *Because they know what is in their hearts* but instead he said, "There are some who wish to be friends. These must be sought out and encouraged."

Episode 6: Deaf Chief

Deaf Chief, a Potawatomi, was a common sight in many haunts around Vincennes. He had attended the grand council without an invitation but the Governor quickly made him feel welcome when he saw him. As his name stated, the Potawatomi was deaf but during the excitement of near battle during the council Deaf Chief knew there was serious disagreement between the Governor and Tecumseh. It was not until the following day that Deaf Chief learned the Shawnee had called Harrison a liar. This greatly angered the Potawatomi and he told all his friends, Indian and white, that had he known what language had been used he would have confronted Tecumseh and thrown the words back in his teeth.

"Be careful," an Indian cautioned Deaf Chief in sign language "lest The Prophet have you killed. Come with me. Let us hunt a while."

"I KILL FALSE PROPHET!" he yelled as he walked down the street. There were more soldiers than civilians. "TECUMSEH TOO!" His friends tried to control him but could not.

The Potawatomi went to his little camp, entered his tent and put on war paint. With great care he put on his feathered headpiece and armed himself with rifle, scalping knife, tomahawk, and war club. He walked to his canoe, boarded, then paddled to the Indian encampment. "I MEET EVIL TECUMSEH!" he shouted, attracting as much attention as possible.

Deaf Chief walked into camp, saw Tecumseh standing outside a tent, conversing with Interpreter Barron. The Prophet, Jainai, and many others saw the bold Deaf Chief stride up to the leader and begin tongue lashing him: "You and your men... kill white men's hogs, call them bears! You afraid face a warrior!" He continued in this vein, Tecumseh looking at him once then ignoring him completely. "You puppet slave of British redcoats!" persisted Deaf Chief.

Tecumseh continued his conversation with Barron, saying nothing to the Potawatomi. He could not have heard him anyway. Deaf Chief finally let out a warhoop, raising his rifle and tomahawk in triumph. He strode triumphantly back to his canoe and left.

Tecumseh ignored the man but The Prophet had watched in seething anger. He said something to Jainai, who quickly walked to his tent and emerged minutes later, his face painted black. He followed the Potawatomi to the river as the sun began to set, the dark wings of night beginning to veil the world.

That night Deaf Chief was missing from his usual haunts at Vincennes. No one ever saw or heard of him again.

Episode 7: Destroy Tecumseh!

In the weeks that fnllowed the council Governor Harrison assured the populace there was no cause for alarm. The frontiers were peaceful and would remain so. Politics took up his time and the letter from Secretary of War Eustis supported his original ideals. When it was time to address the Legislature he railed against "...the pernicious influence of alien enemies among the Indians. We must remove those enemies from our borders.

"Although much has been done toward extinguishment of Indian titles in the Territory, much still remains to accomplish. We have not yet sufficient space to form a tolerable State. The eastern settlements are separated from the western by a considerable extent of Indian lands. And the most fertile tracts that are within our territorial bounds are still their property. Almost entirely divested of the game from which they have drawn their subsistance, it has become of little use to them; and it is the intention of the government to substitute, for the pernicious and scanty supplies which the chase affords, the more certain support which is derived from agriculture and the rearing of domestic animals.

"Gentlemen of Indiana and the United States, let us not falter before our duty toward the march of civilization. Are those extinguishments of native title, which are at once so beneficial to the Indian, the Territory, and the United States, to be suspended upon the account of intrigues by a few Individuals, Indian or white? Is one of the fairest portions of the globe to remain in a state of nature, the haunt of a few wretched savages, when it seems destined by the Creator to give support to a large population, and to be the seat of civilization, of science, and true religion..."

Governor Harrison did not confide his intentions in anyone as the months wore on. *Tecumseh was probably the most dangerous Indian in history.* Still, the United States would have no part of naked aggression.

There had to be justifiable reason for striking at Prophet's Town at Tippecanoe. Not that there wasn't already, if Harrison wanted to use various killings and horse thefts. He ordered swords from the War Department, specifying the weapons must be able "...to attack the naked skull of a savage as well as the leathern cap of a British dragoon." Tecumseh had met his arguments boldly and sagaciously. How, from an unlettered savage?! He ordered five hundred rifles, stating his militia "...were extremely awkward with the musket." He had never met such an Indian before! Here was a savage who could not be debauched or intimidated. And he was constantlx on the move, speaking to all the savage nations, never resting! Such a man posed extreme danger for the United States. What if the savages got enough weaponry from the British and formed their own country? The United States would have to fight a bloody war. The price of expansion would be a river of blood. And if the British fought alongside the savages? Perhaps they would indeed form a country and manage to keep it. Worse yet, what if the savages and British together conquered the United States and made everyone stay south of the Ohio?! Such an abomination was sacrilege to Governor Harrison. He must mobilize his forces and strike Prophet's Town! There was no other choice. But it was risky business. If he should fail he was finished in politics. But if he won... he would not allow himself to consider how far he would rise with his countrymen. Yes, when the time was right, he would strike Tecumseh at Tippecanoe! A sound thrashing of his forces would end his grandiose league. And if it brought on war with the British? Well and good. The United States would throw them out of the North American continent, annexing Canada without delay. *But first he must destroy Tecumseh!*

Episode 8: Devil's Tools

"It matters not to me who they are, who are devil's tools, whether men or angels, good or bad," said the man addressing the crowd. "In the strength of God I mean not to spare! I used leniency once to the Devil because he came in the guise of a good man. But my God respects no man's person. If they trouble you I would they were cut off! The Shakers indulge in extravagant emotion during the bacanals they call religious expression! Yet they effect outer discipline, and such an all encompassing discipline! Worse, The Millenial Church, as they call themselves, has gone on record helping the savages which terrorized this country years gone by and are apt to run it crimson again without warning. The lives of our women and children demands that this BE STOPPED! If the Shakers want to live with the Indians they should be encouraged to remove themselves from the society of civilized folks. They are holding a camp meeting at Union Village. I mean in the name and strength of God to lift his rod of Almighty truth against the viper!" Thompson went to his horse, mounted up, and rode toward the camp meeting, everyone in the crowd following him and picking up greater numbers on the way, each bdcoming more aggressive with each step of horse or walker, talking as they went:

"I heard tell them Shakers castrated all their males so as not to have children. I'd like to see their necks in a forest of gallows!"

"Those people have no modesty whatsoever! They strip naked in their night meetings and dance till the wee hours when they blow out all the candles and debauch each other. And the women are just as willing as the men!"

"They murder all the poor little babes born to them!"

"The men say each one of them is a Christ! Can you imagine such blasphemy? They tell us to throw our Bibles away!"

"They say they're against marriage and attach criminality to that for which we have the express command of God."

"The men are all lechers, having their way with any woman after the dancing."

"They encourage men to beat and otherwise abuse their wives then turn them away when another strikes their fancy."

"They have testified they will never die!"

"They are hypocrities, worldly minded cunning deceivers. Their religion is license for everything earthly, sensual, or devilish."

The gathering now took on the demeanor of a roving mob bent on destruction. There were more than five hundred armed men, led by officers in military array, giving the impression the march was planned instead of being a spontaneous surge. Hundreds of people followed, some of which were friendly to the Shakers and wished them no harm but the far greater number were either entire strangers or decided enemies who came to support the military in case of necessity. The latter were armed with guns and swords, bayonets fixed on poles, sharp sticks of various lengths, staves, hatchets, knives, clubs. Together they formed a motley multitude of every description, from ragged boys to hoary-headed old men. The mob was grotesque and appeared the more ruthless as the sun began to set.

The Shakers, involved with their campmeeting, were unaware of danger until the huge crowd encircled their small numbers.

"They are liars!" yelled Thompson at the speakers, "they are liars!

The Good Book tells us 'A liar is not to be believed, even when he speaks the truth!' "

A bold individual went up to one speaker and told him "Go to hell!" in his face.

John Meacham was spat upon openly by a man who yelled out, "Let us make a big fire and roast these false prophets!" Everyone around laughed and encouraged him.

Richard McNemar went up to Thompson and asked, "What is the meaning of this? We are peaceably assembled, as is our right. You have no authority here, legal or divine."

"Sinner repent!" said Thompson as he pointed an accusing finger at McNemar. "Have you not sinned in many sacriligeous ways?" The finger was now between McNemar's eyes. "You stand accused of taking children away from their rightful mother, to wit, Polly Smith; that the education of children among you is a sham and pretense; that you whip your underlings severely, and also your children; that you consider it no sin to have carnal knowledge of many women; that your Elder David Darrow, like the Roman pope, exercises unlimited authority over all under his control, living sumptuously on the labors of others; that you knowingly and willingly aided the savage Indians, knowing full well they were vile enemies of the United States and the liberty which they represent. You stand accused and we await your answers!"

"Tar and feather him!" yelled someone and up went the chant, "TAR AND FEATHER, TAR AND FEATHER!"

An Indian was found among the Believers, pounced upon by several men and severely beaten. He lay senseless on the ground and when other Shakers came to attend his wounds they were slapped roughly.

"Now see here," rang out the voice of State Circuit Judge Francis Dunlavy, "there will be no violence in this village without punishment by the law!"

"I am willing to refute all charges," said Reverend McNemar calmly, "if the procedure is conducted according to precedent. We can confer in yonder wood, if the accusers will step forward."

A man stepped up to McNemar and slapped him in the face. He was surprised by the sudden assault but he didn't move, staring calmly at his assailant. The man slapped him again, with the same result. A third slap pushed him backward but the non-violent McNemar did not reply in kind. Some of the man's friends pulled him away.

"Let us repair to yonder grove," said Judge Dunlavy, incensed that the Reverend had been struck but grateful he had been Christian enough to take it. A spirited defense quite probably would have been the beginning of open warfare and the Shakers would have been annihilated.

The council was held around a fire, Amerindian style. All charges were answered by a small group of three Shakers, opposed to twelve inquisitors. The thrust was to make the Shakers move away from Union Village and McNemar summed up his peoples' feelings when he concluded: "Respecting our faith which we hold in the Gospel, we esteem it dearer than our lives and mean to maintain it, whatever the consequences. And as to our leaving the country, we are on our own possessions which we purchased with money obtained by our honest industry. It is our endeavor not to owe anything to anyone. We have not a cent of anyone else's money. We enjoy our peaceable possessions in a free country. We are entitled to those liberties, including the freedom of conscience, which the laws of our country grant us." As Reverend McNemar stood momentarily in front of the fire which was dying down he evoked visions of Tecumseh and The Prophet.

Episode 9: Jainai's vow.

"I do not understand why you feel the way you do, brother," said The Prophet to Jainai as they ate privately in the latter's wegiwa. "The woman has not offended you, has she? She has not caused you some injury? Stolen your property? Slandered you? I would have you explain once and for all."

"The witch should have been executed long ago," said Jainai in his icy fashion. "She is a vile person ruled by lust."

"Her husband has made no charges," pointed out The Prophet.

"Spybuck is no better," replied Jainai. "They are a pair of fornicators!"

"They are married. What they do for their relationship cannot concern us. Have you seen the woman with anyone else?" Jainai shook his head. "The man? Neither have I. We have no grounds for charges."

"Why is it everyone fears Spybuck?"

"I fear no one," said The Prophet as he stopped eating momentarily and scrutinized his disciple, assuredly his most valuable one. "Spybuck does not deal in evil magic. He is a healer. He was of immense help to me during my younger years. He has been a friend of Tecumseh since before that."

"The people fear him."

The Prophet shrugged his shoulders. "I do not.. and you don't."

"I will not abide with fornicators."

"That emanates from your Christian background, I would surmise," said The Prophet. "Brother, you have performed most valuable services

412

for me and I cherish you. From the beginning I was able to depend on you and nothing has changed. This matter causes me to ask you a personal question. I hope you will answer it candidly. Do you desire the woman?"

Janinai stopped eating. "Desire? I would blacken my face and execute her, that is my desire! Why do you ask such a thing? You know I am vowed to celibacy."

"Could that also be a holdover from your Christian years?" asked The Prophet.

"I live the way I choose. I have no regrets."

"It is good to know one's self," observed The Prophet. "Sometimes we are governed by subconscious drives, totally unaware. I understand how you might feel. Flame used to bother me, at one time," he confessed. "Apart from her pale skin she could represent the essence of passionate femininity in a man's subconscious. Men resent what they cannot control, especially in women."

"She was a paywoman among the Christians," said Jainai. "I cannot desire what is sold to anyone with gold in his hand."

"Years ago I was a worthless drunk. Why resuscitate the past? It is the road to futility."

"She will be allowed to live down her evil among us, then?"

"I cannot move against her unless there is just cause. The same for Spybuck or anyone else. If it was otherwise we would be put to shame by the beasts of the forests. I want you to get the woman out of your mind. She and her husband are innocuous and have performed good services for our welfare. They have not been as instrumental as you, brother, I am not asking you to suffer comparison. Your paths should not cross many times. Now I must be going."

Jainai hardly paid attention to his leader as he exited from the wegiwa. He set aside the bowl of stew and searched his mind... the woman had been accused of witchcraft and he had brought her in. But Tecumseh and Spybuck saved her. Had he taken this as a personal defeat? He had watched her at various times, though she totally ignored him, snubbing him as she had done in the Christian period of his life. Jainai's eyes opened as if in recognition: was he bitter that she had never even noticed him? She, a whoring paywoman, refusing to acknowledge his devout existence. Some of the other paywomen had been kind to him... not Dawn, the red wench, the popular, expensive... she didn't even know the Indian-turned-Christian was alive. To this day he would wager Flame did not remember him.

So what did he want from her? It was not as The Prophet suggested, he

413

did not want to possess her. Yet she had been in his dreams, a fact he shared with no one. Together they had gone over a sparkling waterfall, arm in arm, laughing merrily until he was underwater, Dawn swimming above him sensuously, her voluptuous legs moving rhythmicly, beckoning. At that point he was startled into awakening. Since then he had refused to consider the implications, submerging them until his subconscious unchained him.

The Christian world had been severe with Jainai. It had filled him with inexplicable contradictions. And pain. Much pain, physical and mental, emotional and spiritual. Flame would pay for so much mortification! Execution was too good for a Christian paywoman! She wanted lust? He would give her all she could take. First he would rape her. Yes, he would kill Spybuck and take his woman. Jainai's repression had been finally unbridled by The Prophet. Lust was the only language Flame understood. He would rape her then *blacken his face and execute her!*

Episode 10: Within one moon.

James Galloway filled the ceremonial pipe Tecumseh had given him years ago, lit it, then passed it to the chief. Tecumseh took a few puffs, the aromatic kinnikinick smoke ascending slowly.

"Sir, I have a most serious request for your consideration," said Tecumseh. As he returned the pipe to Galloway.

"Yes, what is it, my friend?" returned Galloway before he puffed on the pipe.

"I desire the hand of your daughter Rebecca in marriage."

Galloway looked at the chieftain. There it was finally, dignified, properly serious, totally confident, at least on the surface. He took another puff and looked closely at Tecumseh. He had expected it for a long time, what with the birchbark canoe, the large comb of pure silver, expensive furs, the many gifts from over the years.

"My friend, I would not have the slightest objection in becoming your father-in-law," said Galloway. "But I cannot speak for my daughter. She has a mind of her own, as you well know, so you must ask her."

"With your permission, then," said Tecumseh as he directed his moccasins toward the cabin.

"You have it," said Galloway, "and good hunting," he added with a smile.

Tecumseh maintained his dignified mein, knocked softly on the cabin door and quickly saw a delighted Rebecca standing in front of him. "I did not know you were here!" exclaimed the young woman. "Oh that father of mine! Why did he not call me! Come in, come in."

"No, if you don't mind, let us go for a ride in the canoe for a while."

"Of course." Rebecca had not seen Tecumseh for months and elation ran through her entire being.

The two walked to the canoe where it was secured until desired and shortly the couple was floating softly down the river. "Rebecca, our settlement on the Tippecanoe is far from this place. I wish you to come there with me and be my wife. On our wedding day I will give you fifty broaches of silver. You will always be the Star of the Lake. I ask you to be my wife."

Rebecca was taken aback with such directness, but only for the barest instant. She kissed him softly. "I have waited so long for you!" she confessed. "You have always been my Mr. Tikomfa Chief. I thought I would be an old maid spinster before you told me your heart!"

"You are no where close to being an old woman," chided Tecumseh. "I had to wait until you knew exactly what you wanted."

"You are what I want," she said and Tecumseh kissed her. "You are what I will always want. I accept your proposal with all my heart."

"I know there are great differences between us," said Tecumseh. "I am older than you. We are of different backgrounds, people, traditions."

"There is nothing that can't be worked out," returned Rebecca. "But I do love you and there are things on my mind that..."

"Tell me what they are and they shall be resolved."

"You know that I am a Christian," said the woman, "and I could not handle it if you took another wife. I would never be able to tolerate polygamy as is practiced by some of your race."

"I will take no other wife," said Tecumseh directly, "you have my promise on that."

"Another thing, not as important but... I have seen how hard Tecumapease and other women work. I do not know that I could do all they do. You might not be too happy with me."

"You will be the wife of the chief. You shall have help. I will see to it."

"And what will you expect of me?" asked Rebecca.

"You must read to me every day," said Tecumseh, a smile on his face.

"What a delight that would be. Have you told Tecumapease?"

"I had nothing to tell until now," said Tecumseh.

"How far is Tippecanoe from here?"

"Very far. You will miss your parents, I know, but we will return to visit often. Or perhaps they might want to move there. The land is wide and rich. Could you live away from your parents and brothers?"

"I guess so, if I had to. Is there any chance you could live here?"

"Ohio is the land of my birth. I would like to come back, if possible."

"Come," said Rebecca with renewed enthusiasm, "let us go tell mother!"

The canoe was directed toward shore and the happy couple broke the news to the Galloways. Father Galloway had already prepared his wife so they both knew what was transpiring on the river. Mother Galloway's eyes were bright with held-back tears when her daughter informed them of the proposal and her acceptance. Food was prepared and enjoyed but nevertheless Tecumseh felt a certain hesitation, especially on Mother Galloway's part.

"There is talk of war," said the woman in the course of conversation.

"Now mother," chided Father Galloway, "one can't go by rumor."

"You will never have anything to fear from my people," soothed Tecumseh.

"Indiana is so far away," said Mother Galloway.

"Tecumseh said he would like to move back to Ohio," said Rebecca, very aware of her mother's feelings.

"That would certainly be ideal," commented Father Galloway. "Besides, we could hunt together. Ah, there is no real danger of war, is there?"

"Not from my people," said Tecumseh. "We are in no position to begin a conflict." He looked at Rebecca. Was she a bit--subdued? Her enthusiasm did not seem to be as high. "Your daughter would be well taken care of in any case."

"Let us not even mention war," said Father Galloway. "We should go tell your brothers the news."

The rest of the evening was spent in lighter conversation. Tecumseh and Rebecca went outside into the moonlit evening. He told her about the many trips he was making, talking to so many chiefs about the land.

"I would hate to see you gone for such a long time," commented Rebecca. "What would I do if your're gone for a week, a month? I don't know a soul at Tippecanoe. Could we not live in Old Chillicothe?"

Tecumseh looked at his Star of the Lake. What would she do during his long absences? Love would see them through.

"Could we not?" repeated Rebecca. "Tell me yes, my sweetheart, and I'll marry you tomorrow!"

Tecumseh was impassive, silent. "Is it such an important issue to you" he asked finally, "as important as the two you mentioned on the river? You know I want you to be happy."

"Of course, my dearest Shooting Star, and I want the same for you. Could you not work for peace from here? I do not ask you to put on white clothes and live as the whites do, all of a sudden. But together we could work for your ideals and when you go off to distant tribes I would have family to be with until your return, causing you no worry. Would that be too much to ask?"

Tecumseh would give almost anything to return to Ohio and live in peace. What his bride said could be true. Governor Harrison was inimical to him but Governor Kirker of Ohio had been most friendly. He was absolutely certain of one thing, he wanted Rebecca to be his wife. "Perhaps not," he said in response to her question. "Tecumapease is always after me to return. She says I could work for the people just as well from Ohio. She does not like it when Wasegoboah is at my side instead of hers."

"I do not blame her. My heart dies a little when you are gone. Tell me we can live here! Tecumapease is right."

"Give me time to reflect, pumpkin flower." He kissed her, holding her to him in a passionate embrace. "I shall return with my answer within one moon."

To be continued in the
Conclusion
of
I AM TECUMSEH!